ST ANTONY'S SERIES
General Editor: Alex Pravda, Fellow of St Antony's College, Oxford

Recent titles include:

Mark D. Alleyne
INTERNATIONAL POWER AND INTERNATIONAL COMMUNICATION

Daniel A. Bell, David Brown, Kanishka Jayasuriya and David Martin Jones
TOWARDS ILLIBERAL DEMOCRACY IN PACIFIC ASIA

Judith M. Brown and Rosemary Foot (*editors*)
MIGRATION: The Asian Experience

Alex Danchev and Thomas Halverson (*editors*)
INTERNATIONAL PERSPECTIVES ON THE YUGOSLAV CONFLICT

Anne Deighton (*editor*)
BUILDING POSTWAR EUROPE: National Decision-Makers and European
Institutions, 1948–63

Simon Duke
THE NEW EUROPEAN SECURITY DISORDER

Y Hakan Erdem
SLAVERY IN THE OTTOMAN EMPIRE AND ITS DEMISE, 1800–1909

Austen Ivereigh
CATHOLICISM AND POLITICS IN ARGENTINA, 1910–60

Leroy Jin
MONETARY POLICY AND THE DESIGN OF FINANCIAL INSTITUTIONS
IN CHINA, 1978–90

Matthew Jones
BRITAIN, THE UNITED STATES AND THE MEDITERRANEAN WAR,
1942–44

Anthony Kirk-Greene and Daniel Bach (*editors*)
STATE AND SOCIETY IN FRANCOPHONE AFRICA SINCE
INDEPENDENCE

Jaroslav Krejčí and Pavel Machonin
CZECHOSLOVAKIA 1919–92: A Laboratory for Social Change

Leslie McLoughlin
IBN SAUD: Founder of a Kingdom

David Nicholls
THE PLURALIST STATE: The Political Ideas of J. N. Figgis and his
Contemporaries

J. L. Porket
UNEMPLOYMENT IN CAPITALIST, COMMUNIST AND POST-
COMMUNIST ECONOMIES

Charles Powell
JUAN CARLOS OF SPAIN: Self-Made Monarch

Neil Renwick
JAPAN'S ALLIANCE POLITICS AND DEFENCE PRODUCTION

William J. Tompson
KHRUSHCHEV: A Political Life

Christopher Tremewan
THE POLITICAL ECONOMY OF SOCIAL CONTROL IN SINGAPORE

Stephen Welch
THE CONCEPT OF POLITICAL CULTURE

Jennifer M. Welsh
EDMUND BURKE AND INTERNATIONAL RELATIONS: The
Commonwealth of Europe and the Crusade against the French Revolution

The German Question and Other German Questions

David Schoenbaum

and

Elizabeth Pond

St. Martin's Press
New York

in association with
ST ANTONY'S COLLEGE, OXFORD

St. Martin's Press, Scholarly and Reference Division,
175 Fifth Avenue, New York, N.Y. 10010

First published in the United States of America in 1996

Printed in Great Britain

ISBN 0–312–16048–8

Library of Congress Cataloging-in-Publication Data
Schoenbaum, David.
The German question and other German questions / David
Schoenbaum and Elizabeth Pond.
   p.   cm. — (St. Antony's series)
Includes bibliographical references and index.
ISBN 0–312–16048–8
1. Germany—History—Unification, 1990.   2. Germany—Foreign
relations—1990–   3. Germany—Economic conditions—1990–   4. Germany
(East)—Politics and government—1989–1990.   5. Political culture–
–Germany.   I. Pond, Elizabeth.   II. Title.   III. Series.
DD290.29.S364   1996
943.087'9—dc20   96–2600
                                                              CIP

To
Fritz René Allemann
the 70,000 Leipzig demonstrators of 9 October 1989
and in memory of
Walter Henkels, Ursula Henkels-Schäfer
and
Wellington Long
who all taught the authors some important things
about Germany

Contents

Acknowledgements   ix

1 The Once and Future Kingdom   1

2 Old Germans and Young Turks   43

3 From Industrial Park to Theme Park?   87

4 Revolution, East German-Style   148

5 European and Foreign Policy   174

6 Whither Germany?   230

Bibliography   237
Index   243

Acknowledgements

In 1991, the editors of *Past and Present* invited one of the authors to help think about 'Boundaries and Border- Crossings' at a conference in Oxford the following June. This book is an indirect result of that salutary kick, plus the welcome interest of Mr Alex Pravda, editor of the St Antony's College series. But above all, it reflects the current state of a conversation between the authors that began in 1979, and shows no sign of ending. The common denominator is Germany, and why it matters fifty years after the Second World War and five years after unification. Both the 'whence?' and the 'whither?' dimension have caused us to think some new thoughts and ask ourselves some new questions. If our book causes readers to do the same, we believe it will have served a useful purpose.

As only authors can appreciate, acknowledging how much they owe to others is one of the nicest parts of writing books. We are therefore grateful for an opportunity to thank:

- Klaus Becher, J. D. Bindenagel, Peter Katzenstein, Mária Kovács, Gerhard Loewenberg, Michael Mertes, Ursula Müller, Franz Urban Pappi, Ernst-Jörg von Studnitz, Angelika Volle, and Elisabeth Wendt for unblinking editorial rigor when confronted with draft chapters;

- The libraries of the German Society for Foreign Affairs, the University of Iowa, the Bologna Center of the Paul H. Nitze School of Advanced International Studies of The Johns Hopkins University, and the Library of Congress, and especially Gisela Gottwald, John Williams and Gail Martin, as well as Mitchell Ash, Françoise Globa, Gabriella Poggi, for bibliographical support above and beyond the call;

- Michael Schoenbaum, Gesine Gerhard, for research assistance where and when it mattered;

- Robert Cooper, Ralf Dahrendorf, Warnfried Dettling, Gisela Erler, Franz Eschbach, Andreas Falke, Eva Gerigk, Elisabeth Hirte, William Horsley, Karl Kaiser, Angelika Legde-Jaskolla, Ulrich

Littmann, Hans Meyer, Klaus Richter, Hermann Rudolph, Erwin
Scheuch, Roland Ullrich, Angelika Volle, Stephanie Wahl, for
collegiality, patience, expertise and bright ideas;

- Eduard Ackermann; Manfred Ackermann; Rudolf Adam; Bernd
Albani; Hans Ambos; Joachim von Arnim; Alexander Arnot;
Robert Beecroft; Kurt Biedenkopf; Dieter Bingen; Joachim Bitter-
lich; Ilva Boden; Hans-Otto Bräutigam; Birgit Breuel; Nigel Broom-
field; Fraser Cameron; Dominique Chassard; Jürgen Chrobog; John
A. Cloud; Klaus J. Citron; Alexander Dijckmeester; Burkhard
Dobiey; Michel Duclos; Claus J. Duisberg; Willem van Eekelen;
Heinz Eggert; Frank Elbe; Thomas Enders; Hans-Joachim Falenski;
Beatrice Fromm; Karl Furmaniak; Jens Fischer; Charles Gati;
Helmut Geiger; Hans-Dietrich Genscher; Bronislaw Geremek; Wolf-
gang Gibowski; Sir David Gillmore; Carl Ernst Grummt; Artur
Hajnicz; Daniel Hamilton; Wojciech Hann; Martin Hanz; Peter
Hartmann; Martin van Heuven; Richard Holbrooke; Jerzy Holzer;
Karl-Heinz Hornhues; Berthold Huber; Robert Hunter; Erich Iltgen;
Wolfgang Ischinger; Gerhard Jahn; Marlies Jansen; Robert John-
son; Reinhard Junker; Uwe Kästner; Dieter Kastrup; Catherine
Kelleher; Reinhard Keller; Robert Kimmitt; Klaus Kinkel; Michael
Koch; Valentine Kosch; Eberhard Kuhrt; Adam Krzeminski; Die-
trich von Kyaw; Michael Koch; Helmut Kohl; John Kornblum;
Gerd Langguth; Sir Christopher Mallaby; Hubert Marquitan; Tho-
mas Matussek; Markus Meckel; Thomas Meyer; Andreas Meyer-
Landrut; Gerd Mielke; Jerzy Milewski; Bowman Miller; Hans
Misselwitz; Gebhard von Moltke; Hubertus von Morr; Klaus
Murmann; Klaus Naumann; Klaus Neubert; Pauline Neville-Jones;
Henning von Ondarza; Janusz Onyszkiewicz; Mark Palmer; Hein-
rich Pfeiffer; Ulrich Pfeiffer; Friedbert Pflueger; Hans-Friedrich von
Ploetz; Gerd Poppe; Konrad Porzner; Hans-Joachim Queisser; Peter
Radunski; Charles E. Redman; Rolf Reissig; Janusz Reiter; Josef
Rembser; Edzard Reuter; Hermann Rudolph; Volker Rühe; Jacek
Saryusz-Wolski; Gunter Schabowski; Wolfgang Schäuble; Fritz
Scharpf; Cornelia Schmalz-Jacobsen; Barthel Schoelgens; Franz
Schoser; Richard Schröder; Jörg Schönbohm; Wilhelm Schönfelder;
Volker Schroer; Horst Schulmann; Eberhard Schulz; Franz-Joseph
Schulze; Berndt Seite; Konrad Seitz; Jamie Shea; Horst Siedschlag;
Thomas Simons; Helmut Sonnenfeld; Uwe Stehr; Gerrit Stein;
Manfred Stolpe; Jerzy Sulek; Henryk Szlajfer; Jerzy Szmajdzinski;
Karol Szyndzielorz; Jan G. van derTas; Horst Teltschik; Wolfgang

Thierse; Mieczyslav Tomala; Wolfgang Ullmann; Edward Unger; Hans-Joachim Veen; Alexander Vershbow; Dietrich Vogel; Heinrich Vogel; Wolfdietrich Vogel; Wolfgang Vogel; Karsten Voigt; Ruprecht Vondran; Jenonne Walker; Norbert Walter; Vernon Walters; Henning Wegener; Werner Weidenfeld; Hans-Heinrich Weise; Hans Georg Wieck; Michael Weller; Thomas Weston; Inge Wettig-Danielmeier; Peter Wild; Anna Wolff-Paweska; Vera Wollenberger; Roland Wötzel; and others, for answering questions with authority, good humor and candor.

- Christopher N. and Bonnie E. Moon, and the Graduate College of the University of Iowa, each in their respective way, for help with the index.

- Tamara Schoenbaum-Holtermann, because she's there.

- Thanks go also to the *Wall Street Journal Europe* for permission to reprint excerpts from an article by Elizabeth Pond from October 1994, and to McKinsey and Company, Inc., for permission to quote from McKinsey Global Institute's 1993 study of 'Manufacturing Productivity'.

Iowa City   DAVID SCHOENBAUM
Bonn   ELIZABETH POND
November 1995

1 The Once and Future Kingdom

The Germans 'come from the day before yesterday or the day after tomorrow,' Friedrich Nietzsche declared in 1886. 'As yet, they have no today.'[1] A hundred years later, on the downward slope of an uncommonly strenuous century, it appeared that Germans had turned Nietzsche, and themselves, upside down. Once they had aspired to be great, if not good. Now, West Germans, at least, appeared to live in the best of all possible presents, and wanted, in principle, to be just like everybody else. To their own and other people's surprise, they also showed a startling aptitude for it.[2] On the threshold of a new, twenty-first century, the combination of 'carpe diem' and 'sufficient unto the day' seemed to suffice as never before in living memory.

In 1933, the grandparents and great-grandparents of today's Germans had made a pact with the devil. Twelve years later, the deal had virtually brought German history itself to an end, and divided the country into successor states conceived in the image of their occupiers. 'No more excitement,' a just-demobilized 19-year-old officer replied, when asked his plans for the future.[3] Now, after nearly half a century, one Germany, at least, was safe, civil, prosperous, democratic, a solidly unassertive international citizen.[4] A place people shunned half a century earlier, it now attracted immigrants from around the world, even Jews from the Middle East and Eastern Europe, who came not only to work, and remit one of the world's most desirable currencies, but to bring their families, start businesses, and settle down. Polled in June 1986 on how they viewed their neighbors, 55% of the citizens of the European Community (now Union) expressed some or much confidence in the Germans, compared to 56% in the Dutch, 52% in the Danes and Belgians, and 50% in the Luxemburgers.[5] Britain, France and all others trailed behind.

This time there was no need, and still less temptation, for a pact with the devil. Yet things were better than they had ever been before. 'When in this century have Germans had it best?' the pollsters asked. In 1951 only 2% had answered 'today'. By 1959 the figure had risen to 42%, by 1963 to 63%, by 1970 to 81%. A decade later the figure was virtually

1

unchanged.[6] Where the old days had so obviously been bad, and even the nation's Green and procreative instincts hinted at strong reservations about the future, Germans, to a greater degree than most people, lived in, and certainly for, the present.

'This convention takes place at a time of unexpected happenings and social transitions . . .' declared a major German labor leader in his keynote address to his nominally leftwing union, in Berlin, the hitherto divided city, in November 1989, the very month the Wall came down, liberating 16 million fellow Germans from a 40-year dictatorship, and ending a Cold War that had brought the world to the brink of nuclear war. 'In such a situation, where insecurity and fear of the future are all around us, truth and candor are indicated,' he continued. He then delivered a litany of impending environmental catastrophes.[7] Five years later, half of all Germans acknowledged fear of a nuclear accident, 40% fear of damage to their health from chemical wastes, over 30% fear of global warming, 20% fear of genetic engineering, 10% fear of the electromagnetic fields generated by high tension wires and cellular telephones.[8] Overall birthrates were at record lows, East German birthrates below even the record lows of World War II and the depths of the Great Depression.[9] Governments, parties, candidates, deported themselves accordingly.

'Not without tensions, but thoroughly middle-class, rather conservative than innovative, perhaps a bit boring and, all things considered, amazingly "normal",' an astute Swiss journalist reported as early as 1956.[10] He was speaking, of course, of West Germany, the Federal Republic created in 1949 from what had only recently been American, British and French zones of occupation. But it was already clear that the terms Germany and West Germany were merging, in ways that enhanced the legitimacy of one postwar successor at the slow but ultimately corrosive cost of the other.[11] 'Germany 2, German Democratic Republic 1', a young Leipziger replied matter-of-factly in summer 1974 when asked by a visitor about a soccer game in progress between the Federal Republic and 'the first socialist state on German soil', of which he was an unwilling citizen.[12] Yet 85 per cent of West Germans in 1973, and 93% in 1983, viewed a united Germany as unlikely or out of the question.[13] East German responses would probably have been similar – had the likelihood of a unified Germany been a question East German pollsters asked.

Like Goethe's Faust, that most proverbially German of German literary personae, twentieth century Germans had yearned for generations for the day when they could finally say 'Abide, you are so fair.'[14]

Now, if opinion surveys were a guide, they said it whenever the pollster asked them. The question was whether, and how long, they expected their luck to hold. That Germans paid only 5% of GNP as private insurance, compared to 8% in the United States and 11.4% in Britain,[15] could be read as an expression of confidence in their public insurance, established since Bismarck in one of the world's most respected and comprehensive social security systems. But, when the 5% was added to gross savings that had grown from 20% to 27% of GNP between 1982 and the first half of 1990, the combined investment suggested at least a hedge against an increasingly uncertain future.[16]

Even domestic observers noted that stress (pronounced 'shtress')-prone West Germans, cushioned by some of the world's most generous health insurance, engaged the services of 9000 academically-trained psychotherapists, and countless other ad hoc practitioners. West German hospitals, their favorite news magazine reported in 1994, also maintained some 7000 beds for psychiatric and mental health patients, more than the rest of the world put together.[17] Tourism, two thirds of it outside Germany, accounted for 4% of German consumer spending. Americans, by comparison, spent 1% of their consumer dollars on tourism.[18] But it was anybody's guess how much of this *Wanderlust* represented traditional German yearning for classical art and monuments, post-modern longing for fun in the sun, or a shared need to escape from what many seemed to view as intolerable social and occupational tensions.

Yet few realities in life are harder to resist than tomorrow. In May 1989, with the following November still barely visible over the horizon, George Bush, the President of the United States, appeared in Mainz in the company of Helmut Kohl, the German Chancellor. Like millions of his contemporaries half a century before, Bush had fought in a war to liberate Europe from Germans, and incidentally liberate Germans from themselves. Now, on Kohl's home turf, he addressed the Chancellor's constituents as 'partners in leadership', noted the opening of the Hungarian-Austrian border, and called for the same openness in Berlin. The Wall 'must come down', he declared in what was obviously meant to be an applause line.[19] As the cameras turned squarely on the representative face in the crowd, viewers around the world could hardly help notice his implacable expression and folded arms. Yet by early 1990, what had seemed unthinkable barely half a year before showed every likelihood of becoming inevitable.[20]

On 11 July 1994, as the once unchallengeable dollar plunged by a full 1 per cent against the Deutschmark, another American President appeared, this time in Berlin, to encourage Germans to 'become America's main partner' in reintegrating the East and Central European countries that Americans had helped liberate from Germany half a century before.[21] Like it or not, for better or for worse – and views were mixed[22] – Germany and Europe again were one. Both Germans and Europeans would have to live with it. The only question left was how. For, as Strauss's and Hofmannsthal's Marschallin rightly points out in Act I of 'Der Rosenkavalier,' 'It's how it's done that makes all the difference.'[23]

THE PAST AS PROLOGUE

If the twentieth century could reasonably be called the American Century,[24] its first five decades could as plausibly be called the German Half-Century. Yet, even measured against the dramatic standards of the first half-century, the second was only slightly less remarkable. Now, on the threshold of a new, twenty-first century, Germans again found the world's eyes turned expectantly and apprehensively in their direction.

Between 1870 and 1945, the span of a single lifetime, Germans had twice been pariahs. They had witnessed the collapse of a kingdom, a republic, a fascist and a communist dictatorship; two world wars and the runaway inflations that followed them, and the loss of up to a third of their national territory to eastern neighbors. They had inflicted on themselves a loss of intellectual capital[25] like none, perhaps, since the fall of Byzantine Constantinople to the Ottomans in 1453. They had seen the destruction of their factories and cities by Allied bombs and invading armies. Almost one German in five had been expelled from ancient homes by vengeful East and Central European neighbors. Three million more had fled as voluntary refugees from the Communist east. The delivery of their politically and morally bankrupt country into international receivership after World War II had led to 40 years of national division. Yet their position at century's end – and the malaise, ambivalence and self-doubt that attended it – were in many ways uncannily similar to what they had been when the century began. From empire to postwar republic to totalitarian dictatorship and one and another postwar republics, the eagle had survived on bills, coins, pennants and official seals as Germany's totemic bird of choice. The phoenix seemed at least as appropriate.

Identified *post facto* as a perennial and constant of European history, the German Question was really nothing of the kind. It was, on the contrary, a relatively recent discovery, the product of a world that had learned from Americans and Frenchmen to regard the national state as a natural corollary of the pursuit of happiness. For the next 200 years, the war of attrition between dynasty, class and nation dominated European affairs. All three had ancient roots and powerful champions, not least in Germany. But nation was the clear winner. Stirred and energized by the power of steam, the magic of the market, and the truths others already held to be self-evident,[26] Germans too acquired a taste for more perfect union. What they wanted in principle differed only marginally from what others around them wanted too, among them Serbs, Belgians, Poles, Italians, Czechs, Hungarians, Roumanians, Bulgarians and Irish. But history, geography and numbers made Germany an aggravated case.

On 8 May 1945, Germans surrendered unconditionally to a coalition of American, British, French and Soviet forces. Historians have debated ever since whether what followed was really an end of history, a midnight from which the 24-hour clock resumed at zero. But be it '*Stunde Null*' or watershed, the moral and physical devastation at the epicenter of history's greatest war was powerful evidence that the 75-year experiment in German national unity had failed in ways that made the German Question everybody's question – save, perhaps, the Germans'. The most German of all wars, World War II had cost upward of 50 million dead, among them some 3.5 million German soldiers, twice as many as in World War I, plus a million German civilians.[27]

Like anybody else's, the German future makes no sense without the past. But to an even greater degree than most, the German present makes no sense without the watershed experience of World War II. Even after half a century, the lessons and legacies were still piled high around for all to see. To the survivors, including both the prostrate Germans and their conquerors, it seemed obvious that the so-called German Empire, the fully sovereign quasi-national German state created in 1870, was just one more casualty. A year later, Prussia, the resilient North German dynastic state that had first delivered the Empire, then dominated it from birth, had joined the casualty list too.

Philosophers had interpreted the world in their various ways, the young Karl Marx declared in 1845. What mattered now was changing it.[28] The world had interpreted – and tried to coexist with – Germany in various ways, the nominally United Nations declared in much the same spirit almost exactly a hundred years later. What mattered now was changing it – and doing the job themselves.

The possibilities included loss of sovereignty, dismemberment, partition, deindustrialization, even Germany's disappearance from the map. Nothing like this had happened in Europe since the eighteenth century, when Poland, a state of great magnitude and far greater antiquity, was partitioned by its neighbors, or since 1814–15 when most of Europe combined to contain and restrain a revolutionary France. The consensus of 1941–5 soon crumbled. Yet as the Western Allies and the Soviet Union learned again to coexist and even cooperate in the 1950s, the residue of improvisations, faits accomplis, pragmatic understandings and summit-level agreements to disagree, acquired a life of its own, and people even found it good.[29] If there was no settlement like Versailles or Vienna to show for the greatest war in history, a peace treaty emerged as incrementally as the British Constitution. Untried, untested and initially crisis-prone, the intricate improvisation became the status quo, including two German successor states, one West, one East, both united and divided by a common history,

On 3 October 1990, the two German states – successor states, client states, little brother states to respective superpower-big brother states – again became one. Wistfully recalling the French sociologist Ernest Renan's definition of nationhood as a community of shared memories, a senior official in the federal chancellery later recalled sitting with his mother, wife and 10–year-old son in front of the family TV. It only occurred to him in stages, he said, how differently the people in the room perceived what was happening on the screen.

The experience had made him want to write an essay about the nuances and comparative use of 'unification' and 'reunification'.[30] The prefix re-, and the anxieties so obviously contained in it, subsumed nearly two centuries of German history, and four decades of heated debate on the nature and direction of German statehood. If reunited, Germany was again the house that Bismarck built and Hitler destroyed, with all its attendant territorial, treaty and legal claims, traditions, legacies, dilemmas, ambivalences and, not incidentally, debts.[31] If united, it was neither more nor less than the postwar Federal Republic plus five new federal states and some 17 million people, that is, a liberal democracy, and market economy, deeply rooted in postwar soil, with its face turned squarely to the West. Was the new Germany, in fact, a new Germany? Both Germans and non-Germans found it natural, even irresistible, to scrutinize the current scene for traces of 'assertiveness'[32] and generally consult the Lessons of History. But it was soon clear that there was a lot of history to consult, and that a lot of very different lessons could be learned from it.

THE COURSE OF GERMAN HISTORY

'The history of the Germans is a history of extremes', the English historian A. J. P. Taylor proclaimed in 1946. 'It contains everything except moderation, and in the course of a thousand years the Germans have experienced everything except normality.'[33] As time passed, the author even substituted 'German' for 'world', as in 'First German war' and 'Second German war'.[34] The usage failed to catch on. Yet innumerable Germans too had meanwhile concluded that there was something endemically rotten in the state of a Germany that had twice devastated itself and much of the world around it within little more than a generation.

Germany was 'a special case', Taylor emphasized in a preface for American readers, 'an alien body in the structure of European civilisation'.[35] Still in print two decades later, the Taylor's-eye view of Germany history, like a kind of historiographical equivalent of the ubiquitously parodied New Yorker's view of America, had become both an icon and an optical chart for Germans and German-watchers alike.

Young German historians, who would dominate the field for the next two generations, reached similar conclusions. Dismissing any thought that the Nazi era was an 'accident,' they combed and scoured archives for the fatal flaws that had destroyed the Weimar republic, the tectonic faults that guided Bismarck's empire to World War I, and the original sin of 1848 that ended in the Prussian-led unification process. 'A difficult fatherland', the sober and candid Gustav Heinemann called the country that elected him its third postwar president in 1969. Asked if he loved his country, Heinemann replied that he loved his wife. In 1971, on the eve of the first postwar election in which an incumbent Social Democratic Chancellor directly appealed to German pride, only 42 per cent of Germans admitted pride in being German. By 1981 the figure had fallen to 35%. The same year, in a comparative survey of national pride in fifteen nations, including a variety of Europeans, Icelanders, Finns, Japanese and Mexicans, Germans led from the rear.[36]

Foreigners conventionally assumed that Germans ducked their history. The truth was quite the contrary. By the 1980s, the 'special case' was an established orthodoxy, enshrined in a joyless vision of the past that criss-crossed the entire modern era.[37] It was virtually impossible to imagine a non-German, or an East German, equivalent for the *Historikerstreit*, the 'historians' war', of the mid-1980s. Ignited by the quirky Ernst Nolte's effort to 'historicize' the German genocide as a reaction to prior, Soviet, mass murders, the controversy soon blazed away on its own, while fascinated outsiders watched.[38]

On the fortieth anniversary of the postwar Federal Republic, and the very threshold of the remarkable events that were to make Berlin the capital of a united Germany for the first time since World War II, James Joll, another distinguished English historian of Germany, recalled a recent whirlwind tour of the city. His guide, a former student, had recently been appointed founding director of a newly-authorized Museum of German History that itself was to be twin and complement of a newly-authorized Museum of the Federal Republic in Bonn. The chosen itinerary was an unrelieved, but emblematic, parade of debacles and calamities. They had first visited the place where the writer Kleist killed himself in a suicide pact in 1811. They then looked at the window where the abortive Weimar Republic was proclaimed in 1918. After that they inspected the place where Rosa Luxemburg's body was dragged from the Landwehr canal a few months after her murder in early 1919. Then came the courtyard where the anti-Hitler conspirators had been executed in 1944, and the site where young Peter Fechter had bled to death after trying to escape over the Wall from East Berlin in 1962. 'Well,' Joll concluded cheerfully as he described it to another former student, 'that's German history for you.'

Yet even as Germans pursued their 'special way', this time in retrograde, foreigners increasingly found German experience less alien, more familiar, even more attractive than they once assumed.[39] Writing in 1916, an ambivalent American Progressive acknowledged his respect, even affection, 'for the orderliness, finish and perfection of administration that makes for personal comfort and convenience', 'the generous provision for art, music, drama and the cultural things of life', 'the wonderful elementary, vocational and high schools', 'the far-seeing legislation for the protection of the worker from the costs of industrial and urban life . . . and the many municipal services . . .that explain in large measure the charm of the German city.'[40]

Writing nearly 80 years and all the multitudinous vicissitudes of a turbulent century later, a French economist turned insurance-executive, and a reflective British journalist came to similarly positive conclusions. 'The economic and social superiority of the Rhine model is manifest', the economist declared.[41] 'Given a free and informed choice, where would most people rather be born if they did not know which class or ethnic group they would belong to, Detroit or Cologne?' the journalist asked.[42]

BENCHMARKS

By the end of the twentieth century, Germany was in some ways startlingly similar to, in other ways startlingly different from, what it had been when the century began. But in a land where tomorrow had arrived so suddenly and with so little advance notice, both the similarities and differences seemed somehow to come as a surprise.

On the threshold of the new century, a united Germany, with eight neighbors and its capital in Berlin, had been a continental power with global reach, global interests, and a receptive audience for the newly composed symphonies of Gustav Mahler. Now, on the threshold of the twenty-first century, a united Germany, with nine neighbors and its capital in Berlin, would again be a continental power with a global reach, global interests, and a receptive audience for the Mahler symphonies, that had meanwhile become both ubiquitous and classic.[43]

In 1910 a German Empire, extending from Aachen to Königsberg, was home to 15% of the population of a continent that was itself home to about a quarter of the human race. The empire's population of 65 million people, compared with Britain's 45 and France's 39 million, had itself grown from 56 million in a decade, reflecting an average birthrate of over four per thousand women between 15 and 50. Over 40% of Germans were under 20, fewer than 10% over 60. An ethnic or linguistic count, including some 16 million Germans in the Habsburg Empire, Switzerland, the Balkans, the Russian Empire, etc., brought the German total to nearly one European in five.[44]

Eighty-four years later, a newly united Germany extended from Aachen to Frankfurt/Oder; and there was even talk, though also concern, again about Königsberg[45]. Some 88 million German speakers, including almost 80 million citizens of the Federal Republic, most Austrians, the majority of Swiss, and sprinklings of German-speaking French, Italians and Luxembourgeois, compared to 60 million Anglophones and 60 million Francophones, were still the European Union's largest ethnic-linguistic community.[46] But of Germany's 80 million people including resident foreigners, barely 20% were now under 20; over 20% were over 60; and Germans represented about 11% of a

European population defined to include the former republics of the Soviet Union that now constituted the Community of Independent States (CIS). With even the populations of Armenia and Kirghizstan thus added, Europeans now made up barely 12% of the world's population.[47]

Firmly astride a Europe that was itself the world's powerhouse and center of gravity, Germans in 1900 had as much reason as anyone to see the new century as theirs, and themselves as generic Europeans. After the fact, it was easy to rediscover, amplify, even savor, the ambivalence, malaise, misgivings and *angst* of artists, philosophers and composers, the dark intimations of poets, and the partiality of the young Thomas Mann for death and social entropy. Yet the indestructible monumentality of then-new *gymnasien*, borough halls, even synagogues – still robust a century later – delivers a very different message about public priorities, civic style and national self-assurance.

Even Germans conceded that their country could be difficult to love. Though they had last gone to war in 1870, their armies were the continent's and world's most potent, their efficiency proverbial, their uniforms alone an object of emulation from West Point to Chile.[48] On the threshold of the new century, an international expeditionary force set off for China under German command, the emperor's injunction that they cause their adversaries to remember the ancient Huns echoing after them. Meanwhile, a fleet, intended to deter and challenge a pace-setting Britain in order that Germany too might be a global power, was already well under construction. By the early twentieth century, containment of Germany was the only strategy that made sense to most of its neighbors.[49]

Yet even while fearing Germany, contemporaries found it equally difficult not to respect, admire, imitate, let alone do business with it. On the very eve of World War I, Britain and Germany were one another's major trading partner. French and German businessmen, who were to collaborate in one kind of Europe after 1940, and a very different one after 1950, already felt comfortable enough in one another's company to make their governments anxious.[50]

Even in an era of general and legendary growth, German growth rates were a wonder of the world. Between 1885 and 1913, Britain's economy, the world's most mature, grew by 2.1%. Over the same period, Germany's average annual growth was 4.5%, compared with America's 5.2% and Russia's 5.7%. But American growth was favored by waves of immigrants, tidal currents of foreign investment, and virtually bottomless domestic demand; while Russia's enjoyed the statistical amplification that goes with threshold baselines. German figures impressed absolutely as well as relatively. In 1900, German miners produced 149 million tons for 65 million people, as opposed to Russia's 16.2 million tons for 111 million. They had incidentally increased production by nearly two-thirds since 1890, making them third only to headstart Britain and a thunderously dynamic America. Between 1900 and 1910, production again rose by more than half. Iron production, another of the era's other leading indicators, was already approaching British levels. In steel, Germans already surpassed British production, leaving a substantially larger America as Germany's only peer.

But *Kultur* was Germany's real comparative advantage. For anyone with academic aspirations, German was as self-evidently the *lingua franca* of scholarship as French was the language of diplomacy, Italian the language of opera, and Latin the language of the Catholic church.[51] From agronomy to zoology, Germans not only advanced, but practically defined, the natural sciences. From Göttingen and Halle to Berlin and Strassburg/Strasbourg, Germans virtually invented the modern research university.[52] By 1900 it was imitated from Dorpat (now Tartu) on the Baltic to Iowa City and Tokyo.

The newly established Nobel prizes reflected the magnitude of German achievement. From their creation in 1901 to the eve of World War II, Germans, including an occasional Austrian, led all comers with 11 laureates in medicine, 13 in physics and 17 in chemistry. They also left their mark on the prize for literature. From 1901 and 1912, four of thirteen prizes went to German writers, including the historian Theodor Mommsen, the philosopher Rudolf Eucken, the poet Paul Heyse and the playwright Gerhard Hauptmann. It was 1929 before another German writer, Thomas Mann, was so honored. It was 1946 before he was followed by Hermann Hesse. But Hesse by then had been a Swiss citizen for 25 years, and Mann, expatriated by the Nazis, had successively become a citizen of Czechoslovakia and the United States.

For good measure, there was even a sprinkling of German peace laureates – Gustav Stresemann, the annexationist-turned-diplomat, who shared the 1926 prize with his French colleague Aristide Briand for their common efforts at Franco-German reconciliation, the pacifist parliamentarian Ludwig Quidde in 1927, and Carl von Ossietzky, the leftwing editor, who blew the whistle on illicit rearmament, and eventually paid with his life, in 1936.[53] Since the recognition of Ossietzky was seen as an affront to the national honor, neither he nor any other designated German laureates were allowed to accept the prize, and the prize itself was declared un-German.

As a relatively young man on the eve of World War I, the photographer August Sander undertook a taxonomy of German social types in a series of portraits as penetrating as any since Dürer and Cranach. In 1929, the first 60 of a projected 540 appeared in Munich as *Antlitz der Zeit* (*The Countenance of the Times*). The collection confirmed the photographer as one of the century's masters. On taking power in 1933, the Nazis confiscated and destroyed the plates and unsold copies. Sander's son, arrested for distributing Communist handbills, subsequently died in a Nazi jail. In 1935 Sander undertook a collection of cityscapes, conceived as 'Old Cologne'. Ten years later, amidst the debris of both Old Cologne and the German Half-Century, Sander turned his camera on the devastated and British-occupied city like an archaeologist in the ruins of Angkor Wat or Chichen Itza.[54] The postwar Cologne he now portrayed was another countenance of the times, a wasteland only the eerier for the seeming absence of human beings. By the end of the war, the city's population had shrunk from over 750,000 to some 40,000.

Warning and benchmark alike, the devastation left such an impression that half a century later postcard photos of the ruins could be bought at newsstands in big city rail stations. But just as Germans had set world-class standards in destruction and self-destruction, they now proved equally adept at digging out and cleaning up. The ruins were virtually gone by the mid-1950s. A little more than 40 years after Sander's moonscapes, a British and an American visitor retraced his footsteps en route to the opera, itself built between 1954 and 1957, in what was effectively a new city. Lifetime students of German history, both were struck by what they saw. The house alone was a demonstrative statement of postwar priorities.[55] The production of Mozart's *Die Entführung aus dem Serail* was interesting too. In a city as Catholic as any north of Italy, where even Protestants till recently considered themselves a diaspora, Turks were now the tailor down the street, or the grocer around the corner and Islam was taught in school. The Neumarkt was now a blur of homebound traffic. Among the well-stocked department store windows, sidewalk purveyors peddled ethnic fast food to Germans, whose parents could not easily have distinguished a pizza from a paella. Regarding the scene over a slice of stand-up pizza, the older man recalled looking out on it from the same place in 1945 when he was a precocious major in the British army. 'You know,' he reflected, 'you couldn't even believe there would ever be a city here again.'

In Cologne at the time, like the rest of the British and American zones that later made up the core of the Federal Republic, official rations for 'normal' consumers ranged from 1500 to under 1000 calories daily.[56] Yet only a few years later there was once more fire in the ashes.[57] Ten years after midnight, 'economic miracle' was both a fact of life and a part of the vernacular language. A few years later, in the first good study of postwar German politics, Fritz René Allemann, who had tracked developments in Germany since his student days in the early 1930s, reported a panorama of 'clear, easy to follow curves, all pointing upward' to sovereignty, stability and prosperity.[58] Disgracefully, his book was never translated into English. But its title, *Bonn ist nicht Weimar (Bonn is not Weimar)*, soon became a household phrase.

Forty years after their creation and nominal disarmament at the hands of the wartime Allies who were now their patrons, both postwar Germanies had again acquired a serious military presence. But this time it was confined to a very small space. As respective pillars of the contending alliance systems that were designed to contain them as well as defend them, Germans were also more or less reluctant hosts to some of the world's densest military concentrations forces, with some 400,000 troops from America, Britain, France, Belgium, the Netherlands and Canada on one side and 380,000 from the Soviet Union on the other side, of the German–German border. Equipped with everything the modern conventional armorer could offer, German armies, including 490,000 Western and 172,000 Eastern troops, were second only to those of their superpower patrons.

But in contrast to the early years of the century, it was Germans themselves who were scared and irritated by it. For the first time since World War II, German generals again commanded international forces as senior partners in NATO. Yet for most Germans, the idea of deploying expeditionary forces beyond their borders, let alone recalling the Huns, was as remote as the thought of a battleship navy. If they again fantasized about sovereignty, as they had in the 1920s and '30s, this time the point was not rearmament but disengagement, even disarmament. In an age of middle- and short-range missiles, the idea that their Allies might actually defend them was as terrifying as the fear that they might not. By 1988, one in eight young Germans availed himself of one of the world's most permissive conscientious objection laws, and roughly 40% of draft-eligible West Germans classified their own army as 'potential murderers'.[59]

In the late 1960s, Germans had viewed the Nuclear Non-Proliferation Treaty as a potential obstacle to rapport with France, and a potential handicap in the acquisition and development of what was then assumed to be a leading-edge technology.[60] Thirty years later, the reservations of 1968 made odd reading. In a country where Greens had flourished as nowhere else,[61] disposal of nuclear waste was a perennial political hot button. Despite one of the world's lowest thresholds of nuclear sensitivity, West Germans had nonetheless learned to generate 12% of their electricity in nuclear plants.[62] But when an American strategic intellectual insisted that post-unification Germany would need its own Bomb,[63] most Germans regarded him as someone from another planet.

The economic figures, by comparison, were limpidly straight-forward. The world's third largest economy when the century began, West Germany alone was again the world's third largest economy, second only to the United States and Japan. Second only to the Soviet Union, its East German sibling led its bloc too. Contingent on exchange rates, West Germany was also the world's first or second biggest exporter, far ahead of Japan, despite the Bundesbank's proverbially cautious management of what had long become one of the world's most desirable currencies. Per capita GNP was second only to the United States, Luxemburg and Switzerland. Inflationary pressures were among the world's lowest – 2.8% in 1989, up from 0.2% two years before. The work week – 37.5 hours with 40 days of holiday and paid vacation - was among the developed world's shortest. Wages and benefits were among the world's highest, time lost to strikes was among the world's lowest.[64]

The scene of some of the academic world's most spectacular upheavals before and after 1968, perennially overcrowded, under-equipped and underfunded,[65] the German university had admittedly lost much of its legendary sheen. Like *Angst*, *Weltanschauung* and *Blitzkrieg*, occasional German neologisms – *Ostpolitik*, *Gastarbeiter* – still made their way into international usage. But in the ever more comprehensively anglophone world of software, air travel and rock singers, the German language too had lost much of its international mystique.[66] Nobel laureates, made in Germany, no longer rolled off the academic production lines either. Between 1944 and 1990, Germans carried away only three Nobel prizes in medicine, ten in chemistry and eight in physics. A grim but telling measure of achievement, the physics total might have reached eleven or higher, had emigration and exile not caused such laureates as Wolfgang Pauli, Max Born and Hans Bethe to earn their Nobels as citizens of other countries. The good news, testifying to the sturdy recovery and high quality of basic research, was that four of the German prizes were won between 1985 and 1989. While some of the work took place in universities, a large part went on in the 64 modestly financed but impressively productive Max Planck Institutes, whose accessibility to foreign colleagues testified to another of the nicer traditions of German science.[67]

German writers won two postwar prizes for literature. But one of the two was the Jewish poet Nelly Sachs, who had continued for decades to write in German from her Swedish exile.[68] The other was the novelist Heinrich Böll, a lifelong resident of Cologne. Since World War II, a single German had won a peace prize, Chancellor Willy Brandt in 1971, after a trail-blazing campaign to normalize Germany's relations with eastern neighbors. In 1990, the Nobel committee then honored one of the executors of German unity. But it was Mikhail Gorbachev, the Soviet leader, not Helmut Kohl, the West German leader, nor any of the nameless thousands of East German demonstrators, whose courage in the streets of Leipzig and Berlin caused the Wall to come tumbling down in November 1989.

Yet even after school wars that shook Germany as they did the rest of the developed world, the *abitur*, the traditional college-preparatory certificate, remained the Mercedes of secondary school diplomas, and German vocational education was still acknowledged as 'the envy of the rest of the world'.[69] Comprehensive, well-funded public services from health and transportation to museums, theater and music again made German cities liveable in ways Americans could only covet. Public spending on the arts in 1989 alone amounted to DM 9 billion, the equivalent of $6 billion, most of it state (in the US sense) and local.[70] Meanwhile, a generation of postwar German directors captured the attention of cinéastes from Paris to Tokyo and, by 1995, German conductors presided over no fewer than three of America's five premier orchestras.[71]

But it was German normality, a phenomenon that hitherto seemed a contradiction in terms, that struck even Germans as the most remarkable achievement of all. 'I know France, Italy, Britain and the United States fairly well,' a thoughtful German political scientist concluded in 1989 at one of the typically international symposia, convened to observe West Germany's fortieth birthday. '. . .Who would want to claim that they are better equipped, as modern democracies than we are?'[72] Paradoxically, the unified Germany that would soon issue from another of the century's geopolitical earthquakes could also be plausibly described as 'the first normal state in German history'.[73] But what was new about paradox in German history?

FORWARD TO THE PAST

A disastrous year for prophets, 1989 was at least a banner year for those historical benchmarks from which people measure their progress, direction and options: 50 years since the outbreak of World War II, 60 since the crash of the Wall Street market, 70 since the Versailles treaty and 75 since the outbreak of World War I, 200 since the great French Revolution. It was also the fortieth anniversary of the two postwar Germanies that had once been one, and whose borders, fortunes, parameters, style, monuments, icons, coins and even language, collectively bore witness to all the year's other commemorations. Together, the Federal Republic of (West) Germany, with its capital in Bonn, and the (East) German Democratic Republic, with its capital in (East) Berlin, had already outlived their Nazi predecessor (1933–45) by 28 years, and its Weimar republican predecessor (1919–33) by 26. As late as August, when Poland's first non-communist government in 40 years made dominoes shiver from the Baltic to the Elbe, the two postwar Germanies still showed every promise of overtaking, then outliving, Bismarck's so-called empire (1870–1918). With only another eight years to go, the two Germanies between them would then constitute the most durable German regime since Napoleon dispatched the decrepit Holy Roman Empire after 1006 years in 1806.

In fact, a very different, post-postwar era was already forming below their feet. Yet for most people, even at the faultline, the future remained as abstract as an actuarial table and as unpredictable as a California earthquake.[74] In a book that appeared before the remarkable year was over, but still far short of its dénouement on 3 October 1990, David Marsh, the Bonn correspondent of London's *Financial Times*, left a fortuitous benchmark for measuring what followed.

An interviewer of uncommon energy and enterprise, who covered his beat with what might be described in any other context as German thoroughness, Marsh was basically concerned with sounding out his interlocutors on the restive state of the national psyche after 40 years of prosperity and democracy. But he made a point of reserving a final question for their views on the likelihood of reunification. Art for its own sake between early 1988 and February 1989, the results made humbling and ironic reading afterward.

'I do not believe in reunification,' said Joachim Fest, a senior editor of the relentlessly establishmentarian *Frankfurter Allgemeine*. 'We gave up reunification as a solution thirty years ago,' said Werner Holzer, the editor of the forthrightly left-of-center *Frankfurter Rundschau*. 'The idea of reunification is completely hopeless,' said Manfred Rommel, the maverick Christian Democratic mayor of Stuttgart. 'I reject the word reunification,' declared Daniel Cohn-Bendit, a surviving monument of the Parisian student revolution of 1968, and now an active West German Green. 'No one thinks of reunification,' said Edzard Reuter, the chairman of Daimler–Benz, and son of Ernst, the mayor who led West Berlin through the heroic months of the Soviet blockade some 40 years before. 'I have not used the word 'reunification' for thirty years, said Helmut Schmidt, the former Social Democratic chancellor. Karl Otto Pöhl, the president of the Bundesbank, was apprehensive of a 'unitary German state, which would certainly alter the balance of power in Europe, not so much from the military as from the economic point of view.' But he hoped the German–German border would someday resemble West Germany's border with Belgium.[75]

A very few with seismographic ears heard tremors that escaped most others.[76] Yet despite the prodigious efforts of their reader-friendly, market-sensitive publishers to get their books to reviewers and bookstores in less time than it normally takes a cat to deliver kittens, even they were buried in the rubble of collapsing paradigms when things began to move.[77]

Meanwhile, history itself was on display. In Bonn, the unassuming postwar capital where 20 years of studied architectural neglect were followed by 20 years of furious construction, lines formed for a large and imaginative exhibition of German capitals from the present back to Charlemagne. In West Berlin, where the huge, jamboree-like, biennial convention of the German Protestant church overflowed the fairgrounds, a panel on the course of German history filled the hockey arena. Part seminar, part Chautauqua, part sermon, the occasion featured French, Polish and American panellists, Theodor Mommsen's great grandson, a retired pillar of the East Berlin historical establishment, and the bitterly self-flagellant daughter of Albert Speer, once Hitler's armaments minister.

In Bonn a few weeks later, while everything and nothing still seemed possible, a German economist sat patiently under the trees on the Kaiserplatz, listening to an American visitor expatiate on the future of the Federal Republic of Germany. 'It all depends on immigrants, R&D

(research and development) and structural change,' he announced with a self-assurance that both remembered years later. 'And what if East Germany collapses?' she asked disarmingly. Stalled in mid-sentence, the American had the grace to concede the shrewdness of her question. 'Well, what?' he asked. In fact, she admitted, she had no idea either. But it took only another few weeks to confirm that her question was as prescient as the bafflement was universal; that reports of history's end[78] were premature; that even the best of historical educations was dubious preparation for a career in prophecy; and that anyone interested in where the world was going was nonetheless well-advised to think again about where the Germans had been.

Demography, migration and national identity were not the worst place to start. If experience was any guide, their impact on German history might be assumed to correspond to the impact of gravity on the behavior of planets. None of the three, of course, had gone unnoticed. Well before 1989, German identity had become a staple on international conference menus, and demographers, actuaries and social planners needed little reminding that Germans too were aging. An established population of nominal guests, plus successive waves of ethnic German immigrants, were a reminder that borders too were no longer what they used to be. Yet the conventional division of social scientific labor, compounded by the traditional separation of Historical Then from Journalistic Now, more frequently avoided or obscured the basic continuities and discontinuities. Only now, in the perspective of a new and ambivalently united Germany, was their cumulative impact finally attracting some attention from foreigners.[79]

Given their collective impact in the past century alone, the question of their collective impact on the next one was increasingly likely to interest Germans too. 'I've had enough of these old clichés,' the editor tells his staff in a classic American newspaper joke. 'What we need around here are some new clichés.' In the face of an unprecedented conjunction of immigration pressure, demographic decline and national ambivalence, a salutary jog of the historical memory could at least help distinguish real choices from phantoms and phonies.

THE SUM OF THE PARTS

For the student of Germany history, German or non-German, the unresolved and perhaps unresolvable paradoxes of German identity – *Ossi* or *Wessi*, *grossdeutsch* or *kleindeutsch*, east, west or *mitteleuro-*

paeisch – have been among the conundrums of national existence since Germans first concluded they were a modern nation. The first of its kind in history, Bismarck's eccentric, but recognizable, German national state excluded millions of Austrian and East European Germans and included millions of Polish, Alsatian and Danish non-Germans. It was also seen by both Germans and foreigners as a secular achievement.[80]

Yet by 1914, millions of Germans, for a variety of reasons, had concluded that the deliberately circumscribed, this-far-and-no-further, Prussocentric solution of 1870 was itself among their problems. The ambiguities of national identity and the horrific metamorphoses of self-image that followed the disasters of World War I were even more dramatic than those that preceded it. For the moment, at least, millions of Austrian, Bohemian and other Germans, who had been deliberately excluded from Bismarck's 'Lesser Germany', welcomed Hitler's 'Greater Germany' as the answer to their own 'German Question'. Each for their own reasons, Britain and France, then the Soviet Union, then the United States, took a different view.

This time, the ensuing catastrophe seemed to answer 'the German Question' once and for all. It was a literal article of constitutional faith that the Federal Republic of (West) Germany was a provisional entity,[81] pending free elections in the (East) German Democratic Republic, born of Soviet occupation, and a peace treaty that would determine the status of those formerly German territories east of the Oder-Neisse line that had been consigned at the end of the war to Poland and the Soviet Union. It was also an article of diplomatic principle that West Germany's allies would support, if not actively pursue, the West German claim to unification. Yet relations between the Germanies became increasingly and pragmatically conciliatory, approaching *de facto* recognition, by the early 1980s. Far from exerting themselves to isolate and subvert the other Germany, most West Germans now inclined to coexist with, and even support, it. For some, the other Germany behind the Wall was a simple fact of postwar life, to be tolerated, even respected, on its own peculiar merits, as an alternative German society. For others, it was a lesser evil, an alternative to the instability or worse that could be expected to result from its collapse. Either way, Erich Honecker's quasi-state visit to Bonn in 1987 was the crest of mutual accommodation. For most, his red-carpet reception by a Christian Democratic chancellor confirmed that 'the German question' had not only been answered, but had effectively ceased to exist.[82]

That it should now rise from the tomb, like Barbarossa from the Kyffhaeuser, was one of the many surprises of 1989. But that it should be accompanied by an unprecedented wave of immigrants from the remotest and unlikeliest places, was another. What was the German's Fatherland after 40-odd years of national partition, triumphant *Ostpolitik*, European unification, a voracious domestic labor market and a perennial bad conscience? For the gourmet of German history, it was just another three-star irony that Ernst Moritz Arndt, the professor–poet–publicist, who was the first to pose the question 'What is the German's Fatherland?' in a poem millions of children had learned in school, had ended his days in Bonn, not Berlin.

THE BEST OF TIMES, THE WORST OF TIMES

By comparison with the dilemmas of national identity, the challenges of an aging and declining population on a country with a robust reproductive past have been relatively recent. Yet most understand their potential impact on health care and tax base, social stability and international equilibrium. The same applies to the newcomers known, instructively, by a variety of different names including *Gastarbeiter* (hired, non-German labor), *Aussiedler* (ethnic Germans from Eastern Europe), *Umsiedler* (Germans from the former German Democratic Republic) and *Asylbewerber* (applicants for political asylum, both successful and unsuccessful, from all over the world). With evidence of German immigration readily available from the Black Sea to Australia, Germans for centuries have considered themselves a nation of emigrants. But they have been slow and reluctant to acknowledge that they have repeatedly been an immigrant country too.

On the eve of the nineteenth century, Germany was an aggregate of baronies, bishoprics, free cities, duchies, principalities and kingdoms, extending from somewhere west of the Rhine to somewhere east of the Vistula. Most of these were subsumed, in turn, in a Holy Roman Empire of the German Nation that was neither Holy, Roman nor imperial, and whose self-definition subsumed Danes, Poles and Czechs. Since 1700, the population of what was later to call itself a Second Empire, and that still constitutes the greater part of Germany, had grown from perhaps 15 to over 20 million people. Theologians, musicians, architects, philosophers, scientists and, increasingly, writers, bore witness to a real German culture of real international quality. German soldiers and statesmen left their marks on the continent too, whose estimated 120 million people in 1750 constituted perhaps 13–16% of the world's population.[83] Yet in the absence of *a* German state, and in the presence of dozens and hundreds of them, to speak of German politics was an academic abstraction. By the standards of the national state, that was soon to become the inernational norm, Germany was a nation without a country, where borders proliferated and both intra and international border crossings were the order of the day.

Economically, Germany's weight was close to zero, though, given the nature of German geography and statehood, some German states were more, and others less, equal. For centuries the multi-national empire called Austria had been a major power in both Germany and Europe. But Germans constituted only a fraction of its population, and the empire's German properties were only a fraction of its dynastic patrimony. An early practitioner of what would now be called industrial policy, Protestant Prussia was also an early protagonist of what would now be called a multi-cultural society. It had only recently attained some international status as a military power. But generations would pass before it discovered a strictly German mission.

On the contrary, compared with such historically demonstrable tribes as Hessians, Saxons or Bavarians, each with their indigenous landscape, dialects, costumes or cuisine, a Prussian people could hardly be said to exist. In part a civic identity, being Prussian was above all a state of mind, personified by a legendary corps of officers and civil servants, who devoted themselves to the state as Japanese might devote themselves to their company or Jesuits to their order. Though their greatest king spoke French, the majority of Prussians were, or became, Germans. But this was neither a sufficient, nor even a necessary, condition for being Prussian. In fact, with the annexation of Silesia, and the partition of Poland among Austria, Russia and Prussia, Prussia's Polish population momentarily outnumbered its German population, and the state acquired a rather substantial Jewish population into the bargain. Turning windfall contingents of French Protestant, Jewish, even Polish talent, capital and labor to its peculiar dynastic advantage, Prussia meanwhile resettled thousands of Saxon and Swabian colonists in its East Elbian territories. Yet paradoxically, the acquisition of both Jewish and Polish Catholic minority populations only made Protestant Prussia a more credible and even inevitable challenger to Catholic Austria as Germany's second state.

Then came the other states in a mini-world more like today's Latin American or Arab world than is usually imagined. Bavaria, Austria's adversary, was France's ally. Hanover, for dynastic reasons, was linked to Britain. Certain southwestern principalities were linked, in turn, to Austria. Yet despite the common denominators of language, history, religion and culture, German soldiers and princes could take arms against each other with no apparent sense of civil war, while southwest German economic immigrants could settle in Prussia, Russia, various Habsburg territories and even America with no obvious sense of existential displacement.[84]

In the very nature of this scene, losers, minorities, and underdogs of every kind were both compelled and allowed to vote with their feet. Respectively persecuted as Jews, Catholics, Protestants and non-conformists, liberals, Socialists, anti-Nazis and anti-Communists, refugees to, from and within Germany have been among the most familiar of emigrants and immigrants.

Economic emigrants, usually the great majority of the outward-bound, are hardly a novelty either. On the contrary, Germans have been mobile for centuries, usually for reasons that would hardly distinguish them from today's Anatolian *Gastarbeiter* or *Aussiedler* from Kazakhstan. German traces can still be seen as far from home and one another as Latvia, Romania, Brazil, Australia, South Africa, and the Iowa River valley.[85] Then came Napoleon and Bismarck.

On the eve of the twentieth century, Germany had changed almost beyond recognition. Endowed with a dynamic economy, a dynamic military, a dynamic culture and a dynamic foreign policy, the new Germany was also endowed with a dynamic population. In 1900 fewer than 5% of Germans were over 65. But more than a third were under 15, a figure now characteristic of countries like Algeria. Between 1815 and 1826 alone, the population grew by an average 16% a year, an awesome figure by any standards. In ways that were re-enacted in other places, the incapacity of a pre-industrial Germany to find jobs and housing for its proliferating population was a major factor both in the coming, and the anticlimactic outcome, of the 1848 revolutions. Despite the explosive industrialization that began in mid-century, the disproportion between jobs and people had led to at least two giant waves of emigration by the 1890s. Despite the departure of nearly 2.5 million Germans in the 30 years after 1870, most of them to the United States, the German population had nearly tripled since 1800.

Yet defining both who and what was German was always harder than it seemed. Like population growth, the growth of national feeling was among the century's long-waves. An aggregate of Rhinelanders and Bavarians, Saxons and Swabians, Friesians, Pomeranians and Tyroleans when the nineteenth century began, most Germans, and some Austrians, had agreed that they were Germans by the time it ended. 'What is the German's Fatherland?' Arndt asked rhetorically in 1813 in endless stanzas of breathy verse. His answer was understood to cover an area extending from the Eifel and the Alps to the Black Sea and the Gulf of Finland.

In reality, as engineered and practised between 1864 and 1870 by Bismarck, his collaborators and supporters, the nominal unification of Germany was actually a division of Germany. It deliberately excluded millions of German speakers in Austria, Switzerland, Luxembourg, the Baltic provinces of the Russian Empire, and beyond. Yet despite the cautiously balanced Lesser German borders of Bismarck's new Reich, Germans continued to lift their glasses to August Heinrich Hoffmann von Fallersleben's 'Deutschland über Alles', whose Great German borders extended by definition 'from the Meuse to the Memel, from the Adige to the Belt'. Only after World War II, when circumstances caused (West) Germans to find a more suitable national anthem, did anyone remember that Hoffmann, in the last of his three stanzas, had also appealed for justice and freedom as well as unity.

What did Germans see in one another that they apparently missed before and after? Like many nation-building processes, their experience is both interesting and a puzzle after the fact. Was the national state a result of Germans wanting to be German? Or did they only become Germans, as opposed to Saxons, Bavarians and Swabians, for the fact of living in a national state?[87] The answer would seem to be yes to both. The consequent ambiguities can be seen in the moraine of juridical nuances like *Staatsangehörigkeit* (formal citizenship), *Volksangehörigkeit* (historical ethnicity) and *Nationalität* (national identity)[88] left behind by the unification process and the idiosyncrasies of Central European history. Alone among the great European states on the eve of the twentieth century, Germany was both an emigrant and an immigrant country. Internally inconsistent until the victory of *jus sanguinis* in 1913, German citizenship was part territorial, part hereditary, in contrast to the unqualified *jus soli* of Britain and France. Despite opposition from Social Democrats, Progressives, Poles and some Catholics, the new law effectively separated citizenship from territory. Henceforth, Germans could remain German even if born abroad, while foreigners remained foreign even if born in Germany. Still opposed by Social Democrats, the descendants of the Progressives and some Catholics, the 1913 law was still valid 80 years later, witness to a state only imperfectly linked to a nation, and ambivalent as ever about taking in poor immigrants.[89]

Born alike of classical liberalism, romantic historicism, and a streak of authentic chauvinism toward neighbors both east and west, German nationalism remained 'Western' in its approach to constitutionality, free trade and national self-determination – in any case its own[90] – until the early 1860s. But from at least the end of 1848, German Liberals felt increasingly constrained to join Conservatives they couldn't beat against Socialists, Catholics, radical democrats and others that each regarded as challengers, adversaries or obstacles.

Till 1813, a deeply conservative Prussian monarchy regarded nationalism with deep suspicion. Then, under extreme Napoleonic duress and, in Wendish and Polish as well as German, a Prussian sovereign appealed 'to my people'. Now, for essentially conservative reasons, Prussia wrapped itself in the national flag, gave itself a constitution and yielded equivocally to both liberalism and parliamentarism. Yet there was always both more and less to this than met the eye. From the 1860s on, an ambivalently liberal understanding of 'national' turned increasingly conservative.[91] Previously associated with citizen soldiers, free trade and parliamentary government, the word now came to mean defence of a highly peculiar status quo against putative threats of all kinds, both internal and external – from France, Russia and Britain, Jews, Masons, Catholics, Socialists, intellectuals and modern artists.

Yet Prussian inertia too was potentially dissonant in a federation of republics, duchies and monarchies, where the press was basically free; the rule of law was basically secure; and parliaments were heard as well as seen, i.e., a national state quite different from its neighbors to the east as well as west. If a united Italy could be said to extend from Switzerland to Libya, Prussia already extended from Eastern France to Eastern Poland. Its Huguenot, Jewish and Polish legacies were already evidence of its ambiguous German identity. The wars with Denmark, Austria and France then added Alsatians and Danes to the mix, while deliberately excluding millions of Catholic Germans.

Meanwhile, the dynamics of the new economy led to systemic internal migration, and a growing appetite for cheap imported labor. As whole cohorts left the farms, mines and construction sites of the agrarian East for the industrial West, they were increasingly replaced by foreigners. In 1871, about 200,000 registered foreigners, over 40% East European, constituted about 0.5% of the German population. By 1910, there were more than 1.25 million resident foreigners, *Gastarbeiter* in all but name, 200,000 of them born in Germany. Over 60% were from Eastern Europe. Together, they constituted nearly 2% of the population.

Locally concentrated, these were impressive figures, compared even with the United States, where the railroads imported Italians and Chinese in much the way German mines and agriculture imported Poles and Ruthenians. Yet in contrast to the United States, there was not even a hint that the huddled masses had come to stay, and still less that they were welcome.[92] Strictly controlled and policed, Poles were engaged like *braceros* to work the Junker estates,then go home across the Russian or Austrian border. If anything, the presence of large numbers of Silesian, i.e., juridically Prussian, Poles in the mines of the Ruhr was itself a deterrent to employing more, and juridically foreign, Poles in Prussia's Western provinces. Yet cascades of official rhetoric to the contrary, the assimilation of Ruhr Poles was as successful and uneventful as their americanization in Milwaukee or Detroit, and the process itself was remarkably similar.[93]

In the aftermath of a war that scrambled Eastern Europe, and cost Germany some 7% of its prewar population in casualties and lost territories, immigration resumed where it had stopped before the war. By 1925, registered foreigners, more than 77% of them East European, and the majority from the newly-constituted Austria, Poland and Czechoslovakia,[94] again constituted 1.5% of the German population. With the coming of the Depression and the Nazis, the number of foreigners again declined – at least at first – while 'German' itself was redefined more radically, exclusively and demonstratively than ever before in history. According to the Nuremberg laws of 1935, full citizenship was biological, although, for all the measurement of noses and crania, the practical definition remained strictly genealogical.[95] But the effect was the same: fathers or no fathers, the children and grand-children of Jews could no longer be German citizens.

With the coming of economic recovery by the mid-1930s, and the war economy that followed, a new and involuntary immigration nonetheless began in earnest. As before, Germans continued to stream from rural East to industrial West, and from there into armies deployed from the Arctic to the Sahara. As usual, foreigners, including as many as two million Poles, were conscripted to fill the gap. By 1943, as much as 40% of the workforce at Flick, Krupp and IG Farben, and 80–90% of the workforce in aircraft production, was foreign, including prisoners of war and concentration camp inmates.[96] The collapse of the Nazi régime and empire then led to more migrations. As the occupying powers dispersed and repatriated hundreds of thousands of West and East Europeans – some of them less, some of them more voluntarily – the 'displaced persons' were replaced by a still larger wave of immigrants from hitherto German homelands now reassigned to Poland, Czechoslovakia and the Soviet Union. Between 1945–46 and 1950, over 12 million Germans – 18% of the prewar population – crossed the borders of what still remained of Germany. Of these, about 60% arrived in the Western zones that were to become the Federal Republic of Germany (FRG), the rest in the Soviet zone that was to become the German Democratic Republic (GDR). But for all that they had nominally moved from Germany to Germany, countless thousands felt, and were made to feel, as alien as any immigrant.[97] By 1961, the year of the Berlin wall, another six million refugees then made their way from the GDR to the FRG.

In effect, only one German border now mattered. Yet border crossing remained, as it had always been, a fact of German life. The dynamic was part political, part economic. According to Article 116 of the new Basic Law, anyone eligible for citizenship within the 1937 borders of the Reich, as well as anyone, including spouse and offspring, who was subsequently accepted as an ethnic German refugee or expellee, automatically qualified for FRG citizenship. Enacted in law, this subsumed the 12 million Germans from the pre-war territories now controlled by Poland and the Soviet Union; and Germans from 'Danzig, Estonia, Latvia, Lithuania, the Soviet Union, Poland, Czechoslovakia, Hungary, Romania, Bulgaria, Jugoslavia, Albania or China',[98] but also the 16 million postwar East Germans – or at least those of them disposed and able to assert their claim.

Mindful of the recent past, the constitutional assembly not only wrote political asylum into the new Basic Law,[99] but demonstratively included it among the basic rights. This effectively excluded asylum from political control. Both a blank check and a well intentioned time bomb, Article 16, Paragraph 2, exploded some 40–odd years later, detonated in turn by revolutionary changes that could themselves be regarded as aftershocks from at least as far back as the great upheavals of World War I. In 1989, the number of applicants for asylum in the Federal Republic – 21% of them from Poland, 16% each from Turkey and Yugoslavia – exceeded the number of applicants for asylum in the United States and Canada combined.[100] By 1990, the total would reach almost 200,000, by 1991 250,000, by 1992 an estimated 438,000 – more than half from Romania and what had once been Yugoslavia[101] – and with growing pressure in Bonn to amend the constitution as just one more incentive for the figure to keep on rising while it could.

In fact, as the publicist Sebastian Haffner noted long before 1989, emigration has always been the characteristically German form of revolution, and both refugees and emigration have been among the existential facts of German life for centuries. As a Nazi era refugee in Britain, and postwar re-emigrant to his native Berlin, Haffner could testify from personal experience that emigration is linked to immigration. But for most Germans, the idea that Germany might therefore be an immigrant country took some getting used to.[102] In 1992, revealingly, the computerized subject catalogue of the European University Institute library in Fiesole listed only 'Emigration – Germany,' as though 'Immigration – Germany' were a contradiction in terms.[103]

As defenders of freedom of movement since the end of World War II, as well as an archipelago of the free and rich, the Western democracies, including Germany, nonetheless made sure in 1975 that the right to emigrate was included in the Helsinki Final Act. A quasi-peace treaty 30 years after the war, the Helsinki document legitimized borders that till then had been only provisional. Yet at the same time it consolidated them, it also opened them. With the implied right of East European Jews to move to Israel and ethnic Germans to live in (West) Germany, a generic human right had become a matter of national principle with the sanction of international law. Written into successive bilateral treaties, the quasi-repatriation of ethnic Germans from Poland, Hungary, Romania, the Soviet Union *et al.* to (West) Germany was properly seen as one of the successes of *Ostpolitik*. Between 1976 and 1980, of 216,000 Soviet immigrants, about 134,000 went to Israel, under 40,000 to Germany; in 1989, of 236,000 emigrants, about 106,000 would go to Israel, about 100,000 to Germany.[104]

With the end of the Cold War, opportunities to emigrate gained ground on incentives to emigrate for the first time since the Cold War began. By the early 1990s, it was estimated that as few as 10 million, and as many as 500 million refugees were fleeing war, poverty, persecution and environmental disaster in search of rights and opportunities that Westerners officially took for given.[105] It was also only logical that the Western democracies should become a preferred destination for emigrants of every description, both legal and illegal, although, of the 17.7 million refugees registered with the United Nations High Commissioner for Refugees in 1991, the vast majority were in Asia and Africa, with only 1.3 million in Europe. Yet the 'only' could hardly be more relative. Before Helsinki, in all of Western Europe, the average annual volume of applications for asylum was 13,000. It was 10 years after Helsinki before the volume first exceeded the number of legally issued work permits. From there, the curve continued upward: 92,500 in 1984, 156,500 in 1985, 440,000 in 1990.[106]

Given the dynamism of West Germany's economy, the attractiveness of its social benefits, the comprehensiveness of its treaty commitments and, not least, its porous borders and accessible airports, it was not surprising that Germany should become a favored goal. Of the half million and more annual applicants for European asylum in the last decade, by far the greatest number – 44% of all applications filed in the 1980s, and an estimated 60% of all applications filed in 1991 – were now filed in the Federal Republic.[107]

In practice, the procedure was unpleasant for everyone: an increasingly resented burden on local police and budgets; a trial for the applicants themselves, who were excluded from the job market and all but interned, pending review of their cases by an overworked judiciary. Mayors were inevitably among the first to feel the heat.[108] Laborious but formally correct, the review itself became so rigorous that fewer than 5% of applicants were accepted. Even before the 1993 reform, the actual refugee population was estimated at barely two for every thousand Germans[109].

Yet deportation was not that easy either. Of 155,000 applicants who would be rejected for asylum in 1991, only 4000 were actually deported. The rest were allowed to stay for reasons including illness, commitments undertaken under the Geneva convention on refugees, and the requirements of German law itself.[110] Comfortable and safe in a world of rapidly proliferating and increasingly desperate people, West Germans, like their European neighbors, sought and applied a variety of deterrents and disincentives to hold off the huddled masses knocking at their doors.[111] Yet even today, after the great debate and drastic restrictions of 1993, the Federal Republic remains the only country where political asylum is an established constitutional right – at least in theory.[112]

Of course, the German labor market too has had something to do with immigration. One of the postwar world's great economic success stories, West Germany reached full employment in 1960, the year before the Wall. But as early as the 1950s, German industry already needed all the labor it could get. Between 1945–46 and 1970–72, the German economy had absorbed Eastern refugees, returning prisoners of war and refugees from East Germany. From 1961, with East Germany behind the Wall, West German employers turned to foreigners. Between 1960, when recruitment began, and 1973, when the oil shock stopped it in its tracks, the number of employed foreigners grew from about 280,000 to 2.6 million. Last hired and first fired, the new '*Gastarbeiter*,' or guest workers took the same low-rung and entry-level jobs in services, construction and unskilled manufacturing that immigrants had always taken, and natives had learned to reject.

At first, the newcomers came from such traditional reservoirs of underemployment as Italy, Spain, Portugal, Greece and Yugoslavia, then Turkey. But for the October war and the oil shock that finally brought the process to a halt, North Africa would have followed. Between 1960 and 1973, as the number of Turkish workers in Germany rose from 2500 to 605,000, 'foreigner', 'Moslem' and 'Turk' approached identity in German awareness, and 'Turk' and *Gastarbeiter* became virtually interchangeable.[113] But the mutual dependency took years and even decades to appreciate. Even in the recession after the oil shock, initiatives to persuade the guests to leave were soon superseded by incentives to keep them. Some of the new immigrants accepted German government premiums to return to Turkey. But most chose instead to stay, particularly after the law was prudently amended to let them bring their families. By 1982, the Turkish presence would grow to 1.5 million, by 1993 to 1.8 million, twice as many as the ex-Yugoslavs, who by then constituted Germany's next largest immigrant population.[114]

Both demography and social structure confirm how a generation of German life transformed an army of *Gastarbeiter* into a more or less normal immigrant community, on the one hand, and a kind of national minority, on the other. In 1972, 89% of the Turks in Germany were men, and 91% of the Turks in Germany lived on wages. A generation later, 45% of the Turks resident in Germany were women, and 29% were self-employed, including the proprietors of some 35,000 Turkish-owned businesses with some 125,000 employes and an estimated annual turnover of DM 25 billion. Higher education, a common index of social mobility, was also a revealingly ambiguous one. On the one hand, there were only 14,500 Turkish students matriculated at German universities. On the other hand, 4500 of them were women, 80% graduates of German schools, and 60–80% of them from working class families. Despite complaints about advising, academic deficiencies and handicaps of culture and language, two thirds also expected to work in Germany after graduation, compared to only 15%, who expected to work in Turkey. Nationality figures suggested a comprehensive ghettoization – or self-ghettoization. Among Algerian mothers in France, the figure for those bearing children by non-Algerian fathers rose from 6.2% in 1975 to 27.5% in 1990. Among Turkish mother in Germany, the proportion bearing children by German fathers rose from 0.5% in 1975 to 1.2% in 1990.[115] Yet of about two million resident Turks and Kurds in Germany, the vast majority regarded Germany as home. In fact, 74,000 were already living in Germany as old-age pensioners.[116]

Yet for different but complementary reasons, the result was a challenge. On the one hand, both law and culture assured that foreigners remained foreign, both *de jure* and in varying degrees *de facto*. On the other hand, barring circumstances and calamities currently unimaginable, the immigrants had become part of the landscape. Of the foreign population, Turks, in turn, had become the biggest single group, and West Berlin had became the world's third biggest Turkish city.

Meanwhile, it appeared that the original 'German Question' was lost from view, subsumed in the palladian architecture of a global alliance system that was seemingly made to last forever. Not only had 'the German Question' lost its power to make people angry. But for a tiny minority of researchers, editorial writers, graduate students and, mostly West German, Chautauqua promoters, it had even lost its power to hold people's interest. Obviously East Germans paid a higher price for its apparent disappearance than did West Germans. But each after its fashion, and within its limits, East and West Germany enjoyed their share of creature comforts, declared themselves the sole legitimate heirs to the nicer sides of German history, and successfully indulged the national preference for a life without surprises.

Of course, tomorrow was already stirring. Well before the drama of September, October and November 1989, unfamiliar stirrings, irritations or malaise already ruffled the surface of today. Rather a mood than a movement, the phenomenon included displays of national feeling unseen for decades. As compelling to foreigners, who were regularly invited to join in, as it was to Germans, the public introspection even went on at public expense, sponsored by the deeply establishmentarian party foundations that were themselves a German speciality, in such remote and congenially un-German venues as Washington, Long Beach and Honolulu.

Surely among the oddest, but most revealing, symptoms of change were recurring spasms of rebellion against the price and consequences of the NATO relationship that had been at the heart of today for 40 years. By 1988–9, random events were regularly transformed into miniature psychodramas, joining both Left and Right in a common distrust of Washington.[117] Unanticipated and only partially perceived by most Americans, the phenomenon suggested deep ambivalence about a special relationship with a globally activist and anti-Communist America that had itself been a keystone of postwar German identity. Still more remarkable, intellectuals, who for decades had only wanted to be 'good Europeans', discovered they were German, usually to their surprise. For the first time, Germans come to consciousness since 1945 discovered how much they wanted and welcomed unity, while others discovered how much they feared and deplored it. Significant again, some of the country's most prominent intellectuals, who had kept their distance from the Bonn republic since its largely Christian-Democratic and resolutely anti-Communist creation, discovered they were patriots. But in contrast to anything in modern memory, their new-found patriotism was strictly West German. The philosopher Juergen Habermas called it *Verfassungspatriotismus*, i.e., a civic patriotism that tied traditional feelings of flag and anthem to the unpretentious civility and democracy that distinguished the Federal Republic from all its predecessors.

Yet the confusions of identity took other forms too. In January 1989, Franz Schönhuber's hitherto marginal Republicans scored a first breakthrough in West Berlin, the island city, where for more than 40 years immobility, stress, federal handouts, immigrants, counter-culture, an aging population and endemic national malaise had met as nowhere else. By summer, they had left more marks on Hesse, North Rhine-Westphalia and the European parliament. Targeted at Turks, the Berlin TV spots came closer to 'Germany for the Germans' than anything seen in decades. But while survey data showed little patience for lawyerly distinctions, they also showed little sympathy for the world according to Ernst Moritz Arndt. For Republican voters, resident Turks, Polish-speaking descendants of Germans from across the Oder, and newly arrived East Germans were all foreigners.

With the first rumblings across the Wall, the malaise vanished abruptly. At first, unification seemed a distraction from the politics of immigration. Yet ironically, immigration was the crucial dynamic. In Germany too, events inevitably echoed what happened – or failed to happen – in the Soviet Union. Yet their German form was as indigenous as the Reformation. As so often in the past, disaffected (East) Germans were given a chance to vote with their feet. From September on, they went with a will, using Hungary as their launching pad en route across Austria to (West) Germany.

Suddenly, 860 miles of sensors, bunkers, arc lights, watch-towers and 10-foot barriers, secured by 47,000 border guards at an estimated cost of almost half of one percent of the East German budget, became a kind of Maginot line in reverse.[118] From here on, it should have been clear in East Berlin that non-intervention and intervention were about equally hopeless. In the first week of October, in what could have been a scene from Brecht, a superannuated Erich Honecker tottered to the microphones one final time to proclaim his Germany, a socialist East Germany impervious to *glasnost* and *perestroika*, the Germany of youth and change. Then came 9 October and 9 November. The state of the nation, for 28 years a matter of speculation and theory, had again became a matter of daily practice. For better or worse, tomorrow had finally arrived.

Notes

1. Friedrich Nietzsche, *Jenseits von Gut und Boese*, quoted in Peter Pulzer, 'Unified Germany: A Normal State?' *German Politics*, April 1994, p. 1.
2. See Franz Urban Pappi, 'Die deutsche Gesellschaft in vergleichender Perspektive' in Karl-Heinz Reuband *et al.* (eds), *Die Gesellschaft der Bundesrepublik in vergleichender Perspektive* (Opladen, 1995).
3. Fritz René Allemann, *Bonn ist nicht Weimar*, (Cologne, 1956), p. 103.
4. In 1995, the German government even announced plans to issue new bonds to American investors, stuck with German government bonds on which Germany had defaulted in 1933. The new bonds, which were to mature in 2010, paid 3% plus interest accrued until 1990. (The new agreement only applied to interest payments. The Bonn government had paid off the principal between 1953 and 1980.) 'Six Decades Later, Germany Will Pay War Debt', *New York Times*, 6 January 1995.
5. Eurobarometer No. 25, June 1986, quoted in Erwin K. Scheuch, *Wie Deutsch sind die Deutschen*, (Bergisch-Gladbach, 1992), p. 101.
6. Institut für Demoskopie, Allensbach, quoted in ibid., p. 189.
7. Franz Steinkühler, president of the IG Metall, Berlin, November 1989, quoted in Konrad Seitz, *Die japanisch–amerikanische Herausforderung* (Munich, 1991) pp. 378–9.
8. 'Die Angst kommt ins Wohnzimmer,' report of a study by the Institute of Applied Socialpsychology, Düsseldorf (*Informationsdienst des Instituts der deutschen Wirtschaft* 39), 29 September 1994.
9. In Brandenburg, where live births had fallen from c. 38 per thousand in 1989 to nearly 10 per thousand in 1993, the state government announced plans for incentive payments of DM 1000 (about $650) for each new baby, in addition to existing comprehensive obstetrical coverage and a nationwide children's allowance. Stephen Kinzer, '$650 a Baby: Germany to Pay to Stem Decline in Births', *New York Times*, 23 November 1994. See Nicholas Eberstadt, 'Demographic Shocks in Eastern Germany, 1989–93', *Europe–Asia Studies*, Vol. 3, 1994. Cf. Rainer Münz and Ralf Ulrich, 'Was wird aus den neuen Bundesländern, Demogra-

phische Prognosen für ausgewählte Regionen und für Ostdeutschland', Lehrstuhl Bevölkerungswissenschaft, Humboldt Universität, Berlin, 1994.

10. Allemann, *Bonn ist nicht Weimar*, p. 101.

11. Pulzer, 'Unified Germany . . .', pp. 9–10.

12. In 1989 the same young Leipziger, now in his mid-30s and joined by his wife and two small sons, was among some 40,000 East Germans, who first made for Hungary, then for West Germany, across the Austrian border.

13. Scheuch, *Wie Deutsch sind die Deutschen?* p. 201.

14. Goethe, '*Faust: der Tragödie Erster Teil*,' line 1700. The translation is by Walter Kaufmann, *Goethe's Faust* (Garden City, NY, 1963), p. 185.

15. *The Economist*, 13 August 1994, p. 93.

16. Herbert Giersch, Karl-Heinz Paque and Holger Schmieding, The *Fading Miracle* (Cambridge, 1992), p. 247. In 1994, savings constituted some 25% of GNP, behind Luxembourg, Japan, Austria and the Netherlands, but ahead of all other EU and G-7 members. In fact, Luxembourg's savings to GNP ratio, which approached 60%, included an estimated $150 billion in German deposits that had ended up across the border in order to avoid a 30% witholding tax on interest income at home. *Financial Times*, 18 May, 1994; 'Germans in Tax Revolt Embrace Luxembourg', *New York Times*, 25 November 1994.

17. 'Das Dasein wird seziert', *Der Spiegel*, 1 August 1994, See *Health Care in Germany* (Federal Ministry of Health, Bonn, 1994), p. 49.

18. 'Endless Run for the Sun Keeps German Tourists on the Go', *International Herald Tribune*, 29 July 1994.

19. Speech in Mainz, 31 May 1989, quoted in *George Bush, 1989, Public Papers of the Presidents* (Washington, DC, 1990), pp. 651–2.

20. A few exemplary titles from an already voluminous literature on how the unimaginable became inevitable: see Elizabeth Pond, *Beyond the Wall* (Washington, 1993); A. James McAdams, *Germany Divided* (Princeton, 1993); Horst Teltschik, *329 Tage* (Berlin, 1991) Wolfgang Schäuble, *Der Vertrag* (Stuttgart, 1991), Theo Waigel and Manfred Schell, *Tage, die Deutschland und die Welt veränderten* (Munich, 1994).

21. See Thomas L. Friedman, 'Clinton Calls on Germany to be Partner', *New York Times*, 12 July 1995. Given the size of its economy, Germany had no choice but to assume a leadership role in the world, Clinton emphasized in an interview with foreign correspondents, including Kurt Kister of the *Süddeutsche Zeitung*. Even were it to try, the vacuum thus created would again cause Germans to take action. Quoted in *Süddeutsche Zeitung*, 4 July 1994.

22. According to an *Economist* survey, 45% in France, 61% in Britain and America, favored unification. Yet 50% in France and Britain and 29% in America were also concerned that a united Germany would dominate Europe. Quoted in Scheuch, *Wie Deutsch sind die Deutschen?*, p. 222. Between March and June 1990, West Germans found the pace of unification too fast and much too fast by a 2:1 ratio, support for unification varied directly with age. Scheuch, ibid., pp. 222 and 334.

23. Hugo von Hofmannsthal, *Der Rosenkavalier* (Frankfurt, 1962), p. 41.

24. The expression, in intention hortatory, idealistic, anti-isolationist and anti-Nazi, was coined by the American magazine publisher, Henry R. Luce, in an extended editorial-essay that first appeared in *Life* on 17 February 1941; also Henry R. Luce, *The American Century* (New York, 1941).

25. 'Germany has paid a high price for Hitler's war . . . Three consequences stand out: first, the disappearance of the Jewish population through the Holocaust; second, the exodus . . .of distinguished writers, artists and scientists – every autumn when the Nobel prizes are announced this becomes painfully apparent; third, large population losses . . .' Jochen Thies, 'Observations on the Political Class in Germany', *Daedalus*, Winter 1994.

26. Cf. Harold James, *A German Identity* (London, 1989), Chapters 2–3.

27. Peter Calvocoressi and Guy Wint, *Total War* (Harmondsworth, 1972), p. 552.

28. Eleventh thesis on Feuerbach in Karl Marx and Friedrich Engels, *Ausgewählte Schriften* (Berlin, 1953), p. 378.

29. Cf. David Schoenbaum, 'The World War II Allied Agreement on Ocupation and Administration of Post-War Germany' in Alexander L. George, Philip J. Farley and Alexander Dallin (eds), *US–Soviet Security Cooperation* (New York and Oxford, 1988).

30. See Michael Mertes, 'Germany's Social and Political Culture', *Daedalus*, Winter 1994.

31. A practical, and remarkable, example is the German government's intention, announced in early 1995, to pay off loans incurred by their predecessors in 1924. Floyd Norris, 'Six Decades Later, Germany Will Pay War Debt', *New York Times*, 6 January 1995.

32. The expression, then a cliché, enjoyed its fifteen minutes of currency after unification, as diplomats, columnists and editorial writers tried to decide whether and how unity had changed the Germans. In January 1992 one of the authors was kind enough to book the other for a briefing with a senior British official. The briefing, a masterpiece in all respects, ended with a resumé of presumed assertivenesses, from language and monetary policy to the treaty of Maastricht and disintegration of Yugoslavia. But the finding was basically positive. For better or for worse, Germans were looking after their interests, the official concluded. But they were not being unduly 'assertive'.

33. A. J. P. Taylor, *The Course of European History* (New York, 1946), p. 13.

34. He was also not alone in it: 'Our primary interest in Europe, as shown during the Napoleonic and the two German Wars, is that no European power should emerge which is capable of aggression outside of the European continent.' Walter Lippmann, *US Foreign Policy* (Boston, 1943), p. 164.

35. Taylor, *The Course of European History*, p. 7.

36. Scheuch, *Wie Deutsch sind die Deutschen?*, p. 85.

37. Not that the thesis itself was intrinsically new. The difference was that the presumed 'special way', that had once been a source of pride, was now understood exclusively as a source of chagrin and embarrassment. Cf. Heinrich August Winkler, 'Abschied von den Sonderwegen', *Evan-*

gelische Kommentare 1994; *Deutscher Sonderweg – Mythos oder Realität* (Munich and Vienna, 1982); Wolfgang Sauer, 'National Socialism: Totalitarianism or Fascism?' *American Historical Review*, December 1967.

38. For a representative overview of the issues, see Dan Diner *et al.* (eds) *Ist der Nationalsozialismus Geschichte?* (Frankfurt, 1987); *Historikerstreit*, (Munich, 1987); Rolf Kosiek, *Historikerstreit* (Tübingen, 1987), Charles S. Maier, *The Unmasterable Past* (Cambridge, 1988).

39. See David Blackbourn, *Class, Religion and Local Politics* (New Haven, 1980), *The German Bourgeoisie* (London and New York, 1991); David Calleo, *The German Problem Reconsidered* (Cambridge and New York, 1978), Geoff Eley, *From Unification to Nazism*, (Boston, 1986), David Schoenbaum, *Zabern 1913* (Boston and London, 1982) for a representative sampler.

40. Frederic C. Howe, *Socialized Germany* (New York, 1916), pp. 1–2.

41. In fact, the author understands his 'Rhine model' as a generic product, characteristic of West Germany, Switzerland and the Benelux countries. But his argument makes clear that he sees its intellectual sources – Christian social doctrine as espoused by Germany's Christian Democratic Union, and social democracy as espoused by Germany's Social Democratic party – as peculiar to Germany. Michel Albert, *Capitalism against Capitalism* (London, 1993), p. 169.

42. David Goodhart, 'The Reshaping of the German Social Market,' (Institute for Public Policy Research, London, 1994), p. 80.

43. See Alessandro Barrico, *L'Anima di Hegel e le Mucche del Wisconsin* (Milan, 1992), pp. 86 ff.

44. These figures, as well as the economic figures that follow, are quoted from A. J. P. Taylor, *The Struggle for Mastery in Europe* (Oxford, 1954), pp. xxv-xxxi, and Harold James, *A German Identity*, p. 30.

45. See Marion Gräfin Dönhoff, 'Königsberg – Signal der Versöhnung,' *Die Zeit*, November 15, 1991; 'Marion Gräfin Dönhoff, 'Offene Türen', and Ernst Müller-Hermann, 'Zukunft: Hafen', *Die Zeit*, 1 May 1992, Heike Dörrenbächer, *Die Sonderwirtschaftszone Jantar von Kaliningrad*, Deutsche Gesellschaft für auswärtige Politik, Bonn 1994. 'Kaliningrad Opens its Fortress Gates,' *Financial Times*, 15 February, 1995. The concern, expressed in Moscow and publicly acknowledged by the German foreign ministry in an interview on North German Radio, had to do with a neo-Nazi editor from Schleswig-Holstein, active in an organization concerned with resettling ethnic Germans in Kaliningrad, presumably as the first step toward a territorial claim. *German News*, 19 March, 1995.

46. 'Building Babel in Brussels', *The Economist*, 6 August 1994.

47. Birthrate, cohort and global population figures from Meinhard Miegel and Stefanie Wahl, *Das Ende des Individualismus* (Bonn, 1993), pp. 67 ff.

48. Contemporary Europe knew five perfect institutions, according to one such proverb: the British parliament, the French Académie, the Roman *curia*, the Russian ballet and the Prussian general staff. On uniforms see John Mollo, *Military Fashion* (New York, 1972), p. 219. Though Prussia-Germany's success in the war with France was duly noted in

1871, and West Point faculty had no problems adapting to the spiked helmet, it was 1941 before German language teaching was introduced at the US Military Academy. Craig W. Nickisch, 'German and National Policy', *Teaching German in America* (Madison, 1988), pp. 76 ff.

49. For entry-level access to a vast literature, see George F. Kennan, *The Decline of Bismarck's European Order* (Princeton 1979), Samuel R. Williamson, *The Politics of Grand Strategy* (London and Atlantic Highlands, NJ, 1990).

50. On 1914 and before, cf. Harold James, *A German Identity* (London, 1989), p. 106, Raymond Poidevin, *Les Relations économiques et financielles entre la France et l'Allemagne de 1898 à 1914* (Paris 1969), passim; on 1945 and after, see Herman Van Der Wee, *Prosperity and Upheaval* (Berkeley and Los Angeles, 1987), pp. 359 ff. On Hitler's, as it were, Greater European Co-Prosperity Sphere, see Eberhard Jäckel, *Frankreich in Hitlers Europa* (Stuttgart, 1966).

51. 'The doctor, the student of art, of architecture, the engineer, the clergyman and men engaged in many other occupations, are constantly finding out that German scholars have something . . .in their particular field it is essential they should know,' as one American academic reported. 'It is expected of every educated man that he should understand the position occupied by Germany in the civilized world, and there is no better way to learn to appreciate the best the German civilization has to offer us, than by studying the German language . . .'. Elijah W. Bagster-Collins, *The Teaching of German in Secondary Schools* (London, 1904), p. 5. As though to prove the point, the philosopher Josiah Royce apparently thought nothing of referring to Goethe, Schiller, Novalis, the Schlegels, Jean Paul, Heine and Hoffmann in a series of popular lectures at Harvard in 1890. See Jeffrey Sammons, 'Some Considerations on our Invisibility' in Walter F. W. Lohnes and Valte Nollendorfer (eds), *German Studies in the United States* (Madison, 1976), p. 17.

52. See C. E. McClelland, *State, Society and University in Germany 1700–1914* (Cambridge, 1980).

53. See István Deák, *Germany's Leftwing Intellectuals* (Berkeley, CA, 1968).

54. Winfried Ranke (ed.), *August Sander, die Zerstörung Kölns* (Munich, 1985). For a verbal equivalent of Sander's photos, cf. Franz Josef Schöningh, 'Is it still worth living?' *Süddeutsche Zeitung*, 6 October, 1945: 'The foundations of our lives are shaken. Many of the cities we knew and loved are destroyed, the basic conditions for our previous occupations devastated, our families torn apart. Many loved ones will not return or we have no idea whether they will ever return. We fear for the next day's nourishment and the roof over our heads. The Reich that once seemed an unchallengeable political reality has become thoroughly doubtful. To what reality can we now cling, from what happenings or sources of strength can we find hope or consolation? Is it even worth living?' The answer is, in fact, both positive and instructive. 'How can we face our grandchildren, unless we do all we can to clear away both the moral and the physical debris our generation has created?' the writer continues. 'Our grandchildren will never understand what we did, but

they will at least not despise us if we now atone for our guilt toward them by working and sacrificing whatever is required.'

55. A kind of brick tent, known locally as 'the tomb of the unknown general manager', its architect had designed it to be as different as possible from the Wilhelmine monumentality of its prewar predecessor. The production was also noteworthy, though rather for what it was not than what it was. Given the style and reflexive political correctness of latterday German stagecraft, the older man half-expected that Bassa Selim, the master of the seraglio, would appear in olive fatigues as leader of the local Third World Liberation Front. He was both surprised and relieved that the director had resisted the impulse.

56. The figures are somewhat misleading, since 'normal' consumers were a minority, and large numbers of people bartered with farmers, raised food on their own, etc. But the caloric deficit was real enough to boost absenteeism and cut productivity with ripple effects throughout the economy. See Alan Kramer, *The West German Economy 1945–55* (New York and Oxford, 1991), pp. 75–80.

57. For an engaging eyewitness account not only of German, but West European recovery, See Theodore E. White, *Fire in the Ashes* (New York, 1953).

58. Allemann, *Bonn ist nicht Weimar* p. 101.

59. David Marsh, *The Germans: Rich, Bothered and Divided* (London, 1989), pp. 187–94. Of c. 345,000 young men eligible for military service in 1994, 125,700 opted for alternative service; and, of the 160,000 who joined the Bundeswehr, only 7% declared themselves willing 'to serve in any capacity, including in missions outside of Germany', according to the annual report of the Bundestag's ombudsman. 'Young Men Increasingly Prefer Civil to Military Service', *The Week in Germany*, German Information Center, New York, 10 March, 1995.

60. George C. McGhee, *At the Creation of a New Germany* (New Haven, 1989), pp. 207–12.

61. See Marsh, *The Germans . . .*, Ch. 13.

62. The figure is for 1992. The equivalent East German figure for 1990 was 2%. *Zahlen zur wirtschaftlichen Entwicklung der Bundesrepublik Deutschland* (Institut der deutschen Wirtschaft, Cologne, 1993), Table 117.

63. See John Mearsheimer, 'Back to the Future: Instability in Europe after the Cold War', *International Security*, Summer 1990.

64. *Zahlen . . .*, Tables 150, 151, 155, 156, 157.

65. See Hansgerd Schulte, 'Les Universités allemandes entre l'Est et l'Ouest', *Géopolitique*, Winter 1993–4; Norbert Lammert, 'Wie sollte die Hochschulpolitik reformiert werden?' *Wirtschaftsdienst*, May 1994.

66. Once the premier foreign language of choice in American high schools, German had long ago given way first to French, then to Spanish. By the early 1980s, it was estimated that only 1% of American high school students were enrolled in German classes, and most of these for only two years. Henry Marx, *Deutsche in der Neuen Welt* (Braunschweig, 1983), pp. 273–74. 'We ought in principle to take cognizance of the fact that German is at present a semi-exotic language in the United States and

employing it is rather like dropping a *Tarnkappe* over a publication'. J. Sammons, 'Some Considerations . . .', op. cit., p. 21.

67. Specifically directed at new and syncretic research areas as yet unaccommodated in university curricula, the Max Planck Institutes in 1990 consumed DM1.1 billion, about 2% of total German research spending. Or, for a rather different standard of comparison, spending on Germany's premier research institutes constituted about a seventh of annual public support levels for agriculture and the coal industry. Of the 200 institute directors, 26 were foreigners from 12 different countries. Of supervisory board members, 15% were Americans, 33% non-German Europeans. See *Die Max-Planck Gesellschaft und ihre Institute* (Max-Planck-Gesellschaft, Munich, 1991), pp. 26–32.

68. In yet another variation on German identity, a third Nobel laureate, Elias Canetti, a Sephardic Jew from the Balkans long resident in London, wrote in German, but had never been a German writer.

69. The quote is from Lester Thurow, *Head to Head* (New York, 1992), p. 275. See also Bill Clinton and Al Gore, *Putting People First* (New York, 1992), p. 87, proposing a 'national apprenticeship-style program' as grist for the 1992 US presidential campaign mill, and Hedrick Smith, 'Challenge to America', originally made for WETA, Washington, DC, then shown on National Public television and released on five videocassettes (Princeton, 1994). C.f. W. R. Smyser, *The Economy of United Germany* (New York, 1992), pp. 76–7, Stephen F. Hamilton, *Apprenticeship for Adulthood* (New York and London, 1990) and Alain Lattard, 'L'apprentissage à l'allemande' in Anne-Marie Le Gloannec (ed.), *L'Etat de l'Allemagne* (Paris, 1995), pp. 351 ff.

70. Pascale Laborier, 'Une politique culturelle polycentrique' in Le Gloannec, *L'Etat de l'Allemagne*, p. 110. Berlin alone, with a population of circa 3.5 million, invested about $800 million in its cultural institutions. By comparison, in its budget for fiscal year (FY) 1996, the Clinton Administration proposed about $167 million each for the National Endowments for the Arts and Humanities in all of the United States.

71. Masur in New York, Dohnányi in Cleveland, Sawallisch in Philadelphia.

72. Kurt Sontheimer, 'Speech on One's Own Country' in Wilhelm Bleek and Hanns Maull (eds), *Ein Ganz Normaler Staat?* (Munich, 1989), p. 304.

73. Pulzer, 'Unified Germany . . .' passim.

74. Cf. Gebhard Schweigler, 'Normalität in Deutschland, *Europa-Archiv*, 25 March 1989.

75. Marsh, *The Germans . . .* , pp. 272–3.

76. See Anne-Marie Le Gloannec, *La Nation Orpheline: Les Allemagnes en Europe* (Paris, 1989).

77. See 'Wall Notwithstanding', *The Economist*, 18 November 1989.

78. See Francis Fukuyama, *The End of History and the Last Man* (New York and Toronto, 1992).

79. For early examples of efforts to address all three, see Angelo Bolaffi, *Il Sogno Tedesco* (Rome, 1993); 'Ein einig Volk von Blutsbrüdern,' *Der Spiegel*, 15 March 1993 and F. Stephen Larrabee, 'Down and Out in Warsaw and Budapest: Eastern Europe and East–West Migration', *International Security*, Spring 1992.

80. For an authoritative and original synthesis, see Harold James, *A German Identity*, Chs 2–4.
81. According to the preamble of the Basic Law of 23 May 1949, 'the German people in the Western-occupied Länder, by virtue of their constituent authority, adopted this basic law in order to confer a new order on their public life *for a transitional period* [author's italics] . . . It has also acted on behalf of those Germans unable to participate . . . The whole German people is called upon to achieve Germany's freedom and unity by means of free self-determination.'
82. Like the consensus on '*Westpolitik*' that preceded it, the consensus on Ostpolitik was obviously a significant achievement. For equally obvious reasons, it was also a considerable embarrassment after 1989, when newly-elected East Germans demanded a parliamentary inquiry into the crimes and misdemeanors of the former East German state. Their West German colleagues could hardly say no. But, unsurprisingly, they were less than eager to say yes, knowing full well where such an inquiry could lead. In a letter to Chancellor Helmut Kohl, that drew a testy answer, former Chancellor Willy Brandt warned preemptively against any *post facto* revisionism, e.g., of the Honecker visit. It also seemed no coincidence that only one West German joined the committee of inquiry. A. James McAdams, 'Revisiting the Ostpolitik in the 90s', *German Politics and Society*, Fall 1993, pp. 49 ff. For a full and persuasive discussion of theory and practice of German–German *Ostpolitik*, see Timothy Garton Ash, *In Europe's Name* (New York, 1993), Ch. 4.
83. Carlo M. Cipolla, *Wirtschaftsgeschichte und Weltbevölkerung* (Munich, 1972), p. 91.
84. See Peter Marschalk, *Bevölkerungsgeschichte Deutschlands im 19. und 20. Jahrundert* (Frankfurt, 1984), p. 21. Though the modest interpretations are the author's, he is indebted to Marschalk for virtually all the figures in this section.
85. Ingeniously resolved to remind his readers that Germans too are ubiquitous *Ausländer*, and that they still settle around the world just as Turks, Italians, former Yugoslavs *et al.* have variously come to settle in Germany, Helmut Herles, editor in chief of the *Bonner General-Anzeiger*, produced a whole supplement to his Christmas Eve 1992 edition, consisting of letters and addresses from former Bonners in 54 countries.
86. Cipolla, *Wirtschaftsgeschichte* . . . , p. 91.
87. For a general statement of the thesis see Lord Acton. 'A State may in course of time produce a nationality; but that a nationality should constitute a State is contrary to the nature of modern civilisation.' John Emrich Edward Dalberg-Acton, 'Nationalism' in *Essays in the History of Liberty* (Indianapolis, 1985), p. 427. For an interesting theoretical treatment of the German case, cf. John Breuilly, 'Sovereignty and boundaries: Modern State Formation and National Identity in Germany', paper for 'Boundaries and Border-Crossings', a conference sponsored by the journal *Past and Present*, Oxford 25 June 1992. In the German case, Breuilly argues, politics not only superseded both culture and religion, but favored new forms of German statehood, whose

approach to both sovereignty and boundaries was quite different from anything known before Napoleon. This then favored unification by a modernized, liberalized Prussia, which in turn left its marks on German identity and borders. John Breuilly (ed.), *The State of Germany* (London and New York 1992), passim.

88. For their historical origins, see Rogers Brubaker, *Citizenship and Nationhood in France and Germany* (Cambridge, MA), and London, 1992), pp. 50–1.
89. Ibid., pp. 114 ff.
90. Polish nationalism was an early and obvious exception. Until at least the 1830s, German liberals were sympathetic to the Polish struggle. Confronted with Polish claims to West Prussia in 1848, they then reconsidered. See Sir Lewis Namier, *1848: The Revolution of the Intellectuals* (Oxford and New York, 1992).
91. 'It was only through Bismarck that German patriotism became respectable and Conservative, with the result that many men who had become Liberal because they were patriots became Conservatives for the same reason.' Bertrand Russell, *Freedom Versus Organization, 1814–1914* (New York, 1962), p. 362.
92. In fact, it can be argued that a main incentive for defining legal citizenship was exclusion of immigrant poor. Brubaker, *Citizenship and Nationhood* pp. 70–1.
93. See Richard C. Murphy, *Gastarbeiter im Deutschen Reich* (Wuppertal, 1982), passim.
94. Given the German populations of the latter two, let alone of Austria, many of these may, in fact, have been ethnic Germans. But Marschalk's figures are silent on the subject (Marschalk, *Bevölkerungsgeschichte Deutschlands . . .*, p. 175).
95. C.f. Brubaker, *Citizenship and Nationhood*, p. 167.
96. Klaus J. Bade, *Vom Auswanderungsland zum Einwanderungsland?* (Berlin, 1983), pp. 52 ff. Though there were no reparations to individuals, Daimler–Benz commissioned a study of its slave-labor policies in 1986, donated DM 20 million to agencies that care for surviving victims of the Nazis in 1988, and dedicated a memorial to slave workers at company headquarters in Stuttgart–Untertürkheim in 1989. 'Vorsorgen für das Nachkriegsgeschäft', *Süddeutsche Zeitung*, 1 June 1994.
97. See Albrecht Lehmann, *Im Fremden ungewollt zuhaus* (Munich, 1991), passim.
98. Quoted from Article 1, Paragraph 2, no. 3 of the Federal Law on Expellees and Refugees (Gesetz über die Angelegenheiten der Vertriebenen und Flüchtlinge) of 19 May 1953.
99. The text says 'Victims of political persecution enjoy the right of asylum.'
100. Uta Knight and Wolfgang Kowalsky, *Deutschland nur den deutschen?* (Erlangen, Bonn and Vienna, 1991), p. 56.
101. Volker Ronge, 'Ost–West Wanderung nach Deutschland,' in *Aus Politik und Zeitgeschichte, Beilage zur Wochenzeitung Das Parlament*, 12 February 1993, Table 3, p. 20.

102. Significantly, it was only in the mid-1970s, after the realization that millions of *Gastarbeiter* were both an economic necessity, and likely to stay, that the German federal government created an office of commissioner for integration of foreign labor. Significantly again, the incumbent Liselotte Funcke chose to quit in July 1991, after submitting her annual report, charging a government dominated by her fellow Christian Democrats with inadequate support. Her FDP successor, Cornelia Schmalz-Jacobsen, succeeded in having the office renamed. As commissioner for foreigner affairs, she also saw to it that it got more money, as well as official assurances that it would be involved in all deisions regarding foreigners. (Gert Krell, 'Migration und Asyl', HSFK Report 4 (Frankfurt, 1992), p. 16. In 1994, she then published the office's first annual report, despite opposition from the majority Christian Democrats, and particularly the Christian Social Union, the party's Bavarian wing.

103. In 1995, on the other hand, the entry 'k = germany and immigration' produced 1397 entries from the computerized Research Libraries Information Network, going back as far as 1847. For a standard of comparison, the entry 'k = germany and emigration' produced 1477.

104. Sture Oeberg and Helene Boubnova, 'Ethnicity, Nationality and Migration in Eastern Europe' in Russell King, *Mass Migration in Europe* (London, 1993), p. 246.

105. The figures quoted here – including estimates from the International Red Cross, the Worldwatch Institute, the International Labor Organization, and the United Nations High Commissioner for Refugees – are from Gert Krell, 'Migration . . .', pp. 2–3. For a general discussion of both global and European migration, cf. Peter J. Opitz, 'Rahmenbezug I: Weltbevölkerung und Weltwanderung' and Rainer Münz, 'Rahmenbezug II: Bevölkerung und Wanderung in Europa', *Das Manifest der 60* (Munich, 1994).

106. Krell, 'Migration', p. 5.

107. Krell, 'Migration', p. 14; 'Allarme immigrazione per la Cee', *La Repubblica* , 2 November 1991.

108. For a case study overview by the mayor of Pforzheim, see Joachim Becker, 'Die Städte sind überfordert', *Aus Politik und Zeitgeschichte, Beilage zur Wochenzeitung Das Parlament*, 12 February 1993.

109. Knight and Kowalsky, *Deutschland nur den deutschen?*, p. 57.

110. Aufzeichnung zur Ausländerpolitik umd zum Ausländerrecht in der Bundesrepublik Deutschland', Bundesministerium des Innern V II 1 – 937 020/15, January 1991, p. 64. Nomura Research Institute Deutschland, 'Rebuilding Europe: Germany's Contribution', February 1992, p. 37.

111. These include a court decision in December 1985, denying recognition to Tamils as a group on grounds that persecution in the constitutional sense applies only to individuals, and a general consensus that economic distress and civil war do not contitute 'political persecution'. See Barbara Marshall, ' "Migration into Germany": Asylum Seekers and Ethnic Germans,' *German Politics*, April 1992, pp. 126–8. For a comparative

overview of Portuguese Italian, British, Greek, Swiss, Swedish and Austrian theory and practice, cf. Krell, 'Migration', pp. 6–10.

112. C.f. 'Sie kommen, ob wir wollen oder nicht', *Der Spiegel*, 15, 6 April 1992, pp. 26 ff.

113. Figures quoted by Bade, *Vom Auswanderungsland* . . . , p. 70. For comparative perceptions of foreignness, religion and ethnicity, see Scheuch, *Wie Deutsch sind die Deutschen*? pp. 106–7.

114. See Ali Gitmez and Czarina Wilpert, 'A Micro-Society or an Ethnic Community? Social Organization and Ethnicity amongst Turkish Migrants in Berlin', in John Rex *et al.* (eds), *Immigrant Associations in Europe* (Aldershot, 1987).

115. 'Klage über Benachteiligung,' Agence France Presse in *Süddeutsche Zeitung*, 8 June 1994, Ian Davidson, 'Divide and Rule', *Financial Times*, 30 August 1995.

116. Interview with Professor Farouk Sen of the Institute for Turkish Studies at the University of Essen; *La Repubblica*, 17 June 1993; 'Weder Heimat noch Freunde', *Der Spiegel*, 7 June 1993, pp. 16 ff.

117. Among the practical examples were the crash of an Italian stunt flier at Ramstein, the American base in the Palatinate, killing and injuring several hundred spectators, and the crash of an American bomber on a residential area in Remscheid. Cf. Marsh, *The Germans* . . . , pp. 185–6.

118. Until 1984 automatic firing devices and mine-clearing had to await unification. Ibid., pp. 300–3.

2 Old Germans and Young Turks

'Bliss was it in that dawn to be alive, but to be young was very Heaven,' the English poet, William Wordsworth, reported of the great events in 1789 that left indelible marks on him and his contemporaries.[1] 'Bliss was it in that dawn to be alive, but to write opinion pieces was very heaven,' he might have written 200 years later.

The collapse not just of the Wall, but of the whole, incrementally-constructed international order that it symbolized, set imaginations free on a global scale. But even among a bumper crop that sometimes seemed nourished on pure oxygen, Conor Cruise O'Brien's reflections in *The Times* of London were among the most remarkable. A maverick Irish intellectual from a family with a long history of 'cussedness,'[2] O'Brien rightly grasped the immensity of what he referred to as the 'processes' already underway, i.e., 'the dissolution of the Soviet empire and German reunification'. The combination, he prophesied, was 'likely to result' in 'the advent of a German economic hegemony' from the Aran islands on Ireland's Atlantic coast to Vladivostok on the Pacific.

Yet only here did the prognosis became truly interesting. 'We are on the road to the Fourth Reich,' O'Brien announced. Reunification would be greeted with 'an explosion of nationalist enthusiasm'. '*Reich*' would supersede '*republik*' because the latter was 'associated with defeat and the ascendancy of alien values'. Berlin would become the capital of a united Germany. The old imperial flag, red, white and black, perhaps even a Hohenzollern from the old imperial family, would follow. The Third Reich would be rehabilitated, racial science and all. Jews would be expelled, diplomatic relations with Israel would end. Germans would dispatch a military mission to the Palestine Liberation Organization, and there would be 'a statue of Hitler in every German town'.[3]

In an unique tribute to the power of such historical thinking, Britain's Prime Minister Margaret Thatcher summoned an ad hoc symposium of senior Germanwatchers to Chequers a few months later to explain what was really happening. British and American, the list included such old, and not so old, guildmasters as Fritz Stern, Gordon Craig and Timothy Garton Ash. The guests did their best to convince her that the Germans had changed for the better. With no sense of mission, no lust for conquest, no militarism, the only question was how things might look in 20 years. Polite and interested, the hostess remained skeptical. '. . . the way the Germans were currently using their elbows and throwing their weight around in the European Community gave reason to suspect that they had not changed all that much,' the minutes reported.[4] As P-words like 'power' and 'patriotism' were again heard publicly for the first time in almost half a century, German intellectuals too strained their ears for the distant sounds of Weimar or worse.[5]

An instant book by Arnulf Baring, once a young liberal hope, and now the bard and prophet of a bleak but remunerative neo-conservatism, was widely understood as at least a distant early warning that the Right was about to ride again.[6] Between March and August 1991, Baring, then 59, rounded up his publisher Wolf-Jobst Siedler and a substantially younger associate, switched on the tape-recorder, and let conversational nature take its course. Self-irony was not conspicuous in what followed. Between subtitles including 'The East European vacuum', 'Are there German interests?' 'We need to rediscover something as basic as power', and 'German decline', the conferees considered the future of Berlin, Germany's new responsibilities in Poland, the legacy of history, and the proper understanding of Goethe. They even conceded a certain, admittedly long-range, optimism. But for the moment, at least, they agreed that Germans, called once again to greatness, were heading instead for the beach. Unless Germans were ready to confront the external, particularly East European, challenges with a kind of national sense of destiny, Baring reaffirmed a few years later, the challenges could quickly turn to crisis. But it was out of the question that this would happen, he added quickly, given the 'spoiled, hedonistic individuals, with whom we have to deal over much of our society'.[7]

Bells rang again in 1993 with the appearance of a bellwether anthology by an ad hoc assemblage of New Right intellectuals. The very title, 'The Western Connection,' proclaimed the intention to challenge what the editors claimed was the nation's last taboo.[8] Friedbert Pflüger, a young, liberal, and occasionally rambunctious Christian Democratic Bundestag deputy,[9], fired back with a paperback collection of speeches and articles on subjects ranging from Maastricht to Salman Rushdie to 'The Dead End of Nationalism'. But the title, *The Future of the East is in the West*, and cover design, a montage of the American and European Union flags, already left little doubt where he stood.[10]

Yet it appeared that the New Right's real problem was the editors' failure to find authors who could agree on what the New Right was Right about. Several contributors, for example, spoke warmly of Adenauer, the father of the 'Western Connection' the editors regarded with such misgivings. Another, Ludwig Watzal, blasted at Brussels, supranationality and the European Union's proverbially extravagant Common Agricultural Policy like a German Thatcherite. But it was only, it turned out, because he favors free trade. Germany's real interests, in Watzal's view, are economic integration of Eastern Europe plus solid resistance to French anti-Americanism.[11] Still another contributor deplored Germany's tendency to circle the wagons against a hostile world instead of facing up to its nationhood like everyone else, and getting on with it. The New Right was certainly out there looking for something, one reviewer concluded. But it seemed equally certain that they were a long way from finding it.[12]

THE ART OF THE POSSIBLE

Himself a PhD in history, Chancellor Helmut Kohl could hardly overlook the more obvious historical dimensions of what was happening. But after 40 years of Cold War, partition, selective inattention and secular change, even the most familiar landmarks – the Prussian customs union, 1848, Bismarck, the Third Reich – were little help, and some were positive distractions. As Germans struggled to cope again with Germans, the economic burden, already vastly higher than expected, was matched only by the psychic burden imposed by new and unfamiliar thoughts. 'We are the people,' East Germans chanted in euphoric October. 'We are one people,' they chanted only a few months later. Both seemed almost self-evident at the time. But tested against reality, neither was as self-evident as it appeared.

The future began in Leipzig on 9 October 1989, when some 70,000 ordinary people took to the streets, undeterred by a show of potential force unseen since spontaneous rioting had nearly capsized East Germany in 1953. Come what may, the demonstrators were resolved to show that they had had enough.[40] In the course of a few hours what could as plausibly have turned into a Central European Tiananmen Square instead become a kind of real-life *Nabucco* or *Fidelio*, where nature, for once, had imitated art.

Inadvertently resonant of the preamble to the US constitution, their watchword 'We are the People' soon became proverbial. In contrast to the communist slogans that had hitherto floated on tattered banners, or the Western variety that were routinely floated by well-paid advertising and public relations agencies, this one had no discernible initiator – or a thousand of them. But like nothing said before or after, it accommodated even non-marchers in a shared community: '. . . we saw that they were entirely normal people . . . and we belonged to them too,' a member of the workers militia recalled afterward.[13] The slogan was to become a shining memento of the first popular, bloodless and successful revolution in German history, but also a nostalgic, and even a rueful one.

Only a few weeks later, it had already undergone a significant modulation. The new version, with the specific 'the' replaced by the gramatically generic but politically specific 'a' or 'one', was several historical chasms remote from the *Deutschland über Alles* of 1848 or 1914, and endlessly remote from the 'One *Reich*, one People, One Leader' of the Hitler years. As 'We are *a* people' or, more literally, 'We are *one* people' it was nonetheless a powerful incentive for political leaders to think faster, and Westerners to think again. In November 1989 52% of East Germans were 'rather' or 'completely' opposed to unification. Yet even without encouragement from Mikhail Gorbachev, 39% had decided by January 1990 that they were 'rather', and 40% that they were 'completely', for it.[14]

Before spring, the new slogan had entirely superseded its predecessor. By 18 March 1990, when East Germans cast their first free votes since 1946, the parties of unification carried almost 80% of the vote, and circa four-fifths of the fewer than 20% of the votes cast in favor of parties more or less opposed to one Germany were for successors to the Communists. On 2 December 1990, when both East and West Germans elected their first common parliament, the results were much the same, although the ex-Communist vote had declined by about a third.

Yet, ironically, unification could hardly have been further from the intentions of October's avant-garde, or even its disaffected establishment. An ad hoc coalition of artists, intellectuals and church activists, the dissidents most closely resembled the Western Greens that many regarded as their models. Unique among the anti-Communist *résistants* of 1989, East Germany's core opposition avoided any claim to national legitimacy – at least in the traditional sense of flags and anthems. Yet, in another sense, they were among the most honorably German of Germans, with antecedents extending backward from the Confessional Church of the Nazi years and the anti-annexationist anti-war movement of World War I to the Reformation itself. Born Protestants, they only felt really at home in the minority. As reflexive anti-politicians, they typically viewed power as evil, and victory itself with deep suspicion. Both West German capitalism and traditional nationalism were the antithesis of what they had in mind when they took to the streets.[15] And so, in contrast to their Czech or Polish peers,[16] they let themselves be shouldered aside, half gratefully, half resentfully, by the fellow-citizens they had helped emancipate. In March 1990, October's revolutionaries polled under 3%, compared to the former Communists' 16.4%, in December 1990 6% to the former Communists' 11%. Just as the Weimar Republic in the aftermath of World War I could be called a republic without republicans, East Germany *in extremis* soon became a kind of revolution without revolutionaries. Neither Communists nor dissidents, the majority of East Germans had again become east Germans, keen above all for the normality – and prosperity – denied them 40 years earlier. Given a choice not simply of government but regime, they voted with their feet, heads and stomachs, but only marginally with their hearts,[17] for annexation by the Federal Republic, and a currency reform that raised their wages to Western levels.

Their opportunism, pragmatism and sobriety were rewarded. Yet, in a post-Communist east Germany increasingly populated by the psychically and structurally displaced, the price seemed to grow from day to day. Depressingly but predictably, dawn's bliss withered as hitherto unacknowledged realities were seen by light of day.[18] But to be young, it seemed, was very Purgatory. Seen from outside, young East Germans, adaptable and uncompromised, might logically have expected more from the future than their parents. Yet, as their identification with East Germany plunged, they seemed instead to declare themselves a lost generation. Strangers at home, about half of East German boys and a third of East German girls announced that they were 'bothered' by a modest contingent of resident foreigners. True, 65% of East German 15 and 16-year-olds acknowledged pride in being German, compared to 56% of their West German contemporaries. But even here, the East German young fell far short of the average, 79%, let alone of senior citizens, whose pride peaked at 89%.[19]

A generation earlier, the psychiatrist Alexander Mitscherlich had noted and deplored the social consequences of a West German

'inability to mourn'.[20] Now an apparent 'inability to celebrate' exacted
its own toll. Each for their own reasons, both Easterners and Westerners found it difficult to honor, let alone savor, the achievement of
people with whom neither felt fully comfortable. Standing in the ruins
of what they had brought down, Easterners agreed only that they
wanted to put the past behind them. With much of the East threatening
to arrive momentarily in Düsseldorf or Frankfurt,[21] politically responsible Westerners preferred like Hamlet to bear those ills they were
accustomed to than fly to others that they knew not of. As an anti-
heroic and reflexively managerial political class[22] took over, national
catharsis and self-discovery turned imperceptibly into crisis management.[23]

Significantly, it was 3 October, the end of the process, not the
beginning, that was finally declared the national holiday.[24] Equally
apprehensive of national and international disorder, Western leaders
preferred the half-loaf incorporation of five new East German states in
an existing Federal Republic to the whole-loaf option for a constitutional new beginning.[25] Like Eastern pragmatism, Western pragmatism
too was rewarded. Without body counts, public disorder or a day's
default on a public payroll, an unprecedented transformation, only
recently unimaginable, was accomplished within a year. But Easterners, who had risked and won like no previous Germans in history,
behaved increasingly like country folks, talked out of the family farm
by slickers from the city.[26] Within a year of heroic 9 October, the
neutral '*Wende*', i.e., a change of direction without agent or motive,
was used by most east Germans to describe Germany's first popular,
successful and bloodless revolution. 'They wrote off the tradition of
1989 as though it hadn't happened,' Joschka Fischer, the West German
Green, told a university audience in ex-East German Magdeburg in
1994. 'As though Germans had such a surplus of democratic tradition,
that there was no further need for a success story,' the news magazine
Der Spiegel concurred.[27]

West German reservations not only reflected, but anticipated, the
state of a nation so ambivalently reborn. Few West Germans were
overtly opposed to unity. But surveys confirmed that positive support
declined consistently and dramatically by generation, from 80% among
respondents over 60 to under 60% among respondents under 30. While
virtually no one considered the pace too slow, three-fifths to two-thirds
considered it too fast. For forty years, East Germans had borne the
heavy end of the nation's history, Lothar de Maizière, East Germany's
post-Communist prime minister, declared. He appealed to West Ger-

mans to help reconstruct East Germany. Surveys confirmed that barely a quarter of West Germans shared his views, while more than half were in overt disagreement.

In a triumphant campaign for election as first chancellor of a united Germany, Chancellor Helmut Kohl promised 'blooming landscapes'. But there were no clearly audible calls for solidarity, let alone for blood, sweat and tears. Initial estimates of what it would take to fix the East German economy already ran to DM 500 billion. 'Prosperity is likelier to lead to envy than solidarity,' Wolfgang Schäuble, Kohl's former chief of staff, interior minister, and now majority leader in the Bundestag, announced in a reflective and revealing popular lecture on the state of the nation.[28] It was a remarkable thing for an elective politician to say, both about West German democracy and the people who elected him.

Within four years, the Federal Republic had taken on more than the initial estimates of what it would cost to reconstruct East Germany in new public debt. In 1992–94, annual transfer payments alone averaged upward of DM 150 billion in public funds alone, almost DM 10,000 per year per East German, with no end in sight.[29] Yet fewer than a quarter of West Germans reported great willingness to sacrifice for the sake of national unity, while over half denied any, with a sharp generational slope in favor of the status quo. If 36% of respondents over 60 declared great willingness to sacrifice, only 16% of those under 30 followed suit, and 63% were firmly opposed to the idea.[30] Hitherto divided by a common language, east and west Germans now seemed increasingly bonded by their common differences.[31]

Hypothetically, any of four familiar and widely respected figures – Richard von Weizsäcker, the Christian Democratic federal President, Kurt Biedenkopf, a former Christian Democratic party secretary and later governor of Saxony, or either of two former Social Democratic chancellors, Willy Brandt or Helmut Schmidt – might have sought some greatness in the occasion, or at least anticipated, and pre-empted, the hangover that inevitably followed the champagne. Kohl, who had survived or bested all of them, was a very different man. Bismarckian only in girth, he was the born practitioner of a middle-class *realpolitik*, the medium of 'middle Germany' in much the way Ronald Reagan had been the medium of 'middle America'. Like Reagan, Kohl too had his short-list of sincerely-held priorities, among them a 'United States of Europe' around a Franco-German core, a special relationship with the United States, and a 'normal' Germany that was neither at its neighbors' throats nor knees.

Where indicated, or unavoidable, he was, in fact, capable of initiative, even courage. During the party's desert days, he had first opened the governor's office in Mainz, then party headquarters in Bonn, to liberal, original and independent thoughts and people. In 1982, he had confronted and faced down Europe's largest peace movement in compliance with a NATO resolution calling for deployment of American cruise missiles. In late 1989, while the opposition dithered, Kohl was among the first to see where things were going, and act on it preemptively.

But it was equally clear that he was a graduate of the Lyndon Johnson school of statecraft, aware to his fingertips that politicians who want to be statesmen first have to be elected. Kohl was at his happiest doing political business on the telephone, an aide noted. Growing numbers of challengers, doubters and former associates, some from as far back as his days in Mainz, could also confirm from personal experience that he could be purposeful, ruthless, even vindictive when challenged or tested. Briefed for an appearance at Harvard on the 'neo-realism' of the political scientist Stanley Hoffmann, he was characteristically bemused by what was presented to him as profundity. 'Where we come from, every mayor knows that,' he told an aide. For a man who was to become the winningest electoral politician in German history, appeals for sacrifice, challenge and austerity were as improbable as a campaign appearance in a spiked helmet. A child of the postwar Federal Republic, he was a natural pragmatist, inclined, as even a close and admiring aide described him, to see imprecision as a political virtue, and disposed to see the future as an extension of the past.[32]

THE FACTS OF LIFE

In the wake of the confused and traumatic debates on Germany's role in the Gulf war in 1990–91; its aggressive support for the Maastricht treaty on accelerated European Union, and Bonn's early recognition of Slovenian and Croatian independence[33] in December 1991; the Bundesbank's subsequent decision to raise interest rates without apparent regard for the impact on Germany's neighbors and the world economy[34]; a cascade of rightward election returns from north to south in April 1992; a series of violent assaults on foreigners from East German Hoyerswerda in September 1991 to West German Mölln in November

1992 and Solingen in May 1993; and even the public unveiling of a Franco-German brigade in apparent disregard of NATO, policy makers and commentators again found it easy to see 'a Germany of 80 million' as a loose cannon on Europe's deck, and Germans, after a 40-year truce or interregnum, as once again – well, German.[35]

Yet none of this was really any clearer than before. If Germany's role, or lack of one, in the Gulf War, was an embarrassment, which it was, it was still only fair to ask what useful role German troops might have played there. If the implosion of Yugoslavia was a debacle, which it was, Italians, even Danes, held similar views on Slovenia and Croatia, without causing veins to throb in neighbors' foreheads. Electoral slippage toward the right, and a continuing series of assaults on foreigners justifiably caused the world to look at Germans, and Germans at themselves. But similar attitudes, election returns, assaults and outrages happened elsewhere with only minimal foreign media attention.[36] In the real and interactive world of global capital flows, Bundesbank rates can undeniably constitute a heavy foot on other people's brake pedals. But while neighbors, allies and the world in general only rarely ask the question, it was hard to see how German inflation was in anybody's interest either.

What were increasingly clear, on the other hand, were certain facts of Central European life, both recent and historical. Some were consciously concealed, or lost from view behind the Wall and Iron Curtain. Other were legacies of the postwar era. But after 40 years of speculation on 'third ways', 'Fourth Reichs' and whole atlases of alternative *Sonderwege*,[37] virtually all of them were rich in irony.

The first was the continuing, even enhanced, centrality of a Germany its neighbors had fought two world wars to contain. Yet, as Adenauer had realized decades earlier, Germany is only as strong as its alliances. Already a European, an Atlantic and a global center, the new, enhanced and formally sovereign Federal Republic is now not simply what one analyst calls 'the East of the West and the West of the East'.[38] It is all of the above and more, with all the ambiguous consequences. So contrary to what many Germans dreamed, and even believed, before 3 October, unification and recovered sovereignty meant more, not less, foreign policy, with harder, not easier, choices.

Attitudes toward NATO were a revealing test. For more than 40 years, NATO membership had been seen by some as a national affront and gratuitous provocation, by others as a necessary evil or even an alternative form of patriotism. But its origins as such were not controversial. NATO was to the Warsaw Pact as West Germany was to East Germany. It seemed reasonable to assume that the end of one was the end of the other. Now the Warsaw Pact and East Germany were gone. Yet not only was NATO still there, it was also virtually uncontested, and Germans, not to mention their Eastern neighbors, even wanted to see it extended eastward.

The rediscovered centrality of the German economy was a second, related fact. Failure to understand this would be the cause of endless trouble, J. M. Keynes warned in a famous book after World War I.[39] In the aftermath of 1945, German recovery was generally recognized not only as a necessary condition for west European recovery, but of peace itself. Now, in the aftermath of 1989, it was clearer than ever that German capital, technology and markets were a necessary condition for the recovery of post-Communist Europe too. In 1993, east and central Europe consumed barely 5% of German exports, and provided less than 6% of German imports.[40] On the face of it, the relationship was as caboose to locomotive. In fact, as Kohl was quicker to appreciate than most, Eastern Europe was to Germany as Mexico to the United States. Once Germans dreamed that Eastern Europe could make them rich. Now they feared, and understood, that it could make them poor. But, just as in North America, this involved expensive and complicated choices about open markets and open borders.

A third fact, after generations of presumed and authentic aberration, was Germany's new normality, with all its consequences. Normal in health, life expectancy[41] and creature comforts, Germans were normal too in their susceptibility to the 'normal pathology'[42] of modern life in all its variety, from racism, violence, divorce,[43] delinquency, family breakdown, AIDS and drugs, to organized crime, hazardous wastes, even obesity.[44] Like any other 'normal' country, middle-class, middle-aged, export-dependent Germany also faced the puzzles and vicissitudes of an ever more competitive, ever more globalized economy, in a world where 'the Rio Grande is everywhere'.[45]

If educational attainments, cultural standards and general civic habits are any index, Germans so far have met the test as well as most, and better than many. But two supplementary challenges have arguably made the German case more normal than most. One is the post-modern reprise of the national question imposed by unification. Alone among the industrial democracies, Germany has not only gathered in a diaspora, but chosen to absorb, accommodate and learn to live again, with 16 million once and future citizens.[46] Projected on the United States, the equivalent effort would mean integrating some 50 million new Americans.

Employment figures before and after 1989 affirm both the problem and the achievement. West German unemployment, 7.7% in 1983, had declined to 6.2% in 1988. But, as elsewhere, the improvement masked a growing number of presumably low-paid, part-time service jobs, and a high level of long-term unemployed. Of the registered unemployed, long-term unemployment, 21% of the total at the beginning of the decade, had increased to nearly 50% at the end. Then came unification. In 1994, west German unemployment was 8.3%, east German almost 15% – and in a federal election year, at that. Figures scarcely higher than these had sunk the Weimar Republic by the early 1930s.[47] Yet all that happened this time was a modest rearrangement of parliamentary seats, and the reelection of the incumbent government.

The concurrent challenge is the post-modern reprise of what might be called the imperial question, imposed alike by history, economics and geography. As its large resident populations of Turks and Kurds, Croatians and Serbians confirm, Germany stands not only on one, but on two, of the world's most active fault lines. The first and more obvious runs between the West and the post-Communist East, extending from the Brandenburg Gate to the Pacific. The second, and less obvious, runs between the West and the post-Ottoman Middle East, extending from Bosnia to the Persian Gulf. This is not the first time that two of the classic 19th century conundrums, the Eastern and the German Questions, have merged in German awareness. On the contrary, the antecedents include Germany's greatest writer, and the foreign policy that led to World War I.[48] But this is the first time the two have merged in the streets of the Frankfurt Westend or Berlin–Kreuzberg.

Their merger leads to a fourth, fifth and sixth fact: the perennially unresolved debate about German identity; its continuing importance to non-Germans as well as Germans, and the concurrent metamorphosis of the national state per se. Once believed sovereign beyond its borders, the national state now seems less and less sovereign even within them, while real decisions are negotiated somewhere else – or not at all.[49]

Alan Milward and like-minded colleagues have argued that supra-nationality, as practiced by Europeans since World War II, has actually saved the national state. First, it deputized the national state to send delegates and civil servants to the CSCE, EU, IMF, NATO, WEU, WTO, WHO, and all the other institutional jots and squiggles that now fill the days of policy-makers, editorial writers and conference organizers. Second, it left, allowed, even required, the national state to deal with the consequences.[50] German experience is a laboratory case for the ingenuity and plausibility of the argument. Defined by the political scientist Karl-Dietrich Bracher in 1986 as a 'post-national democracy among nation-states',[51] the Federal Republic derives a fair degree of its 'post-national' identity and even legitimacy from connections that pool its sovereignty and put its military under foreign command. Yet today's unified Germany, the closest approximation of a 'normal' national state in German history, has done nothing different, and, if anything, more of the same, since its national epiphany in 1990. Both for better and for worse, its experience to date is de facto confirmation that unification is not *re*unification, and a practical example of what can happen when a post-national national state with an unresolved identity problem and a passion for 'Abide, you are so fair', meets the challenges of secular change.

FACING THE MUSIC

Certainly, the new German national state could hardly be more different from Arndt's and Hoffmann von Fallersleben's. 'From the Meuse to the Memel,' etc., their explosive Germany extended in principle 'wherever German tongue is heard'. In a sense, the same applies to the new, essentially implosive Germany. Only now, at least for political purposes, the German tongue that was once heard as far away as Riga and Romania, is essentially confined between the Rhine and Oder, and Germans like it that way.

The irony, according to Wolfgang Schäuble, was that 1989 again made Germans central, but left them without an identity, alienated and seduced by prosperity, and disoriented by political change. The purely civic patriotism endorsed by certain west German intellectuals was too abstract for most people, he added. It had not been loyalty to the constitution that caused the patriotic conspirators of 20 July to try to assassinate Hitler.[52] If Germans were again to play a responsible part in a world where 'boundaries no longer divide, but also offer no protection', Schäuble insisted, they needed the sense of historical kinship that only the nation could give.[53]

The irony, according to the authors and signatories of a widely noted 'Manifesto' on immigration, was that Germany, already an immigrant country since at least the 1970s, now faced a mass of 'strangers,' some foreign, some domestic. Yet it refused to face reality, as it had since the 1970's, and adopt a coherent immigration policy.[54]

Who were the Germans, and what was the German's Fatherland under the circumstances? 'Wherever German complaints are heard' seemed, for the moment, as plausible an answer as any. In the golden age of *Ostpolitik*, it had been fashionable to describe Germans as 'One nation, two states'. Unification now seemed to have turned it into 'One state, two nations'. Reading habits were a revealing barometer. In the first flush of freedom, Western hopes and newspaper circulations soared. Yet despite strenuous efforts to sell their product and double their coverage in the East, it was soon clear to Western editors that they were still behind a Wall.[55] Less than two years after unification, *Der Spiegel* estimated that it sold circa 60,000 of its weekly edition of 1.2 million copies in former East Germany.[56]

Not only was there little real interaction between East and West Berliners, visitors noted with bemusement that they even found it difficult to find their way around the other part of town. In 1991, according to *Der Spiegel*, about a hundred West Berlin women had married Africans. Only 46 had married East Berliners. Although an estimated 20,000 young East Germans accepted West German apprenticeships, high rents, inadequate housing, and what the potential applicants themselves described as 'a rough climate and competitive pressure' were steadily reducing the number of applicants.[57] Kurt Biedenkopf, the governor of former East German Saxony, warned of an impending east German *mezzogiorno*, i.e. a perennially depressed, corrupt and handout-dependent equivalent of the Italian south, whose principal exports would presumably be crime and immigrants.

Hitherto surrounded by nine neighbors, with open borders to seven, the formally united, but only imperfectly reunited, new Germany now had nine neighbors, and open borders to all of them. The respective legacies of their colonial and Communist pasts made as many as six – France, Belgium, Holland, Poland, Austria and the Czech Republic – potential funnels for unwanted, and frequently illegal, immigrants. But the former Soviet Union; the rest of the former Communist empire, and the Arab-Moslem world from Turkey to Algeria were more of the same. The self-destructive Yugoslavia was already a case unto itself. Some 600,000 of its citizens[58] lived in the Federal Republic before the disintegration even began. By 1992, the number exceeded 900,000.

With its open-ended obligation to extend political asylum;[59] its pledge to resettle up to two to four million ethnic Germans who might wish to leave Poland and the former Soviet Union – as many as 80% of them in need of German language instruction[60] – as well as Romania, the former Czechoslovakia and Hungary;[61] a treaty commitment to open EC borders in 1993, and the gravitational pull of its economy on the desperate and enterprising from virtually everywhere, it was small wonder that immigration became a matter of fierce political controversy in Germany as it did in other countries. But the inertial state of German law did little to address the anachronisms, ambiguities and inequities of civic 'we' and 'they' in a country where the foreign presence was so established that one in every ten marriages was now binational.[62] As both domestic and foreign observers regularly noticed,[63] immigrant Polish speakers who could produce a grandfather's Waffen-SS papers were already almost Germans.[64] The vast majority of an ever-growing number[65] of German-born, German-speaking, German-educated Turks were not.

The costs and stresses of unification amplified the stresses of immigration. But the reverse was also true. In 1989, Interior ministry officials cited a cabinet resolution from 1982, the year of Kohl's election as chancellor. It reaffirmed that 'the Federal Republic is not now, and shall not become, an immigrant country'. The same year, German immigration officials noted a net increase of almost 333,000 foreign entries over departures from the Federal Republic. Two years later, the net gain had risen by over 27%, including an increase of almost 450% in new arrivals from the former Yugoslavia alone,[66] and a Bundespost brochure explained the new five-digit postal codes in German, English, French, Spanish, Italian, Turkish, Greek and Croatian,

In fact, as any schoolbook history, morning paper or evening TV program confirmed, Germany had not only become an immigrant country, it had always been one. Successive Brentanos had flirted with Goethe, compiled a classic anthology of German folk poetry and served as Adenauer's foreign minister. Hans-Jürgen Wischnewski, a close associate of Chancellor Helmut Schmidt, had played a crucial role in the famous Mogadishu rescue mission that saved German air passengers from terrorists in 1977. Klaus von Dohnányi served as mayor of Hamburg; his brother Christoph conducted the Cleveland Orchestra. Lothar de Maizière was East Germany's first, and only, post-Communist prime minister; his cousin Ulrich had served as General Inspector of the Bundeswehr. Although Oskar Lafontaine failed to get himself elected Germany's Social Democrat chancellor in 1990, he was regularly reelected governor of the Saar. Spiros Simitis, a Frankfurt law professor, first wrote West Germany's first privacy law. He then became Germany's first state privacy commissioner. Helios Mendiburu, the son of Basque Communist refugees to Communist Germany, was elected, and reelected, post-Communist mayor of the

East Berlin borough of Friedrichshain.[67] Now Akif Pirincci, one of Germany's best-selling novelists, was a naturalized Turkish immigrant, brought to Germany by his textile-worker parents when he was 10.[68] Perhaps the nicest irony of all was Willy Millowitsch, the Cologne dialect comedian. On the very eve of unification, Millowitsch finished second to the prototypically German film actor, Heinz Rühmann, in a survey of Germans whom other Germans perceived as 'typically German'.[69]

Language, as always a clue to social movement, reflected the effort to catch up. Just as the coldly pejorative *Fremdarbeiter*, foreign worker, had given way to the more hospitable *Gastarbeiter*, the latest transformation too reflected the evolving scene. Anywhere else, the expression *ausländische Mitbürger*, foreign fellow citizens, might have seemed an oxymoron. In Germany by the early 1990s, it was ubiquitous and used without irony.[70]

The new expression testified to a changing social and demographic landscape. Of the reunited Germany's c. 78 million residents in 1992, six and a half million, about 40% of them women, were not Germans at all. This worked out to an average foreign population of 8.0%. But the average was doubly misleading. First, the foreign population was located almost entirely in the West, and there in locally formidable concentrations. In Hesse alone, almost 12% of the population was foreign; in Munich and Stuttgart nearly 20%, in Frankfurt almost a quarter.[71] Second, by the end of 1991, 40% of the migrant population had already lived in Germany for at least 20 years, 40% for more than 15, 55% for more than 10,[72] and 80% of immigrant children – a population of some 700,000, or nearly 15% of the foreign total – were German-born.[73]

In relative figures, Germany's foreign population was roughly equal to France's and Belgium's, and double Britain's. Yet this too was ambiguous in at least two ways. On the one hand, thanks to the enlightened self-interest of both business and labor, legally employed foreign workers enjoyed shopfloor equity with their German colleagues, including social services, job protection and union representation. In fact, foreign workers themselves held up to 30% of the labor seats on factory councils. A model of conscientiousness, the giant IG Metall alone ran a comprehensive support program for foreign members, organized conferences to represent their interests, and bought display ads spelling out why immigrants were a net plus.[74] On the other hand, under French and British, not to mention American *jus soli*, many of Germany's foreigners would not count as foreign at all. The crucial difference was the traditional German – though also Italian, Irish, Israeli, Arab, Turkish, Tamil and Singhalese[75] – *jus sanguinis*. The secondary difference was persisting reservations about dual citizenship that deterred all but about 200,000 resident foreigners from applying for naturalization since the mid-70s.[76]

As over half a million German Jews discovered after 1933, citizenship, dual or otherwise, is itself no assurance of civil rights and coexistence. Nor should naturalization be necessary to protect people against murder, arson and physical violence. But citizenship has invariably been understood as a necessary condition of acculturation and social integration, not least where large numbers fear multiculturalism, as many Germans do.[77] It seems equally likely that a law, conceived for the Reich of Wilhelm II, perpetuates social distances that many of today's Germans might well prefer to narrow.

Effective 1 July 1993, the latest reform allowed foreigners in the Federal Republic the right to apply for citizenship after 15 years of residence, with corresponding reductions in the residence period for 'second and third generation foreigners'. It also reduced the relatively stiff administrative fees required of applicants. After the murderous assault on a Turkish family in Solingen in May 1993, Kohl also urged more, if unspecific, reforms, to make the existing process more attractive. But he not only avoided the question of double nationality, he omitted the single reference to it in the advance text.[78]

Although efforts to establish local suffrage for resident foreign nationals in Hamburg and Schleswig-Holstein were ruled unconstitutional, pending reciprocity within the EC, survey data showed significant shifts in public opinion. According to an Emnid poll taken shortly after the murders in Solingen, 62% now favored local suffrage for foreigners, with only 28% opposed. There was also a 53% majority for dual nationality, even a plurality of support among Kohl's fellow Christian Democrats, Bavarians included.[79] Yet Germany, with its 14,000 optional naturalizations in 1991, remained significantly less tolerant of dual citizenship than virtually all its neighbors, including the Swiss, whose views on aliens and immigrants were proverbially exclusive.[80]

It was easy to link post-unification *tristesse* to the question of open borders, beginning in 1989. On their very arrival from Hungary, the first East German wave found 350,000 *Aussiedler* plus 100,000 *Umsiedler*, themselves only newly arrived since the start of the year, already waiting for them. The newcomers were first celebrated. But they were increasingly resented as more and more East Germans followed. By early 1990, the rush to unification and the economic union that made it possible had clearly become a massive effort to bring the Deutschmark to East Germans before another 15 million East Germans came to the Deutschmark. Between 1989 and 1992, an estimated 1.23 million East Germans moved west, compared to an estimated 233,000 West Germans and returning east Germans moving east.[81]

By March 1992, according to official reports, a further 340,000 former East Germans, mainly young and male, commuted to jobs in what was hitherto West Germany. Of these, 100,000 came home only on weekends, and 45% at intervals of more than two weeks. But the real commuter traffic was believed closer to 600,000. Over half indicated their willingness to move definitively 'under certain conditions', 10% to move immediately, if they only could.[82] Although young volunteers were uncommon, a few West Germans too – bankers, entry-level civil servants, any number of lawyers, and a few retired politicians – heeded the urgings of duty, opportunity or, more rarely, a sense of adventure, to take jobs in the east.[83] Among them was a dedicated band of self-declared 'Wossis', who intended to stay in the east. Their ability to translate 'Ossi' into politically credible 'Wessi' made them increasingly valuable intermediaries. But their numbers, let alone profile, hardly matched the commuters from East to West.

As might be expected, reservations grew with the swelling numbers. According to surveys, majorities of Germans expected the newcomers to encourage public housing; rejuvenate the population;[84] make Berlin once more a metropolis; fill vacant jobs; enliven political debate, and stimulate the economy. But virtually comparable majorities also expected them to produce a housng shortage, increase unemployment; inflate welfare figures; clash with the indigenous population; work below union scale; fill day-care centers, and radicalize politics.[85]

For Christian Democrats in Bonn, under pressure from the Republicans, the *Aussiedler* were a natural client constituency, well worthy of the DM 7 million and four advertising agencies already enlisted by the government's public information office in October 1989 for a first appeal to national solidarity and self-interest.[86] Not only did they meet traditional standards of ethnicity, with high birthrates, respectable job skills[87] and old-time German virtues, they represented a claim on the national conscience that even Social Democrats had to acknowledge.[88] Anti-socialist to the roots of their hair, and German by definition and self-image, they also seemed likely to vote CDU.[89]

For the swelling numbers of Republican voters, on the other hand, Germans from Kazakhstan were simply 'the Russians'.[90] Where jobs, apartments, income supplements and tax allowances were at stake, they were as self-evidently competitors for jobs, apartments, income supplements and tax allowances as any Turk from Anatolia; and candidates for political asylum were the functional equivalent of Ronald Reagan's 'welfare queen'.[91]

If modestly endowed, middle-aged West Germans made their statement at the polls, young and initially East German thugs took theirs to the street, where their age and socio-psychological profile proved at least as alarming as their ideology and organization. More worrisome still, the offenders were only minimally accessible to police, courts, social workers, even the deterrent effect of social obloquy. Predominantly male, disproportionately unemployed, and consistently unremarkable, virtually all were under 30, and 70% under 21. It was understandable, but too easy, to see them as a neo-Nazi cadre. On closer inspection, they appeared to be hateful, vengeful, mindless and pathetic in roughly equal parts, requiring only a charge of beer to turn them into walking fire bombs.[92]

At first, their assaults on foreigners were effectively ignored by elected officials and public agencies at every level. Ineffectual in virtually all cases, police resistance in some varied from the risible to the complicit. Although post facto investigations confirmed that the police had been warned of impending violence, the authorities in Rostock had virtually looked the other way, and even tried to negotiate with the perpetrators.[93] The passivity, even applause, of spectators was still more alarming. But arguably most alarming of all was the passivity of a conservative government in Bonn that looked on in apparent helplessness as law and order, nominally a conservative government's comparative advantage, were mugged in the street.

By 1992 it was estimated that aggregate membership in neo-Nazi grouplets, had grown from circa 20,000 in 1982 to 65,000. Between 1989 and 1992, recorded acts of violence increased at a quasi logarithmic rate: 103 in 1989, 270 in 1990, 1483 in 1991, 2285 in 1992.[94] Only the murders of a long-resident Turkish family in West German Mölln in November 1992 led to a dramatic shift of public opinion – and an impressive decline in the ascending curve of police statistics. Beginning in December, as many as four or five million ordinary Germans assembled in the streets of Munich, Hamburg and other cities with lighted candles. The demonstrations, all locally organized, were as spontaneous as the Leipzig demonstrations three years before. This time, no one was at risk, and few put themselves to the risk of guarding foreign neighborhoods or refugee shelters. The demonstrations were nonetheless a clear and unmistakable statement to both the thugs and elected officials that people had had enough.

Reinforced by the appalled reaction from foreign editorialists and domestic boardrooms, Minister of the Interior Rudolf Seiters finally cracked down on the proliferating grouplets.[95] In 1993 recorded acts of violence fell to 529. Before Mölln 20% of east Germans and 12% of west Germans acknowledged 'understanding' for violent attacks on refugees; in January 1993 10% of east Germans and 5% of west Germans.[96] According to an Emnid survey taken in the following June after a subsequent firebombing in West German Solingen, 73% of Germans and 82% of German women now considered the danger from the radical right to be 'great' or 'very great'.

As the shock waves from the right successively buffeted the Bavarian Christian Social Union, a pillar of any Christian Democratic government, Kohl's Christian Democrats themselves, and the ambivalently liberal Free Democrats (FDP), it was only a matter of time before they finally reached the opposition Social Democrats (SPD). After state elections in spring 1992 that shook all the established parties,[97] even then party chairman Björn Engholm, the governor of Schleswig-Holstein, began to rethink the hitherto unthinkable. 'Anybody who thinks an effort to hear and take aboard what people say is immoral and conformist, has a very elitist approach to things,' Engholm enjoined the party faithful.[98] 'There are relatively few referenda initiated by Social Democrats or anybody else that say: Please, build a shelter for refugees in our part of town,' his predecessor Hans Jochen Vogel added.[99]

The collective reappraisal led successively to a special convention, an all-party consensus, an emotional debate, and finally, on 26 May 1993, an ambivalent compromise to amend the constitution. Successive Social Democratic 'essentials' – an immigration law, special status for civil war refugees and the possibility of double nationality for those 'foreign fellow citizens' – were left in the dust. Short-term special status for civil war refugees was linked to a consensual decision by state and federal authorities on what constituted a civil war; liberalized naturalization was the trade-off for a debate on citizenship; it was agreed that German-descended East Europeans would no longer enjoy automatic inheritance of German citizenship; and an annual limit of 100,000 was set on contractual *Gastarbeiter*.[100] The crucial sentence 'Politically persecuted persons enjoy the right of asylum' also survived the reform. But what had hitherto been unqualified was now qualified by five extended paragraphs.

Besieged and blockaded by thousands of demonstrators, a number of deputies could only reach their seats to vote by helicopter or boat from the opposing Rhine embankment. But there was never any doubt about the outcome. 'For the first time since the creation of the Federal Republic, a basic right was cancelled de facto,' wrote Heribert Prantl the next day in the *Süddeutsche Zeitung*.[101] While the new version continued to assure qualified applicants the right to political asylum, it was equally clear that a parachute would be immensely helpful. According to the new law that accompanied the amendment, applicants from 'secure countries of origin' – including Romania, Bulgaria, Ghana, Gambia and Senegal, though not, under protest from the SPD, Turkey and India – would be assured of a speedy hearing, presumably meaning immediate deportation.

On the other hand, according to a stipulation introduced by the CDU in November 1992, and later reluctantly accepted by the SPD, applicants from 'secure third states', meaning Germany's neighbors and Scandinavia, would no longer have a claim on any hearing at all. They would just be sent back where they came from.[102] Since such a formula inevitably required the compliance of eastern neighbors, who were themselves in the path of mass migrations from still further eastward, it was obvious that money would change hands. As a first installment, both the 1993 and 1994 budgets allocated DM120 million as an incentive for Poland. Similar arrangements were then concluded with the Czech Republic, Bulgaria and Romania. 'Subcontractors for Fortress Europe,' said Janusz Tychner of the Warsaw weekly *Prawo i Zycie*.[103]

In 1994, the number of asylum-seekers fell by 60% from its 1993 total, itself 26% below the total for 1992, Interior Minister Manfred Kanther reported proudly. On the other hand, 7.3% of the processed applications were now accepted, compared with 4.25% in 1992. Above all, Germany was still at the head of the line with more than 125,000 applications in 1994, compared with 55,000 in the Netherlands and 24,000 in France. Yet even in elections to the European parliament, where voters often cast ballots as they might otherwise scrawl graffiti, the Republicans polled only 3.9% in 1994, compared to 7.1% in 1989. In Hoyerswerda, in fact, where all the trouble began, Republicans polled only 2.8%.

By now, only 21% of voters still saw immigration as a major issue.[104] Yet the issues remained as obscure and conflicted as ever. According to an Emnid poll in July 1994, just days after the Federal Office for the Accreditation of Refugees on June 30 rejected an 18-year-old Tutsi's appeal for asylum on grounds that 'the reasons offered do not exceed the political, economic and societal conditions common to all Ruandan citizens', a plurality of Germans, including a majority of east Germans, favored taking in refugees from Ruanda. As church groups threatened civil disobedience, state-level officials squabbled with federal officials over the equity and costs of deportations. In 1994 alone, the chief justice of the supreme court complained, there were 800 requests for injunctions, as the courts struggled to do the right thing, for example, about Kurds, who had been jailed in Germany for anti-Turkish violence, but were only too likely to be tortured if deported to Turkey on their release from German jails. In March 1995, the Turkish and German interior ministries solemnly agreed that Turkey would notify German authorities if charges were pending, assure deportees due process, and require medical exams before and after interrogation. There was an equally solemn assurance that a standing committee of officials from both countries would look into charges of abuse.[105]

Yet the immigration issue persists, and with it the still more basic question of distinguishing 'us' from 'them'. Polls before 1989 confirmed a traditional German rule of thumb. There were, in effect, *Edelausländer*, i.e., first-class foreigners, including other north and west Europeans. Then there were neutral foreigners, like Spaniards or Italians. Finally, there were poor non-Europeans, primarily from North and black Africa, of the sort that Italians refer to euphemistically as *Extracommunitari*.[106] Up to the moment of unification, Germans also inclined to equate German with *West* German, i.e., Germans were those who lived within the borders of the Federal Republic. Confronted with similar challenges, neighboring countries tended to act similarly. By another nice coincidence, just weeks after the Bundestag amended the right of asylum, and on the same day Kohl promised unspecifically to move German procedure away from *jus sanguinis*, a new, conservative French government proposed a fundamental reform of France's traditional *jus soli*. Meanwhile, the immigrants, unlike the babies, kept coming, while 1913 receded ever further behind the historical horizon.

THE FUTURE LIES AHEAD

In principle, there is nothing remarkable about the state of German demography save, perhaps, the reluctance to talk about it. In fact, actuaries and insurance specialists talk about it a lot, one leading German social scientist notes. But with labor not currently a problem, even economists find the subject easy to dodge. Revealingly, it even failed to come up at a book party in Bonn, where a blue-ribbon panel of academics discussed the so-called Delors White Book on the future of the European economy. Pressed from the floor, six of the seven panelists avoided the question altogether. The chairman answered mildly that the subject would probably come up before the end of the decade.[107]

Unsurprisingly, politicians too have been slow to volunteer. Underwritten by a grant from the Federal Ministry of Research, a comprehensive study of the likely impact of declining population on German life and public policy was recently turned down for official publication by the Federal Ministry of Interior because, one of the authors assumes, they preferred to avoid public debate on the subject.[108] It is not hard to imagine why Kohl himself has avoided the issue. Like anywhere else where the future funding is delicate, a national debate on the impact of population on pensions is nobody's idea of good politics.

Yet the real difference between German figures and their neighbors' is marginal. In 1986, German birth rates were the lowest in the EU. But of 12 EU members, only Ireland, exceeded the 2.1 needed to maintain a stable population anyway. In 1981, 29% of the West German population lived in single-person households. But 30% of Denmark, 25% of France, and 23% of Britain did the same. In 1985, 21% of West Germans were already 65 or older, compared to an EU average of 20.1%. By 2025, the number of Germans 65 and older was expected to reach 39.3%. But by that time, the EC average too was expected to reach a substantial 31.6%.[109]

German ambivalence about immigrants is hardly unique either.[110] Since Hoyerswerda in October 1991, there have been similarly nasty episodes in Italy[111] and elsewhere. Nor, for all the ugliness of individual instances, have public order or basic democratic consensus come close to breaking down. German election returns too are well within European norms, viz. regional turnouts of 20% for Jean-Marie Le Pen's *Front National* in France; 25% for the separatist-xenophobic *Vlaamsblok* in Belgium; almost 30% for Jörg Haider's aggressively anti-immigrant Freedom party in Austria. If rightward tides in Bremen, Baden-Württemberg et al. in April 1992, were unlovely, California voters expressed quite similar anti-immigrant views in November 1994, and immigration has meanwhile become a high-profile issue in Italy, Austria and much of the United States.[112] Yet the smarmily avuncular Schönhuber has vanished without a successor, and German Republicans have totally failed to make the cut in recent federal and state elections. In Hesse, with Germany's densest foreign population, Republicans in February 1995 scored only 2%.

In 1930, the combination of political paralysis and economic crisis turned the hitherto marginal Hitler into a respectable option for distraught and rudderless voters. Sixty years later, what failed to happen was at least as interesting as anything that did. In contrast to their Weimar predecessors, business leaders resisted an impulse to hedge bets, let alone cozy up to thugs. Senior military officers showed minimal tolerance for xenophobic violence in uniform. University students, who had been a favored constituency of the nationalist right for generations, were conspicuous among the millions joining hands and lighting candles in the street.[113]

It was true that German conservatives and party strategists, both Bavarian and otherwise, were at least as quick as foreign counterparts to make hay of the issue. 'SPD-*Asylanten*,' then-CDU General Secretary, later Defense Minister, Völker Rühe sneered publicly – until voter backlash began to take its toll on the CDU. But no German came close to France's former President Valéry Giscard d'Estaing in legitimizing populist wog-bashing, or Austria's Haider in sounding horns unheard in public since the end of World War II.

In May 1994 there was another explosion of popular lynch-lust, this time in Magdeburg, where 150 adolescents chased five Africans into a Turkish-run café. Police then released 47 of 48 arrested rioters on their own recognizance, *not* including a Turkish waiter, who allegedly stabbed an attacker in self-defense. But if the Magdeburg incident was an internationally-visible challenge,[114] the media, and still more the political response, were at least as significant. On 1 July 1994 both the new and the departing federal president addressed the issues head-on at the inaugural ceremony in the Berlin Reichstag. In his farewell address, Richard von Weizsäcker pointedly confronted what Kohl and others had equally pointedly avoided. 'Anyone who turns the word 'immigration' into a taboo for fear of xenophobic violence is turning things on their head,' Weizsäcker declared. 'We need new provisions for immigration and citizenship to direct the flow of immigrants according to our own obligations and interests,' he continued to silence from his fellow Christian Democrats, but cheers from the rest of the hall. 'Anyone who doesn't know that you don't set fire to living people, beat them to a pulp and chase them through the streets, will just have to learn that lesson with all the force the law can bring to bear,' his successor, Roman Herzog, added. That, at least, drew unanimous cheers.[115]

As interesting as the failure of the New Right was the unanticipated success of the old Left. But revealingly, foreign media virtually ignored it. It was true: eastern voters were rebellious. But what had not been so clearly foreseen was that they would scavenge to the left, not right, for a vehicle for their protest. In June 1994 the Party of Democratic Socialism (PDS), east Germany's old Communists, or at least their institutional heirs and successors, swept local elections in the shadow of a new Coca Cola plant. In October, they established themselves as a substantial third party in eastern state parliaments, and made themselves heard as far as Bonn.[116] Represented by the CDU as an unreconstructed band of dedicated Marxist–Leninists, they were, more plausibly, a kind of regional support group, representing nearly a third of the 18-to-24-year-olds, the 46% of former East Germans unhappy with their economic fortunes, and literally countless fellow citizens nostalgic for subsidized rents and bus tickets that had vanished with the old régime, and fed up with feeling inferior to West Germans who invariably claimed to know more and better.[117]

German reservations about the brave new European world are unremarkable too. Once disposed to regard 'Europe' as their definitive standard of respectability, many Germans have become Eurosceptics in much the way Americans flirt with global abstinence. Even a combined CDU/CSU-FDP-SPD resolution hailing the Maastricht treaty on more perfect European union acknowledged subliminal anxieties in declaring that a strong and competent Europe was needed to fight crime, as well as poverty and environmental hazards.[118] Polls confirmed further reservations ranging from fear that the Deutschmark might be sacrificed on the altar of what Peter Gauweiler, a Bavarian conservative, called the 'Esperanto money' of a united Europe;[119] to resentment of the most-equal-animal status that caused Germany to pay 28% of the EU's costs;[120] to concern for the peculiarly German vocational certificates and restrictive shop hours that were believed to shield Germans against invading battalions of Spanish plumbers, Greek dentists and Turkish grocers. Yet of the 12 EU members in 1994, Germans were first only (87%) in their willingness to admit Sweden, Finland, Norway and Austria, third (52%) in questioning the EU's effectiveness, fourth (with 62%) in their readiness to vote in the European election, and fourth again (with 52% and 67%) in their readiness to admit Poland, the Czech Republic, Slovakia and Hungary, and their opposition to a united Europe with a central government. They were also second only to Luxembourg in the number of citizens who regarded themselves exclusively or primarily as Europeans, and 9th of 12 in the number of citizens who identified themselves only by their nationality.[121]

What distinguishes Germans from their neighbors in this case is a matter of scale, not quality. Long before 1989, Germany had again become the midpoint of concentric – East–West, North–South, trans-Atlantic and intra-European – rings, and an economy that reached around the world. So regarded, 1989 only meant more of the same, with more obligations, more history to digest, and more surfaces exposed. For Germans, confronted by ever more and different challenges to think big after decades of learning to think little and liking it, both the ancient concept of *kleindeutsch* and Chancellor Konrad Adenauer's brilliantly effective 1957 campaign slogan 'No Experiments!,' assumed new dimensions of meaning.

'We have a deep nostalgia for the present,' another departing federal president, Walter Scheel, observed on leaving office in 1979. Like the peace movement of the early 1980s, the Gulf War debate of 1990–91 suggested a country that really wanted to be Greater Liechtenstein. Yet, as most Germans reluctantly concede, self-denying isolation is no solution either for a country with a major stake in international cooperation, an economy dependent on global markets, and a society whose best of all possible services and living standard depend on the skills of its workforce, the competitiveness of its products, and a favorable ratio of insurance contributors to beneficiaries.

As in most other advanced countries, the linkages are bound to challenge an aging country, where pension, health and welfare costs are bound to rise, and the ratio of contributors to beneficiaries is already in rapid decline. As elaborated by the economist Meinhard Miegel, two alternative scenarios are easily imaginable. In the first, population continues to fall without compensating immigration. At least through the year 2030, per capita productivity nonetheless stays constant, or even rises, contingent on capital investment; reduced labor costs; reduced social costs, including public debt; appropriate infrastructural accommodations, e.g., more bus services, more nursing homes, fewer kindergartens; more efficient use of labor, and a comprehensive system of adult education for which, he laconically adds, no precedent currently exists.

In Miegel's second scenario, working-age immigrants balance the declining population, but the population continues to age – unless Germans are prepared to let their population rise to 100 million by the year 2030, which is an unlikely possibility. Even so, the scenario presupposes the will and capacity to work productively as well as an economy prepared to accommodate them. This again leads to an educational system, capable of training and integrating increasing numbers of immigrants – 300,000 a year in this decade, 450,000 a year in the next decade, 600,000 a year thereafter, according to Miegel's projections. But it also implies a substantially different Germany, populated by substantially different Germans.[122]

Again as elsewhere, the policy options include increased taxes on everyone, increased contributions by beneficiaries, more general employment of women, and longer working lives. But neither higher taxes nor increased contributions, i.e., diminished benefits, is an easy political sell, particularly to the well-organized and intensely interested voter cohorts that will increasingly dominate the electorate, and increasingly make themselves felt in all parties. As American experience may prove better than most, incremental increases in productivity also come progressively harder in a service economy.[123]

Within the limits of declining numbers, increased employment of women is a more positive possibility – at least in West Germany, where a 50% reservoir is potentially available,[124] in contrast to the hitherto inefficient and featherbedded East where 90% of all women were employed outside the home before unification . On the other hand, British, Italian and German work lives would have to be extended ten years to keep taxes in the year 2040 at 1994 levels; and extending work lives creates further problems of mobility and motivation for the young. By 2010, Japan anticipates three older supervisors for each young worker.[125] All things being equal, it is hard to imagine the German scene would be very different. The impact on social investment is even more alarming. As large numbers retire, and relative savings presumably decline, it is not hard to imagine what will happen when investments in the young and the future such as housing, education and R&D, collide with increasing demands on pensions, health and social services, particularly from an electorate dominated by people who need and want them. By 2030, overall social spending could rise from its present third to half of of GDP; by 2040, pensions alone could consume 10–13% of US, Canadian, British, Japanese and German GNP.[126]

At this point, according to such distinguished and politically ecumenical Germans as former President Richard von Weizsäcker, Heiner Geissler, the former CDU party secretary, Gerhard Schröder, the Social Democratic (SPD) minister-president of Lower Saxony and Dany Cohn-Bendit, the onetime Parisian student revolutionary turned

Frankfurt commissioner of multi-cultural affairs, a prudent and comprehensive immigration policy might not only do a world of good, there is hardly a rational alternative to one, considering the jobs Germans prefer to leave to others, and the cost of maintaining the services they like and want. According to Dieter Oberndörfer, the Freiburg political scientist, there is virtually no problem from manpower to tax base that, say, 15 million immigrants over the next 40 years would not help solve. 'The idea that Germany can survive as a garden city rest home, with automated production plant turning out more and more export goods to compensate for a receding domestic market, while people from the Third World and Eastern Europe pile up outside the gates, is unrealistic and inhumane,' says Oberndörfer.[127]

But this only leads back to the issue of immigration. In fact, since 1992, the obligatory declarations that Germany is not an immigrant country, have all but vanished, even from government statements. A more practical obstacle, as the SPD proved again en route to the asylum compromise, is a general consensus on what to do next. As with *Ostpolitik* in the 1960s, *tout Bonn*, even including close advisers of the Chancellor, concedes that change is coming. But while increasingly acknowledged as desirable, a rational, equitable and comprehensive immigration policy means authentic moral and political dilemmas. It therefore means authentically difficult and divisive choices from politicians, who are rarely masochists. For the Greens, Republicans, even the PDS, as generic opposition parties with coherent clienteles, the choices are fairly simple. Determined as ever to prove themselves 'good' Germans, Greens seem rarely to have met a non-German immigrant they didn't like. As parties of the socially aggrieved and resentful, both Republican and PDS voters are unlikely to have met any immigrant they do like. In this respect, at least, the PDS can be regarded as the Republicans of the east.

But for the big parties, with their mixed constituencies and real responsibilities, the trade-offs are more complicated. For historical reasons, Kohl's CDU depends on the Bavarian Christian Social Union (CSU). The CSU, in turn, is perennially terrified of guerrilla attack from the Right. Like other center-right parties, the CDU also not reluctant to speculate in traditional patriotism either. But domestic and foreign considerations alike require an equal concern for an image of responsible moderation. Tax receipts from resident Turks, including DM3.4 billion in general revenue and another DM3 billion in insurance contributions, are reason enough why Turks are not for burning. An estimated 100,000 immigrant entrepreneurs, and DM10 billion in retail sales to immigrant consumers is a powerful reminder that immigrants are good for business.[128] Foreign opinion is an unavoidable reminder that violence is bad.[129]

The result has been an irresistible temptation to fudge.[130] 'We must not allow *Aussiedler* and *Übersiedler* and foreigners and applicants for asylum to be mixed and merged,' one CDU position paper declared. But a senior aide conceded with heavy irony that it would probably be necessary too to pre-empt claims on German citizenship by the 'third of the Polish population with shepherd dogs whose ancestors served in the SS.'[131] In an election-year interview with the BBC's William Horsley, Kohl could legitimately have pointed to the size and integration of Germany's immigrant population as grounds for pride in the success and attractiveness of German democracy, or an asset to German industry and trade, or the last best hope of an aging population with a fragile pension system. Instead, he grew positively truculent when asked about the status of resident foreigners.[132] In Schäuble's own election-year contribution, a book with the title *Der Zukunft Zugewandt* (*Facing the Future*),[133] the only mention of immigrants is sandwiched between paragraphs on international crime, including drugs, counterfeiting and prostitution, and the implied need for European union as a surrogate form of border control.[134]

In contrast to the CDU, national leaders of the opposition SPD not only held out for the constitutional status quo till well into 1992, while attacking the more-equal status of East European *Aussiedler*. At the same time, local officials like Munich's former mayor Georg Kronawitter, who actually lived with the logistical and electoral consequences of the unamended Article 16, Paragraph 2, were acid to the threshold of aggressiveness about SPD support for the foreign and foreign-born. In Kronawitter's view, his party should have led the charge toward reform.[135] Instead, they let their own voters lead the rightward tide.[136] Plagued alike by loss of support and loss of profile, the bantam FDP, Germany's traditional swing party, leaned all along toward compromise, 'As much realism as necessary, as much circumspection as possible,' one observer put it prudently.[137] What this means in practice, says Cornelia Schmalz-Jacobsen, Germany's outspoken commissioner of immigrant affairs, is that, whenever she feels the urge to tell voters 'that Germany's six million disenfranchised foreigners should have more rights,' party leaders tell her 'to stop talking about the need for dual citizenship'.[138]

In the aftermath of the 1994 election, Johannes Gerster, a CDU conservative, for the first time proposed full citizenship for German-born children of resident foreigners – but only until age 18, when they would need to choose between their parents' nationality and their own. Challenged to reply, Minister of Justice Sabine Leutheusser-Schnarrenberger, FDP, swayed gently in the wind. Yes, she acknowledged, a new law was indicated; and yes, it was only four years since her party had come out foursquare for dual citizenship. Yes, she conceded, what happened to people when they reached 18 would also require some thought. 'But we all know that our current constitutional law makes it very, very hard to deny people their German citizenship against their will,' she added.[139]

With any promise of a meaningful consensus on immigration still barely visible, it is not surprising that its surrogate, the asylum debate, should have consumed such vast political energies. For Schäuble, solving the asylum problem was an absolute good, both for the Federal Republic and the CDU. Yet even the late Willy Brandt agreed that a status quo so obviously an incentive to illegal immigration with all its abuses and social pathologies,[140] and so readily manipulable for so many reasons by so many interested parties, was badly in need of reform.

Yet this still leaves the basic question of controlling the numbers with minimal damage to international conventions and commonly professed political and human values. How, in fact, does an increasingly service-based '*Zwei-Drittel-Gesellschaft*' (two thirds society), as Germans like to call theirs, socialize, educate, employ and house the remaining third, i.e., the resentfully poor and unskilled? How does a rich, free Northern, and Western hemisphere as addicted, for example, to farm subsidies as it is allergic to development aid, interact and coexist with a poor and desperate Southern and Eastern one, as the gap grows wider and distances grow shorter? How, when it comes to that, does a Germany that is increasingly home to both Turks and Kurds respond effectively, and even coherently, when Germany itself not only becomes a theater of the increasingly bitter war between them, but of the collateral skirmishes between secularized and religiously-politicized Turks, and moderate and radical-nationalist Kurds?

The grim reality is that the subliminal concerns of both voters and politicians have some objective legitimacy. The respective experiences of Canada, Belgium, the former Czechoslovakia and still more former Yugoslavia, not to mention Lebanon, Sri Lanka, and the southern margins of what was once the Russian empire, may not be the last word on the possibilities of coexistence in culturally and ethnically diverse communities. But they are at least cautionary examples. Given Germany's continued willingness to accept refugees on a scale its neighbors would never dream of,[141] it is also unfair to dismiss German concerns as simple, let alone uniquely German, racism. Neither election returns, survey data nor practical results suggest that Germans are more racist or xenophobic than others. With their own and other people's experience in view, doubts about both their will and capacity to assimilate large numbers of North African Moslems or black Africans, for example, are not totally unreasonable either.

To date, to be sure, such concerns have been largely theoretical. In reality, the great majority of recent applicants have been both white and European. As objects or victims of civil war and ethnic conflict in such genuinely riven countries of origin as Romania, ex-Yugoslavia, or the former Soviet Union, the newcomers have also been driven by real need. Refugees from ex-Yugoslavia were, in fact, received and even welcomed, as though the elections in Bremen, Baden-Württemberg *et al.* never happened.[142] Given some luck and free choice, the odds are also good that most refugees would leave again as soon as possible.[143]

Yet any credible policy must start from the premise that most future immigrants will come to stay, and that white, more or less West and Central European immigrants, will be increasingly scarce. Kohl's government would like to limit immigrants from outside the EU. Its rationale surely makes sense to a majority of ordinary Germans. But the parallel decline of EU birthrates is evidence enough of why little is likely to come of this. The second most favored pool, the remaining reservoir of potential *Aussiedler*, has limits too.[144] The remaining options extend from Poland to North Africa, as well as East Asia, where the immigrant potential is greatest, but so are the political and cultural resistance immigrants are likely to encounter.[145]

Under the circumstances, imaginable outcomes include a new *Wirtschaftswunder* with its reflorescence of *Gastarbeiter*; and Los Angeles on the Rhine or Main, even a Central European Beirut, as Turkish, Polish, *Aussiedler* and *Ossi* kids wage gang war in the streets of Rüdesheim and Chemnitz. A new republic is conceivable, where the young still answer to Uschi, Eva, Wolfgang and Klaus, but also to family names very different from Schmidt and Meyer. So is a kind of neo-Prussia with former Soviet Jews in the role of the Huguenots, and Turks, not to mention Poles, as the Silesian Poles. But a German Kuwait, or unreconstructed South Africa, is imaginable too; where the aged and *ausgestresst*, maintained by pools of savings, are serviced, and even defended, by a transient or resident *Gastarbeiter* population, vastly larger than the population it serves. In a world where Europe's global weight will be at its lowest point in several centuries, it is hard to imagine what the international role, and relative political, economic, military, cultural or scientific weight, of such a Germany might be. But blond, blue-eyed columns, swinging eastward in spiked helmets and black shirts to the tune of 'Heute gehört uns Deutschland, morgen die ganze Welt' ('Today we have Germany, tomorrow the world'), are surely among the least likely possibilities. Whatever other problems such a Germany might cause and face, that much, at least, should be good news for practically everyone.

Notes

1. Save for the language, which could come from another planet, the much quoted passage, written in 1805, is an uncannily evocative impression of how it felt to countless thousands of others to be alive in the last months of 1989. *The Prelude*, lines 108–23.
2. Conor Cruise O'Brien, *The Great Melody* (London, 1992), p. ix.
3. 'Beware, the Reich is reviving', *The Times*, 31 October 1989.
4. A transcript can be found in *Der Spiegel*, 16 July 1990, pp. 109–12. Nothing at all on the meeting can be found in Mrs Thatcher's memoirs. There are, however, innumerable observations on German character, culture and history, as well as a frank concession of defeat on the question of unification, and an assessment of bad things – a 'rush to European federalism', a 'Franco-German bloc' and 'gradual withdrawal of the US' from a 'German-led federal Europe' – likely to result from it: Margaret Thatcher, *The Downing Street Years* (New York, 1993), pp. 813–14.
5. Viz. Günter Grass, 'Rede vom Verlust' in *Reden über Deutschland* (Munich, 1992).
6. Arnulf Baring, *Deutschland, was nun?* (Berlin, 1991). For a cruel, cogent and devastatingly funny review, see Gerhard Spoerl, 'Unsere Existenz in der Tiefe', *Der Spiegel*, 18 November 1991.
7. 'Sind die Liberalen noch zu retten?', *Die Woche*, 17 March 1994.
8. Rainer Zitelmann *et al.* (eds), *Westbindung: Chancen und Risiken für Deutschland* (Frankfurt and Berlin, 1993).
9. In Spring 1994, Pflüger mounted a loud and effective campaign against Steffen Heitmann, his own party's nominal candidate for the largely honorific but visible office of federal president, and a particularly conservative East German, who seemed to have learned nothing and forgotten nothing since at least the 1920s. See Warnfried Dettling, *Das Erbe Kohls* (Frankfurt, 1994), Ch. 4.
10. Friedbert Pflüger, *Die Zukunft des Ostens liegt im Westen* (Düsseldorf, 1994).

11. Cf. Ludwig Watzal, 'Nationalstaat und Nationalismus', *Europäische Rundschau*, 2/94.
12. Heinrich A. Winkler, 'Westbindung oder was sonst?' *Politische Vierteljahresschrift*, March 1994.
13. Elizabeth Pond, *Beyond the Wall* (Washington, 1993), p. 118.
14. Quoted by Peter H. Merkl, 'German Nationalism, National Identity and the Generations,' Working Paper 3.4, Center for German and European Studies, University of California–Berkeley, November 1992.
15. Pond, p. 134. Cf. Bärbel Bohley *et al.* (eds), *40 Jähre DDR... und die Bürger melden sich zu Wort* (Frankfurt, 1989); Jurek Becker, 'My Father, The Germans and Me,' *German-American Cultural Review*, Winter 1994. Cf. Dirk Philipsen, *We Were the People* (Durham, NC, 1993), passim. For a generous appreciation of the dissidents' dilemma from a political adversary, see Wolfgang Schäuble's reference to Bärbel Bohley in *Reden über Deutschland*, p. 131.
16. See Timothy Garton Ash, *The Magic Lantern* (New York, 1990); Gale Stokes, *The Walls Came Tumbling Down* (New York and Oxford, 1993), pp. 125 ff., pp. 148 ff.
17. Surveys reported that 45% of East Germans polled in December 1989 believed that the German Democratic Republic was being *vereinnahmt*, swallowed up, by the Federal Republicr. But they also noted that 17%, many of them over 60, also considered this was a good thing. Merkl, 'German Nationalism . . .' p. 11
18. Air quality was a practical example. One of the signal achievements of the recent events in Berlin and Leipzig was regular smog reports on local radio, an East German academic told a Western visitor in November 1989, after the visitor referred discreetly to a pall so thick that it caused him trouble crossing streets. The bad news was, of course, the smog itself, a seemingly inevitable by-product of the antediluvian chemical industry, that was a pillar of East German exports, and the combustion of local peat as the fuel of preference. The good news was official recognition, for the first time ever, that smog was smog. 'Why did we take East Germany so seriously?' a prominent West German publicist asked her peers a year or two later at a post-unification conference in Weimar. The answer, she reported, was icy silence. The silence was only the more remarkable for its comprehensiveness. Intellectuals can, of course, be notoriously selective tourists. Cf. Angela Schwarz, *Die Reise ins Dritte Reich* (Göttingen, 1993); Robert Silverberg (Paul Hollander), *Political Pilgrims* (New York, 1981); Silvia R. Margolies, *The Pilgrimage to Russia* (Madison, 1968). But of all the Bloc states, East Germany had been the most accessible to visitors of all kinds, with an established Western media presence by the 1980s, and five to six million West German visitors alone every year, one to every three inhabitants. The visitors also included experts of every sort, as well as countless family contacts.
19. Merkl, 'German Nationalism', pp. 21 ff.
20. Alexander Mitscherlich, *Die Unfähigkeit zu trauern* (Munich, 1967).
21. Between November 1989 and July 1990, an estimated 400,000 East Germans moved West, both confirming and assuring the collapse of the East German economy, plus a serious West German backlash. See

Otto Singer, 'The Politics and Economics of German Unification, *German Politics*, April 1992.

22. For the classic statement, see Ralf Dahrendorf, *Gesellschaft und Demokratie in Deutschland* (Munich, 1965). For a contemporary corroboration, cf. Thies, 'Observations on the Political Class in Germany', *Daedelus*, Winter 1994, passim.

23. 'The people are frustrated, government and opposition without elan and vision,' a group of unhappy establishmentarians protested in a widely-noted pamphlet. 'Almost everything is left to chance.' Marion Dönhoff *et al.*, *Weil das Land sich ändern muss* (Reinbek, 1992), p. 11.

24. 9 November, a plausible alternative, was disqualified because it also happened to be the anniversary of the so-called *Kristallnacht* of 1938, when organized mobs harassed and brutalized Jews, and burned and plundered Jewish property; Hitler's attempted *coup d'état* against the Bavarian government and 'march on Berlin' of 1923; and the collapse of the imperial regime and proclamation of a republic in 1918.

25. For an efficient résumé of the choices see Jürgen Kocka, 'Crisis of Unification', *Daedalus*, pp. 177 ff.

26. Anecdotal but representative are the young East Berliner who consistently used the English name 'Germany' to avoid association with a 'Deutschland' he regarded as foreign; or the young man from Rostock, who argued five years after the events of 1989 that there been no revolution, on grounds that no one had been killed, no new dictatorship had been created, no Hegelian 'realm of freedom' had been attained, and the putative revolutionaries had made straightway for the flesh-pots – actually banana stands – of West Berlin. Anyway, he added, Germans just didn't make revolutions.

27. 'Der Hunger nach Sinn', *Der Spiegel*, 6 June 1994.

28. Wolfgang Schäuble in *Reden über Deutschland*, p. 136.

29. Viz. Jean-Paul Picaper, 'L'Allemagne en quête de son Identité', *Géopolitique*, Winter 1993–4, Fred Klinger, 'Aufbau und Erneuerung', *Aus Politik und Zeitgeschichte, Das Parlament*, B 17/94, 29 April 1994; Rémi Lallement, 'L'Aide publique à'l-ex RDA', *L'Etat de l'Allemagne* (Paris, 1995), p. 331

30. From Allensbacher Archiv, August 1980, quoted in Erwin K. Scheuch, *Wie Deutsch sind die Deutschen?*, p. 436; Institut für Demoskopie, Allensbach Archiv, February 1990, p. 334; from various agencies Allensbacher Archiv, p. 413; Institut für Demoskopie, Allensbach Archiv, p. 434. By comparison, Polish willingness to accept further personal sacrifice 'if it advances the cause of reform' increased consistently from 40% among respondents 60 and over to almost 65% among respondents 29 and under. The comparison is as interesting for what it suggests about West as well as East, and adult as well as young, Germans as for what it says about Poles. Hans Peter Haarland and Hans-Joachim Niessen, *Der Transformationsprozess in Polen*, Arbeitspapiere zur Internationalen Politik 85 (Deutsche Gesellschaft für auswärtige Politik, Bonn, 1994), pp. 50–51.

31. See Helga A. Welsh, 'The Divided Past and the Difficulties of German Unification', *German Politics and Society*, Fall 1993.

32. Cf. Warnfried Dettling, *Das Erbe Kohls*, pp. 20–38.
33. For specimen claims of particular, even unique, German responsibility for the Yugoslavian debacle, see. Dino Frescobaldi, 'Il ponte (distrutto) die Mostar', *Politica Internazionale*, January-March 1994, pp. 29–30, Misha Glenny, *The Fall of Yugoslavia* (London, 1992), p. 112, pp. 179–80.
34. For an ingenious analytical linkage of Maastricht, Yugoslavia and the Bundesbank, see Wolfgang Krieger, 'Toward a Gaullist Germany?', *World Policy Journal*, 1994.
35. For a representative example, see William Horsley, 'United Germany's Seven Cardinal Sins: A Critique of German Foreign Policy', *Millennium*, Summer 1992.
36. Since the early 1970s a 'Eurobarometer' has tracked the electoral potential of far-right parties in EU states. In 1989, it was assessed at 5–14%, going up in Denmark and Greece, at a lower level in France, and in long-term decline in Germany and the Netherlands. Änne Ostermann, 'Rechtsextremismus und Gewalt im neuen Deutschland', *Friedensgutachten 1993*, Hessian Foundation for Peace and Conflict Research (Münster and Hamburg 1993), p. 65.
37. '. . . the anti-Western Sonderweg of the German Reich, the postnational Sonderweg of the old Federal Republic, and the internationalist Sonderweg' of the German Democratic Republic . . . ' Heinrich A. Winkler, 'Rebuilding of a Nation,' *Daedalus* (Winter 1994).
38. Quoted by Garton Ash, *In Europe's Name*, p. 381
39. J. M. Keynes, *The Economic Consequences of the Peace* (New York, 1920).
40. *L'Etat de l'Allemagne*, (Paris, 1994), p. 307.
41. In 1986–8, 72.2 for men, and 78.7 for women, compared with 71.5 and 78.3 in the US (1987), 72 and 80 in France (1987) and 75.9 and 81.8 in Japan (1990). *Japan 1992: An International Comparison* (Tokyo, 1992), p. 8.
42. The expression can be found in Änne Ostermann, 'Rechsextremismus und Gewalt . . .', p. 62.
43. In 1989, there were 6.4 marriages and 2.1 divorces per annum per thousand population, compared to 9.7 and 4.8 in the United States, 6.9 and 2.9 in Britain, 5.8 and 1.3 in Japan. *Japan 1992*, p. 93.
44. According to a World Health Organization study carried out by the Institute for Nutrition Research in Potsdam on a representative sample of 1400 Germans, 40% of Germans are overweight. *This Week in Germany*, German Information Center, New York, 10 February 1995.
45. Hans-Joachim Hoffmann-Nowotny, 'Wanderungen in unserer Zeit', unpublished lecture, Cologne, 11 June 1994.
46. The closest equivalent is probably the accommodation of 12 million German refugees from the Baltic, Silesia, the Sudetenland, and other historically German communities. Approximate, but still remote, equivalents might be the resettlement of a million French *colons* at the end of the Algerian War, and significantly smaller British and Dutch colonial populations from India, Indonesia *et al.*; Polish and Czech

ethnic minorities in consequence of border changes after World War II; or, still more remote, Israeli resettlement, e.g., of Jewish newcomers from Ethiopia and the former Soviet Union.

47. Stefan Huckemann and Ulrich van Suntum, *Beschäftigungspolitik im international Verleich* (Gütersloh, 1994), pp. 76–7. 'Mühsamer Weg aus dem Tal', *Informationsdienst des Instituts der deutschen Wirtschaft*, 22 December 1994. Cf. B. R. Mitchell, *European Historical Statistics* (London, 1980), pp. 175 and 178.

48. As so often, the endlessly cosmopolitan Goethe got there first with a collection of poems on 'oriental' themes called '*Der westöstliche Divan*'. Then, *inter alia*, came the *Realpolitiker*, the Congress of Berlin, the Berlin-Bagdad railroad, the Liman von Sanders mission, and a disastrous alliance in World War I. See Curt Hohoff, *Johann Wolfgang von Goethe* (Munich, 1989), pp. 477–84; Ulrich Trumpener, *Germany and the Ottoman Empire* (Princeton, 1968); Jehuda L. Wallach, *Anatomie einer Militärhilfe* (Düsseldorf, 1976).

49. See Fritz W. Scharpf, 'Die Handlungsfähigkeit des Staates am Ende des zwanzigsten Jährhunderts' in Beate Kohler-Koch (ed.), *Staat und Demokratie in Europa* (Opladen, 1992); Jean-Marie Guéhenno, *La Fin de la Démocratie* (Paris, 1993); Alan S. Milward, *The European Rescue of the National State* (Berkeley, 1992).

50. See Milward *et al.*, *The European Rescue*, passim. 'In order to achieve a European awareness, we need national identity as a transmission belt', Schäuble told interviewers in late 1994. But this was only a transitional stage, Schäuble added. 'I don't claim that the nation is history's final goal.' 'Das Nationale als Mittel zum europäischen Zweck', Interview with Wolfgang Schäuble, *Süddeutsche Zeitung*, 28 December 1994.

51. Quoted by Winkler, 'Rebuilding of a Nation', p. 107.

52. Wolfgang Schäuble, *Der Zukunft zugewandt* (Berlin, 1994), pp. 217–18. In 1994, on the fiftieth anniversary of the failed attempt to assassinate Hitler, Kohl made the same point in his own way by not only attending, but virtually dominating, the official commemoration in Berlin. His presence was remarkable in at least four perspectives: first, previous CDU chancellors had kept their distance from the 20 July commemoration; second, Kohl had made a point of appearing with France's President François Mitterrand on the battlefield of Verdun and then, less successfully, with America's President Ronald Reagan at a military cemetery in Bitburg; third, Kohl had attended the funeral of Alfred Herrhausen, the president of the Deutsche Bank, in 1989, and Detlev Karsten Rohwedder, the director of the East German privatization agency, in 1991, both victims of leftwing terrorists; fourth, he had not attended the funeral in Solingen of Turkish residents killed by local arsonists in 1993. The first was a signal that it was now safe, and even good politics, to identify with safely-dead, and thoroughly conservative, anti-Nazis. The second was a signal that a post facto anti-Nazi Federal Republic was now reconciled with, and on the same side as, its adversaries in two world wars. The third put the chancellor on the side of outraged order in the war with leftwing terrorism. The fourth implied that association with recent, poor and foreign victims of German rightist

terror was politically risky – and made clear that Kohl was not about to take the risk.

53. Since the translation is free, the key phrases are 'Die Menschen suchen . . . den Rückhalt in der nationalen Gemeinschaft' and 'Wenn sie sich der Schutzfunktion des Staates. . . nicht mehr sicher sind, wachsen Ängste, Unsicherheiten.' Schäuble in *Reden über Deutschland*, passim. The nation is a 'community of protection and destiny', Schäuble amplifed a few years later. Even if Germans found it hard to agree on common principles, they needed it to enhance their 'feeling of national togetherness'. Schäuble, *Der Zukunft zugewandt*, pp. 219–21.

54. Klaus J. Bade (ed.), *Das Manifest der 60* (Munich, 1994), p. 18.

55. Interview with Hermann Rudolph, editor in chief of *Der Tagesspiegel*, January 1992.

56. Price, of course, could well be part of the explanation. Nominal wage parity notwithstanding, the newsstand price of DM 5, about $3.00, was still a lot of money for most East Germans. See David Schoenbaum, '*Der Spiegel*, une institution', in Le Gloannec, *L'Etat de l'Allemagne*, pp. 280–81.

57. 'Privat geht vor Katastrophe', *Der Spiegel*, 20 July 1992, p. 51, Radio interview with Regine Hildebrandt, social welfare minister of Brandenburg, *Frankfurter Allgemeine Sonntagszeitung*, 18 July 1993. '34,000 Lehrstellen fehlen in Ostdeutschland,' *Frankfurter Allgemeine Zeitung*, 28 July 1993.

58. It could even be argued that the tide of refugees was catalyzed, albeit inadvertently, by a German policy that was moved in turn by a tide of public sympathy for Slovenia and Croatia that caused German policy makers to anticipate their European Community partners in recognizing their independence. See Heinz-Jürgen Axt, 'Hat Genscher Jugoslawien entzweit? Mythen und Fakten zur Aussenpolitik des vereinten Deutschlands', *Europa-Archiv*, 25 June 1993.

59. In 1990, the number of potential refugees in the world, some political, many more as victims of vast environmental catastrophes, was already estimated at 17.6 million. See 'Fermate il baby boom', *La Repubblica*, 29 April 1992.

60. Czarina Wilpert, 'Migration and ethnicity in a non-immigration country', *New Community*, October 1991.

61. See 'Aussiedler', *Information zur politischen Bildung* 222 (Bonn, 1991), p. 1.

62. Interview with Cornelia Schmalz-Jacobsen, federal commissioner for refugee affairs, 26 July 1994. The figure incidentally included two of her own three sons, she added.

63. See Garton Ash, *In Europe's Name*, p. 235; Pulzer, p. 12.

64. C.f. Krell, 'Migration', Pulzer, 'Unified Germany', *German Politics*, April 1994, p. 21.

65. In 1991, according to the annual report of the Federal Commissioner for Integration of Foreign Labor, 80% of school-age foreigners in the Federal Republic finished secondary school. Liselotte Funcke, 'Bericht der Beauftragten der Bundesregierung für die Integration der ausländischen Arbeitnehmer und ihrer Familienangehörigen', Bonn, March

1991, p. 11. According to a 1988 study, 72% of the young Turks, and 85% of the young Yugoslavs, compared respectively with 28% and 40% of their parents, also spoke good to fluent German. Quoted by Scheuch, *Wie Deutsch*, p. 172.

66. Funcke, 'Bericht der Beauftragten', p. 98.

67. For a portrait of Mendiburu, see 'Der Mann aus Spanien fühlt sich längst als Einheimischer', *Der Tagesspiegel*, 21 July 1990.

68. The novel, *Felidae* by Akif Pirincci, appeared in 1989, had gone through four editions by 1990, and sold between 1.3 and 1.5 million copies by the end of 1994. See Craig Whitney, 'Novel of Feline Revenge and Germans Lap It Up', *New York Times*, 30 December 1994.

69. Among the also-rans were Max Schmeling, Steffi Graf and Heinrich Böll. Quoted by Elisabeth Nölle-Neumann, *Demoskopische Geschichtsstunde* (Zurich, 1991), p. 189.

70. In conversation with visitors, Schäuble pointed to his own use of the expression, in contrast to the ultra-conservative Afred Dregger, who invariably said 'guest worker.' Interview, 17 June 1994.

71. Rudolph Wassermann, 'Plädoyer für eine neue Asyl- und Ausänderpolitik', *Aus Politik und Zeitgeschichte: Beilage zur Wochenzeitung Das Parlament*, 21 February 1992, p. 14, Aufzeichung, op. cit., p. 16. By comparison, Amsterdam in 1987 had 21.4%, Brussels 23.8%, Geneva 29%, and Luxemburg 42.6%. Paul White, 'Immigrants and the Social Geography of European Cities' in Russell King (ed.), *Mass Migrations in Europe* (London and New York, 1993), p. 67. Cf. Xavier Bougarel, 'Francfort, un modèle multiculturel?' in Le Gloannec, *L'Etat de l'Allemagne*, p. 217.

72. *Bericht der Beauftragten der Bundesregierung für die Belange der Ausländer* (Bonn, 1993), p. 16 and Table 7.

73. Ibid., p. 8.

74. 'Foreign employees secure our social security system,' declares one ad, featuring a German and a Turkish moppet, companionably nibbling ice-cream cones. 'Without them, we would long ago have had to raise the rates.' 'Here on the shop floor they know me, and I belong,' says Ali in another, co-featuring a beaming Hans. 'Hans knows that too,' the text continues. 'Without Ali things would be worse, at the plant and for the whole economy.' Interview with Berthold Huber, IG–Metall, Frankfurt, 19 July 1994. See 'Protokoll: 3. Ausländerkonferenz der IG-Metall,' *Travemünde*, 7–9 May 1992, for an overview of style, issues and resolutions.

75. See Dieter Oberndörfer, 'Vom Nationalstaat zur offenen Republik,' *Aus Politik und Zeitgeschichte, Beilage zur Wocheneitung Das Parlament*, 21 February 1992, p. 23. Cf. 'A Survey of Germany,' *The Economist*, 23 May 1992.

76. Cited in *The Economist*, 31 July 1993, p. 46.

77. 'Multikulturelle Gesellschaft mehrheitlich nicht erwünscht,' *Süddeutsche Zeitung*, 29 December 1994.

78. *Süddeutsche Zeitung*, 17 June 1993. Cf. *Frankfurter Allgemeine Zeitung*, 17 June 1993. He also refused to attend the funerals in Solingen because, as a spokesman explained, he was not a 'condolence tourist'. In fact, as

another aide explained, he was sincerely afraid that his presence would incite a public scene, if not real violence. But it was a bona fide PR problem, the aide conceded, for a man who punctiliously balanced every reference to the dangers from the right with a reference to the dangers from the left.

79. *Der Spiegel*, 7 June 1993, p. 21.
80. Cf. Funcke, 'Bericht der Beauftragen . . .', p. 21.
81. Münz and Ulrich, 'Was wird aus den neuen Bundesländern' (Berlin, 1994), p. 23.
82. 'I pendolari del dopo-Muro', *La Repubblica*, 7 March 1992.
83. When asked about their friends, a representative young Düsseldorf couple, he in banking, she in public relations, could think of only one contemporary, a Protestant minister's son, who had voluntarily moved to Dresden. He was considerably more conservative than themselves, they said. They also admired his idealism. Of the couple, the young man, a native of Cologne, had been sent by his company to Zwickau in Saxony, and enjoyed the assignment. He might even have stayed, he added, had he not been offered a job as personal assistant to a senior executive in Düsseldorf. He now wanted to move to New York, which was also unusual. Personal interview, 30 July 1994. Cf. 'Du passt nicht mehr in unser Weltbild', *Der Spiegel*, 13 July 1992, pp. 32–35.
84. Thus, for example, Helmut Kohl. He was 'pleased about the many German children', who could only 'improve the miserable demographic statistics', the chancellor told a television interviewer in August 1991. Quoted by Krell, 'Migration', p. 21.
85. Nölle-Neumann, *Demoskopische Geschichtsstunde*, pp. 93–4. There is, in fact, an objective case for both positions. Compared to the host population, the newcomers are relatively young. Compared to West German unemployed, the newcomers are also relatively well qualified. The result is a measurable plus: immigrants generate substantially more income than they cost in public services. At the same time, it can be plausibly argued that they push hard on an anyway torpid housing market; flood the market for unskilled labor, and overwhelm the welfare system. Cf. Arne Gieseck *et al.*, 'Wirtschafts- und sozialpolitische Aspekte der Zuwanderung in die Bundesrepublik', Horst Afheldt, 'Sozialstaat und Zuwanderung', in *Aus Politik und Weltgeschichte, Beilage zur Wochenzeitung Das Parlament*, 12 February 1993.
86. Author's interview with Dr Wolfgang Bergsdorf, *Bundespresseamt*, 10 August 1989. Cf. 'Ihre Heimat Sind *Wir*', an elegantly produced brochure, published in Bonn in 1991 by Aktion Gemeinsinn, an establishmentarian public-interest lobby. 'Sind Aussiedler Ausländer?' ('Are *Aussiedler* Foreigners?') the authors ask, distinguishing in a subtitle between Staatsbürgerschaft (formal nationality) and *Volkstum* (ethnicity). As might be imagined, their answer is No.
87. For example, 30% and more of the *Aussiedler* are under 30, compared to under 20% of the indigenous population; and nearly half are in employed in industry and crafts, compared with 36.5% of the indigenous population. Quoted by Marshall, 'Migration into Germany', *German*

Politics, April 1992 p. 133. Cf. Stefanie Wahl, 'Wer sind die Neuankömmlinge?' Das Parlament, No. 35, 25 August 1989; Knight and Kowalsky, *Deutschland nur den Deutschen*?, p. 9.

88. Of course, she would prefer to see the ethnic Germans stay where they were, one SPD deputy emphasized. She was even persuaded it might work, given adequate assurances to Mennonites and Baptists. But she was also impressed by a determination to be German that extended even to local productions of Schiller, and an eagerness for German media internships, in Alma Ata. What worried her was the discrepancy between the old German virtues the *Aussiedler* brought – punctuality, industriousness, personal honesty, etc. – and the reality they were likely to meet in the real-world Germany. Their disillusionment, she feared, would then make them easy prey, e.g., for Republicans. Author's interview with Gerlinde Hämmerle, MdB, 4 August 1989.

89. On the other hand, this had never been empirically proven, according to Franz Urban Pappi of the University of Mannheim, in part because the population was too small for reliable samples, in part because their German was too shaky for interviews and questionnaires. Interview, January 1995.

90. Bergsdorf interview, op. cit..

91. As might be expected, survey data only confirm that attitudes on political asylum vary directly with education and social status, i.e., that blue-collar workers are most hostile to large numbers of foreigners, while civil servants and higher-level mangerial personnel are the most tolerant of them. See Krell, 'Migration', p. 22.

92. Michael Mertes, a senior aide in the Chancellor's office, actually recalled seeing a recent interview with a Turk-bashing, Germany for the Germans-spouting, Ruhr skinhead, whose name ended in -ski. See survey data, pp. 25–6, 'Hau ab, du Flasche,' *Der Spiegel*, 7 June 1993. According to a study for the Federal Ministry for Youth Affairs by three social scientists from the University of Trier, youth violence tended to be both local and unorganized, with a far stronger tendency in the former East than in the West German *Länder* to emerge spontaneously in crowd situations. Borne on the waves of the immigration debate, the youthful offenders assumed they enjoyed public support. Revealing in itself, the authors were also at pains to address and invalidate the political correctnesses of both right and left. No, they insisted, there was no demonstrable correlation between current youth violence and the 'anti-authoritarian' style of childrearing practiced in the 1970s and 1980s. But there was no visible correlation either between current youth violence and the presumed alienation and disintegration of capitalist society. See 'Asyl-Diskussion stachelte zu Gewalttaten an', *Süddeutsche Zeitung*, 30 June 1993.

93. The violence in Hoyerswerda led to the formation of a Saxon special commission on rightwing extremism. By June 1994, it claimed to have solved 90% of 200 cases, and issued arrest warrants against 185 suspects. *Süddeutsche Zeitung*, 4–5 June 1994.

94. Ostermann, 'Rechtsextremismus', p. 60.

95. See 'Der Bundesminister teilt mit', 27 November, 9–10 December, 1992.

96. Martin Greiffenhagen, 'Rechtsextremismus in Deutschland', *Europäische Rundschau*, February 1994, p. 99.
97. In Bremen, Schleswig-Holstein and Baden-Württemberg, radical right, i.e., anti-immigrant parties won 6–11% of the vote; Kohl anticipated 12–14% if nothing happened, and Bavarian polls indicated a Republican potential of 15–20%.
98. *Der Spiegel*, 9 November 1992, p. 34.
99. Speech by Hans-Jochen Vogel, special Social Democratic convention, Bonn, 16 November 1992. The equivalent position, expressed at local Christian Democratic party caucuses, were proposals that Heiner Geissler, a former party chairman and leading Christian Democratic liberal, put up a 'gypsy container' in his garden. Gerd Krell, 'Die Asylfrage zwischen Grenzen der Moral und grenzenloser Unmoral', *Friedensgutachten 1993*, p. 70.
100. See ibid., p. 73.
101. Heribert Prantl, 'Der Versuch, politische Schuld zu begraben', *Süddeutsche Zeitung*, 27 May 1993.
102. For an analysis and text, see *Frankfurter Allgemeine Zeitung*, 27 May 1993.
103. Quoted by Krell, 'Die Asylfrage . . .'.
104. *Süddeutsche Zeitung*, 14 June 1994.
105. 'Number of Asylum-Seekers Dropped Sharply in 1994,' *This Week in Germany*, German Information Center, New York, 13 January 1995; German News, 10 March 1995. Cf. *Der Spiegel*, 7 February 1994, pp. 45 ff., 'Churches Take on Bonn over Asylum-Seekers,' *International Herald Tribune*, 18/19 June 1994, 'Spur verloren', *Der Spiegel*, 1 August 1994, p. 17, German News (compiled from German radio sources, and circulated on H-German) 18 February 1995.
106. Scheuch, *Wie Deutsch*, pp. 167 ff.
107. Panel discussion at European Community offices in Bonn, 9 June 1994, interview with Fritz Scharpf, Max Planck Gesellschaft, Cologne, 28 July 1994.
108. Interview with Stephanie Wahl, 27 July 1994.
109. 'Les consequences', pp. 1–13.
110. In a survey of current concerns facing their respective EC-member countries, 23% of Danes and 9% of Dutch but only 8% of Germans listed 'Foreigners' as a major problem. Eurobarometer, 'Rassismus, Ausländerfeidlichkeit und Intoleranz', November 1989, quoted by Scheuch, *Wie Deutsch*, pp. 159–60.
111. Cf. Krell, 'Migration', pp. 7–8.
112. See Craig Whitney, 'In Europe, the Right also Rises', *New York Times*, 14 November 1994.
113. Polled in 1991 on whether the unification as the bottom line under the Nazi past, 50% of West German and 67% of East German students said yes. Polled again after Hoyerswerda and Mölln, 70% of west German and 71% of East German students said no. Paul-Ludwig Weihnacht, 'Studenten in Ost und West', *Die Politische Meinung*, May 1994.
114. See 'Hate Crime in Germany', *Washington Post* editorial in the *International Herald Tribune* of 20 May 1994.

115. See the texts of both speeches as reprinted in the *Süddeutsche Zeitung* of 2–3 July 1994. In a pre-election interview, Herzog, an advocate of double-citizenship, avoided the issue of *jus soli*. But he left no doubt where he stood on *jus sanguinis*. 'The idea that we're all of one blood is historical nonsense,' he declared. 'Only an old Nazi could hit on an idea like that.' 'Ich liebe dieses deutsche Volk', *Focus*, 19/94, p. 23. Cf. Weizsäcker's definition of 'nation' as 'common responsibility for the past and a common will to face the problems of the present and future.' Neither skin color or even language were crucial to the definition, Weizsäcker added. 'Wir waren oft zu bequem', interview with Weizsäcker, *Der Spiegel*, 17 June 1994, p. 29.

116. In June 1994 the PDS vote in Hohenschönhausen was 46.3%. In October 1994, PDS candidates in Thuringia won 16.6%, in Mecklenburg-Vorpommern 22.7%, second only to the SPD and CDU. They also carried four Bundestag constituencies directly, which translated into 30 seats, equivalent to 4.4% of the national vote.

117. She had had a fine time as a first-time tourist in Sweden and France, a secretary in one East Berlin borough mayor's office told a visitor in early 1993. The only place she didn't feel at home was West Berlin. Cf. Evelyn Roll, 'PDS wählen, damit es jeder sehen kann', *Süddeutsche Zeitung*, 18–19 June 1994, 'Auferstanden aus Ruinen', *Der Spiegel*, 27 June 1994, pp. 18–19; 'Das Gespenst der DDR', *Der Spiegel*, July 4 1994, pp. 28 ff.

118. Resolution of 12 December 1992, quoted in Hans-Wolfgang Platzer and Walter Ruhland, *Welches Deutschland in welchem Europa?* (Bonn, 1994), pp. 20–21. Of course, the crime theme also acknowledged a conservative goverment's political sensitivities – and campaign priorities. By the European parliament election of 1994, the SPD too featured mafia-busting, as well as job-creating and generic security-related, motifs in its campaign posters.

119. Ibid., pp. 66 ff.

120. See Brandon Mitchener and Tom Buerkle, 'Germany's EU Burden', *International Herald Tribune*, May 30, 1994.

121. Quoted in *Der Spiegel*, 23 May 1994, p. 134, *Financial Times*, 1 June 1994. Cf. 'England und Deutschland vereint gegen Europa', *Süddeutsche Zeitung*, 3 June 1994, p. 10, 'More-or-less European union', *The Economist*, 25 August 1995, p. 46.

122. Meinhard Miegel, 'Die Zukunft von Bevölkerung und Wirtschaft in Deutschland' in *Das Manifest*, pp. 118 ff.

123. Cf. Mario Pirani, 'Il Welfare State è caro come suonare Mozart', interview with William J. Baumol, *La Repubblica*, 29 April 1992.

124. 'Working women and the rise of the house-husband', *Financial Times*, 27 July 1992.

125. R. L. Cliquet, 'Economic and Social Consequences of Current Demographic Developments in OECD Countries', Draft for OECD Directorate for Social Affairs, Manpower and Education, King Baudouin Foundation, Brussels, 15–16 December 1986, p. 37.

126. See Pensions Survey, *The Economist*, 13 August 1994, Germany Survey, *The Economist*, 21 May 1994. Miegel himself proposes, e.g., that income currently allocated to child support – DM11,000 per child per year in

1992, or DM100 billion total – be reallocated to old-age support. Miegel, *'Die Zukunft'*, p. 124.

127. Oberndörfer, op. cit., p. 25. Cf. Stefanie Wahl, 'Ist der Weg in die multikulturelle Gesellschaft vorgezeichnet?' *Informaionen zur Raumentwicklung, Bundesforschungsanstalt für Landeskunde und Raumordnung*, Heft 7/8 (Bonn, 1991), pp. 387–93.

128. Funcke, 'Bericht der Beauftragen . . .', p. 10; 'Unser Algerien am Bosporus', *Süddeutsche Zeitung*, 31 March 1995.

129. According to one commissioned study, 78% of all Germany-related American TV stories in the first half of 1993 were negative, while a Foreign Ministry study reported that 'pictures of burning houses and refugee shelters' dominated news coverage even in 'traditionally germanophile Asia'. 'Alle kennen Mölln', *Der Spiegel*, 22/1994, pp. 27–8 .

130. 'Helmut Kohl has a fine gift for seeing both sides of a question when political expediency requires it.' *The Economist*, 14 May 1994, p. 33.

131. Quoted by Knight and Kowalsky, *Deutschland nur den Deutschen?*, p. 131.

132. Horsley: 'We have three million people from the Caribbean an the subcontinent and black parts of the world, Herr Bundeskanzler. . . Is that not comparable with your three million?' Kohl: 'No, no, no, that is not comparable.' BBC Interview, broadcast 27 May 1994. *Ethnische Minderheiten in Großbritannien* (Ethnic Minorities in Britain), a handsomely produced German-language brochure laid out in the British embassy for visitors to take home, was a practical example of the differences. Produced by the Foreign and Commonwealth Office in London, the brochure celebrated the contribution of immigrants in general, and individual immigrants in particular, among them a TV journalist from Trinidad, a union president from Jamaica and an MP from Ghana. Whether and to what extent the brochure did full justice to the immigrant experience in Britain was debatable. The difference was that the British Foreign Office clearly saw immigration as a public relations plus, while any comparable German document in a German embassy was unimaginable.

133. The title was taken directly from J.R. Becher and Hanns Eisler's old East German anthem, 'Risen from the Ruins'. Asked point blank about this by visitors, Schäuble smiled a wicked little smile. Interview with Wolfgang Schäuble, op. cit.

134. See Schäuble, *Der Zukunft Zugewandt*, pp. 201–3. Ironically, Europhobe British Conservatives sought to make the case that the European Union, one bugbear, was the natural ally of immigration, a second bugbear. In fact, as the European Council on Refugees and Exiles reported, EU policy was not only punitively inhumane but counter-productive. 'Safe Third Country', (European Council on Refugees, 1994), see Edward Mortimer, 'The Final Frontier,' *Financial Times*, 22 February 1995, p. 18.

135. 'Die flotten Enkel und die Toskana,' *Der Spiegel*, 13 April 1992, p. 44. Crusty old Herbert Wehner, the longtime Social Democratic leader in the Bundestag, who spent years of his own life as a political refugee in the Soviet Union and Sweden, had reached the same conclusion in 1982.

'If we keep failing to impose some limits on the refugee problem, the voters will sweep us away, our own voters included,' Wehner told the party executive committee. Quoted by Erwin Scheuch, ' "Fremdenhass" als akute Form des Rechtsextremismus' in Konrad Löw (ed.), *Terror und Extremismus in Deutschland* (Berlin, 1994).

136. See Klaus Dieter Frankenberger, 'Protest der "Kleinen Leute," ' *Frankfurter Allgemeine Zeitung* 11 October 1991. On the other hand, the CDU too has taken its knocks. In April 1992, 40% of Republican voters in Baden-Württemberg and a third of the hard-right German People's Union (DVU) votes in Schleswig-Holstein were CDU defectors; while only a quarter of their respective votes came from previous supporters of the SPD. Matthias Jung and Dieter Roth, 'Der Stimmzettel als Denkzettel', Die Zeit, 10 April 1992. For a comprehensive sociology of the new right voters see Claus Leggewie, 'Die Stunde der Populisten – Auf dem Weg ins Fünfparteiensystem' in Jochen Buchholz (ed.), *Parteien in der Kritik* (Bonn, 1993), pp. 64–9.

137. Knight and Kowalsky, *Deutschland nur den Deutschen?*, p. 136.

138. Judy Dempsey, 'On the Brink of Irrelevance', *Financial Times*, 19 February 1995. A well-attended Sunday morning street party in July 1994 on the congenially leafy grounds of the Foreign Ministry might be regarded as one more variation on FDP ambivalence, and also an object lesson in the prevailing division of political labor. Under the patronage of Klaus Kinkel, the foreign minister and current party chairman, the event featured a cavalcade of gospel singers, African dancers, Russian gymnasts, ethnic fast food, mini-interviews with such resident foreigners as an Iraqi-born bus-driver, and a T-shirt proclaiming 'Operation Tolerance'. Foreign service officers spend a good deal of their working life as foreigners, a poster added, implying that diplomats are just another sort of *Gastarbeiter*. As might be imagined, Manfred Kanther, the Christian Democrat responsible for immigration (and deportation), did not sponsor anything similar on the grounds of the Interior Ministry in a different, and considerably less attractive, part of town.

139. 'Herumfummeln an einigen Vorschriften genügt nicht', *Süddeutsche Zeitung*, 29 December 1994.

140. In October 1991, the interior ministry estimated that there were already 'at least' a half million illegal immigrants in the country, with 200,000 more expected by the end of the year. Krell, 'Migration,' p. 15.

141. As of 1993, of 700,000 refugees from the former Yugoslavia, Germany had taken 300,000, France 58,000, Italy 17,000 and Britain 4,000. *International Herald Tribune*, 29 June 1993.

142. With predictable reluctance, the Federal Republic had accepted 5000 Bosnian refugees by the end of July. Since the beginning of the year, it had nonetheless accepted 275,000 refugees from former Yugoslavia alone, compared with 1600 in neighboring Italy, 900 in France, and none in Britain . Viz. 'Eine Million auf dem Sprung', *Der Spiegel*, 27 July 1992, p. 21, 'No land is an island', *The Economist*, 1 August 1992. But this only did half justice to the confusions and ironies of the German situation. As minister of defense, Rühe, the former CDU general secretary who had sneered about 'SPD-Asylanten', now favored a Ger-

man role in aiding Bosnian civilians and imposing sanctions on Serbia – if necessary, without NATO constraints. Meanwhile, the opposition Social Democrats, who had no problem accepting refugees, challenged the constitutionality of any German military role in an effort to stop the war the refugees were fleeing. See 'Nahe dran am echten Krieg', and 'Das ist keine Drohgebärde,' *Der Spiegel*, 20 July 1992, pp. 27–9 and 32–4; Albrecht Müller, 'Entritt nur mit Schusswunden?' *Die Zeit*, 17 July 1992.

143. Cf. 'Rebuilding Europe', Nomura Research Institute Deutschland, pp. 36–7, 'Sie kommen, ob wir wollen oder nicht', *Der Spiegel*, 6 April 1992, p. 33.

144. Cf. Czarina Wilpert, 'Demographische Entwicklung und Migration zwischen den Mitgliedstaaten der europäischen Gemeinschaft und in sie hinein,' in Ingrid Gogolin (ed.), *Kultur- und Sprachenvielfalt in Europa* (Münster, 1991).

145. Viz. Rafael Biermann, 'Migration aus Osteuropa and dem Mahgreb', *Aus Politik und Zeitgeschichte, Beilage zur Wochenzeitung Das Parlament*, 21 February 1992.

3 From Industrial Park to Theme Park?

Looking at campaign posters on the eve of the European elections in 1994, the viewer could almost believe the voters had hung their psyches out to dry. 'Jobs, jobs, jobs,' was one popular motif. Gangbusting, featuring shackled hands behind a pinstriped jacket, was another. But security, spelled out in red letters, was the clear favorite of both major parties. In the Christian Democratic version, a grandparent and grandchild were seen from the rear, hand in hand, bathed in autumnal light, with the parent generation conspicuously missing. In the Social Democratic variation, a young father, himself a disappearing species, was snoozing in a rowboat, with his young son, no common species either, snoozing on his chest. Tied securely to the pier, the boat was going nowhere.

'Take advantage of an opportunity *here*? Are you kidding?' one civil servant asks. Seconded to a Bundestag committee staff by the Ministry of Research and Technology, he has already spent years helping ambivalent Social Democrats draft legislation on both. The experience has at least encouraged a highly-developed sense of irony. 'Why does it take us 12 years to put synthetic insulin on the market?' he asks, as though he were really in doubt about the answer. 'We developed the stuff.'

If DNA and the integrated circuit are the future, Germans, and not only Social Democrats, are Melville's Bartleby the Scrivener, he had concluded, the acidulous clerk who said only 'I prefer not to.' They are not necessarily opposed to science. They are also not bad at it. But the days when Social Democrats said 'Knowledge is Power' with a confident smile are long gone. Today their first reflex is to associate it with Big Brother, Nazi war criminals like Josef Mengele, the birth defects once caused by an inadequately-tested prescription sedative known as thalidomide in English-speaking countries and as contergan in Germany, and Frankenstein's monster.

The national aversion to things nuclear is legendary. Unlike the French, from Gaullist right to Communist left, who staked their national sovereignty on nuclear-generated power, energy-dependent

Germans coexist with it only reluctantly. The economic, political, even psychic trade-offs between industry, jobs, fossil fuel consumption, CO_2 emissions, coal subsidies, the comparative costs of alternative energies, and endemic nuclear anxieties, are perennial, even insoluble. In the mid-1970s, German reactors in Brazil caused trouble with the proliferation-sensitive United States. But where they really caused trouble was at home. For post-postwar Germans, reactor and, still more, designated nuclear waste sites from the Lower Rhine to the Bavarian Forest have been the symbolic battlefields of a generation.[1]

Wonderful irony in itself: in one of its last displays of technocratic machismo, the Communist regime in East Germany assembled a giant nuclear plant near Greifswald, where their Nazi predecessors once tested rockets. On completion, its eight reactors were to generate 3500 MW of electricity, enough for a city of 3.5 million people. The *Treuhand*, i.e., the trusteeship encharged with privatizing former East German properties, tried in vain to find a buyer. Daunted by the intimidating costs of bringing the plant up to Western safety standards, investors were unwilling even to let themselves be bought. The authorities have therefore decided to dismantle it – over 15 years, at an estimated cost of DM 5.4 billion – with every likelihood of a moderate boom in local employment, and the acquisition of marketable skills and experience. These can then be put to good use in the business of dismantling still more such plants all around former Communist Central and Eastern Europe.[2]

Bioengineering is more of the same on a European scale. Eduard, the competent, luckless, basically likeable nebbish of a recent Peter Schneider novel, watches his mouse, his experiment and just possibly the cure for AIDS evade his grasp.[3] Pursued by family ghosts, mistaken identities and guerrilla attack by anonymous animals rights activists, Eduard is another emblematic figure in a country where reports on the development of a new, genetically-engineered, disease-resistant potato drew 3000 protest letters.[4] Bounded by elaborate legal restraints and some of the world's toughest data protection provisions at home, plus the European parliament's inability to reach a coherent consensus on the subject,[5] both public and private-sector Germans continue to pursue research – but preferably in the United States or Japan.[6]

Computer habits are a variation on the theme. PCs have been generally visible since the late 1980s, when they were discovered as status symbols. But even Nixdorf, the largest German maker, is only major by the standards of a notoriously fragmented European industry, and the kind of zippy young software firms familiar in America,

Israel, even Britain, have been few and far between. In 1993 there were about 30 computers per 100 people in the United States, about 13 in Germany – fewer than Britain, Sweden, Switzerland, Holland and France.[7] The Party of the Democratic Left, i.e., the former Communists, in the Emilia Romagna have made Internet access a public utility. Until recently, Social Democrats in Germany were not even sure if they wanted their offices wired for modems. Social acceptance has crept slowly upward. In 1984, 40% of West Germans felt 'positive' about computers, by 1994 56% of west, and 64%, of east, Germans.[8] But while 82% of American, over 60% of British, just under 60% of French users actually enjoyed them, according to a 1995 Gallup poll, only 20% of German users found them fun.[9] Even kids held back. Though every second teenager had a PC, according to a 1993 study, they were optional but middle-priority on boys' wish lists of consumer electronics, optional but lowest priority on girls'.[10]

'Why is there no socialism in America?' the sociologist Werner Sombart asked as the century began.[11] 'Why is there no E-mail in Germany?' a visitor asked first himself, then others, as the century ended. The replies were a medley of incomprehension, frustration, despair, even occasional hilarity. When asked if they could imagine their employer, Rudolf Scharping, the governor of Rhineland-Palatinate and leader of the Social Democratic opposition, declaring equal access to the information superhighway an essential condition of equal opportunity, and making it a campaign issue, two legislative assistants just laughed and laughed. Yet Chancellor Helmut Kohl, a voluble exponent of the new technologies, hardly came off better. Asked about the 'information superhighway' in a much-quoted interview on the commercial channel RTL, he could only answer at prolix and stammering length about highway congestion being a matter for the respective federal states.[12] Put to the test by a visitor's E-mail address, one uncommonly young and demonstratively modern CDU deputy even needed to be shown the @ on his office keyboard. He then confessed that not only had he never heard of E-mail, he had never used a computer either.

Reflecting on the common denominators, respondents pointed to politics, economics, technology, law and culture. But virtually all of the answers either began or ended with Deutsche Telekom, the giant utility, whose monopoly was written into the very constitution,[13] and whose long-delayed privatization had only just come up for debate. Telecommunications, almost everyone agreed, was not only the key to modern business, but a big, and potentially very good, business in itself. Second only to Japan's NTT, Deutsche Telekom was very big too, in 1993 some 20% larger than America's AT&T, half again as large as British Telecom.[14] Yet it was also perennially overstaffed and undercapitalized, and half its work force of almost a quarter million was tenured. Their current contract included access to vacation resorts on the North Sea and Côte d'Azur, eight minutes in the hour to excuse themselves, a cold drink when temperatures rose above an agreed maximum, and a hot drink when they fell below an agreed minimum.[15] Though the post office was nominally divided into three autonomous units, of which Telekom was one, it was also the minister's favored piggy bank when it came to covering deficits in the others. Finance ministers milked it for general revenue too.[16] As public attention shifted nervously from *Modell Deutschland*, i.e., postwar Germany as a place for pride and emulation, to *Standort Deutschland*, i.e., post-Cold War Germany as an expensive and bureaucratic place to do business, the modernization and privatization of Telekom became at once a test case, a metaphor, even a moment of truth.

Telekom, it was credibly reported, was already eight years behind its foreign competition, and steadily losing ground. Marketing, for obvious reasons, was low priority. Advertisements read like user's manuals. As happened in America years earlier, business increasingly inclined to solve its own problems. First, with the help of a 1992 court ruling that allowed normal phone as well as data traffic for the purpose, it leased lines from Deutsche Telekom. It then created its own internal networks, despite leasing fees well above the European Union average, and over six times the prevailing US rate;[17] rates per phone line exceeded only in Italy, and yearly inland service bills exceeded only in France.[18]

Actually, there is E-mail of sorts, for business, for government – though not the Bundestag, where the respective party caucuses are only now connecting their members.[19] There is every likelihood of more as one of the world's densest fiber optics networks[20] expands, particularly eastward toward the five new states, where a phone system left over from the 1930s is already being transformed both into a leading edge and a comparative advantage. In a population of 80 million, an estimated half a million to a million were linked by business networks.[21] There were also about 150,000 Internet hosts, with perhaps a half-million users, compared, e.g., to America's two million-plus hosts,[22] with an indeterminate number of users that nonetheless includes virtually every regularly-matriculated college undergraduate. Modem prices had fallen from c. DM800 to DM200. But Compuserve, the only commercial service generally available, still charged a hefty monthly fee.

By 1 January 1998, free enterprise is supposed to ride to the rescue by order of the European Union.[23] Meanwhile, like so many dance partners at a ball, BellSouth and Thyssen, Northern Telecom and German Aerospace, British Telecom and Viag, Cable & Wireless and Viab, Bertelsmann and America Online, are lining up, just waiting for the music to start. So are Telekom and Sprint.[24] With Germany the world's third largest market after the United States and Japan, it stands to reason that it will be worth the wait. There is no question that Germans will telephone in one way or another. Total phone volume was already growing by 7%, east German volume by 26%, a year. By 2003, volume is expected to grow by 75%. The only question is who will get the business, who will provide what service, and whether a Telekom and even Germany still struggling with the nineteenth century will be ready in time for the twenty-first.

In the end, despite a flurry of slow-downs and postal strikes, privatization passed, with the understanding that the public sector would retain a majority of the shares for at least five years. Has Germany exchanged a public monopoly for a quasi-private one, one legislative staffer wondered? Has Telekom, in its eagerness to reconstruct East Germany, to extend Europe's densest cable system and establish mobile phone networks, actually deterred investors by taking on more than it can deal with, including a burden of debt in excess of DM107 billion, i.e., 70% of its corporate assets?[25] It is too soon to answer either question. But in a country where secondary schools still teach 'Faust' thoroughly and well, but typing hardly at all, it is certainly reasonable to ask them.

ECONOMY AND SOCIETY

In 1895 Max Weber was appointed to his first professorship in Freiburg. He was just 31, an age at which many Germans a hundred years later are still students. His inaugural lecture addressed the dilemmas of economics and national interest, not least in West Prussia, where an ancient German agrarian economy both feared and depended on Polish workers.[26] A full generation and a lost war later, Weber devoted what was to become an even more famous lecture to the moral and practical dilemmas of professional, and not just German, politics.[27]

By 1945, successive test cases from Bismarck to Hitler had persuaded even many Germans that the German dilemmas were too serious to leave to the Germans themselves. For the moment, Allied planning pointed in any of three directions. The first was the Morgenthau Plan,[28] that briefly captured Anglo-American imaginations and even attracted the attention of policy-makers. It foresaw a 'pastoral', deindustrialized Germany that would presumably threaten no one. The second was the Potsdam Accords, that envisaged an intact and unpartitioned economic Germany, despite the zonal divisions and military government of the victors. The third course, warmly endorsed by the State Department, Wall Street, and even military government, was the incremental reintegration of Germans in the European, global, and even human, family after the disasters of 1919–39.

Of the three, only the last turned out to be a practical long-term option. Over a public life that included two world wars, two post-war inflations and famines, and history's greatest depression, former President Herbert Hoover had learned a thing or two about the facts of European life. Keeping Germany in economic chains, he reported after another postwar survey, meant keeping Europe in rags.[29] It was a hard political sell in 1945. But by 1947, his argument looked virtually self-evident. Keen for their own piece of the Ruhr, even the Russians agreed that west German industry was a locomotive of postwar recovery. Pressures from home to cut the costs of occupation were incentive enough to let British and American military governors push, and permit, Germans to pay their own way.[30] With Foreign Minister Robert Schuman's proposal for a West European common market for coal and steel of 1949–50, France too came around. Hitherto the principal obstacle to German economic integration, the French now acknowledged that a reconstructed Germany was also a key to their own recovery, with political payoffs for both countries. With the extra incentive in 1948 of a legendary currency reform,[31] West Germans needed little persuading that work was both in their nature and in their best interest.[32] They soon concluded that it was in their own best interest to cooperate with the victors too.

The results have long become part of the landscape. Guided in part by American, British, then French expectations, in part by their collective reading of recent history, Germans reached their own conclusions. Undiminished and unqualified by the challenges of unification, any number of them can still be seen in a constitution whose Article 14 stipulates that private property has obligations as well as rights, and whose Article 20 declares that Germany is federal, democratic, and committed to the social welfare of its citizens.[33] As time went on, significant numbers of Germans also revealed an aversion to inflation and central planning.

What was expected of Germans was that they reconstruct their economy, and resume doing what they traditionally did best, i.e, make substantial and familiar things. They were supposed to pay their way with exports. They were supposed to dig coal and produce steel in their neighbors' interest as well as their own. They were supposed to surrender their advanced technologies – and technologists – as intellectual reparations to the victors.[34]

Favored by a reservoir of cheap, skilled labor, seemingly limitless demand, an undervalued currency, insulation from both the demands and competition of the East, and start-up capital from America, the results astonished everyone, including Germans themselves. In 1950, Marshall aid constituted only 1.4% of German GNP, compared to 2.5% in France, 2.1% in Italy, and 1.8% in Britain. Yet average annual growth – of GNP by over 13.3%, of industrial production and capital formation by over 20%, of exports by over 50% – was not only the highest of the fifteen recipient countries, but far ahead of all the rest.[35] The structure and direction of exports were significant too. In 1955 78.5% of all German exports were manufactures, 60% of them finished goods. In 1950 72%, in 1955 65% of all exports, went to a rapidly-growing Western Europe.[36] In 1992, almost 75% of their exports still went to Western Europe, although the world's commercial center of gravity had moved dramatically toward an even more rapidly-growing East Asia, and Germans knew and worried about what they were missing.[37]

The reconstruction of Germany's intellectual and institutional infrastructure was no less impressive than the reconstruction of its physical plant. Neither historically liberal, traditionally conservative nor conventionally socialist, postwar Germany assimilated reminiscences of all three, including Prussian paternalism and Catholic social doctrine, guilds, estates and public monopolies, plus a new, improved labor movement that substituted sixteen comprehensive industrial unions for a mixed bag of some 200 pre-1933 predecessors, organized according to craft, religious denomination and political affiliation.[38]

The result was soon labeled and packaged as 'social market economy'. The *cuvée* turned out to have a wide general appeal. Its basic elements included a real market, in which consumer choice determined production and prices; organized employee participation in both corporate and factory-floor decision-making to moderate historical adversary relationships; competition, but with regulations to limit temptations and tendencies that might lead to concentration and new monopolies; full employment assured, if necessary, by government subsidy; and income redistribution mechanisms to benefit those in need.[39]

The return, rehabilitation, even renaissance, of the hard-faced men from the orderly jungles of organized German capitalism initially gave the impression that nothing had happened. Yet the result was considered a miracle – at least until similar miracles followed in France, Italy and Japan a few years later. Within a decade, apparently irreparable devastation had been transformed into what now looked amazingly like humming normality. Yet what mattered, as Mancur Olson was to argue another generation later, was not the continuity, but the discontinuity of German economic life. Total defeat, according to Olson, had loosened the deadly grip of historical vested interests. It thereby allowed the explosion of entrepreneurial energy that accounted for German dynamism as opposed, for instance, to British inertia.[40] His explanation made sense post facto. But contemporaries were slow to notice any new deals or new departures.[41] On the contrary, the impression of normality, alternatively understood as a pervasive postwar 'restoration', acquired its own reality. Voters, who liked it, returned incumbent Christian Democratic governments with growing majorities. A gifted generation of postwar novelists and film-makers, who did not like it, became adept and internationally successful at packaging and marketing their alienation.[42]

Yet the less things seemed to change, the less they remained the same. For the first time, Germany had really became a liberal country. Markets worked. Productivity,[43] demand and purchasing power soared. Labor moved. Capital flowed. Borders opened. Trade barriers fell.[44] The traditional hegemony of coal, steel and hard-faced men between Düsseldorf and Essen, yielded to manufacturing, services and south Germans, including a quasi-Texan Bavaria. Germans discovered cars with a passion, then asserted their right to drive them without speed limits with the passion of Americans asserting the right to bear arms.[45] Discovered in turn by the oil multis, they also discovered cheap, non-German and internationally marketed oil as their new fuel of preference.[46] While farming and mining jobs fell perpendicularly, service and public-sector jobs multiplied.[47]

Since none of this was foreseeable, previous, disastrous experience was inevitably taken as the standard of comparison. Unsurprisingly, there was endless speculation on what would happen when the postwar order encountered its first heavy weather. From oil shocks to political terror to unification itself, the challenges came and went, among them tests that would have rattled the foundations of the ill-fated Weimar republic. Yet Bonn never came close to becoming Weimar. The first real recession, in the late 60s, responded to a mild dose of Keynesianism; the second, after the oil shock of 1973, to budget tightening and a productivity program; the third, an aftershock of the second, to moderate pump-priming and a counter-cyclical change of course.[48]

Despite an export-driven recovery, median unemployment, most of it structural, remained high in the 1980s, at least by German standards. Yet unemployment was still below the OECD, and substantially below the European Community, average on the eve of 1989,[49] and those Germans who worked outearned anyone else in their economic weight class save Danes, Norwegians, Swiss and, just barely, Japanese, while working less than Britons, Americans and Japanese.[50] Counting supplementary benefits that amounted to 86% of wages, Germans were actually in a class by themselves, with inflation substantially below European Community and OECD levels.[51] Measured against a 'misery index', created by adding annual inflation to annual unemployment, Germany's average score between 1971 and 1992 was 7.5%. This was still above Japan's. But it was substantially below Sweden's, America's, Australia's, France's, Britain's and Italy's, while gross capital formation between 1969 and 1989, at circa 22% of GNP, was second only to Japan's among the major economic powers.[52]

Yet measured against the proverbial virtues – elevated savings, intensive investment in education, public restraint *et al.* – associated with Asian tigers, the German economy has been unremarkable. At an average 24.4% of GNP in 1986–90, Germans savings are impressive by US standards, but only slightly above European Community and OECD averages.[53] Per capita household spending on education, recreation and culture (9.2%) was slightly higher than in America (8.6%) and France (7.6%), but behind Britain (9.7%) and tied with Italy. As a percentage of GNP, overall educational spending, at 5.4% in 1991, was, in fact, the lowest in the European Community, behind Finland (6.6%), Hungary (6.7%) and the United States (7.0%) – though ahead of Japan (5%).[54] Public debt in 1989 was 22.5% of GNP, substantially below American (30.4%) and OECD (31.3%) levels. But it also was well above Japan's 14.7%, and almost twice the German level of just ten years before. By the late 1980s, public budgets not only constituted 46% of German GNP, but enterprises administered, subsidized or otherwise protected by the public sector generated an estimated 40% of German added value – and this even without manufacturing, where direct public ownership is minimal.[55] 'In quantitative terms, German liberalism can certainly be judged among the more temperate,' one recent French observer notes ironically.[56]

In principle, the same applies to Switzerland, Scandinavia, the Benelux countries, even Japan, where a similar product flourishes.[57] Yet, if a German *Sonderweg* exists, the social market economy is the likeliest place to look for it. Baffling to foreigners, self-evident to Germans, it is rather a product of recent history than conscious design, although the basic elements go back to Bismarck, even Hans Sachs.[58]

'Social', as Germans understand it, is neither left nor right, but the common denominator of a world where liberals joined, not beat, conservatives, Catholics and socialists. Spelled out in a variety of public and private-sector, federal and local agencies, its practical definition includes comprehensive health, old-age, unemployment and, most recently, nursing and home-care coverage for virtually everyone. Yet paradoxically, at least by Anglo-American standards, it runs with a minimum of direct state intervention.[59]

The health system alone is not just an example, but practically a case study, of German style and trade-offs. Funded by employers, private households, private-sector insurance companies, a proliferation of locally-organized statutory health and accident funds, several nationally-organized pension funds, and state governments, absolute health expenditures increased by about fivefold between 1970 and 1990, while the cost of living and producer-price index rose by 2.3.[60] Even admirers and defenders admit that the system offers few incentives to save. In an intensely particularized system, some 1100 local insurance funds compete with one another and private insurers. Like their counterparts elsewhere, their trustees and administrators tend to defer to experts, overbuild hospitals and overbuy the latest new machines to equip them, as Karl Furmaniak, a sociologist in the federal ministry of health cheerfully acknowledges. Quality controls, including morbidity statistics, are selective or unavailable. Prophylaxis is unremunerative – even prohibited in the case of water flouridation since, as the courts have ruled, it would constitute involuntary treatment. And yet, he notes, for all that Germans drink and smoke too much, their life expectancy continues to rise.[61]

Dental prophylaxis, in turn, might be seen as a relatively small but illuminating metaphor of the health system. In 1993, dental treatment accounted for DM12.8 billion, 6%, of all expenditures by the statutory health insurance system. Tooth replacement then cost an additional DM6.3 billion.[62] Of the services dentists provided, according to Dr Joseph Kastenbauer, president of the Bavarian Dental association, tooth replacement was the biggest item. Prophylaxis, he added with concern and puzzlement, was the smallest – although the ratio of significantly cheaper periodontal treatment to actual tooth replacement had improved from 1:64.5 in 1975 to 1:7.3 in 1992, he added. He further noted that periodontal treatment, the prophylactic maintenance of gum tissue that represents a low-cost alternative to tooth replacement, was underdeveloped in Germany, but a staple in neighboring countries like Switzerland.[63]

On closer inspection, the explanation might qualify as a test question in a business school course on market theory. As accountable public agencies, the statutory insurance funds pay German dentists for what they do, e.g., replace teeth. Equally, as accountable private practitioners, not state employees, German dentists are not paid for what they do not do, e.g., the routine, and significantly less remunerative job, of periodic periodontal treatment. What is regularly done by hired dental hygienists in Switzerland, Holland and the United States is, in fact, rare in Germany, and current law makes no provision for hygienists at all, although the most recent version of the law for the first time offers the patient a modest incentive for prophylaxis. Instead, the law establishing a point system providing for direct payment to the practitioner for services rendered. The dentist accordingly has no incentive to volunteer services that pay substantially less for more effort.[64] Certification of salaried hygienists as their employers' agents is evidently no option either.[65] Yet, for all its apparent wastefulness, the German system, with its virtually universal coverage, high quality and general accessibility, consumed 8.1% of GNP in 1990; 1.9% more than the British system, but without its notorious bottlenecks; and 4% less than the nominally market-driven American system, that still excluded up to 15% of the population from any coverage at all.[66]

Hitherto at least, the German version of 'market' has been similarly successful in similar ways. With its proliferation of self-regulatory agencies, public intervention and industrial codetermination, it has also been about equally remarkable to foreigners. David Goodhart, who learned his way around the German scene as Bonn correspondent for the *Financial Times* between 1988 and 1991, sorts the elements of the German system into four generic categories. The first is the relationships between companies and capital; the second between companies and labor, circa 42% of it unionized;[67] the third between companies and the state – and states; the fourth between companies and other companies. But common to all four is a system that both links and separates business and politics. Admirers, of whom there are many, point to the ways the system levels playing fields, and favors social equity, collective responsibility and long-term planning. Critics, of whom there are also many, point to the ways it also favors oligarchy, inertia, even entropy. Both are right.

The national preference for long-term, low-risk financial support is a practical example. If British and American companies look first to the stock market, and pay out their earnings as dividends, German companies look first to their earnings and then, like their nineteenth-century predecessors, to the bank. In 1994, some 2000 British companies were listed on the British market. Of some 370,000 limited liability companies (*Gesellschaften mit beschränkter Haftung*) 2300 joint stock (*Aktiengesellschaften*), some 600 were listed on the German market – including only half of the hundred biggest companies.[68] In the United States, some 20% of household savings is in equities. In western Germany, where over 60% of savings gravitates to such real property as lots, houses and condominiums,[69] the equivalent share is about 4–6%. Over 40% of all shares traded on a relatively small market are owned by companies themselves. Rather than answer to an annual assembly of external owners, German management first responds to a supervisory board that includes white as well as blue-collar employees, suppliers, and sometimes even customers. To a degree uncommon and even unknown elsewhere, the bank is a major player. Hostile takeovers are rare. But so, say some knowledgable critics, are the entrepreneurial 'gazelles' that have recently accounted for 70% of American job growth;[70] the occasional entrepreneurial comet like Ted Turner or Bill Gates, as well as a large measure of accountability, transparency, flexibility and, to judge by some notable recent cases, critical judgment.[71] The 1995 OECD report is quite explicit in associating the relative underdevelopment of Germany's high-tech sector with its conservative style of corporate governance, while Edwards and Fischer find the bottom-line results even in traditional sectors overrated and inconclusive.[72]

Consensus – or inertia – is established again in what is revealing called the *Betriebsverfassungsgesetz* (roughly industrial constitution act) that defines relations between labor and management. Based on Weimar Republican precedents, the principle of labor codetermination was rendered only the more attractive by the top-down brutality of the

Nazi era. In the aftermath of Hitler, the idea of industrial power-sharing not only became a union priority, it was welcomed by British and even American occupiers, who could hardly have imagined, let alone proposed, anything like it at home. In 1951, codetermination was introduced in the coal and steel industries. In its original form, it provided parity representation for labor and shareholders in companies with over a thousand employees, plus an elected labor representative as a kind of senior vice-president of the company. A year later, a modified bill extended the principle to all other joint stock companies. although reserving only a third of the seats on the board to labor, and established elected factory councils to govern working conditions in all enterprises with more than 20 employees. In 1972, with Social Democrats again in power for the first time since the 1920s, elected factory councils were established in 98% of all manufacturing, as well as 75% of all wholesale and retail firms. Four years later, codetermination was then extended to all firms employing over 2000.[73]

While bargaining is strictly autonomous, the state and states nonetheless stand by as arbiter, initiator and regulator. A fact of German life before and after Hitler, the public sector subsumes and reflects an anthology of legacies. As in much of continental Europe, its presence begins with a pervasively codified legal system, applied by an army of legally trained civil servants[74] and interpreted by professional judges in elaborately differentiated courts. From time to time, it is even reinforced by a quasi-militia of entrepreneurial citizen volunteers.[75] Federalism adds another layer of public sector. German states and localities are allowed, even encouraged, to underwrite technology transfer, invest in infrastructure, and otherwise promote business; to regulate broadcasting and higher education,[76] and to exercise a virtual monopoly over elementary and secondary schooling. The regulatory culture is amplified, in turn, by the political parties, which favor controls – and public jobs – consistent with their own view of the public interest; by a ministerial bureaucracy disposed, and even mandated,[77] to act autonomously; and whole pyramids and networks of 'self-governing' bodies – chambers of commerce, professional associations, trade associations, employers associations, unions *et al.* Although all are private sector, they have effectively been deputized to act as agents of the state. The recent case of a small-town Thuringian baker is at once quaint, representative, and ironic for what it says about one former East German's experience with the West German market economy held up for 40 years as a model. In a test of consumer-friendly enterprise, the baker, Helmut Bernart, rose early on Sunday to

produce fresh breakfast rolls for a market otherwise constrained by law
to buy its Sunday breakfast rolls before shop-closing at 2 p.m. on
Saturday. His initiative was well-received by customers in Coburg. But
it brought him an injunction from the district court in Meiningen on
behalf of the local baker's association. Under threat of a DM500,000
fine or half a year in jail, Bernart was enjoined to stop producing fresh
rolls for Sunday breakfast – though the rules did allow him to continue
producing cakes and pastries for sale during the predetermined Sunday
afternoon shop hours like his competitors.[78]

'Self-government' leads to the last, and perhaps most remarkable
premise of the German model, again, at least, as seen, from English-
speaking countries. This is the relationship between company and
company. German companies combine to lobby. They even send
deputies to the Bundestag.[79] They negotiate and police[80] industry-wide
labor contracts based on qualifications, seniority and nationally-bind-
ing wage scales. They own one another's shares, collaborate with
suppliers, and cooperate both with state governments and one another
in research, development, technology transfer and export promotion.
They define and enforce industrial norms and standards.[81] They claim
to level the playing field by imposing some of Europe's most restrictive
closing hours, requiring both department stores and the mom and pop
stores alike to shut their doors at 6.30 p.m. four nights a week, by
8:30 p.m. on Thursdays, and at 2.30 p.m. on three of four Saturdays a
month.[82]

Inconvenient, unpopular, a burden on working parents, and politically untouchable, shop hours too are a part of the 'German model',
passionately supported by retail employers and employees alike. 'I
can't understand that people go shopping at night in America,' one
retail clerk was recently quoted. 'Logically speaking, why should
someone need to buy a bicycle at 8:30 p.m.?'[83] In part unwilling, in
part unable to compete in service, price or convenience, corner shops
are nonetheless vanishing like other endangered species: of 45,000 in
1989, it was estimated that as many as half were out of business five
years later. The irony of a law defended as the last hope of the small
against the large is that the service station, not a chain like Aldi, has
proven to be their nemesis.[84] Not even most retail clerks would ask
why, logically, people might want to fill their tank at 8.30 p.m. Thus
exempted from the closing time imposed on corner grocers, service
stations can sell gasoline at any hour, plus bananas, milk and breakfast
rolls at an appropriate markup.

More explicably, business supports a vocational education system that keeps apprentices in school, trains them to national standards in some 400 fields, qualifies them for industry-wide employment on completion, and is generally regarded as a wonder of the world. Since wages are negotiated industry-wide, labor-poaching is not a problem. Since apprentice wages are low, and a fungible pool of skilled labor is regarded as a sensible investment, there are few disincentives to train on grounds that it will only benefit competitors. Over 80% of the German, compared with some 40% of the French or British, population therefore claims certified job skills[85] – though none of this, it should be added, guarantees a job.

A genuinely open economy, whose huge export dependency alone assures a passion for free trade,[86] German business offers practical examples of virtually every known entrepreneurial form from the yuppy consultant and family farm to the multinational corporation. But machines and brewing might be seen as especially emblematic of the German style.

An ancient German specialty, metal-working still reflects its craft origins in a proliferation of small, family-owned firms that are another German specialty. Around half of German metal-working jobs in 1987 was in firms employing between 100 and a thousand, another quarter in firms employing fewer than 100. Unlike Japan where the fifty largest firms controlled 78%, and America, where the fifty largest firms controlled 65%, in Germany the fifty largest firms controlled only 43% of the market.

Like similar industries elsewhere, German makers too since the early 1980s have had to face a new world of automation, miniaturization, computerization in the design of products rather different from the saws, lathes and milling machines of an earlier industrial era. Like their Japanese and American competitors in a world where specificity and flexibility are also a comparative advantage, they have also had to reconcile the conflicting demands of economies of scale with the special requirements or innovations of particular customers.

According to McKinsey Global Associates, which calculated metal-working productivity (value added per hour worked) in Germany at 100 (Japan 119, United States 100) the German industry in 1990 generated $12.9 billion worth of goods (Japan $40 billion, United States $11.6), and employed 163,630 (Japan 239,250, United States 119,900) who worked 1,604 hours (Japan 2,197, United States 1,963). Since 1987, McKinsey noticed, Japan had also gained a productivity advantage of about 20% by standardization of products, increased automation, plus economies of scale and outsourcing, while their German and American competitors stuck to relatively small volumes of highly specialized products.

Predictably, the German strengths were in the fundamentals: fewer customers, products and suppliers, shorter lines of communication, and superior labor skills related, in turn, to intensive training. Predictably again, they paid off in exports, an inevitable matter of German concern. In 1990, German machine tool makers exported almost 60% of their product (Japan 36.4%, United States 26.9%), over half of it to Europe. No less predictably, German weaknesses were seen as a function of German strengths: including fragmentation and specialization that minimized incentives to standardize and invest in productivity-enhancing equipment.

In its rather different way, brewing too could be viewed as the German economy at its most German. In Germany in 1990, c. 1000 breweries produced 12.5 billion liters of beer. In America c. 67 produced 23.1 billion. Quality was no issue – at least for McKinsey, which calculated American labor productivity (in' liters per hour worked) at 100, Japan at 69, and Germany at 44. Beer, it was argued, is a simple and homogeneous product, particularly suitable for large-scale processing and packaging. The roughly equivalent sizes of Beck's in Bremen and an average American plant shows what Germans could do, the argument continues. Yet not only are Germans disposed, for the most part, to produce in smaller units, and maintain inefficiently localized distribution systems, customers are also prepared to pay the price at the tap and support up to a thousand locally-owned and locally-operated monopolies against consolidated production and nationally-advertised competitors.[87]

WHAT IS TO BE DONE?

Mother of parliaments and then industrial revolution, Britain for at least a hundred years had also been the first to fall behind, while others caught up, then overtook it, in ideas, energy, skills, productivity and, finally, market share. Since the end of World War II, British authors excelled, if nothing else, in self-doubt and self-examination as the pound sank and the trade gap climbed. Meanwhile, the devastated economies of Western Europe took off and soared in what appeared to be a contagion of miracles.

Then came the 1990s. These days, Americans look earnestly at Germany, and vice versa. But both Americans and Germans look especially earnestly at Japan.[88] In the 1930s, communists and fascists around the world had seen the Great Depression as history's last word on liberal democracy and capitalism. Now, both fascism and communism are dead. Democracy and capitalism have survived and conquered. With its 380 million potential producers and consumers, the freshly-constituted European Union is the world's biggest and richest single market. Yet German unemployment, currently at 1950 levels, seems once more a way of life for millions of other West, let alone post-communist Central and East Europeans too. Long familiar as over-night presences in London storefronts and on Washington subway grates, the homeless can even be found now in Bonn, passing the night in the Foreign Office subway station. In early 1995, even in Germany, some five million people, over 6% of the resident population, was on welfare.[89] Was it possible, a British commentator recently asked, that Britain has again been a leader, this time as the first to face the post-modern, post-colonial and post-industrial facts of life? Was it possible that the 'British' disease is actually generic, that widening circles of rustbelt decay, unassimilable immigrants, functional illiteracy and disfunctional families, familiar from Gary, Indiana, to Wolverhampton, England, are the common future of the West?[90]

Imposed by a world of global markets and open borders, and the imponderable trade-offs that come with both, once-British dilemmas have certainly become common property, defined by common coordinates of national state and world economy, domestic tranquillity and market discipline, getting it right and getting elected. But as so often in German history, idiosyncrasies of identity, location, magnitude and culture add a particular spin to the general case.

In a radio broadcast in October 1939, Winston Churchill described Russian policy as 'a riddle wrapped in a mystery inside an enigma'.[91] Half a century after World War II, five years after unification, and on the threshold of a new century, the German economic scene could as plausibly be described as 'A stalemate wrapped in a dilemma inside a paradox.' Asked to reflect on their situation, Germans invariably look thoughtful. Their answers then tend to fall in three directions. The first, widely encountered among such would-be modernizers as professional technocrats and entrepreneurial consultants, is 'Yes, and it's even worse than you imagine.' The second, a specialty of thoughtful conservatives around the chancellor, is 'Yes, no different from any-where else, which proves we're finally normal.' The third, a staple of business leaders, gazing out on splendid views from the windows of their high-rise offices, is 'Yes, we know, and we're going international.'

In fact, none of the powerful gravitational fields of politics, business and government has completely inhibited authentic, even dramatic expressions of national will and political purpose. But under normal, i.e., most imaginable, circumstances, the system makes it easier to follow than to lead. Under six different postwar chancellors, Germans have taken and sustained such major initiatives as the decision to rearm; to join the Atlantic alliance and pursue a supranational Europe with their Western neighbors, even at the cost of national sovereignty and early unification; to pursue détente with the Soviet Union, *Ostpolitik* with their eastern neighbors, and even coexistence with a communist German state.

Domestic politics has yielded its flowers too, including school and university reform, industrial codetermination, continued prosecution of Nazi murders,[92] and the first wholesale revision of the criminal code since the Second Empire. But like amendments to the US constitution, all presumed broad public and parliamentary support, and allowed for years of gestation and national debate.

The options for economic, then political, unification in 1989–90 were especially momentous, eliciting energy and decisiveness, not least from Kohl himself. Yet earthquakes determine their own agenda and calendars. Much of the post-unification *tristesse* and *malaise* can be traced not only to the real and enormous difficulty of doing so much so quickly, but of confronting it without the psychic preparation of a cathartic national debate.

In contrast to such secular benchmarks, successive elections in Britain, America and Germany between 1979 and 1982 not only display the natural inertia of the normal political process, but reveal with almost laboratory precision how Germany resembles, yet also differs from, even its closest allies. In all three countries, roughly similar electorates turned against roughly similar center-left governments for roughly similar reasons, replacing them with roughly similar center-right governments by roughly similar margins. In all three countries, the winners proclaimed their intention to reverse a secular tide of public regulation, intervention and dependence, if necessary, with the slaughter – or at least auction – of some of their predecessors' most sacred cows. Like the new administrations in London and Washington, the new government in Bonn was quick to see the outcome as a mandate for change, and to proclaim a '*Wende*', a new direction. East Germans later applied the same word to the unification process of 1989–90.

But Britain's winner-take-all voting, plus the constitutional hegemony of the House of Commons, let Margaret Thatcher turn a 47% plurality into a genuine change of course. America's electoral college, plus a Senate majority, and the inherent prerogatives and mystique of the US presidency, let Ronald Reagan turn a 51% majority into a quasi-revolution. Ironically, Kohl's 49% plurality was a landslide by German standards. But nothing remotely comparable happened in Germany. For all its declared dedication to tax cuts, deregulation, market priorities and personal responsibility, the new government in Bonn tended to ratify, not reverse, the decisions of its predecessors.[93]

That Kohl has been consistently rewarded and reelected to the point of becoming postwar Germany's longest-serving chancellor is rather a tribute to his mastery of the powerful statics than the rather less developed dynamics of German politics.[94] Recruited from the university like most company employees, German parliamentarians work their way up in the business like most other German professionals. Lateral entry and exit are not unknown in German public life. But, as in the private sector, both are uncommon.

For many, parliament really is a career. Wages, benefits, even job security are genuinely attractive. In 1992, they included a basic monthly stipend of DM10,128, a monthly allowance of DM5765 for travel, housing and office costs, another allowance of up to DM12,960 for staff, travel, phone, data processing, and a pension at 35% of the basic stipend after eight years and rising to 75% after 18.[95] To a considerable degree, the money is public, all the more so after a series of Italianate affairs in the 1980s, when corporate donations got out of hand, almost, but not quite, carrying away a few of the country's most illustrious party treasurers.[96] At election time, the parties enjoy self-evident access to the public TV channels they help govern. To the extent the system thereby relieves them of the need to beat the bushes for campaign funds and TV time, individual deputies are independent of their constituents in ways American colleagues can only envy.

With their well-defined committee and caucus assignments, and the job security that comes with indirect election,[97] German parliamentarians in many ways resemble civil servants. Be it as judges, local officials, professors, teachers, police officers, or rail and post office workers, about half actually are public employees, secure in the knowledge that nothing very bad can happen to them. In still other ways, they resemble the middle managers of a large, diversified company, providing a variety of political services to customers of questionable brand loyalty. By their nature, the parties pursue their comparative advantage in a basically oligopolistic market.[98] Like most German employees, the deputy shares the risks, but also rewards, of what is meant to yield both a secure return and a regular occupation. Representative even in the organization of their offices, most leave technology to the experts, or their secretaries, who use their PCs as very superior typewriters.

The business of politics nonetheless differs in notable ways from the business of business. Though not unknown, business people are rare in public life. Those who have been there report that their experience is not looked down on. But it also seen less as a qualification in itself than a kind of ancillary skill, like competence in an unfamiliar, but occasionally useful, foreign language. Irrespective of history, voter profile and constituency, even the smaller and more monochromatic parties favor brokerage over entrepreneurship, and political over economic priorities.[99] A party of big and small business, employers and employees, the competitive and the subsidized, not to mention Lutherans and Catholics, the governing Christian Democrats would be hard to mistake for American Republicans or British Tories, even in the unlikely event that a Reagan or a Thatcher appeared to lead them. A party of aging trade unionists and middle-aged teachers, the opposition Social Democrats more commonly remind even their friends of American Democrats. What his employers are good for, says one of their legislative assistants, is redistributing wealth, not producing it. Rooted respectively in the social status quo, and in states and regions that frequently regard one another with something like cold war suspicion, Social Democrats are hardly a party of movement either.[100]

Like their peers in other countries, business leaders bewail the heedlessness of politicians and their own deficient political influence. Given the prestige that business still enjoys,[101] and the elaborate consensual mechanisms that link and coordinate public and private interests, much of the argument is clearly disingenuous. Yet no less than elsewhere, political agenda really are self-generated and media-amplified, political attention spans really are short and, in a federal country where someone somewhere is almost always about to vote next Sunday, the election cycle is itself an inevitable guide to political priorities.

Yet for all their frustration with regulation, taxes and the natural inertia of the public sector, business leaders concede the hegemony of politics, if only by omission. 'What we expect from government is that it take the lead in explaining the need for technology and innovation,' the president of the German Chamber of Industry and Trade declared recently in the presence of the chancellor.[102] In America or Italy, each for its own reasons, it is generally left to society itself to fill the empty spaces.[103] Similar civic spontaneity is not unknown in Germany – although even then it frequently takes an anti-technological or anti-technocratic turn.[104] But it is not exactly German nature either. Despite the quasi-rebellion of the newspaper publishers against the monopoly of the public sector, private broadcasting and consumer choice are characteristically limited, and fantasy uncommon.[105] Though business people regularly grouse about the quality and product of German schools and, still more, of German universities, private universities accommodate an estimated 1% of all matriculees.[106]

Although public philanthropy exists, even such visible presences as the Volkswagen, Thyssen or Bertelsmann foundations subsist in the shadow of the public sector, including the party foundations, which have no real equivalent elsewhere.[107] A populist suspicion of 'elites',[108] and equally populist aversion to rewriting the tax code to favor private-sector sponsorship, both confirm and perpetuate the disincentives. In a city with aspirations to be a global financial capital and a country without a Wharton School or Harvard Business, a Frankfurt School of Finance, collectively endowed by the city's banking community, might seem an obvious step, one internationally-respected economist points out. Yet plans for such a project have barely reached the talking stage. Although Germany is vitally interested in the future of Central Europe, a German equivalent of George Soros's privately endowed Central European university in Prague, with its international faculty and students, its common teaching language, its 1:5 faculty–student ratio, and its European studies program, is unimaginable. But a German George Soros is not easily imaginable either.

As a professional elective politician, who has never run a business, never practiced another trade, never drawn a private-sector salary nor even run a ministry, Kohl might actually personify the postwar parliamentary system more perfectly than any of his predecessors. In contrast to the legendary Ludwig Erhard, an economics professor turned politician by circumstance, the formidable Helmut Schmidt, a politician turned technocrat by passion, or even the late Franz Josef Strauss, who acquired a PhD in economics while serving as finance minister, Kohl's instincts, according to a senior aide, are basically communitarian. For Germany's sixth postwar chancellor, he says, social imperatives come first, then economic imperatives. Neither a Reaganite nor a Thatcherite, Kohl takes a pragmatic interest in economic affairs. But he leans heavily and gratefully on a staff of 10–15. Schmidt, who liked the motto 'What's good for business and labor can't be bad politics,' regularly summoned representatives of all three to join him around a common table.[109] Uncomfortable himself in such company, according to a former close associate, Kohl prefers to talk to business and labor only when he has to.

Acknowledging the general sense of lagging competitiveness, he has nonetheless taken to appearing recently at labs, industrial expositions and trade fairs, to preach the gospel of research and innovation.[110] Yet his support for the creation of a new German-American Academic Council, with offices in Bonn and Washington, tells at least as much about his priorities and approach as his appearance in bright new labs. A basic political concern for post-Cold War links with the United States is certainly a conspicuous sub-text of the new foundation. Access to, and interaction with, advanced American science and scholarship is presumably another. But most conspicuous of all is how even the by-laws and statutes of a small, German-funded public agency under a retired official of the ministry of research and technology confirm a primal reflex to organize innovation. The director's ambivalence about a hired fund-raiser, like his insistence that he is not there 'to pass out scholarships', but to coordinate decision making in a basically centri-fugal, ad hoc federation of professional guilds, both illuminates and reflects the political process.[111]

A short-lived campaign initiative in 1994 to create a kind of civil peace corps is another clue to the depth and limits of Kohl's own and German conservatism. Distantly inspired by American models, Kohl proposed a civil relief corps for natural disasters, auxiliary support for understaffed local police, even humanitarian missions abroad, as alternatives to military service. Acknowledged with silence by most Christian Democrats, and declared constitutionally, politically and professionally unacceptable by all possible Liberal and Social Demo-cratic speakers, the idea vanished from view within a day of its unveiling.[112]

Further restrained by the courts, an explicitly autonomous Bundes-bank with its own powerful sense of constitutional mandate and public responsibility,[113] an inherently fractious party, and both Free Demo-cratic and Bavarian, i.e., liberal and conservative coalition partners, Kohl is also confined by the Bundesrat, the parliamentary upper house, whose instructed delegations represent the respective federal states. Since January 1991, virtually the morning after Kohl's finest hour, the Bundesrat has been controlled by Social Democrats, who may have lost four national elections, but have also won innumerable state elections, since 1982.

Arguably – and many Germans do argue – the convergent challenges of the post-Cold War era make clear choices more urgent than ever. Looked to expectantly, even impatiently, by allies, neighbors, and even themselves, for authoritative decisions and effective action,[114] Germans nonetheless concede that none of the above is really their national style. On the contrary, for all possible reasons of historical memory, civic consensus and institutional legacy,[115] German government is what it was meant to be after a relatively brief but uniquely disastrous experiment in charismatic leadership. An English garden of local, state and federal, private, public and semi-public agencies and actors, the postwar decision-making landscape is, by design, as lush and diverse as any in the constitutional world.

Yet checks and balances are only a partial explanation for German inertia. Institutions, culture, even technology – or the aversion to it – also play their role. The dilemmas would exist even if the Federal Republic were governed by a cabinet of decision-loving Trumans, De Gaulles or Churchills, with clear majorities in both Bundestag and Bundesrat.

Responses to the demographic conundrum are both generic and instructive in themselves. In order to maintain themselves at current levels, Germans over the next 40 years would have to absorb immigrants on such a scale that their share of the population would rise from its current 8% to 30%; meanwhile, the over-60 cohort would still rise from today's 20% to over a third of the total. If they wish the immigrant component to remain at present levels, Germans would have to accept a 25% reduction of their total population, including a 40% cohort over 60. If they wished to keep the over-60 cohort at current levels, they would have to accept an immigrant component of 50%, and a total population of over 100 million. In fact, as surveys between 1989 and 1992 confirm, the consensus answer to all three options is 'none of the above'. Fewer than 10% of Germans want their absolute population to decline, or expect anything good to come of a declining birth rate. Still, about half reported unhappiness with the size of the existing immigrant population in 1992, and subsequent events made clear that substantial majorities want limits.[116] Since, as Miegel and Wahl point out, no population anywhere has yet experienced absolute decline, rapid aging and accelerated immigration concurrently, German reactions can only be a matter of speculation. 'Probably, however, such a population will change many of its previous assumptions, needs and interests, as well as its perspectives and behavior,' they note. 'The economy, society and state will presumably be transformed from the ground up.'[117]

Yet immigration, with its political implications and consequences, is just one of an anthology of complementary dilemmas. Post-Communist Europe, which begins in Germany and extends indefinitely eastward, is another. Generally seen as a direct challenge, a vital interest, and a potential source of risk and disorder, its normalization, pacification, and political and economic integration in a larger Europe, threaten the security and livelihoods of large, well-organized constituencies of almost every kind. According to Kurt Biedenkopf, the governor of Saxony, the choice on Germany's eastern border is, in effect, a choice between Mexico and Hong Kong. If the European Union continues to exclude Czech and Polish steel, textiles and farm products, the likeliest result is an insoluble border problem at the cost of East German development, he argues. But hard as it is to sell West German and other West European farmers, steel-workers *et al.* on the idea of being their brothers' and sisters' keeper, it is at least as hard to persuade them that they might also be their neighbors' customer.[118] The question of German responsibility east of the Oder also revives the spectre of German centrality and even hegemony in an area where others have nonetheless hardly rushed to invest.[119]

This leads to the dilemma of capital. Germans have, and continue to attract, it.[120] But long-term demands on it from both eastern and western neighbors, domestic constituencies, aging voters[121] *et al.* can hardly help but grow as fast or faster. Until at least the end of the century, West Germans are committed to annual transfers of DM 150 billion (well above $100 billion at 1995 exchange rates) to east Germany alone, financed in part by a stiff domestic 'solidarity' surtax. In addition, Germans have transferred circa DM 80 billion in grants and direct investment to the rest of post-Communist central and eastern Europe, c. 60% of the Western total.[122]

The hunger for capital, in turn, can hardly help but impose more hard choices on a major exporter that is, at the same time *de facto* proprietor of an international reserve currency, and a political culture famously sensitive to inflation. Hardly imaginable, but not impossible, among the possibilities is a Central European variation of the American experience of the early 1980s. Perennially strapped to cover the yawning deficits brought about by generous tax cuts and a capital-intensive military build-up, the Reagan Administration borrowed on a scale unknown since the First World War. In the process, it penalized American farm and industrial exports both directly and indirectly, by overpricing American goods and pushing interest rates to punitive heights in the heartland of American agriculture and industry.

In an equivalent German scenario, other people's money, diverted to Germany, would underwrite the reconstruction of post-Communist Europe. This would naturally include reconstruction of an east Germany, whose infrastructure at unification barely reached 10–25% of the best West European levels; whose telephone system, even in east Berlin, its nominal capital, compared with Crete's and Northern Ireland's; and where per capita investment, despite massive transfusions of capital, had still only reached 76% of West German levels two years after unification.

Yet much of the borrowed money would actually be diverted to basic income maintenance. According to a comprehensive study by the Federal Labour office, about a third of the east German work force had lost their jobs in the five years since unification, and only a quarter had managed to keep the same job throughout the period. The impact fell disproportionately on old people, young people and women. Job loss among workers 52–63 years old in 1989 came to 90%, among workers under 25 in 1989 to 32%. But 80% of workers between 25 and 51 had remained employed. Seven of 10 men had managed to hold their jobs, but not quite six of 10 women.[123] If American experience were any guide, German capital needs would unavoidably sacrifice the export-competitiveness of already-expensive German goods to an ever-stronger DM.[124] In the event, like the junk bond bazaars of the 1980s, German banks and markets would imaginably grow faster than the industrial economy, turning Frankfurt, Düsseldorf, and even the rehabilitated, formerly East German Dresden and Leipzig, into a kind of German sunbelt, surrounded by rust-belt industries and the retired and aging unemployed.[125]

The dilemmas lead to paradox. But in this case it is the paradox of success. Long ago, in a very different Germany, in a very different era, Prussian kings formed reluctant subjects into an army that became a wonder of the world. Then came the moment of truth. At the battle of Jena in 1806, the Prussian army encountered a French army that was not only better, but also fundamentally different. French superiority seemingly began with deceptively simple innovations in infantry tactics, that allowed French skirmishers to move autonomously and independently, while the proverbial Frederician drill and discipline required Prussian riflemen to stand immobile. But the question of tactical differences soon led to reflections on the training and motivation that made them possible. These then led to still more reflections on the social and civic status of French soldiers. These, in turn, led to reflections on the differences between conscripted serfs and armed citizens. And so, it was discovered, tactical reform led logically and inexorably to structural changes of every kind.[126]

Between 1990 and 1993, Germany's share of world exports declined from 12.6% to 10.3%. By 1995, it had resumed its upward course, but at 10.7% it was still a lower rate of recovery than any other any G-7 country.[127] The German giants – Siemens, Daimler-Benz, Deutsche Bank *et al.* – continue to stand tall. But even Volkswagen, the most recent, is a product of the 1930s and most go back far into the 19th century. Still, there has as yet been no economic Jena. On the contrary, to the surprise of Germans themselves, their economy seems to have rebounded from the recession of the early 1990s with familiar resilience, despite labor costs up to 15% above their next G-7 competitor,[128] a work week that effectively ends by Friday noon, and a soaring Deutschmark.[129] West German growth has been impressive, east German growth dramatic.[130] with both exports and investment up, and public deficits in modest decline.

Yet even if a Jena were in view, something currently seen as unlikely, the supermark and a substantial pool of underemployed labor at least afford Germans a cushion that few of their partners can match. If exports are squeezed, Germans, like Swedes, can devalue, says Fritz Scharpf of the Max Planck Institute for Social Research in Cologne. If job markets are squeezed, it should suffice short-term to hire more women.[131] Yet 200 years after Napoleon, and a half century of their own astonishing success, Germans face three new, and very different, revolutions, whose cumulative impact can hardly help but change their world.

One is the squeeze on savings imposed by an aging population, an unreconstructed East Germany that consumes DM150 billion in direct public spending alone every year, and a west German economy, whose competitiveness and productivity point increasingly to the need for comprehensive structural reforms. The second, as a senior diplomat already argued with compelling verve even before the earthquakes to the East that brought down the Wall, are the secular challenges of such new technologies as space, computers and biotechnology, and such new economies and markets as China and the Asian rim, that Germans and other Europeans have consistently left to Americans and Japanese.[132] The third is a post-revolutionary East and Central Europe that in its own very different way arguably poses as radical a challenge to conservative Germans as revolutionary Frenchmen once did to the heirs of Frederick the Great.

Not quite so long ago, in a very different world, postwar West Germans formed themselves into a society, and organized their re-sources into an economy, that were models to the world. Then came the moment of truth. In 1989, Germans encountered neighbors, who were not only worse off, but fundamentally different. Their inferiority began with deceptively simple lags in productivity, management skills, and industrial organization. But speculation on their structural lags led to reflections on their political and economic culture. These led to reflections on what would happen if nothing happened, and East Central Europe, like East Germany, were to fall apart. This then led to reflections on the complementarities of social stability and foreign policy, which led in turn to reflections on the long-term competitive-ness of German exports that supported both. If Germans were to export stability to their neighbors, it was realized, they would have to import East European products that competed with their own – and incidentally persuade their French ally to do the same. And so, it was discovered, Germany's need for political stability and social peace to the European east and south leads logically and inexorably to struc-tural reforms of every kind, including substantially lower social costs and a substantially different line of German products.[133] It therefore requires reluctant Germans to think unfamiliar, even thinkable thoughts. 'If we want things to stay as they are, things will have to change,' says Lampedusa's Prince of Salina as Garibaldi's Thousand thunder down on Sicily.[134] Arguably, the same dilemma now applies to Germany. But this is not a message most electorates welcome.

THE SUNNY SIDE OF THE WAILING WALL[135]

'Germans, we can be proud of our country,' declared Willy Brandt's campaign poster in 1972. A rare and precocious assertion of national self-assurance from an unlikely source,[136] it understandably, if impli-citly, acknowledged that economic performance was among the grounds for pride. Twenty-some years, a couple of oil shocks, a couple of monetary crises, a couple of recessions, and one national unification later, the German economy is a rather different, in many ways tamer descendant of the still relatively young tiger of 1972. Yet the figures are still grounds for pride: in 1972–4 GNP grew by 3.2%, in 1994 by 3%; in 1972–74 exports grew by 9.6%, in 1994 by 9%.[137]

In 1995, one German (Deutsche Bank) and no American bank was listed, with 11 Japanese, among the world's 20 largest.[138] In 1993, eight German companies (Daimler–Benz, Volkswagen, Siemens, Veba, BASF, Höchst, Bayer and Thyssen) were among the world's fifty biggest, compared with fifteen Americans, nine Japanese, and five French.[139] In a *Financial Times* survey of European business leaders, four German companies (Deutsche Bank, BMW, RWE and Siemens) ranked among Europe's 25 most respected, compared with nine British, four Swiss, four French, two Dutch–British, and two Belgian. In eight of 17 enumerated industrial sectors from automobiles (BMW and Bosch) to media (Bertelsmann), one or more German firms also emerged among the three winners; and nine German, (five French, five Swiss, two Belgian, two Dutch, two Dutch–British, one Finnish, one Swedish, one Spanish, one Swiss–Swedish, and 22 British) firms were among the 51 singled out for particular distinction.[140]

The 121 listed Germans, including representatives of Siemens, Nixdorf, Volkswagen, Alcatel, Telekom, Veba, Daimler-Benz, and the IG Metall, comprise 20% of the Europeans and 7% of the total entries in the 1995 directory of the annual World Economic Forum in Davos, Switzerland, a kind of symbolic board meeting of the world's *Who's Who*. By comparison, there were 215 Americans, 120 Swiss and 38 oddly underrepresented Japanese. Of the Germans, 97.5% were male, slightly over two thirds between the ages of 50 and 70, and slightly under two thirds from industry and commerce.

Despite the obligato of doubt and self-criticism about German competitiveness, it is hard to deny that Germans still do some things very well. In 1992 fewer than 80 million Germans produced more than anyone but 125 million Japanese and 250 million Americans; they produced more per capita than anyone but Americans, Swiss and Luxembourgeois,[141] and also earned more per capita than anyone except Americans, Swiss and Luxembourgeois.[142] The annual Hanover fair, the world's biggest, with 7000 exhibitors and an estimated 350,000 visitors in 1995, is another specimen of a German superlative.

In 1991, industry employed nearly 40% of the civilian work force (34.4% in Japan, 27.8% in Britain, 25.3% in the United States), and contributed almost 39% of GNP (41.8% in Japan, 30% in Britain, 29.2% in the United States).[143] German goods constituted 17% of world trade in quality industrial products (America 15%, Japan 14%, Britain and Italy 7%). In 1992 German products comprised 24% of world machine tool exports, a market share unchanged since 1980. American machine tools, which also commanded a 24% market share in 1980, had meanwhile declined by over a third.[144] Overall German exports, 27% of GNP in 1970–75, had grown to 42% a decade later – compared to 38% in Italy, 26% in France, 15% in Japan and 9% in America. But in 1995, the auto and electrical industry exported fully half of what it produced, the machine industry 60%.[145] Despite a $90 billion deficit, c. 5% of GNP, in invisibles (e.g., services, cross-border investment income), and non-commercial transfers (e.g., development aid and EU payments), Germans emerged in 1994 with an overall trade surplus of $45 billion. They also recalled Mark Twain's remark that reports of his death were greatly exaggerated.[146]

That they continue to export competitively, despite some of the world's highest wages, one of the world's strongest currencies, and a growing cohort of the quasi-permanently jobless, only makes their success the more remarkable. What is it, Germans increasingly ask themselves, that they also do right?

Physical infrastructure is an important part of the answer. Road, rail and air transport are ubiquitous (although smog levels associated with road traffic brought the system to a standstill in summer 1994). Public commuter transport is exemplary (although there was no consensus on what combination of subsidies, privatization and market incentives might increase its usage).[147] If the *Datenautobahn*, i.e., the information super-highway, lags considerably behind the *Bundesautobahnen*, i.e., the national expressways, Germany has nonetheless acquired a respectable telecommunications network too. Counting east and west together, 96.5% of German households had TV in 1994, a third had cable access (although most of it is coaxial, not fiber-optic); and 87.3% have phone connections (although it will be 2000 before the current analog system is replaced by a digital system).[148] In 1995, according to a study by International Data Corporation, 28% of German households also had PCs, compared to France with 15%, Japan under 20% and Britain 24% (but also Belgium, the Netherlands, Luxembourg and Denmark with 30%, and the United States with 37%).[149]

With separate depositories for green, brown and clear glass on every street corner, and user-friendly collection schedules and recycling manuals distributed to every mailbox, even garbage collection is something of an art form (although garbage volume, sixth per capita of 18 industrial countries, remained virtually constant between 1980 and 1990).[150] At least in west Germany, housing is both generous and in good repair (although it remains endlessly dilapidated in the East, where, despite a relative boom in the construction trades, 40 years of public squalor, ambiguities of ownership resulting from previous expropriations, minimal purchasing power, plus credit shortages that fall hardest on small business, all favor vicious circles of stagnation and neglect at the expense of rehabilitation).[151] Factored for inflation, environmental investment doubled between 1975 and 1990 with measurable and palpable results. By 1990, dust emissions were down by about half, and sulfur dioxide emissions by about 70% (although carbon dioxide emissions remained high and, but for the collapse of pollutant industry in east Germany, would also have remained virtually constant.)[152]

Human investment is impressive too. In 1991, (West) Germans were second only to the United States in percentage of working-age population (25 to 64) that continued beyond elementary school (United States 83%, Germany 82%, OECD average 55%). With its minimal drop-out rates, secondary education, unsurprisingly, is among the glories of the system. In 1991, with a level of 93.6%, (West) Germany was exceeded only by the Netherlands and Canada in enrollment of 16-year-olds. But with 92.4% and 79.6% respectively, it led the world in enrollment of 17 and 18-year-olds. Vocational education, which accommodates four of every five secondary school students, obviously accounts for the difference. Graduation rates exceeded all but Finland's.[153] Almost 45% of German 18-to-19-year-olds (Finland 62.2%, United States 60.6%, Japan 53.1%, Britain 27.7%) went on to some kind of post-secondary education.[154]

In part anticipating, in part hedging against, a changing job market, 24% of the new university and 70% of the new technical school matriculees in 1993 arrived with a professional certification, up from 16% and 48% respectively in 1985.[155] As critics, of whom there are many, untiringly point out, they will work an average of nine to 15 semesters for their diplomas, one of the longest matriculations in the world. Like all clichés, the image of the understaffed, overcrowded anomie factory is not just a literary convention. It is regularly noted that matriculations doubled between 1970 and 1990 with only a 10% increase in faculty, and only the most marginal increase in classroom, library and laboratory capacity. Yet part of the explanation for the long march from matriculation to diploma can also be sought in the combination of incentives and opportunities for qualified young adults to drop into, as well as out of, the university. With maximal student aid about 20% below the actual cost of living; with only 28% of registrants eligible for student aid, and only a third of these eligible for aid at maximal levels,[156] certified job skills are obviously their own reward. According to the Frankfurt sociologist Karl Otto Hondrich, the shabbily pragmatic, graffiti-covered and thoroughly deromanticized German university is actually one of the unappreciated pillars of the German economy. With its cadre of cheap, trained, and available talent, Hondrich argues, it constitutes a kind of reserve job corps in one of the world's most inflexible labor markets. Among 25 students he recently took on a field trip were a plumber, an electrician, three nurses, a geriatric therapist, a union official, a trained bank employe, and a Christian Democratic city council member. Today's students, as Hondrich sees them, are not 'just' students, but 'also' students, of whom 40% already turn their summer jobs and internships into regular employment.[157]

In 1991, 13.3% of young (West) Germans of theoretical graduation age left universities with the standard first degree (United States 29.6%, Japan 23.3%, Britain 18.4%), compared with an OECD average of 16.4%.[158] Yet the academic product is consistently utilitarian. Of the degrees conferred, 31.7% were in the natural sciences, mathematics, computer science and engineering, a figure exceeded only by Finland (33.2%).[159]

The link between physical and intellectual infrastructure is arguably a national predilection for high – as opposed to very high – technology, i.e., the kinds of products in which research and development (R&D) constitutes no less than least 3, but no more than 8 per cent of the cost of production. So measured, German goods accounted for 18% of world trade in industrial products in 1991 (Japan 20%, the United States 18%, France and Britain 8%, Italy 5%). Sales volume, in turn, reflects a substantial research investment. Germans in 1990 spent over 2.8% of GNP in R&D (Japan 3.07%, France 1.42%), with about a third of it funded by the private sector (Japan 73.1%, France 43.5%). About DM 1 billion of this, a fifth of it from the private sector, found its way to the 46 Fraunhofer institutes for applied industrial research that constitute another German specialty. Jointly supported by Bonn, business and the states, Fraunhofer manages concurrently to develop products; train PhDs; support small business, the source of 60% of its contracts; and even repatriate foreign earnings from Fraunhofer USA near Detroit. A beachhead in Singapore is also under consideration.[160]

The pay-off can be seen in 130 new patents per annum per million employees (Japan 200, United States 110, France 56, Britain 48), and continued export strength in such traditional German fiefdoms and industrial principalities as upscale cars like the Audi and BMW; chemistry, including both pharmaceuticals, and industrial products such as plastics; and measuring instruments, which, revealingly, are virtually the only area in the entire field of materials research where Germans see themselves ahead of American and Japanese competitors.[161]

Of 16 basic research areas studied, Germans considered themselves leaders in only a few. But these, including energy and resource conservation, recycling, forest management, traffic planning and rail technologies,[162] addressed anxieties that others share, but Germans take more seriously than most.

Asked by the European Community's Eurobarometer in 1989 to identify what most concerned them, absolute and even overwhelming majorities of Portuguese, Italians, Irish, French, Spaniards, Danes and Belgians pointed to unemployment. By comparison, over four Germans in ten, when presented the same menu, pointed to 'disadvantages of modern life'. Unemployment followed at some distance with 30%. When 'feeling of insecurity' (10%) was added to 'disadvantages of modern life' (42%), the German total (52%) was exceeded only by Denmark's (83%), a level of anxiety so startling as to give new dimensions of meaning to the concept of 'melancholy Dane'.[163]

Yet, when sublimated in such environmental technologies as water quality equipment, metal-recycling, photovoltaic conversion and high-efficiency furnaces, as Harm Schlüter points out, German anxiety pays off twice: a measurable improvement in environmental quality, and a strong position in an environmental market growing by 6% a year. In 1990, Germans invested 1.6% of GNP (United States 1.4%, Japan 1.2%) in environmental protection; with a per capita investment in the west German states of almost twice the OECD average. In 1994, German products were estimated to comprise 20.5% of world trade in environmental technologies (United States 17.1%, Japan 12.7%, Italy 9.8%, France 7.9%, Britain 7.6%). Gratifyingly labor-intensive, environmental protection promises both a competitive edge in production costs[164] and a lot of jobs. According to *Der Spiegel*, 8500 firms, among them such big and visible ones as German Aerospace (DASA) and Metallgesellschaft, are already heavily engaged in environmental technologies, 680,000 Germans hold environment-related jobs, and the total is expected to reach almost 800,000 by the year 2000. Predictably, the idea of taxing pollution continues to make blood pressures rise at the Chamber of Commerce and the German Federation of Industry.

Yet the German Institute for Economic Research has concluded that even punitive ecotaxes were likelier to create than to destroy jobs, and even companies as visible and potent as AEG have indicated willingness to trade higher fuel, water, waste-management and energy prices against existing fringe benefits.[165]

THE SHADOW SIDE OF THE WAILING WALL

If the 'Historikerstreit' was emblematic of the 1980s, the '*Standortdebatte*', the great debate about German economic competitiveness, is no less emblematic of the '90s. Though neither was the creation of campaign consultants, it is hard to overlook that both took shape and flourished on the eve of national elections, the first in 1985–6, the second in 1993–4.

But unlike the '*Historikerstreit*' with its specifically German resonances, the '*Standortdebatte*' is really generic. Germany might be regarded as an aggravated case. It is hardly a creature from another planet. With its characteristic mix of vision, precision, technocracy, bureaucracy, market liberalism and eloquent silence, the European Commission's so-called Delors White Paper[166] is a definitive statement of the larger European dilemmas, of which Germany is both an example and a part. According to the authors, the centerpiece of the report, a futuristic network of supertrains, pipelines and information superhighways spanning the continent as far as Moscow, and estimated to cost ECU 574 billion (about $757 billion) over a six-year period, is somehow to be privately financed, but publicly managed. The report's recommendations, including more competition, greater ease of payment, equalization of taxes, common technical specifications, incentives for small and middle-sized business, and protection of intellectual property, are unexceptionable. But they are also, and understandably, unspecific. The point of departure is the stagnant pool of underemployment and sluggish job creation that distinguishes Europe from both the United States and Japan, and now even threatens the foundations of postwar security and prosperity. Yet, as more than one observer notes, visionary precision vanishes entirely when the report even approaches such inherently contentious issues as a common ceiling on public spending, a common ratio of investment to GNP, or common standards for telephones, computers and railroad electrification.[167]

Unemployment in the European Union has actually been consistently higher than in Japan or the United States since the early 1980s, while the United States had led both Japan and the European Union in job creation since the middle 1960s. Between 1970 and 1991, public spending in the United States rose from 29.2% to 29.6% of GNP, in Japan from 19.7% to 30.9% of GNP, in the ten-member European Community from 34.4% to 39.6 of GNP. Over the same period, taxes on individuals rose from 8.6% to 16.6% of GNP in Japan, 15.9.% to 19.4% of GNP in the United States, and 16.6% to 23.5% of GNP in the European Community. Within the sub-set, Germans were slightly above the EU average, with public spending at 40.6% of GNP, and personal tax levels at 25.9% in 1991.[168] By 1994, German public spending passed 50% of GNP. The figure was all the more remarkable in a country with an historical aversion to public debt. By 1995, public debt was expected to reach 59.4% of GNP, consuming as much as 18% of tax revenues, according to the German Institute for Economic Research in Berlin, declining only slightly by 1996. Meanwhile, Germany's ratio of household savings to disposable household income, already below Belgium's, Denmark's, Japan's, Italy's , France's, Austria's and Spain's, had visibly receded since 1989.[169]

Five years after the earthquake of 1989, unemployed east Germans comprised about 30% of the national total, although east Germans comprise only 20% of the German population. Registered west German unemployment was still about 8% (Spain 24%, Belgium 14%, France 12%). But official east German unemployment remained about 14%; with nearly a million more east Germans on subsidized public works programs, frequently notional retraining programs, transitional pensions or working part-time. Still, the supply of apprenticeships in 1993–4 exceeded demand by over 60% – and, despite the projected arrival of 250,000 mostly ethnic-German immigrants in 1995, the West German working-age population was already beginning to shrink.[170]

Unification is obviously a necessary, but not a sufficient, explanation for what makes Germany both more and different. It has also been a powerful incentive to think thoughts already long overdue. Care and feeding of the five new states, once known as German Democratic Republic, currently consumes an estimated 80–90% of domestic savings. Rich and stupid can work for a generation, but that's all, Romano Prodi, the Bolognese economist turned reform politician, regularly reminds fellow Italians. 'The financial burdens of unification, plus structural reforms, are as incompatible with the preservation of social vested interests in the west as they are with open-ended subsidy of economic inefficiency and social immobility in the east,' is Fred Klinger's German variation.[171]

Unsurprisingly, considering the magnitude and complexity of the case, the jury on unification is still out. It could well remain out for another generation.[172] New horizon, dead weight, national challenge, red brick *mezzogiorno*? Any one is plausible, and even compatible with the others. Privatization, a direct consequence of unification, can itself be seen as a triumph, an anticlimax, even a calamity. Created in 1990, the *Treuhand* or trusteeship, the agency responsible for selling off East German enterprises, had disposed of nearly 13,000 of them, 95% of the total, by July 1993. It was well on the way to its own liquidation a year later. The bad news included at least one serious miscalculation, and a whole preserve of white elephants. As in the neighboring Czech Republic, East German enterprise might theoretically have been distributed as shares or vouchers. Instead it was sold off – for profit, it was first hoped. But there was none. With east European markets in their own free fall, and competitive production costs lost with the introduction of the Deutschmark, much of East German enterprise was little more attractive than a used model of the old régime's signature car, the tinny little Trabant or Trabi. Depending on the viewer, private investment could be regarded under such circumstances as both the proverbial glass half full and the glass half empty. From 1990 to 1995, (West) German commercial and savings banks invested and estimated DM billion each in East German operations, including a major training programe, an intensive promotional effort, and a work force of 65,000. In 1994, they also lent about DM 90 billion to industry and small business – compared with over DM 150 billion from the public sector. Leaving such direct transfer payments aside, the alternatives at this point were 'passive rationalization,' a euphemism for massive layoffs, and the subsidies, tax-breaks and price cuts common to all economic development agencies. Responding to the warm rain of western aid, eastern productivity had in fact, grown from about a quarter to a little more than half of Western levels since 1990. But wages had risen from 34% to 70% of western levels, leaving behind a trail of expendable wage-earners; and it was obvious that unemployment would be still higher, were it not for the steady stream of public support invested in dubiously efficient job creation and maintenance.[173]

Any of three recent cases both reveal and test the limits of what might now be called 'real existing capitalism' among the ruins of what East Germans once called 'real existing socialism', Common to all three is a calculus of political necessity, economic opportunity and even sentiment, that might have impressed Max Weber.

After multiple rejections and summit-level arm-wrestling with its EU partners in Brussels, the Bonn government and Treuhand managed to sell 60% ownership of the EKO steel works in the one-industry town of Eisenhüttenstadt in October 1994. Contingent on what one knowledgable source called a suitable 'dowry', potential buyers included an Italian and a Russian group, a subsidized shipbuilder from Bremen, and the eventual winner, Belgium's Cockerill-Sambre. In the end, 2000 jobs were saved at the cost of a DM910 billion subsidy – a little less than DM 500,000 per job – and the agreed liquidation of several other nearby plants. Yet it was still questionable how many jobs would be saved for how long, given Polish competition just across the Oder, and the high probability that the subsidy would be turned into new, labor-saving plant.[174]

In a second case, the West German and East German successors of Zeiss, the lens and instrument maker, merged after unification with the help of $400 million in assistance from Bonn – and retention of 49% ownership by the state of Thuringia. Three years later, falling sales and Japanese competition alike pointed to a 20% reduction in the work force. But predictably, it was the eastern plant, the source of an estimated 75% of the company's losses, that faced job cuts of over 50%.[175]

In the third case, the European subsidiary of Dow Chemical announced plans to pay 'several hundred million dollars' for three quarters of the Buna works near Leipzig, in this case a relic of both National Socialism and its East German successor. Gazprom, a Russian natural gas company, would acquire the remaining shares. The German government agreed to contribute $2 billion, i.e., a substantially larger stake than Dow's, for restoration. It hoped thereby to save 3000 of 4600 remaining jobs at a plant that had once employed 18,000. The plant was 'a beachhead for exports to Poland, the Czech Republic, the Ukraine and the Baltics', a company spokesman explained.[176] There was not even any reason to doubt it.

Unsurprisingly, business as usual, both public and private, has led to intense, though frequently conventional, public scrutiny. For the reporter in search of a story, the business lobbyist in search of a speech, or the government deputy in search of an argument, existing wages, hours, paid holidays, taxes, and benefits are irresistible. In a culture of proverbially knowledgable and conscientious civil servants with lifetime tenure and public pensions, eager to do what they are paid to do, regulation too can be an endlessly rewarding target. According to a recent study by the federal Economics Ministry itself, German officials take longer to authorize new plants than anyone else in Europe. Not only do they reserve seven months to do what the British and Belgians are officially supposed to do in four, and the French in six, in practice, they need up to twelve months to do what Belgian colleagues do in five months, British in seven and French in eight. Since regulatory mandates continue to proliferate, things have also only got worse. In 1980, nearly two-thirds of applications were processed within six months, while only 9% took more than a year. In 1993, fewer than half made it within six months, but 21% took over a year.[177] In the process, time and money can become as interchangeable as mass and energy. According to Horst Teltschik, once Helmut Kohl's national security advisor and now one of Germany's rare lateral entries as a senior vice president of BMW, compliance with the multiple requirements of European and national, state and federal, economics, labor, transportation and environmental protection ministries, can then impose supplementary costs of DM50 million on an investment of DM 500 million. For obvious reasons, business is slower to acknowledge the direct, not to mention indirect, subsidies that are invested annually in such traditional sectors as coal, agriculture and ship-building and might be regarded as the industrial equivalent of welfare. But for reasons no less obvious, they regularly engage the attention of external observers like the OECD. Despite a recent court ruling invalidating the 'coal penny', an established surcharge on fuel bills, coal alone is assured its annual boost of DM7 billion from general revenues through the end of the century.[178]

Yet entrepreneurial inertia too has held the future hostage. Young German managers are not outstandingly keen to travel, nor does a foreign tour necessarily promise rewards. In 1991, barely a third of German executives had worked abroad.[179] Of these, only one in eleven had worked in Japan, although Germans understand as well as most that Japan is one of the places where the future happens. For years, the physicist Hans Joachim Queisser, who happens to know Japan quite well, has regularly pointed out to any who will listen that there are more people engaged in semiconductor research in the publicly supported research institutes than all of German industry. Why is it that Germans, who are so good at liquid crystal research, are so bad at liquid crystal products? Because, says Roland Diehl of the Fraunhofer institute for solid state physics in Freiburg, they already surrendered the market to the Japanese, and business itself is unwilling to pay what it takes to catch up.[180]

But more is at stake than money. Compared, for instance, with the United States or even Britain, East Asia is a modest item on the German academic menu. Business is minimally involved in support for Asian studies. The academy, in turn, is minimally interested in business. The message that well-integrated immigrant communities are a business asset, self-evident in America and even Britain, has not yet even dawned on Germans. It is as unlikely as subliminal porno from a government that sees immigrants as a threat, problem, obligation and burden, but only rarely and discreetly as an opportunity. With vocational education as their nominal comparative advantage, state-level economics ministers, who regularly show up in Tokyo to sell the Japanese on the idea of building plants in Germany, try instead to compete with well-trained labor. But, as Queisser notes, they invariably lose out to Britain, where wages are lower, the language is more familiar, and Oxford and Cambridge enjoy reputations German universities have long lost.[181]

The alternative is industry policy as practiced in Dresden, where Siemens, the state of Saxony and the Federal Republic recently unveiled a microchip plant, intended to employ 1200 directly, and perhaps as many as 3000 as suppliers. Both the distribution of costs and the deployment of riot police at the cornerstone-laying said significant things about the current realities of German business in general, east German business in particular. Of DM2.7 billion invested in the plant, DM1 billion was public. Police were preemptively deployed to discourage demonstrators, who were assembled to protest the sacrifice of several thousand trees on the site of the new plant.[182]

Meanwhile, human infrastructure too is shifting. Declining numbers of applicants, apprenticeships, and contracted apprentices, even a potential teacher deficit, already point to the long shadow of demography. Measured from 1986, the apprentice market has declined by up to a third, with supply up to 10% ahead of demand. Meanwhile, 19% of current teachers are scheduled to retire by the end of the decade, and as many as 60% by 2010.[183]

AND YET IT MOVES

Yet even in the seemingly ptolemaic universe of the German status quo, it is hard to overlook the motion, though movement is invariably slow and frequently costly. Well-traveled, well-educated, articulate, even enthusiastic in ways the visitor rarely encounters in Bonn, business leaders in Düsseldorf, Stuttgart, Frankfurt or Munich are hardly impervious to the world around them. According to a 1993 survey by the Dortmund Chamber of Commerce, almost 60% of the producers of capital goods in their own heavily industrial area planned foreign investments. About 13% were already producing abroad. Another 30% intended to begin or increase an existing commitment by 1995. Industry's choices of venue divided evenly: half EU-Europe, just under half in Eastern Europe. By 62.5%, wholesale businesses were especially interested in Eastern Europe. In 1994, German firms spent DM 13 billion acquiring 128 foreign firms, while Americans spent DM 23 billion on 396 firms in Europe.[184]

Under the circumstances, the much discussed ambivalences of national identity are a potential asset. The erosion of historic national identities is an obvious challenge and trauma for French and British Europeans. Their exemplary versions of national statehood set European, then global, standards that Germans tried both vainly and disastrously to match. But the Hanseatic, Schmalkaldic, Holy Roman legacies have very different implications in an age of E-mail and post-nationalism. Germans have often found it difficult to be Germans. But they have always found it fairly easy to be Bavarians, Saxons, Rhinelanders *et al.*, and frequently to be Europeans.

Each in its way, Volkswagen's choice of a Spanish president, Dresdner Bank's and Daimler–Benz's decisions to list themselves on the New York Stock Exchange, even Deutsche Telekom's decision to list itself in Frankfurt, suggest that German business can overcome historical gravity. Skeptics to the contrary,[185] Edzard Reuter has proven that even a firm as richly traditional as Daimler-Benz can merge cars, trains, planes and finance, think global and unconventional thoughts,[186] and turn a profit – though only at the cost of continued slashes in its work force, and increased production abroad, as he also made clear in a bleak farewell address.[187] Once confined to a circle of political professionals, news of the existence of Asia has reached the business community too – though also the inevitable malaise whenever the conversation turns to human rights.[188] Recent experience has shown that wage contracts can, in fact, be renegotiated.[189] Neither the unions nor small business are inevitable Luddites.[190] One paid holiday has actually almost vanished from the calendar.[191] Meanwhile, in a country that not only helped invent the idea of a tenured civil service, but wrote it into its constitution,[192] there was talk of cutting the public sector by 14,400 jobs – of circa 6.5 million – and containing pension costs by reducing the retirement age to 56 in all but senior categories, where it would fall from 63 to 62. There was even talk of liberalizing shop-hours to 10 p.m. on workdays and 6 p.m. on Saturdays – at least after current contracts lapse, with their provision for 55% overtime pay on Thursday nights. The retail trade union predictably feared the worst. But the government parties appeared favorable; even Ms Lilo Blunck, speaking for the SPD, indicated willingness to consider local option, and the public endorsed the idea by 60–40. In fact 30% of Germans declared their willingness to dispense with limits on shopping hours altogether.[193]

Like all such exercises, the *Standortdebatte* tells plenty about Germany and Germans, but rather less about economies, Germany's included. Basically hortatory and heavily political, its premise only makes sense in a world where trade is understood as a mercantile version of football. Can Germans compete in the international major leagues or first division? The probable answer is still yes. There are good reasons why the DM, like the yen, is quoted daily on the world's financial pages as a lingua franca of currency exchange; why German products continue to be bought and coveted, whether they come on wheels, in tubes or in barrels; why chambers of commerce around the world like to see German companies come to their neighborhoods, and the Bundesbank enjoys much of the awe and respect that were once accorded Prussian staff officers with red stripes on their trousers.

There are equally good reasons why the German economy on the threshold of the twenty-first century can hardly help but be very different from the German economy on the threshold of the twentieth. One is magnitude, a second self-image, the third the nature of the world's first genuinely global economy. Forty years after Hans Tilkowski and Horst Szymaniak[194] burned up the playing fields of the Ruhr, 'German' economy is about as meaningful as 'German' football team.

Once again, given the vagaries of political choice, where this will lead is thoroughly speculative, and no outcome is necessarily exclusive of any other. But big German companies, in many ways more international than ever, are likely to remain major players, while growing ever further from their German origins. German executives already insist that 'Made in Germany' will matter less and less. What will matter increasingly, they believe, is 'Made by us'. If this means research in Singapore, marketing in America, data-processing in Mexico, a growing number of non-German colleagues, and board meetings in English, they seem quite unconcerned by it.

Second, the German economy will progressively be seen as part of a European economy in much the way the Californian or Texan economy is seen as part of the American economy. So regarded, it might even be argued that the future has long begun, and that 70% or more of German exports already go to an internal market.

Third, cultural, geographical and historical gravitation promise that Berlin, and at least the southeast of the old East Germany, should enjoy life after Communism as the 'extended work bench', to use a metaphor in current favor, of a natural regional system. They will therefore do what they always did, i.e. provide goods, services and added value to Austrian, Czech, Slovak, Polish and Hungarian neighbors to the east and south. For demographic reasons alone, the outlook is quite different for the underdeveloped and underpopulated northeast of the old East Germany. But then again, it always was.

Fourth, a generation of new technology, plus a population of aging Germans, some rich, some poor, will have an unpredictable effect on both capital and labor markets. Whoever and whatever else, providers of financial, medical and social services, at least, stand to be among the beneficiaries. In a place ever more remote from smokestack industries, imperial fantasies and hard-faced men with student duelling scars, it is hard to imagine what it will be like, for instance, to be young, male and Turkish, Kurdish or Polish. But it could well be a pleasant enough place for Japanese tourists to visit, Chinese violinists to work and Filipina nurses' aides to live. They might even be able to buy fresh breakfast rolls on a Sunday morning or a banana after 6:30 p.m.

Notes

1. See Christian Joppke, *Mobilizing Againt Nuclear Energy* (Berkeley, Los Angeles and Oxford, 1993).
2. Haig Simonian, 'A Monumental Task', *Financial Times* (19 April 1995).
3. Peter Schneider, *Paarungen* (Berlin, 1992).
4. Harm G. Schröter, 'Ou en est la technologie allemande?', *Géopolitique* (Winter 1993–4), p. 56, Nathaniel C. Nash, 'Germany Shuns Biotechnology', *New York Times*, 21 December 1994.
5. See Caroline Southey and Daniel Green, 'Euro-MPs reject patents for genetic engineering', *Financial Times*, 2 March 1995, 'Bioetica, bocciata la direttiva europea', *Il Sole-24 Ore*, 2 March 1995; Dieter E. Zimmer, 'Freiheit oder Frevel', *Die Zeit*, 3 March 1995, 'Capitol Hill comes to Europe', *The Economist*, 15 April 1995.

6. See Nina Grunenberg, 'Die Diktatur des Zwecks', *Die Zeit*, 10 June 1994; Raimund Hasse and Bernhard Gill, 'Biotechnological Research in Germany, Problems of Political Regulation and Public Acceptance' in Uwe Schimank *et al.* (eds), *Coping with Trouble* (Frankfurt and New York, 1994); Franz Thoma, 'Warum Deutschland zurückgefallen ist' in Dagmar Deckstein (ed.), *Wovon wir künftig leben wollen* (Munich, 1994), p. 30.

7. 'Technology and Unemployment', *The Economist*, 11 February 1995.

8. 'Pluspunkte für den Computer', *Informationsdienst des Instituts der deutschen Wirtschaft*, 19 January 1995, p. 2.

9. *Wall Street Journal*, 10 April 1995, *The Economist*, 15 April 1995.

10. 'Markenbewusst in allen Sparten', *Informationsdienst des Instituts der deutschen Wirtschaft*, 8 December 1994, p. 8.

11. Werner Sombart, *Warum gibt es in den Vereinigten Staaten keinen Sozialismus* (Tübingen, 1906) (trans. *Why Is There No Socialism in the United States*, White Plains, NY, 1976).

12. See 'Go and stop', *Der Spiegel*, 22/1994, p. 99

13. See Article 87, paragraph 1, '. . . posts and telecommunications administration. . . shall be under the direct responsibility of the Federation and have their own organizational substructures'.

14. 'Angriff auf das Monopol,' *Der Spiegel*, 27 September 1993, p. 115.

15. See Dagmar Deckstein, 'Der Streit um kalte Limonade' *Süddeutsche Zeitung*, 9 June 1994, 'Streik gegen die Postreform', *Süddeutsche Zeitung*, 21 June 1994.

16. In 1993, federal law required that DM5 billion, i.e., 10% of current revenues, go straight to the treasury. Another DM1.5 billion was allocated to covering postal deficits, 'Angriff auf das Monopol', *Der Spiegel*, 27 September 1993.

17. 'Go and Stop', *Der Spiegel*, 22/1994, p. 99.

18. Survey on Telecommunications in Business, *Financial Times*, 15 June 1994. C.f. 'The Last One to Draw', *The Economist*, 13 August 1994, pp. 55–7.

19. Challenged in the summer of 1994 to find E-mail addresses, one Bundestag committee staffer for research and technology confidently consulted his file of thousands of business cards, and was able to find only one – in Japan at that. After touring the United States, he then notified his American visitor that he himself could soon be reached on line at a Bundestag address. A half year later, he confirmed the message – via the address of a Bundestag deputy, who had meanwhile subscribed privately to Compuserve. Estimated in summer 1994 at circa 500,000, the total number of German online subscribers was expected to grow to four million by 1998. Interview with Barthel Schölgens, Adenauer Foundation, 26 June 1994, 'Europe's PCs to the phone, please,' *Financial Times* 6 March 1995.

20. 80,000 km in 1994, and a million East German households by the end of 1995. 'Go und Stop', op. cit., p. 100.

21. Barthel Schölgens, 'Medienstandort Deutschland,' *Die Politische Meinung*, May 1994.

22. In July 1994, the Internet Society reported 2,044,401 American Internet hosts, 63% of the world total; 155,706 British and 149,193 German hosts each made up another 5%, and 72,409 Japanese hosts about 2%.
23. The relevant policy paper, known unofficially as the Bangemann report, was presented to the EU Council at its Corfu meeting in June 1994. See 'Europa und die globale Informationsgesellschaft, Empfehlungen für den Europäischen Rat,' Brussels, 26 May 1994.
24. See Nathaniel C. Nash, 'German Telephone Pie Is Just Too Big to Pass Up,' *New York Times*, 30 January 1995; 'Bertelsmann joins up for European online venture', Martin Dickson, 'We're trying to connect you. . .' *Financial Times*, 16 June 1994, *Financial Times*, 2 March 1995, Louise Kehoe and Paul Taylor, 'Europe's PCs to the Phone, Please,' *Financial Times*, 6 March 1995.
25. See 'Lieber gar nicht', *Der Spiegel*, 13 June 1994. Quentin Peel, 'Lean Eagle Fights a Fat Turkey', *Financial Times*, 6 July 1994. Plans for an interactive video system were stiil another example of Telecom's problems. In summer 1995, it was announced that plans to test the new system in 4500 households were stalled till the coming year. The legal and technical complexities of German federalism, reserving responsibility for broadcasting to the respective states, were cited as one obstacle. But critics also charged that the scheme was over-complicated, testing too many new technologies in too many cities. As might be imagined, money was still another bottleneck. In addition to network upgrades, the tests were expected to cost $58 million. But the EU, a major funding source, had not agreed on contract language for the projects (*Wall Street Journal*, 31 July 1995). Meanwhile, for a standard of comparison, the middle-sized, middle-western state of Iowa, with a population under 4% of Germany's, had installed a state-wide fiber-optic network, including an interactive video system, linking schools, state offices and public buildings in all of the state's 99 counties, for an aggregate cost of about $180 million. 'The Wiring of Iowa', *The Economist*, 15 July 1995.
26. 'Der Nationalstaat und die Volkswirtschaft' in Max Weber, *Landarbeiterfrage, Nationalstaat und Volkswirtschaftspolitik*, Vol. 2 (Tübingen, 1993). See Wolfgang Mommsen, *Max Weber and German Politics* (Chicago and London, 1984), pp. 35–40.
27. 'Politik als Beruf', (Tübingen, 1992). Adequately, if not ideally, translated in Hans Gerth and C. Wright Mills, *From Max Weber* (New York and Oxford, 1958).
28. Named for its sponsor, Henry Morgenthau Jr, who was President Franklin D. Roosevelt's secretary of the treasury. See Karl Hardach, *The Political Economy of Germany in the Twentieth Century* (Berkeley, Los Angeles and London, 1980), pp. 91–5.
29. Quoted by Hardach, *Political Economy of Germany* . . ., p. 95
30. See John H. Backer, *Winds of History* (New York, 1983), Ch. 4.
31. See David Schoenbaum, 'Ziehvater der D-Mark', *Die Zeit*, 22 June 1990, Jean Edward Smith, *Lucius D. Clay* (New York, 1990), pp. 481–85, Backer, *Winds of History*, pp. 225–7.

32. Asked to identify their outstanding virtues in 1952, 72% of Germans favored industriousness by an enormous margin; orderliness, the second choice, followed with 21%. Ten years later, industriousness was still in first place with 71%, followed a few years later by first traces of a slow decline. Scheuch, *Wie deutsch sind die Deutschen?*, p. 90.

33. Artikel 20 (1), 'Die Bundesrepublik Deutschland ist ein demokratischer und sozialer Bundesstaat.'

34. See John Gimbel, *Science, Technology and Reparations*, (Stanford, CA, 1990), passim.

35. Greek GNP growth of 9% and industrial production growth of 14.7%, Dutch export growth of 23.9% and Austrian capital formation growth of 16.9% were the respective runners-up. Quoted by Giersch *et al.*, *The Fading Miracle*, p. 98.

36. ibid., pp. 90–91

37. *Zahlen zur wirtschaftlichen Entwicklung der Bundesrepublik Deutschland*, Institut der deutschen Wirtschaft (Cologne, 1993), Table 42.

38. The new unions, in turn, allowed for comprehensive contracts, expedited mediation and minimized industrial disputes. See Hardach, *Political Economy of Germany* . . ., pp. 157–9.

39. See A. J. Nicholls, *Freedom with Responsibility* (Oxford, 1994), pp. 143 ff.

40. Mancur Olson, *The Rise and Decline of Nations* (New Haven and London, 1982), Ch. 4, especially pp. 79–82.

41. See Theodor Eschenburg, *Die Herrschaft der Verbände* (Stuttgart, 1955). Cf. Giersch *et al.*, *The Fading Miracle*, pp. 74 ff., pp. 112 ff., Volker Berghahn, *The Americanisation of West German Industry* (New York and Leamington Spa, 1986, Ch. 3).

42. See the careers, market success and number of dissertations inspired, e.g., by the novels of Wolfgang Köppen, Heinrich Böll, Günter Grass, Siegfried Lenz and Martin Walser, the essays of Hans Magnus Enzensberger, and the films of Wim Wenders, Werner Herzog, Margarethe von Trotta and Rainer Maria Fassbinder. The curious or interested reader, in search of a place to start, might begin with Böll's *Billard um Halb Zehn* (Cologne, 1959; *Billiards at Half-Past Nine*, New York, 1962), Grass's *Hundejahre* (Neuwied am Rhein 1963; *Dog Years*, New York, 1965) or Fassbinder's *Die Ehe der Maria Braun* (The Marriage of Maria Braun) of 1978.

43. Between 1950 and 1960, labor productivity increased by an average 7.3% per year, GNP by 8.2%. Giersch et al., *The Fading Miracle*, pp. 5–6. Cf. Kramer, *The West German Economy, 1945–1955*, pp. 195 ff.

44. Ibid., pp. 110–16.

45. The slogan of choice, '*Freie Bahn dem freien Bürger*' (roughly 'Open roads for the emancipated citizen'), effectively links unlimited speed with life, liberty and the pursuit of happiness. Yet Germans also accept the quasi-monopoly of commercial driving schools, whose certification is required for a license. With private instruction, e.g., by a family member disallowed, school instruction virtually unknown, and Bundeswehr instruction only available to males, driver school fees are accordingly inflexible, high and discriminatory.

46. In 1950, oil constituted 4.4% of West German energy consumption. In 1970, oil constituted 55.2% of West German energy consumption – and total energy consumption had meanwhile almost tripled. Jean-Marie Martin, 'Energie, les incertitudes du long terme', in Le Gloannec, *L'Etat de l'Allemagne*, p. 321.

47. Between 1960 and 1973, jobs in agriculture and forestry declined by 45.7%, between 1973 and 1989 by another 47.9%, while jobs in energy and mining declined by 31.2% and 8.2% respectively over the same period. Meanwhile, employment in insurance and banking increased by 36.8% and 54.1%, in government at all levels by 60.8% and 26.7%. Giersch *et al.*, *The Fading Miracle*, p. 129.

48. For an overview, W. R. Smyser, *The Economy of United Germany* (New York, 1992), pp. 18–31. Cf. Giersch *et al.*, *The Fading Miracle*, Chs. 4–5.

49. Between 1980 and 1984, median German unemployment was 5.6%, compared with an OECD average of 7.4% and an EC average of 9%; between 1985 and 1988, median German unemployment rose to 6.5%, compared to an OECD average of 7.4% and an EC averge of 10.5%. Le Gloannec, *L'Etat de l'Allemagne*, p. 298.

50. Germans worked 1784 hours, Britons 1886, Americans 1963, Japanese 2278. Le Gloannec, *L'Etat de l'Allemagne*, p. 385.

51. *Zahlen zur wirtschaftlichen Entwicklung*, p. 155.

52. Quoted in David Goodhart, 'The Reshaping of the German Social Market', 194), p. 4.

53. Le Gloannec, *L'Etat de l'Allemagne*, p. 301.

54. Ibid., p. 159. Overall, educational spending of every kind, including adult education, universities and research support, constituted 4.2% of GNP in 1991, compared with 3.4% on the threshold of a publicly acknowledged 'educational catastrophe' in 1965, and 5.5% in 1975. *Zahlen zur wirtschaftlichen Entwicklung*, p. 134, *Education at a Glance, OECD Indicators* (Paris, 1993), p. 64.

55. *Zahlen zur wirtschaftlichen Entwicklung*, p. 154. An exceptional case, the state of Lower Saxony owns 20% of Volkswagen. The normal case are public utilities, or public deposits amounting to 50% of the total in publicly-owned financial institutions like the savings banks. Le Gloannec, *L'Etat de l'Allemagne*, pp. 305, 330.

56. Rémi Lallement, 'Une Economie organisée' in Le Gloannec, *L'Etat de l'Allemagne*, p. 328.

57. One warm admirer, the French economist-turned-insurance executive, Michel Albert, in fact, refers to it generically as 'Rhenish' capitalism, as opposed, that is, to the 'American' variety. See Michel Albert, *Capitalisme contre Capitalisme* (Paris, 1991; *Capitalism against Capitalism*, London, 1993).

58. An authentic historical figure, the shoemaker-poet Hans Sachs (1494–1576) is also the real hero of *Die Meistersinger* (1868), Richard Wagner's apotheosis of German liberalism. Sachs presides over a fair competition, making sure that the scene is open to innovation. But he also makes sure that the rules are observed, and that Walther, the gifted but undisciplined outsider, who eventually wins, is properly socialized in the process. Significantly, the opera ends with the chorus hailing not the

victorious Walther, but Sachs, the civic-spirited, quality-conscious and universally respected guild master.

59. In part, the system reflects and perpetuates archaic distinctions of legal and social status. Thus, for reasons going back before the Second Empire, there are discrete and independent pension systems for civil servants, white-collar employees, and others. But it also allows an element of choice, and even competition. Thus, for example, some 6.5 million self-employed beneficiaries and upper-bracket salary-earners insure their health privately, while another five million supplement their state-backed insurance with a private package. See Goodhart, 'The Reshaping', pp. 15–16. In contrast to 'single-payer' systems in Canada, Britain *et al.*, President Clinton's ill-fated health plan of 1993 consciously reflected many elements of the resolutely eclectic German model, with its mix of local, public, and private-sector elements. Yet ironically, it was not only attacked for its complexity, but for what its Republican adversaries claimed to see as an excess of big government and state interference.

60. The figures from 'Health Care in Germany' (Federal Ministry of Health, February 1994), p. 34 and *Zahlen zur wirtschaftlichen Entwicklung*, Tables 55 and 56.

61. Of course, they also eat real, i.e., fiber-rich, bread and still know how to walk, he adds. Interview with Dr Karl Furmaniak, Federal Ministry of Heath, Bonn, 20 June 1994. In 1994, Germans, in fact, ate 81 kg per capita (France 56, Britain 54) from a menu of some 400 different breads produced by German bakers. See 'Well-bread Germans', *The Economist*, 8 April 1995.

62. 'Die größten Ausgabenbrocken', *Süddeutsche Zeitung*, 7 June 1994.

63. And, of course, the United States. The American author first discovered the issue when looking for a dentist in Bonn to maintain his regular periodontal treatment. What impressed the author was that what was ordinarily done in Iowa City by an oral hygienist was being done in Bonn by a highly-qualified oral surgeon. What impressed the oral surgeon, who summoned his entire office staff to look, was that the patient, unlike large numbers of his German contemporaries, had a full set of his own teeth. Actually, as one critical panelist replied to Dr. Kastenbauer, the improved ratio of prophylactic treatment in Germany had less to do with a growing taste for prophylaxis than a 64% decline in the number of prosthetic treatments between 1985 and 1992, presumably due to increased resistance from insurance companies. 'Zahnmedizin heute – von der Prophylaxe bis zur Prothetik', *Süddeutsche Zeitung*, 27 June 1994.

64. See Paragraphs 20–2 of the Health Reform law (1988 version), which cover seminannual visits by 6-to-20-year-olds for caries prevention; group prophylaxis for school children; and 60% reimbursement for tooth replacement if patients can show that they had previously received prophylactic treatment, compared with 50% if they had not.

65. Thus Dr Carl Ernst Grummt, vice-president of the Bavarian Dental association. Grummt nonetheless lays the blame for the current impasse on the public, not the private, sector, and particularly on Social

Democratic parliamentarians, who insist that every contingency be covered, but also on political regulation of fees. Letter to author of 14 September 1994.

66. *Experience of Foreign Nations in Controlling Health Care Costs,'* Hearing before the Committee on Finance, United States Senate, 13 October 1994 (Washington, 1994), p. 171.

67. Albert, *Capitalism against Capitalism,* p. 122.

68. For one standard of comparison, German companies between 1970 and 1989 financed 67% of their investment from retained earnings, British companies 45%. Goodhart, 'The Reshaping', p. 19. For another, there were about 180 new stock issues in Britain in 1993 alone. Between 1984 and 1994, there were only about 200 in Germany. David Waller, 'Frankfurt's Role Consolidated,' German Banking and Finance supplement, *Financial Times,* 31 May 1994. See Andrew Fisher, 'Cracks around the Edges', *Financial Times,* 27 February 1995. Cf. Smyser, *The Economy of United Germany,* pp. 90–2.

69. 'Spar-Präferenzen', Informationsdienst des Instituts der deutschen Wirtschaft, November 1994, p. 1.

71. Steven Pearlstein, 'Fleet Afoot, Firms Restyle US Economy', *International Herald-Tribune,* 5 July 1994; 'Bounding Gazelles', *The Economist,* 28 May 1994.

70. Michael Lindemann and David Waller, 'Insider on the Outside', *Financial Times,* 29 July 1994. Cf. Sylvia Nasar, 'The Oil-Futures Bloodbath', *New York Times,* 16 October 1994, for an entertainingly unconventional post-mortem on Deutsche Bank's intervention in the market operations of Metallgesellschaft, a large industrial client, and the $1.3 billion loss that resulted.

72. See Jeremy Edwards and Klaus Fischer, *Banks, finance and Investment in Germany* (Cambridge, 1994), esp. pp. 228 ff and *OECD Wirtschaftsberichte Deutschland,* OECD, Paris 1995, pp. 152–5.

73. By 1994 the original codetermination model applied to about 30 companies, the revised model to circa 570, employing about 4.5 million. See Peter J. Katzenstein, *Policy and Politics in West Germany* (Philadelphia, 1987), Ch. 3; Smyser, *The Economy,* pp. 80–3; Berghahn, *The Americanisation,* op. cit., pp. 203–30; René Lasserre, 'Les différents modes de cogestion' in Le Gloannec, *L'Etat de l'Allemagne,* p. 349.

74. The nature and magnitude of the relationship between state and law can be inferred a) from the number of senior civil service positions – circa 1.6 million, including judges in 1990; b) the popularity of law as an academic major – third for men behind economics and mechanical engineering, fourth for women behind economics, German literature and medicine in 1990; and c) the link between law and public administration that requires law students to complete a two-year internship as a preliminary to their final bar examination. *Zahlen zur wirtschaftlichen Entwicklung,* Tables 83 and 131.

75. One Frankfurt law student, for example, acting on behalf of a so-called deterrence club (*Abmahnverein*) made a good thing of writing to travel bureaux for information on specials, then informing them by registered letter that they were subject to fine for quoting net ticket prices without

adding incidental transit and airport taxes as the law requires. He then collected a fee for his unsolicited services. Other groups in search of violators have sniffed out dealers who quoted horsepower instead of kilowatts, or quoted the diameter of computer diskettes in inches. 'Die Abmahner', *Der Stern*, 21/1994.

76. For broadcasting, see Kenneth Dyson, 'Regulatory Culture and Regulatory Change' in Kenneth Dyson (ed.), *The Politics of German Regulation* (Aldershot, 1992). For higher education, see Katzenstein, *Policy and Politics*, pp. 76–80. Cf. Goodhart, 'The Reshaping,' pp. 25–7.

77. While specifying the federal chancellor's authority for defining general policy, Article 65 of the German constitution also emphasizes the autonomy and accountability of federal ministers within their respective areas of responsibility.

78. Ruling on a fair-trade suit against the Deutsche Bundesbahn, the German rail system, which leases commercial space at Hamburg's main station, the federal High Court in Karlsruhe also declared that it was illegal to sell shirts or shoes as nominal travel necessities during evening hours or on Sundays (*German News*, 20 June and 24 August 1995). See Dyson, 'Theories of Regulation', pp. 14–18, and Gerhard Lembruch, 'The Institutional Framework of German Regulation' in Dyson (ed.), *The Politics of German Regulation*, 'The German model is a combination of targeted interests, comprising the co-determinative democracy of the factory floor, the negotiated contractual democracy of collective bargaining, and the consultative democracy of electoral politics.' Otto Jacobi, 'Tarifdemokratie – zur Zukunft der Arbeitsbeziehungen' in Warnfried Dettling (ed.), *Perspektiven für Deutschland* (Munich, 1994).

79. A practical example is Ruprecht Vondran, who recently retired to private life after representing the steel industry from 1986 to 1994 as a CDU deputy in Bonn. The long tradition of steel industry activism aside, Vondran defends the principle of direct political participation on grounds that his subsidized industry, while basically competitive, has nonetheless to operate in a highly-politicized and comprehensively subsidized global economy. But he concedes that his eight years in the Bundestag also taught him that amateurs like himself are only minimally effective in a parliament dominated by professional politicians. Interview with author, Düsseldorf, 9 August 1994.

80. Goodhart cites an auto parts maker in Lower Saxony who was thrown out of the local employers association in 1994 for making a special, extra-contractual deal with his 500 employees. Goodhart, 'The Remaking', p. 28.

80. Some 21,000 of them since 1990, though many are now subsumed in EU codes. Rémi Lallement, 'L'arme des normes techniques' in Le Gloannec, *L'Etat de l'Allemagne*, p. 339.

82. By comparison, Irish shops close at 5 p.m. and Danish at 5.30 p.m. On the other hand, French, Greek, Swedish and Spanish shops have no fixed closing time at all. Craig R. Whitney, 'Comfortable Germans Slow to Change', *New York Times*, 16 January 1995. That Germans look enviously at the Dutch, whose shops officially close at 6:30, but who recently allowed so-called evening shops to operate between 4 p.m. and

midnight, is a commentary on German restrictiveness, especially considering that the evening shops must be licensed, and the authorities allow only one per 15,000 residents. 'Holland käuft bis um Mitternacht', *Süddeutsche Zeitung*, 8 August 1994.

83. Daniel Benjamin and Tony Horwitz, 'Store Managers in US and Germany Reflect Big Gulf in Work Ethic', *Wall Street Journal Europe*, 14 July 1994.

84. 'Why should you need to go to a gas station to buy a banana?' one foreigner recently asked. 'Why should you have to lease a gas station to sell a banana?' was the answer. See 'Tankstellen nehmen Tante Emma die Wurst vom Brot', *Süddeutsche Zeitung*, 2 August 1994.

85. See Goodhart, 'The Reshaping', pp. 29–31; Albert, *Capitalism against Capitalism*, pp. 114–16.

86. For a passionate defense of the Uruguay round, a spirited assault on French protectionism, and a ringing declaration that – and why – 'Europe must not become a fortress', see Jean-Paul Picaper's interview with Hans Peter Stihl, president of the German Chamber of Industry and Commerce, *Géopolitique*, Winter 1993–4.

87. See 'Productivity in the Metalworking Industry' and 'Productivity in the Beer Industry', *Manufacturing Productivity* (McKinsey Global Institute, Washington, 1993).

88. Yet another ironic dimension of British leadership is Britain's attractiveness to Japanese investors. Of 728 European manufacturing firms with at least 10% Japanese ownership in 1994, 206 were in Britain, 121 in France, 106 in Germany, 64 in Spain, 52 in Italy. 'Japan kommt näher', *Informationsdienst des Instituts der deutschen Wirtschaft*, 1 September 1994, p. 1.

89. Lothar Julitz, 'In Deutschland bringen Dienstleistungen das Wachstum', *Frankfurter Allgemeine Zeitung*, 21 February 1995.

90. Anthony Hartley, 'O! What a Fall Was There', *The National Interest*, Spring 1994.

91. Quoted in *Bartlett's Familiar Quotations* (Boston and Toronto, 1980), p. 743.

92. See Peter J. Katzenstein, *Policy and Politics*, Chs 3 and 7; David Schoenbaum, 'Nazi Murders and German Politics', *Commentary*, June 1965.

93. Irony again, Thatcher, has nothing very good to say in her memoirs about the nominally conservative Kohl. But she expresses a grudging regard for his Social Democratic predecessor Helmut Schmidt, who, although a 'socialist', has a profound understanding of the international economy, and a deep respect for orthodox public finance. Margaret Thatcher, *The Downing Street Years* (New York, 1993), p. 83. See Katzenstein, *Policy and Politics*, p. 364.

94. For an exemplary examination of the inertial, even entropic tendencies of German parliamentary politics, see Rolf Zundel, *Das verarmte Parlament* (Munich, 1980).

95. 'Leistungen an die Mitglieder des Bundestages', *Zeitschrift für Parlamentsfragen*, 3/92.

96. See Marsh, *The Germans* (London, 1989), pp. 62–8, 79–80.

97. Half of the deputies in the Bundestag are directly elected from parliamentary constituencies. The other half are indirectly elected on statewide party lists. What this tends to mean for most politicians is that survival depends not on the constituency, but on the party, whose convention prepares and votes on the list.

98. For a briskly furious and frequently entertaining tour of the grassroots political landscape by social scientists turned local politicians turned social scientists, see Erwin K. und Ute Scheuch, *Cliquen, Klüngel und Karrieren* (Reinbek, 1992). The bellwether study, of course, remains Robert Michels, *Zur Soziologie des Parteiwesens in der modernen Demokratie* (Leipzig, 1911).

99. The one obvious exception to this might be the PDS, the successors to the East German Communists. Since it exists to represent constituents who are heavily dependent on the public sector, it might be said of the PDS that its economic and political goals approach identity.

100. An obvious example is the adversary relationship between states with coal mines and those with nuclear plants. The latter regularly threaten to cut subsidies amounting to DM 7–8 billion annually to an industry that employs some 120,000 miners. The latter regularly retaliate with threats of sanctions against plants that generate about a third of Germany's power.

100. According to a 1994 poll, 32% of Britons think of entrepreneurs, 32% think of plumbers, and 20% think of company directors as major contributors to society. But 44% of Americans and 60% of Germans see entrepreneurs, and 33% of Americans and 53% of Germans see company directors, as major contributors. 'The Unloved Entrepreneur', *The Economist*, 28 May 1994.

102. Hans Peter Stihl, 'Verweigerung ist ein schlechter Ratgeber', speech delivered at the opening of a conference on 'Initiative der deutschen Wirtschaft zur Verbesserung des Innovationsklimas', 13 May 1994.

103. Toqueville's classic *Democracy in America* is the definitive statement of the American case. Frederic Spotts and Theodor Wieser, *Italy: A Difficult Democracy* (Cambridge, 1986) and Robert D. Putnam, *Making Democracy Work* (Princeton, 1993), are recent statements of the Italian one.

104. For a practical example, not only did high-speed rail service like the French TGV or Italian Pendolino come late to Germany, but local opposition prevented it from stopping in Bonn, the West German capital. Bonn passengers must therefore change, e.g., in Frankfurt or Mannheim. In 1986, organized reservations about the efficacy of laws protecting privacy even caused cancellation of a national census.

105. With its big, entrepreneurial media houses, extensive infrastructure and at least 100 million native German speakers as potential consumers, Germany is made to be a media capital, says Barthel Schölgens of the Adenauer Foundation. At thge same time, while media titans, like Bertelsmann and Leo Kirch battle Disney, Time Warner, Rupert Murdoch et al. for satellite access in a combination gold rush and Star Trek, German federalism, with its considerable stake in the status quo and the respective states' own public channels, has frustrated consensus

in even such basic questions as the relationship of the new media to the existing ones, or who will produce, receive and pay for what when it eventually arrives, e.g., in Saxony or Hamburg. See 'Medienstandort Deutschland', 'There's nothing cooking here,' says Helmut Thoma of the commercial channel, RTL, in a recent interview. 'Who wants all that?' See Petra Pfaller, 'Wea wüh des ois?' *Süddeutsche Zeitung*, 6 June 1994. Detlef Essinger, 'Der neue Goldrausch', *Suddeutsche Zeitung*, 3 September, 1995.

106. See articles by Konrad Schily and Ulrich van Lith in *Wirtschaftsdienst*, May 1994.
107. In the mid 1980s, the author watched with interest as a grants officer of the Volkswagen Foundation appeared almost diffidently at a major historical conference, looking for researchers to take his money. Largely, and lavishly, endowed with public money, the party foundations are part collateral embassies, part collateral cultural institutes, part collateral aid and development agencies, and part service desks for their respective political sponsors.
108. See Peter Glotz, Rita Süssmuth and Konrad Seitz, *Die planlosen Eliten*, pp. 278 ff.; Kurt Biedenkopf, 'Deutschland als internationaler Wirtschaftsstandort', *Europa-Archiv*, 13–14/1994, pp. 411 ff.
109. Quoted in Zundel, *Das verarmte Parlament*, p. 77
110. For an example, see 'Kohl ist mir lieber', *Der Spiegel*, 13 May 1994, p. 18.
110. The German participants include the Alexander von Humboldt foundation, that brings foreign scientists and scholars to Germany; the Deutsche Forschungsgemeinschaft, that distributes grants, and the Max Planck Gesellschaft, that maintains research institutes; the American participants include the American Academy of Arts and Sciences, the American Council of Learned Societies, the National Academy of Sciences and the Social Science Research Council. Document: Establishment of the 'German-American Academic Council' foundation, Bonn, 19 January 1994. Interview with Dr Joseph Rembser, Bonn, 13 June 1994.
112. For both details and reaction, see *Süddeutsche Zeitung*, August 3–4, 1994. The failure did not surprise Warnfried Dettling, a former assistant secretary of Family Affairs in an earlier Kohl government. In the late 1980s, Dettling recalled, he had proposed a corps of auxiliary baby sitters to supervise preschool children in day care between noon and 1 p.m. while regular day care personnel went to lunch. He recalled that the idea had been trampled underfoot by the professionals who were its nominal beneficiaries, on grounds that it opened the door – and presumably job-access – to untrained personnel. Interview, 20 July 1994.
113. See W.R. Smyser, 'America's German Central Bank', *Washington Quarterly*, Spring 1994.
114. '. . . in the third year after the Central European revolution, Europeans in general, but Germans in particular, kid themselves understandably but dangerously about the world they live in. We celebrate the collapse of Communism; but have done nothing to contain the ethnic, economic

and social conflicts the revolution has brought with it. . . . We have not so much as tried to reach a Grand Design – not even one we can reform or reverse at any time. . . ' Peter Glotz *et al.*, *Die planlosen Eliten*, pp. 13–14. The authors are respectively a former general secretary of the Social Democratic party, a former Christian Democratic cabinet minister and speaker of the Bundestag, and a former director of the the foreign ministry planning staff, who later became ambassador to India and Italy. Cf. Marion Dönhoff *et al. Weil das Land sich ändern muss,* whose authors include an editor of *Die Zeit*, a former Social Democratic chancellor, two East German Bundestag deputies, a central banker, the president of a major corporation, and the director of a respected think tank.

115. Conventional wisdom to the contrary, even princely absolutism – of which Germans certainly had their share – was buffered and moderated by the endless particularisms of the Holy Roman Empire; Bismarck, who appealed to 'blood and iron', was compelled by both public opinion and de facto parliamentary majorities to only the most circumspect use of both, and William II's 'personal regime' was rather a testimonial to the weaknesses of the other constitutional actors than to the any inherently superior power of the crown. Only after the disaster of World War I did the philosopher Max Scheler identify 'an unprecedented yearning for leadership – so vast and powerful that it accepts even the wildest, windiest and craziest forms.' Glotz *et al.*, *Die planlosen Eliten*, p. 13. The consequences, including the experience of 1933–45, then created their own precedents, not only for restoration of traditional constraints, but a healthy complement of new ones.

116. See Miegel and Wahl, *Das Ende des Individualismus*, pp. 117–18.
117. Ibid., p. 119.
118. A conference of the 16 state-level German ministers of agriculture in March 1995 both personified and acted out the problem of accommodating Polish, Hungarian, Czech and Slovak farm products without swamping the EU's Common Agricultural Policy, not to mention domestic producers. West German farmers, they noted with concern, work 34 ha., while Czech co-ops work 5000 at lower wages. But there was no consensus on conversion of co-ops to private holdings. Western ministers favored marketing agreements. Eastern ministers, who inherited their own co-ops from their communist predecessors, favored 'a developing common market,' but contingent on unspecified structural reforms over an unspecified transitional period (*German News* online news service, 10 March 1995). Unsurprisingly, Hungary's deputy ministry of agriculture, Jenö Rednagel, complained that EU exports to Hungary had increased by 3 times since 1991, but Hungarian exports to the EU had declined by a third, and Hungarian production now comprised only 1% of the EU's strictly regulated farm imports. He was 'perplexed,' he added, by West European anxiety about being flooded with Hungarian produce (CET online news service, 7 April 1995). Only a few months later, a set of reports by Franz Fischler, the European Union (EU) Commissioner for Agriculture, confirmed that Rednagel's bafflement was, if anything, understated. Far from inundat-

ing Western Europe in hams and slivovitz, the studies found, the 10 post-communist states of Central and Eastern Europe were likely to take until the year 2000 just to reach their pre-1989 agricultural production levels. As their *per capita* income grew, while their farm productivity lagged, they would then become net importers, not exporters, of food and agricultural products, with Hungary, Bulgaria and Estonia as the only exceptions. On the face of it, Fischler's report looked like good news for West European farmers. Yet to post-Communist Central and Eastern Europeans, it must have looked like Catch-22. The report seemed to say that, if they became efficient farm exporters, this would jeopardize their EU application by threatening beneficiaries of the proverbially extravagant agrarian status quo. On the other hand, if their farm sector lagged and stagnated, as seemed probable, this would jeopardize their EU application too. Who in Western Europe wanted to take on another 10 poor cousins and long-term welfare clients? see Caroline Southey, 'East Europe faces painful road to heart of Union', *Financial Times*, 26 July 1995.

119. It would be hard to find a better index of how Europe has changed since World War II than the French decision to leave Poland and the Czech Republic to the Poles, Czechs and Germans. Since 1989, 36.2% of all foreign investment in the Czech Republic has been German, 21.2% American, only 11.7% French. Of new investment in 1994, the German share was 48%, the Austrian and French shares 9% respectively, and the American 4.5%. Volkswagen had meanwhile acquired a majority holding in Skoda, the giant Czech auto company (CET online news service, 13 March and 18 April 1995). See 'Westeuropa endet in Polen', interview with Kurt Biedenkopf, *Der Spiegel*, 4 July 1994.

120. On the other hand, the Japanese case is even more spectacular. Between March 1993 and January 1995, German foreign exchange reserves increased by $8 billion, Japanese reserves by $53 billion. 'Currency Tempests', *Financial Times*, 11 March 1995.

121. For another perspective on what the authors of a recent study call the 'pension time bomb', one need only look at the ratio of people over 65, of retirement age or older, to people between 15 and 64, i.e., of traditional working age. All things being equal, according to a 1995 report of the Federal Trust, the 1990 EU average of 21.4% will rise to 42.8% by 2040. But the 1990 German average of 23.7% will rise to 47.1%, exceeded only by Italy's 48.4%, and the Netherlands' 48.5%. Samuel Brittan, 'Defusing Pension Time Bomb', *Financial Times*, 16 March 1995.

122. Viz. Jean-Paul Picaper, 'L'Allemagne en quête de son identité', *Géopolitique*, Winter 1993–4, pp. 98 ff.

123. Michael Lindemann, 'East Germany's jobs upheaval', *Financial Times*, 20 July 1995.

124. Fred Klinger, 'Aufbau und Erneuerung: Über die institutionellen Bedingungen der Standortentwicklung in Deutschland', *Aus Politik und Zeitgeschichte*, B 17/94, 29 April 1994.

125. For a thoughtful, balanced and very French discussion, see Emmanuel Devaud, 'Perspectives fin de siecle', *Géopolitique*, Winter 1993–4. For the

British equivalent, cf. 'Model Vision: A Survey of Germany', *The Economist*, 21 May 1994.

126. See Peter Paret, *Yorck and the Era of Prussian Reform* (Princeton, 1966), Chs 4–6.

127. David Marsh, 'The costs of competing', *Financial Times*, 6 March 1995, 'Herr Lazarus', *The Economist*, 18 March 1995.

128. Measured against UK = 100, German unit labor costs were 128.8, French 114, Japanese 113, Canadian 99.7, Italian 93.2, American 83.3. Samuel Brittan, 'Three Big Cheers for no "Beef"', *Financial Times*, 26 May 1994.

129. If Germans are losing their edge, as they themselves so regularly complain, how is it that the DM keeps going up, Hans Tietmeyer, the president of the Bundesbank, was asked at a briefing session for American journalists in March 1995? 'In the kingdom of the blind, the one-eyed man is king,' Tietmeyer replied. Cf. 'Herr Lazarus', *The Economist*, 18 March 1995.

130. Since 1993, the west, accounting for circa 90% of German GNP, has grown at 2.5%, while the east, with growth rates of 8–10%. has led all other EU regions. David Marsh, 'The costs of competing'.

131. Interview with the author, 28 July 1994.

132. See Konrad Seitz, *Die japanisch–amerikanische Herausforderung* (Munich, 1991), passim.

133. Hence Kohl's simultaneous discovery of, and attention to, the inadequacies of German competitiveness, and his concern for accelerated European integration, according to a senior aide.

134. Giuseppe Tomasi di Lampedusa, *The Leopard* (New York, 1960), p. 40. The original – 'Se vogliamo che tutto rimanga come è, bisogna che tutto cambi', (If we want everything to remain as it is, everything will have to change) – is even more emphatic than the translation. See Giuseppe Tomasi di Lampedusa, *Il Gattopardo* (Milan, 1960), p. 42.

135. The expression is Kurt Biedenkopf's; see 'Deutschland als internationaler Wirtschaftsstandort', *Europa-Archiv*, 13–14, 1994, p. 409.

136. German Social Democrats had, in fact, been deeply ambivalent about nationhood from their earliest beginnings. Dedicated like all good Marxists to the proposition that the worker has no fatherland, and characterized as 'unpatriotic bums' by the emperor himself, they learned from World War I that their constituents felt otherwise. Rightwingers nonetheless charged with some success that Social Democratic dovishness had been a major contributor to German defeat. Determined after World War II to take and hold the patriotic high ground, they then pushed hard for national unification while the majority of the electorate moved westward toward NATO and European unity. What was new about Brandt's message – and also unique, as it later turned out – was its appeal to productive, democratic *West* Germans to regard Social Democrats as the natural representatives of a new and legitimate *West* German patriotism. See Erich Matthias, *Sozialdemokratie und Nation* (Stuttgart, 1952); Lewis J. Edinger, *Kurt Schumacher* (Stanford, 1965); Carola Stern, *Willy Brandt* (Reinbek, 1988); David Binder, *The Other German* (Washington, 1975).

137. Le Gloannec, *L'Etat de'l'Allemagne*, p. 297, *The Economist*, 18 March 1995, p. 63.
138. *Financial Times*, 29 March 1995.
139. Le Gloannec, *L'Etat de l'Allemagne*, p. 314.
140. 'Europe's Most Respected Companies', *Financial Times*, 27 June 1994.
141. *Zahlen zur wirtschaftlichen Entwicklung*, Table 151.
142. *Education at a Glance*, p. 54 (see n. 54).
143. Le Gloannec, *L'Etat de l'Allemagne*, p. 313.
144. Harm G. Schröter, '*Ou en est la technologie allemande*', *Géopolitique*, *Winter 1993–4*, 'Herr Lazarus', *The Economist*, 18 March 1995.
145. Ibid., p. 298; German News, 6 March 1995.
146. Figures from *The Economist*, 1 April 1995, pp. 48, 89.
147. See 'Verkehrspolitik: die Programme der Parteien', *Informationsdienst des Instituts der deutschen Wirtschaft*, 6 October 1994, p. 6).
148. See Barthel Schölgens, 'Medienstandort Deutschland', *Die Politische Meinung*, May 1994.
149. *USA Today*, 7 March 1995.
150. In 1993 an estimated 43% of synthetic packaging material was recycled, three times the statutory quota. 'Suche nach der perfekten Lösung', *Informationsdienst des Instituts der deutschen Wirtschaft*, 15 December 1994, p. 8. See *Zahlen zur wirtschaftlichen Entwicklung*, Table 113. For comparative figures, Germans produced 333 kg of garbage per capita in 1990, Japanese 411, Americans 721. Thomas Fröhlich, 'Umweltschutz: Jobkiller oder Standortvorteil', in Deckstein (ed.), *Wovon wir künftig leben wollen*.
151. In 1990–91, Western houses and apartments averaged almost five rooms, almost two per occupant; eastern units under four with 1.68 rooms per occupant (*Zahlen zur wirtschaftlichen Entwicklung*, Table 110). In 1990, construction comprised 18.1%, in 1994 32.5% of East German production ('Die Dienste hinken noch hinterher', *Informationsdienst des Deutschen Wirtschaft*, 13 February 1995, pp. 4–5). From the same publication see 'Erste-Hilfe-Paket mit Nebenwirkungen', 6 October 1994, p. 8; 'Defizite beim Management-Know-how', 15 December 1994, p. 2; 'Eigenkapital als Dreh- und Angelpunkt', 12 January 1995, p. 8.
152. Ibid., Tables 112 and 115. Between 1987 and 1993, carbon dioxide emissions also went down by about 15% – but mostly, it appeared, because the East German economy collapsed, and with it the consumption of notoriously pollutant home-dug peat. With 31.3% of the total (Britain 19%, Italy 13.3%), Germany still led the European Union in absolute emission of carbon dioxide; and, with 11.3 tons, was second only to Luxemburg (31.9 tons per capita), in per capita emissions (*The Week in Germany*, 31 March 1995, pp. 5 and 8). On the other hand, the equivalent US figure was 19.53 tons per capita (*New York Times*, 11 April 1995).
153. *Education at a Glance*, pp. 117–18, 120 and 177.
154. Ibid., pp. 126–7.
155. 'Doppelqualifikation', *Informationsdienst des Instituts der deutschen Wirtschaft*, 2 February 1995, p. 2.

156. See Norbert Lammert, 'Wie sollte die Hochschulpolitik reformiert werden?' *Wirtschaftsdienst*, May 1994; Hansgerd Schulte, 'Les Universités allemandes entre l'Est et l'Ouest', *Géopolitique*, Winter 1993–94; *Der Spiegel*, 23 May 1994, p. 87.
157. Karl Otto Hondrich, 'Totenglocke im Elfenbeinturm', *Der Spiegel*, 7 February 1994.
158. But the figure subsumes incommensurates including a thirteenth year of schooling and, for males, up to two years of military or alternative service, that contribute to a calculated graduation age of 25, higher than any save Switzerland, where the equivalent figure is 26. For all other OECD countries, the theoretical graduation age is 21–23. *Education at a Glance*, pp. 179–80.
159. The equivalent figures are 15.3% for the United States, 25.7% for Japan, 25.7% for Britain. The OECD average was 22.5% Ibid., p. 182.
160. 'Collaboration at the Fraunhofer', *Financial Times*, 21 February 1995.
161. *Deutscher Delphi-Bericht zur Entwicklung von Wissenschaft und Technik*, Bundesministerium für Forschung und Technologie (Bonn, 1993), p. 149. See Schröter, 'Ou en est la technologie allemande?'.
162. *Deutscher Delphi-Bericht*, pp. xxvii, 357, 386, 416, 448, 480, 562.
163. The implicit problem of the figures is that they are somewhat incommensurate. Respondents in some countries were evidently allowed only one answer, among them Germans, whose responses add up to 101%. Respondents in other countries were evidently allowed multiple answers, among them Danes, whose responses therefore add up to 200%. If anything, the need to prioritize only emphasizes the salience of German concerns. Quoted by Scheuch, *Wie deutsch sind die Deutschen?*, p. 160.
164. For an example respectfully noted by Audi and BMW, which buy its products, Peguform, a Bavarian auto parts supplier with 800 employees, estimates annual savings of DM1 million on an annual turnover of DM200 million by recycling solvents, containers, dehydrating sludges, etc. Jakob Augstein, 'Sammeln, verwerten – und dabei Millionen ersparen' in Deckstein (ed.), *Wovon wir künftig leben wollen*.
165. Schröter, 'Ou en est la technologie allemande', 'Lieferanten für den Umweltschutz,' *Süddeutsche Zeitung*, 27 June 1994, 'Forsche Schrittmacher,' *Der Spiegel*, 27 June 1994, pp. 82–4. C.f. Volker Wörl, 'Der Umweltschutz: ein Riesenwachstumsmarkt' in Deckstein (ed.), *Wovon wir künftig leben wollen*, German News, 13 September 1994.
166. *Growth, Competitiveness, Unemployment: The Challenges and Ways Forward into the 21st Century* (Brussels and Luxembourg, 1994).
167. Petra Münster, 'Wasch mir den Pelz, aber. . . ,' *EGmagazin*, Nos 1–2, 1994.
168. Eurostat and OECD figures, quoted in Münster, 'Wasch mir'.
169. By comparison, projected British debt was 52.4%, French 53.4%, Austrian 59.9%. Luxembourgeois debt at 9.8% was obviously in a class by itself. But so, in quite different ways, were Sweden at 102.7%, Greece at 125.4%, Italy at 126.8% and Belgium at 138.7%. 'Ecusounder,' *The Economist*, 8 April 1995; *German News*, 30 August 1995, *The Economist*, 26 August 1995.

170. 'Mühsamer Weg aus dem Tal', *Informationsdienst des Instituts der deutschen Wirtschaft*, 23 December 1994, pp. 4–5, 'Noch Überangebot', 19 January 1995, p. 1.

171. Fred Klinger, 'Aufbau und Erneuerung', p. 172. Klaus Murmann, the president of the German Employers association, for example, anticipates a boom in eastern, and therefore central, Europe. But he also expects that it will take another 50–60 years. Interview, Cologne-Bonn airport, 28 June 1994.

173. Andrew Fisher 'Bundesbank criticises DM200 bn aid to east', *Financial Times*, 21 July 1995; Andrew Fisher, 'Banks' big adventure', *Financial Times*, 11 August 1995. See Jörg Rösler, 'Privatisation in East Germany – Experience with the Treuhand', *Europe-Asia Studies*, 3/94.

174. Interview with Ruprecht Vondran. It was only a further irony that EKO, East Germany's only steel plant, like Krakow's Nova Huta, was basically redundant from its construction, a monument to the Stalinist development after World War II that equated steel and socialism.

175. See Nathaniel C. Nash, 'Zeiss bears brunt of German Unity', *New York Times*, 8 November 1994.

176. Nathaniel C. Nash, 'Waking an old East German Giant', *New York Times*, 3 December 1994.

177. 'Beschleunigung in Sicht', *Informationsdienst des Instituts der deutschen Wirtschaft*, 2 February 1995, pp. 4–5.

178. 'Economie entre la politique et les media', Horst Teltschik, interview with Jean-Paul Picaper, *Géopolitique*, Winter 1993–4. See *OECD Wirtschaftsberichte Deutschland*, OECD, Paris 1995, p. 152.

179. Of German managers abroad, almost half had worked in Europe, 23% in North America, 17% in Africa and 14% in Latin America. Only then came Southeast Asia (10%) and Japan (9%) 'Auslandsmüde Manager', *Informationsdienst des Instituts der deutschen Wirtschaft*, 9 March 1995, p. 4.

180. 'Hoffnungslos zurückgefallen?', *Süddeutsche Zeitung*, 23 June 1994.

181. H.-J. Queisser, 'Brief aus Yokahama', *Physikalische Blätter*, 49 (1993), No. 5, p. 385.

182. 'Schon Ende 1995 Chips aus Dresden', *Suddeutsche Zeitung*, 7 June 1994. Horst Sandfort, a German vice president of the American chip-producer LSI Logic, questions the rationality of the investment, both as a job producer and downpayment on a European market share, especially after shutting down two European plants to move his own company's production to Japan and Southeast Asia. In Sandfort's view, chips, like oil, can be imported. He argues instead that the money would be better invested in the application of the chips to new manufacturing than trying to catch up with Americans, Koreans and Japanese ('Eine Art Glaubenskrieg', *Der Spiegel*, 11 July 1994).

183. 'Nachfrageorientiertes Angebot', and 'Der Unterricht ist gefährdet', *Informationsdienst des Instituts der Deutschen Wirtschaft*, 26 January 1995, pp. 2–4.

184. 'Nachwuchskräfte für das Auslandsgeschäft', in *Wirtschaft und Unterricht*, Institut der Deutschen Wirtschaft, Cologne, 16 February 1995.

185.   For an example, viz. Felix Spies, 'Ein Gigant auf tönernen Füssen' in Deckstein (ed.), *Wovon wir künftig leben wollen*.
186.   It would be hard to think of an example of less conventional corporate planning than Daimler–Benz's reported interest in acquiring and restoring Margaret Mitchell's Atlanta house in time for the 1996 Olympics. 'One of the reasons we got into this project is that we. . . are familiar with *Gone with the Wind*,' said Bernd Harling, the company's American PR officer. Jerry Schwartz, 'Margaret Mitchell's Atlanta Home Gets a Reprieve', *New York Times*, 18 December 1994.
187.   By the year 2000, Mercedes estimated, it would build up to 10% of its cars outside Germany, compared with 2% in 1995. Meanwhile, Lufthansa announced plans to shift accounting work to India and maintenance activities to Ireland. Christopher Parkes, '19,000 jobs to go as Daimler–Benz chief warns on costs rise,' *Financial Times*, 13 April 1995. Gillian Tett, Andrew Fisher and Andrew Hills, 'When strength is weakness', *Financial Times*, 9 August 1995. Symptomatically, the proud unveiling of the new Airbus A319 in late summer 1995 only barely drowned out a swelling chorus of anxious employees. Although Airbus had finally reached the promised land of profitable operation, its Dutch affiliate, Fokker, was a loser, and the company looked to DASA to fill the gap. The powerful mark and weak dollar only added to the problem of export competitiveness in a fiercely-competitive and export-dependent industry. Of 4400 DASA jobs in Bremen alone, half were believed at risk, and of 40,000 DASA jobs overall, 7500 of the, Airbus-related, 15,000 were expected to be gone by 1998 (*German News*, 23 and 24 August 1995).
188.   In 1982–3, at Teltschik's instigation, Kohl was the first German chancellor to visit China, Indonesia and Pakistan. In 1995, Indonesia was featured guest at the giant Hanover trade fair. Michael Lindemann, 'Germany begins Indonesia catch-up', *Financial Times*, 5 April 1995. Meanwhile, Osram, the world's second biggest lighting producer, has quintupled foreign sales since 1989–90, a consortium including BMW, Daimler–Benz, Siemens, Telekom, ABB and Lufthansa has announced plans for infrastructural development of the Chinese coast from Shanghai northward, and Daimler Benz plans substantial investments in Vietnam. In summer 1995, a single visit by a delegation including China's party secretary and head of state concluded with eight agreements, covering DM180 million in German development aid, and DM4.1 billion in contracts with German firms, about a third of the total with Daimler–Benz. The price to China included human rights reminders from Chancellor Helmut Kohl, Foreign Minister Klaus Kinkel and Federal President Roman Herzog, presentation of a list of names from Amnesty International, and a small pro-Tibet demonstration. *German News*, 13 July, 1995. See Andrew Baxter, 'Osram Switches Gaze to Far-flung Markets', *Financial Times*, 23 January 1995; 'Daimler–Benz will massiv in Vietnam investieren', *Süddeutsche Zeitung*, 6 July 1994; Victor Mallet, 'Siemens gains stake in Thai rail contract', *Financial Times*, 16–17 July 1994, Angelika Buchholz, 'Aufträge im Wert von fünf Milliarden Mark', *Süddeutsche Zeitung*, 7 July 1994.

189. See 'Es knirscht und knarzt,' *Der Spiegel*, 25 July 1994; 'Angst vorm Risiko,' *Der Spiegel*, 1 August 1994.

190. Both labor, in the person of Bertold Huber of the IG Metall, and management, in the persons of Edzard Reuter, the former president of Daimler-Benz, and Hans Ambos, vice president for corporate technology at German Aerospace (DASA) speak warmly, for example, of a new generation of railroad technology as a job, market, civic and political opportunity all at once (interviews, Frankfurt, 19 July 1994, Stuttgart, 1 July 1994, Munich, 21 July 1994). For a half-dozen examples of Fraunhofer-brokered rendezvous of microchip and machine tools, see Martin Urban, 'Zukunftschancen im High-Tech Bereich: eine Marktnische für den Mittelstand', in Deckstein (ed.), *Wovon wir künftig leben wollen.*

191. Despite appeals and protests from both Catholic and Protestant churches, all states but Saxony agreed in 1994 that 22 November, the traditional Prussian Protestant Prayer and Repentance day, would be sacrificed with effect from 1995 as a trade for employer contributions to the new home-nursing insurance system. In Saxony, where workers will continue to enjoy the holiday, they will also pay the full cost of home-nursing insurance.

192. Article 33, paragraphs 4 and 5, stipulates that 'the exercise of public authority as a permanent function shall, as a rule, be entrusted to members of the public service whose status service and loyalty are governed by public law,' and that 'Public service law shall be based on the traditional principles of the professional civil service.'

193. Judy Dempsey, 'Germany takes axe to the public sector', *Financial Times*, 15–16 April 1995. Andrew Fisher 'Longer German shop hours urged', *Financial Times*, 11 August 1995, *German News*, 11 and 19 August 1995; Nathaniel C. Nash, 'What's in Store for Retailers in German? Later Hours', *New York Times*, 12 August 1995.

194. Pillars of the great German national teams of the 1950s and 1960s, both were obvious descendants of an earlier generation of *Gastarbeiter.*

4   Revolution, East German-Style

When Valentine Kosch went out to demonstrate in Leipzig that chilly October evening in 1989, she thought she might be killed. If she did not return by 10 p.m., her husband was instructed to take the girls immediately to their grandmother in Dresden. There they could start a new life without the stigma of being known as children of an enemy of the German Democratic Republic.

Frau Kosch was a teacher. She admired the Montessori method – and had been dismissed from one school for not being strict enough with pupils. She was fed up with all the petty restrictions and was determined to change things so her 6-year-old and 3-year-old could lead more normal lives. She had been attending the regular Monday prayers for peace at the St Nicholas Protestant Church. She knew that the post-prayer processions that had begun two weeks before were getting dangerous. She had heard warnings that on October 9 there might be a 'Tiananmen' massacre in Leipzig as in Beijing four months earlier. She was scared. But something had snapped. She refused to go on living in fear, and she went out to demonstrate that evening, whatever might happen.[1]

When Socialist Unity (Communist) Party Politburo member Günter Schabowski heard about the regular prayer-and-demonstration night coming up in Leipzig on 9 October he didn't waste much thought on it at all. He was far less concerned about the idiosyncratic protesters who wanted to remain in the German Democratic Republic and reform it, far more concerned about the hemorrhage of able-bodied young East Germans who were fleeing to the West. More than 100,000 had already deserted the GDR since August via the newly opened Hungarian–Austrian border or – after the transit state of Czechoslovakia closed its border with Hungary – by squatting in the West German missions in East Berlin, Prague and Warsaw until GDR autocrat Erich Honecker let them go. A few days earlier the last train evacuating East German squatters from Prague had passed through Dresden on its way to West Germany. Some 10,000 East Germans gathered at the Dresden train station to try to board it too. Molotov cocktails were hurled; one police car was burned. The police used their truncheons freely and made multiple arrests. The 77-year-old Honecker denounced the scum and ingrates who were forsaking this best of all possible worlds. His *Stasi* secret police chief Erich Mielke castigated the 'dirtbags' who were abandoning the GDR under the influence of Western 'swine dogs'. The 82-year-old General Mielke put his men on 'full operational alert' prior to the 9 October demonstration in Leipzig, told them to carry weapons, and ordered them in a 'top urgent' telex to use 'all appropriate means' and take 'offensive measures to thwart and break up conspiratorial assembly'. The *Stasi* then disseminated rumors in Leipzig about staging a 'Tienanmen' to suppress the 'counter-revolution.'[2]

Schabowski had timidly suggested in a Politburo meeting a month earlier that the leaders should say something positive about freer travel and getting everyday consumer goods into shops. On October 8 he and Honecker's heir apparent, Egon Krenz, had drafted, equally timidly, just such a statement to submit to the Politburo. Both Schabowski and Krenz were preoccupied with this maneuver at the heart of power in East Berlin; whatever might happen in Leipzig seemed remote.

When Dietrich Schröder reported to the local news desk of the *Märkische Oderzeitung* in Frankfurt on Oder that 9 October it was a workday like any other. He was, he enjoyed saying, a child of the GDR, born the year the Berlin Wall went up in 1961, 10 years old when Honecker first assumed power in 1971. He was wary of demonstrators and their demands and the 'anarchy' they might stir up; he was not sorry that protests had not spread from the south to his city, hard on the Polish border. He felt at home in the anti-fascist GDR with its socialist goals, the consummation of the best ideals of all previous centuries. He knew the society had faults, but he expected them to be corrected once the hardline East Germany adopted Soviet President Mikhail Gorbachev's sensible reforms. The GDR was his country, the plucky David to the West German Goliath.[3]

When Roland Wötzel, Leipzig's deputy party secretary, rushed to the house of conductor Kurt Masur that 9 October to draft an appeal for non-violence, he knew more than any of his co-signers about preparations for quelling the 'counter-revolution'. The city police chief had been phoning in situation reports to the East German interior minister every half hour, but was getting no new instructions about how to proceed. Mielke's harsh directives remained the order of the day.

Certainly Mielke had the power to stage a bloodbath. The 8000-strong security forces assembling in Leipzig had all necessary means of coercion. The *Stasi* had routed demonstrators in a half dozen cities over the weekend and had updated their eerie plans for interning 13,000 in new concentration camps.[4] The Berlin Wall still stood. Yet on 9 October General Mielke too was puzzlingly silent. No one knew what he was thinking or planning. Wötzel's boss, Leipzig party First Secretary Helmut Hackenberg, couldn't reach Honecker during the day to get any operational guidance. He could get only to Honecker's heir apparent – and Egon Krenz, an opportunist who had risen as high as he had by never taking any chances, was not about to stick his neck out now.

Gradually, the awful truth dawned on Wötzel. In this supercentralized state in which provincial lieutenants had never been allowed (or wanted) to take any initiative, the omnipotent hierarchy above them was now abdicating, without even saying so. The Leipzig lieutenants were suddenly, totally, on their own. If they let the day's drift continue, a clash seemed inevitable. History and crowd psychology alike offer far more examples of a tense atmosphere exploding into violence than discharging itself harmlessly.

The sextet of Gewandhaus Orchestra conductor Masur, Wötzel, two other junior party secretaries, a theologian, and a cabaret actor therefore hammered together a last-minute entreaty for calm, and recorded it for broadcast. The three party secretaries then raced to party headquarters – and were reprimanded by Hackenberg for their *lèse majesté*.

As the prayers finished and demonstrators poured out of St Nicholas and three other churches shortly after 6 p.m., Hackenberg got Krenz on the phone one more time. It was zero hour. Frau Kosch and an unbelievable 70,000 marchers, seven times the previous Monday's record turnout, were already starting around the inner ring road that led right past *Stasi* headquarters. Yet Krenz again equivocated, saying only that he would have to consult his colleagues. Hackenberg hung up the telephone. 'A very, very long time passed,' Wötzel said, recalling the eternity of the next few minutes.[5] Then Hackenberg asked the trio, 'What do we do now?'

Under the circumstances it was marginally less risky to dare insubordination to sacrosanct standing orders than to dare violence. The junior secretaries urged Hackenberg to disengage the security forces. He did so.

'Democracy now or never!' 'We want reforms!' 'Out with the *Stasi*!' the demonstrators roared as they passed the train station unopposed, then the *Stasi* building itself. And again and again, 'We are the people!' At about 7.15 p.m. Krenz finally returned Hackenberg's call. By then it was all over. The hour-long march was finished. The demonstrators were already going home. Germany's first successful revolution in history was bloodless. The Leipzigers had summoned up a moral courage rare in German annals, and won their showdown.

A week later, Krenz and Schabowski would procure a majority vote in the Politburo to oust Honecker, the strongman of 18 years. A month later, the infamous Berlin Wall would fall. Within two months the autocrats in Bulgaria, Czechoslovakia and Romania would also be dethroned. A year later East and West Germany would unite. Ten months after that, 25,000 Muscovites would defy centuries of Russian political passivity, follow the Leipzig prototype, and thwart a hardline Soviet coup. Four months after that the Soviet Union would cease to exist.

And what have the Leipzigers, and the east Germans, gained from their extraordinary bloodless revolution?

Frau Kosch initially brought her enthusiasm and effervescence to the new city government. She thought highly of the mayor imported from the west. She engaged in social work, then got disillusioned by the shunting off of ethnic German immigrants from Russia to desolate barracks evacuated by the departing Russian army. She quit her job and, on her own, organized child care for the new preschoolers, bringing color and cookies to the barracks. Personally, she and her family are now being evicted from their downtown apartment, as the prewar owners from the west reclaim their property.

Herr Wötzel put his earlier legal training to use, attended some seminars in the very different West German system of justice, and went into law practice with a few colleagues. He still lives in his comfortable house in the northwestern residential section of Leipzig. He remains a convinced socialist – by this term he refers more to the old Communist than to Social Democratic precepts – and thinks that something just went inexplicably wrong with the way socialism was practiced in the GDR and the Soviet Union.

Herr Schabowski, by contrast, a stripling in the geriatric Politburo at age 60, broke with the past within a year of his being expelled from the party in December of 1989 – and was ostracized for his change of heart by other ex-officials in his new Berlin apartment house off Potsdamer Platz. The forty years had indeed been in vain, he thought; the open West German system was infinitely better than the claustrophobic one in the GDR. Schabowski now read for the first time some of the Marxist classics and their critics in undiluted form. He discovered Arthur Koestler – and Mario Puzo's *The Godfather*. He went to work for a small newspaper in Hesse in the west. As of this writing he was awaiting trial for the Politburo's permission to border guards to shoot and kill East Germans trying to escape to the West.

For his part, Herr Schröder was sad when his David was swallowed up by the West German Goliath in the unification of 3 October 1990:

'I was convinced that a chance had been forfeited to make a different country. I thought, now everything will be as it is in the FRG [Federal Republic of Germany]. I overheard one west German say to another [in east Berlin], 'We bought this land.' They had this feeling of victory. I had a sense of failure. It wasn't easy for me to deal with this; it took me a long time to get rid of this mood.'

One turning point came for Schröder shortly after unification when he spent a month training at a newspaper in Heilbronn in the west. He was unused to the competitive western 'elbow society' and was leery of it. But he made a discovery when he went to a two-hanky movie there and heard the audience cry just as much as viewers in Frankfurt on Oder would have. 'It sounds stupid now. But I found out that [west Germans] are just as emotional as we are.'

Schröder also experienced at first-hand, as the new editor of city coverage for the *Märkische Oderzeitung*, how civic life in Frankfurt quickened under the new system. He saw some friends succeed, some fail, in starting small businesses. He came to understand for the first time why it was important to have secret ballots, why it was essential for every official to know he could be voted out of power at the next election. Professionally, after a burst of 'too much freedom', in which the paper published virtually anything reporters brought in, he learned to insist on more factual, and less opinionated (or libelous) articles.

'I had a lot of luck with my work,' he comments. He had a steady job that was never threatened, and this job let him observe all the changes and think about them. In large part, he agrees with the school of thought that sees a generational dividing line in eastern Germany. He was 28 in 1989, and he thinks that 'those who were not yet 30 then managed to deal with everything. They were flexible enough to adjust. The real tragedy is, for example, my uncle. He was born in 1937. He knew Germany as a unified land. For him division was unnatural. When unification came, he thought, "Now I can finally use all my capabilities." But he was precisely the one who lost his job' and will probably never get another one. Even though he receives a decent pension, he feels useless. For people his age 'it is too late. For my generation, it isn't too late.'

By now Schröder has made his peace with the professionally more aggressive westerners. Like Schabowski, he is surprised by his own conclusion that the new system is vastly preferable to the old. Yet he is far from idealizing everything western. In particular, he finds missing in his own generation in the west the sense of family responsibility that east Germans take for granted. He himself is married (to a Russian) and has a child in gradeschool. Quite a few of his western colleagues are still sowing wild oats and just beginning to regret that they haven't settled down.

More broadly, Schröder finds the cliché that unification actually divided the 'Ossi' east Germans from the 'Wessi' west Germans greatly exaggerated. He has frequent contact with Russians because of his wife, and with Poles because he is now covering cross-border issues for his newspaper – and he finds that east–west German differences pale beside the differences between Germans and Slavs. 'When you talk with Poles about German-German relations, Poles don't understand why east Germans complain, when they are getting so much money from west Germans. . . .I see that the pillow we lie on is softer than it is elsewhere, but it doesn't satisfy us.'

The even softer pillow in the old Federal Republic also leaves west Germans unsatisfied, Schröder notes. Many of them still haven't been shaken out of the cozy complacency of two generations of ever rising, ever more luxurious living standards. They resent having to forfeit their second vacations and pay higher taxes to jack up their new compatriots. They are not prepared for the low-wage competition that is going to hit them when Poland and the other Central European countries fully join the EU single market. They may soon have to learn from their little-brother east Germans how to be less rigid and more flexible in adapting to a very new world.

Five years after unification, Schröder contends, the real dividing line is thus not between Ossis and Wessis, but between those who have made a go of the new system and those who haven't. And if that phenomenon is most conspicuous today among the Federal Republic's new eastern citizens, it will also become apparent among the old Wessis tomorrow.

'WHAT BELONGS TOGETHER . . .'

On the face of it, unification should have been easy. The Germans' grandparents and their grandparents had lived together in one country for three-quarters of a century before being split in 1945. By contrast to the British and French, they may have been a delayed nation, but long before they formed a single polity, they were a conscious cultural nation. Luther, Lessing, Goethe, even the exile Heine, they all had in common. They spoke the same language (more or less). Sociologically the east and west Germans were remarkably similar. The east might be Protestant, the Rhineland more Catholic, but the postwar mixing of Germans from all regions in the Federal Republic, as well as progressive secularization, had erased the old religious animosities. The only differences wrought by forty years of division, it seemed, were superficial political and economic ones that could easily be overcome. In 1990 the East Germans voted overwhelmingly for west German democracy, and Chancellor Kohl was not alone in thinking that the devastated eastern industry could be salvaged without western sacrifice, by simply dedicating each year's growth in the world's third largest economy to investment in the east. As Willy Brandt phrased it within hours of the opening of the Berlin Wall, 'What belongs together is now growing together.'[6]

Unfortunately, this happy vision was not to be. It turned out that the very frustration and lack of choice – in job, housing, vacation spot, and reading material – that had brought the East Germans onto the streets in 1989 was also a security blanket. The state had been the only employer (with minor exceptions) and made all the important decisions. The resulting standard of living might have been humble as compared with the cornucopia the East Germans saw every night on West German television, but at least there was less open crime in East Germany, rents were a few marks a month, and everybody had work. Moreover (according to the agenda-setting intellectuals in both East and West Germany, if not necessarily according to the man in the street), East Germans led less hectic lives and had more time for leisurely friendships. Life in the GDR was more placid, more 'German'. Theodor Fontane would still have felt at home in Mark Brandenburg. He would not have felt comfortable in the hurly-burly of Hamburg or Frankfurt.

What was certainly true was that ordinary east Germans thrust into the new western 'elbow society' found it bewildering and often threatening. Some 40% of the work-force lost their jobs in the first two years, even if this was disguised by extensive make-work projects. East German production fell 50% in eight months – an achievement it took the US three and a half years to effect in the Great Depression – then dropped still further, to hit a third of old levels before starting to grow again. And if infusions from Bonn meant that east German household consumption simultaneously rose by an incredible 9.7%,[7] this was small comfort to people like Schröder's uncle, who would never again feel needed – or to all the jobless Frau Kosches, as women's employment plummeted from the GDR's old 90% level toward West Germany's 40%-plus figure.[8]

Just the reverse malaise set in among western taxpayers. They had taken in their eastern cousins as a favor, but they didn't expect to have to change their own lives as a result. The burden was tolerable in 1991, as western firms went to full production lines to meet the pent-up consumer demand in the east. It was not tolerable by 1992, when Kohl's economic optimism turned out to have been misplaced, all of Europe went into its worst recession in half a century, and even west Germany started an 18-month decline. Clearly, west Germany's non-existent growth would not be sufficient to resurrect devastated east Germany; instead, east Germany would eat up 5.5% of west Germany's annual GDP,[9] for a bill of $100 billion a year for the entire decade. Taxes and deficits in the west would rise on the same curve as unemployment in the east.

With this double disillusionment, both Ossis and Wessis realized just how great a gulf remained between them. The best indigenous joke of 1990 had the poor-cousin Ossi proclaiming the demand for union of all those east German demonstrations, 'We are one people' – and the Wessi, hand on wallet, responding coolly, 'So are we.' The paradigm of one German people gave way to the paradigm of two incompatible Germans, lazy Ossis and arrogant Wessis. Some Ossis accused greedy west Germans of treating eastern Germany like a colony. Some Wessis accused the easterners of whining because they didn't attain instantaneously the standard of living the westerners had worked hard over forty years to build up. Psychiatric dissections of the differences abounded.[10] The Berlin Wall of concrete and reinforcing bars was replaced by the 'wall in the head'.

Along the way, of course, much transformation went utterly smoothly and was taken for granted. A variety of consumer goods flooded shops immediately; the easterners went on a binge of buying exotic western products, then eventually reverted to showing some loyalty to local, eastern goods. New roadbeds were laid for the entire railway system, and schedules for several years warned passengers to expect construction delays in the east.[11] New-old *Länder* were formed to break up the highly centralized GDR system, and new officials and civil servants were retrained at breakneck speed in the arcane arts of politeness and taking responsibility.[12] Deeds records were reestablished. Ministries and the Central Office for Political Education distributed millions of flyers explaining how to manage credit cards, how much insurance is sensible, how to get loans for renovating apartments. Baden-Württemberg lent droves of civil servants to Saxony; North Rhine–Westphalia did the same for Brandenburg; the west German court system skeletonized itself to send judges on two-year assignments to the east. Local police were recycled away from political control – and new recruits were trained – to learn criminal and riot control. They did not learn soon enough to prevent violence aimed at foreigners in Hoyerswerda and Rostock in 1991 and 1992, but they performed better from 1993 on.

Moreover, countless professionals attended seminars or made study trips to Detmold, Birmingham, or Lyons. Youth exchanges proliferated, so much so that by 1995 a fifth of a group of last-year students in the Plauen grammar school in Dresden would have spent some time in the US, Britain, or France as well as in western Germany (and this wider experience would create its own tensions in the balance of authority within families).

In an incredibly swift nine months, too, the Bundeswehr absorbed the National People's Army. That saga involved shrinking the inflated NVA officer corps, eradicating the nasty hazing of younger recruits, and inculcating *innere Führung,* or moral, democratic leadership, over mere hierarchical authority. It involved as well, *nolens volens,* advising puzzled local mayors about everything from pollution to pricing. And it included such civilities as introducing chairs to the soldiers' mess, installing showerheads in barracks (and replacing them every day as they got stolen) and, on request, donating a full field bakery on two dozen vehicles so that ethnic Germans from Kazakhstan resettled in Kaliningrad/Königsberg might earn some money producing bread for the region.

Along with the successes, there were several spectacular failures. Within months of union, chief West German unification negotiator Wolfgang Schäuble acknowledged two major mistakes in importing west Germany's convoluted legal system into east Germany overnight, and in subordinating indemnification to restitution of old property expropriated by the Soviet occupation or the GDR.[13] The legal system overwhelmed the less litigious easterners – and contests over property clogged the courts and would block investment for a decade, especially in city centers where west German former owners often competed with descendants of Holocaust victims. In some municipalities in and near Berlin, 50% to 80% of real estate is being contested. In one village, Schulzendorf, out of 5911 lots, 5463 have restitution claims, and of these 3763 have claims going back to Nazi expropriation of Jewish property. By mid-1993, 2.2 million claims had already been filed.[14]

The new political system too tended to overpower the easterners. None of the new eastern politicians became a major player in the first five years after unification. And despite the 93% turnout in the GDR's first free election in 1990, none of the major western parties found the right message in the next few years to attract a following in the east as strong as in the west. Membership and votes remained low, and the SPD couldn't even even find enough candidates for local elections in Brandenburg.[15] To the shock of the major western parties, the old East German Socialist Unity (Communist) party, renamed the Party of Democratic Socialism, would gain some 20% of eastern votes in the 1994 general election by an appeal to nostalgia and protest.[16]

Much of the vertiginous new world was exhilarating, at least for the young and the retired.[17] Much of the disorientation was excruciating, especially for those in what should have been their most productive years. East German psychiatrists reported increased disorders among their patients. Outmigration reached one million between 1989 and 1992. The birthrate plummeted in this period from 13.3 to 5.1 per thousand, a convulsion more severe than that in Nazi Germany as it approached unconditional surrender. Marriages dropped from 7.9 to 3.1 per thousand; mortality increased among children, teenagers, young adults, and middle aged – for rates 28% higher than equivalents in west Germany. And these 'historically unprecedented shocks', demographer Nicholas Eberstadt points out, occurred in a period when hope should have been on the rise, as average monthly wages and disposable household incomes both doubled, and goods and services were imported in volumes equal to the entire east German GDP.[18]

In this turmoil one organization quickly became the scapegoat for all grievances, the Treuhand Trust Agency, the world's largest holding company, charged with selling off 8000 firms employing four million people.

Beyond the sheer enormity of the task, the problem was that most of the enterprises were hopelessly inefficient and required major restructuring and slimming down to survive in the harsh world market they were now cast into. In the old days before 1989, the assumption had been that GDR productivity was perhaps two-thirds of Federal Republic levels. As western accountants and managers now inspected books and plants, however, they discovered that the real ratio was probably only a third. Moreover, there had been virtually no industrial investment in the GDR over the previous decade; the infrastructure of transport, communications, and housing was decaying; and environmental degradation would require clean-up on a scale unimagined even by the harshest anti-Communist critic.[19] As the *coup de grace*, the captive Soviet buyers of medium-quality machine tools that might have kept east German plants afloat vanished as the Soviet market collapsed along with the Soviet Union itself.

At first the hope was that West Germany's economic miracle of the 1950s would repeat itself naturally two generations later in the east, that short-term resource transfers would induce a rapid take-off. As the extent of devastation became more apparent, however, the Bonn government decided that gradualism and self-generated growth would be ineffectual and that only a 'Big Bang' could cope with the catastrophe.[20] It therefore ordered 'shock therapy', in that other widely used economists' image, that was far more radical even than what Poland was attempting. To the 40% of east Germans who lost their jobs and saw many of their enterprises disappear altogether, a third image came more readily to mind: slash and burn.

In retrospect, mainstream economists like Manfred Wegner, the first president of the new Institute for Economic Research in Halle, seem to agree that the Big Bang was the proper choice. Although it concentrated the pain, it got the misery over as fast as possible, rather than dragging it out over a decade or more. Treuhand had an enormous task, with no obvious guidelines. It had to proceed by trial and error, at breakneck speed, and it performed its job creditably, with remarkably little embezzlement and fraud along the way.[21]

Economists continue to quarrel about specific decisions, of course. Too many western transfers went into consumption rather than investment, some critics argue. Too much funding was drawn from bonds, too little from taxes, others contend. The artifically high exchange rate for currency replacement in 1990, everyone says, may have conferred purchasing power on East German consumers and averted an even larger migration to prosperous West Germany, but it exaggerated the east's already high production costs and killed off marginal firms. That phenomenon in turn 'deindustrialized' the east so western firms could monopolize the market there, some east Germans assert. On the contrary, tax benefits and Treuhand policy encouraged industry where it was not really competitive, some west Germans charge. Further disputes focused on the selection of mass welfare payments instead of across-the-board subsidies for jobs, on exclusion from restitution of lands expropriated by the Soviet occupation administration before establishment of the GDR,[22] and on the trade unions' insistence on jacking east German wages up to west German levels within four years, even though cheaper labor was the one advantage east Germany could offer investors.

Less cerebrally, east Germans who were being fired demonstrated regularly against Treuhand in the early years. So did the anarchist left in the west. Passions took an especially ugly turn with the assassination, still unsolved, of Treuhand's first president, Detlev Rohwedder.

His successor was Birgit Breuel, a tough Christian Democratic politician whom one admiring Social Democrat describes succinctly with the words, 'I would like to steal horses with that woman!' Under her firm direction Treuhand sold in its four and a half compressed years a total of 22,000 restaurants, shops, travel agencies, and other small and medium sized businesses (70% to east Germans), 43,200 hectares of farmland, 32,000 real estate properties,[23] and (to west Germans primarily) the 14,000 large firms that the original 8000 swelled to as Treuhand broke up giant conglomerates. From purchasers the Trust Agency received DM73 billion, plus guarantees of DM200 billion in investment and preservation of 1.5 million of the 3.5 million industrial jobs that had existed in 1989.[24] Treuhand liquidated 3600 additional enterprises. Contrary to original estimates that east German assets might bring in revenues of DM600 billion, the liabilities far outweighed the assets, for a deficit of close to DM300 billion.[25]

All this did not yet make growth in east Germany self- sustaining, and it still left purchasing power parities there at 35% of the EU average, or below Greece and Portugal. East Germany, with 20% of the country's population, produced only 9% of German GDP. Nonetheless, the economy did begin an upturn in 1992, based on construction, and is now showing 10% growth,[26] the highest of any region in Europe. Productivity rose to some 40% of west German levels. By mid-1993 east German average gross wages were over 70%, by 1994 84%, of west German levels.[27] Rents were 70% of west German levels in 1995, and consumed about 20% of average income, or less than the western 25% average.[28]

By 1995, east Germany climbed back to its output of 1989 and overtook Greece in standard of living. Yet it would take another 15–20 years to approach 70–80% of west German levels, Manfred Wegner thought, and perhaps another 30 years to modernize cities, housing, and the environment. Through the 1990s Germany would continue to be the net importer of capital it had abruptly become after West Germany had contributed up to DM270 billion to world savings in 1989.[29]

Overall, by the time Treuhand closed its doors at the end of 1994, west Germany had transferred DM525 billion (about $350 billion) to the east; that figure would rise to DM680 billion by the end of 1995. The transfers still accounted for 5.5% of west German GDP, 55% of east German GDP.[30] Unemployment in the east had bottomed out, and net jobs had started to grow, even though unit wages were still 140–150% more expensive than in west Germany.[31] Outmigration had stopped. Some 400,000 medium-size firms were operating. And east Germany was on its way to having the most modern telecommunications and lean-production plants in Europe by the turn of the millennium.

The social dislocation was immense. But special provisions softened the impact somewhat by, for example, postponing enforcement of evictions to the year 2000. Indeed, in the case of private dwellings, legislative revisions since the unification treaty have moved so far in the direction of protecting present inhabitants that fewer than half of the former owners – and only a third in Berlin – can expect to repossess their property.[32] Comprehensive social compensation also helped cushion the blow, with pensions and unemployment benefits supplemented by special payments such as the DM550 for former east German political prisoners for every month they spent in jail.

In the end this was no new 'economic miracle', as many had hoped in 1990. But nor had east Germany become a permanently underdeveloped Mezzogiorno, as some had feared.

Beside the central dispute about Treuhand, other east–west controversies in united Germany's first five years raged over *Vergangenheitsbewältigung* and the treatment of old secret-police files.

Vergangenheitsbewältigung, or coming to terms with the past, originally referred to the *Nazi* past and the efforts of post-1945 West Germans to probe and understand this deformation – or, on the contrary, to excuse it and cover it up. The subject of the Nazi past had not arisen in East Germany, since the GDR claimed the Communist heritage of resistance to the Nazis (conveniently ignoring the period of the Hitler–Stalin Pact) and insisted that all the ex-Nazis were in *West* Germany.

East Germany in fact did have its own share of hidden ex-Nazis, but it certainly was true that they were more numerous, and prominent, in the West. Many continued uninterrupted in their old careers there, especially in the courts, schools, medical practice, and business. West German founding father Konrad Adenauer, himself an exemplary opponent of Hitler, made a deliberate point of integrating former Nazi supporters into the political system in order to prevent a new outsiders' 'stab in the back' theory of the kind that festered after Germany's far less traumatic defeat in World War I. On his own staff Adenauer even retained Hans-Maria Globke, one of the drafters of the infamous Nuremberg race laws, until this fact became known and forced Globke's ouster. Adenauer's political calculation in not ostracizing ex-Nazis was only reinforced as the Cold War began and the Western occupation powers welcomed any German allies they could get against the new totalitarian state, no questions asked.

West Germany did prosecute Nazi concentration-camp administrators and guards in a major effort begun in the 1960s, and eventually convicted some 6500 out of 86,000 tried for crimes against humanity.[33] After an initial decade or so of embarrassed silence, it also did a serious job (with considerable local variation) of teaching the horrors of the Hitler era in the schools. One of the major accusations in the 'cultural revolution' of the '68 generation' of university students, however, was that their parents had done far too little to root out Nazi residues.[34] Partly because of the agenda-setting of this young generation in media and the arts in the two decades until the fall of the Berlin Wall, documentaries and features about criminal German passivity in the face of Hitler's atrocities became standard fare on television and in the press in the 1980s and 1990s.

Nonetheless, conspicuous holes in the country's old *Vergangenheitsbewältigung* remained: in the Federal Republic no judge was ever disqualified from serving on the bench for having sentenced political prisoners to death in the Nazi era; medical professional associations for decades avoided discussing responsibility for the grisly experiments doctors performed in concentration camps; deserters from Hitler's Wehrmacht have never been rehabilitated; and not until 1995 was Deutsche Bank willing, in sponsoring an unusually frank in-house history, to admit its own corporate role in the Nazi establishment.[35]

The issue of how to deal with the various crimes and cruelties of the GDR therefore had special resonance after unification. No one maintained that the GDR's inhumanity approached Hitler's monstrosity, but similar moral issues surfaced in finding the proper mix of punishment or integration of those who had collaborated with a repugnant régime.[36]

The basic split in west Germany followed left–right lines, with the old sides reversed. Those on the Right who had sought to bury questions of the Nazi past now tended to be the most zealous in insisting on holding GDR officials to account. Those on the Left who had charged that old Nazis were coddled tended to be the most eager to let bygones be bygones in east Germany and move on to cooperation.

Yet a new differentiation also appeared. In the early 1990s the west German left split acrimoniously over the issue of dealing with the 125-mile long shelves of *Stasi* documents. And in the early and mid-1990s the governing conservatives in Bonn joined the traditional new left in desiring social peace, in not wishing to prolong the days of retribution, either in treatment of the *Stasi* archives or in the later issue of declaring an amnesty against further trials of GDR officials.

Arguably, the debate about *Vergangenheitsbewältigung* was the one issue after unification itself in which ordinary easterners asserted their will. They might feel disoriented and overwhelmed in the realm of jobs and the economy, but they knew what they wanted in terms of personal justice. They demanded access to truth and to their own histories, with the right to see their dossiers and deduce who had informed on them in the *Stasi* system that had deformed so many lives. Whether they then sued their betrayers, divorced them, or forgave them was secondary; the main urge, after years of being treated as kindergartners by the East German state, was to make that choice themselves and not again submit passively to someone else's decision, this time Bonn's.

That, at least, was the kind of self-determination that Rostock pastor and human-rights activist Joachim Gauck advocated, and he was joined by one of Germany's best-known performers, Wolf Biermann. Biermann, a gifted and acid-tongued balladeer, had been the most famous East German intellectual expelled from the GDR in the 1970s. He had been one of the west German Left's stars ever since; and his vitriolic break with the orthodox Left – over the war in Iraq as well as over *Stasi* files – was sensational.[37]

The Bonn government yielded to the strength of eastern opinion on this issue and established the Commission for the Documents of the State Security Service of the Former German Democratic Republic – the 'Gauck Organization', as it instantly became known – with Pastor Gauck as its chief. It was authorized to vet candidates for public office or the civil service, including schoolteachers, to see if they had been among the half million secret *Stasi* informers. It further sorted and administered the unique comprehensive cache of secret-police files that *Stasi* officers never had time to burn or shred because of the speed with which citizens occupied regional secret-police headquarters in December of 1989.[38] Close to a million have applied to see their dossiers so far. And when the question resurfaced of ending public access in 1994, the easterners again protested vigorously.[39]

Less controversy, or at least less emotion, surrounded the legal *Vergangenheitsbewältigung* in the trials of former GDR officials. Border guards were the first to be tried in (west) Berlin courts, charged with firing specified shots that killed identified East Germans among the several hundred who died trying to flee to the West. The young men's defense also echoed the early post-Nazi era: We were just following orders. This excuse was not accepted, and several were sentenced, generally to jail terms that corresponded to the time they had already spent in prison on remand. The precise convictions for manslaughter varied somewhat, but were generally based on existing GDR law as amplified by the concept of 'proportionality' – that is, the judgment that violation of GDR prohibitions on crossing the barbed wire did not warrant mortal shots, even under that East German law. In addition, some convictions were based on international guarantees of human rights that East Berlin had signed.[40]

Once having established the legal liability for deaths at the wall, Berlin prosecutors went up the chain of command to those Politburo members who were on the National Defense Council that gave permission to shoot. Along the way, there were some bizarre detours. Erich Honecker was spirited out of the supposedly sovereign Germany by the Russians and given asylum in the Chilean Embassy in Moscow for months before he was pushed back to Berlin. He was subsequently released from trial for reasons of health, and died in Chile. Erich Mielke was first tried and convicted not for having administered the whole poisonous secret-police system for 32 years, but for having killed two policemen in pre-Nazi 1931. The overburdened prosecutors chose this route to keep the *Stasi* chief in jail while they prepared the real case against him – but the spectacle of a judgment on the basis of evidence compiled by Nazi courts was at best farcical. And Col. Gen. Markus 'Mischa' Wolf, suave East German spymaster and reputed model for John le Carré's fictional 'Karla', was sentenced to six years in jail for treason and bribery of officials. 'Treason against whom?' he demanded rhetorically and successfully appealed against his conviction.[41]

More recently, under a broader concept of culpable neglect, Politburo members who were not on the National Defense Council have also been indicted. The Politburo was the highest organ in the GDR, with state as well as party authority, the indictments charge; under the GDR's own laws it should have humanized the border regime. Günter Schabowski, for all of his newfound admiration for Arthur Koestler, now stands accused of responsibility in the killing of four and the attempting killing of two further East Germans who tried to flee west.[42] In addition, two East German judges who summarily sentenced political prisoners to death in Stalinist-era show trials have been tried and convicted in a way the comparable Nazi judges never were.[43]

BUILDING BLOCKS OF PLURALISM

Germans are thorough, and these trials and their appeals will go on for several years. There is no cut-off point for the courts comparable to the December 1994 deadline for the Treuhand Trust Agency. Yet both of these very public processes of the transitional period are already fading into history. In the realm of law an amnesty for GDR state crimes will be declared at some point, or the ordinary statute of limitations will come into force. In the world of work – apart from interminable property contests – more mundane concerns will take priority. Dietrich Schröder's and Valentine Kosch's generation is more interested in making new beginnings than in exacting retribution for the past. The concentrated high drama of Treuhand and of Politburo trials is now yielding to the tedious, diffuse, private building of all the intermediate networks that were denied the easterners in the centralized command economy and one-party state.

In this burgeoning pluralism, easterners will be disadvantaged, perhaps for another decade. They will lack the institutions as well as the life experience of westerners used to articulating interests in Germany's semi-corporatist democracy. They will only gradually learn the rules, the routes, and the fallback compromises that come instinctively to westerners. Their few high-profile politicians will be tokens; Environment Minister Angela Merkel will continue to be seen as wholly Kohl's creation, SPD Deputy Chairman Wolfgang Thierse as the figleaf to hide lingering Social Democratic distaste for unification, Premier Manfred Stolpe as Brandenburg's adored father figure who cannot rise any higher in politics because of his past dealings with the *Stasi* as a representative of the Protestant church in a very different era.

The next stage of intermediate institution building will be much harder to track than the first half decade of transition. The most one can do is to note some of the early failures, along with attempts by easterners to put these failures behind them and act more effectively in the future.

Certainly easterners, lacking capital, could not participate in purchasing east German industry, except in the odd buy-out by the old Communist managers. Moreover, the fledgling trade unions and business associations they formed in 1989 and 1990 were swamped within a year by the older and much more powerful west German organizations. Characteristically, the heads of the west German umbrella employers' and trade unions' associations met even before unification, in March 1990, and decided (with no easterners present) that they would transplant the existing western bargaining system east and preclude any reforms in the transfer. In the face of this joint action the stronger of the indigenous east German interest groups merged with, and were submerged in, their western counterparts. The weaker ones simply disappeared. The western associations of farmers and housing corporations subsumed eastern associations; trade unions and the associations of doctors and employers established dependent regional branches instead and exported westerners to run them.[44] The newly formed Independent Women's Association and clubs of the unemployed and handicapped, formed more on the model of the old minority protest culture than the new culture of focused lobbies, remained ineffectual.

In a very different field, young east German historians who had kept their distance from ideology in the GDR – and formed the Independent Union of Historians as soon as the system opened up in 1990 – found themselves similarly crowded out of academic posts. As old Marxist–Leninists were fired from university chairs and the east's greatly inflated faculty numbers were reduced, it was west German historians who flocked in to fill the bulk of the vacancies.[45] And even one east German mountain climbers' club complained that it was muscled out of its alpine hut in Tyrol by a (west) German Alpine Club.[46]

The repeated rebuffs in turn reinforced the inclination of many easterners to fall back into alienation and the kind of passivity that had kept them out of trouble in the old GDR. 'Societal transformation of the GDR became a project of external actors possessing superior skills and institutional privileges,' concludes Helmut Wiesenthal, head of the Transformation Process Study Group at Berlin's Max Planck Society.[47]

By 1994 Wiesenthal's study group did detect signs of greater differentiation from west Germany in new east German interest groups – and suggested that this might even modify, partially, the western system. A 'Federation of East German [employers'] Associations' has formed in Berlin and is challenging the branches of western employers' organizations. The same is true in Saxony, where the new federation won investment bonuses from the government for firms that existed in the area prior to 9 November 1989.

' . . . GROWING TOGETHER'

And how different does all this make Ossis and Wessis in the end? Very, says Elisabeth Noelle-Neumann of the Allensbach Institute, a frequent Christian Democratic pollster, and the dean of polling in Germany. Not very much, says Hans-Joachim Veen, director of polling at the Konrad-Adenauer-Stiftung, the Christian Democratic think tank.

Noelle-Neumann's judgment rests essentially on the self-judgment of Germans who answered the question: Do you agree that 'we are one people'? Back when the two Germanys merged, a majority of westerners (54%) and an even split of easterners (45%, with 10% undecided) thought so. By 1994 only a plurality of westerners (47%, as against 44% no's) and a minority of easterners (28%, as against 61% no's) thought so.[48] Contemporaneous EMNID surveys, by contrast, detected just the opposite trend. Easterners who identified themselves simply as Germans grew between 1992 and 1994 from 45% to 61%, it found, while the number who specified that they were east Germans dropped correspondingly, from 54% to 36%.[49]

When 20% of easterners subsequently cast their ballots for the ex-Communist PDS party in October 1994 in a combined nostalgia and protest vote, this seemed to many to confirm Noelle-Neumann's thesis of increasingly separate identities. Veen and co-author Carsten Zelle argue, however, that this transitional PDS support comes essentially from the old GDR cadres and intellectuals and that the PDS has no growth potential among younger voters.

Much more decisive than idealized recollections of a bygone era, they argue, are the easterners' and westerners' strikingly similar personal values and converging political priorities. Both esteem the Federal Republic's successful economy and democracy. And even in one policy area where there was great disparity at the beginning –

support for the North Atlantic Treaty Organization – the ongoing process has already narrowed the difference dramatically. In 1990 only 31% of easterners (as against 64% of westerners) thought that NATO was necessary to ensure peace. In two short years, however, appreciation of the trans-Atlantic alliance leaped to 57% in the east – and, in the wake of the war in ex-Yugoslavia, to an even higher 78% in the west.

The greatest differences remain in general political values, according to Veen, with westerners according freedom and rule of law the highest importance at 74% and 67% (easterners only 58% and 48%), and easterners considering social justice and equal treatment of women the highest virtues at 64% and 65% (westerners only 39% and 49%).

Nonetheless, Veen continues, these divergences do not make the two react differently in concrete political issues. Easterners, like westerners, are 'pragmatic, issue-, and problem-solving oriented', and the choices that are forced upon them are pushing the two together. Nor is it just a one-way street. The west has accommodated to eastern views (and to the harsh recession) in recent years in downgrading the environment from its top political priority to sixth place, below the same main concerns that easterners have always had about unemployment and social security. Veen is convinced that the current economic upswing, education, social modernization, and mobility will all complete the convergence of east and west. And as far as the question of 'one people' goes, Veen sees the future assured, since young east Germans in fact register higher in national consciousness (at 55%) than their cohort in the west (45%).

In Germany's southeastern corner of Saxony, Premier Kurt Biedenkopf – 'King Kurt' as he is known in deference both to the thousand-year history of Saxon sovereigns and to his own landslide re-election in 1994 – goes Veen one better. Not only does he think that east–west strains are greatly exaggerated by the media – and that traditional north–south differences are much more telling. He also proclaims that the easterners are the ones who are flexible, hard working, and innovative – and that sclerotic and complacent westerners should learn from them. 'The revolution must encompass all of Germany,' he likes to preach.

Biedenkopf praises the adaptability and energy of the easterners who plunged into responsible posts with no training and no precedents, and did an admirable job. The first Saxon *Landtag*, made up three-quarters of engineers and scientists from the professions least compromised in the Communist system – but also with the least public experience – had to pass swiftly 180 pieces of legislation to fill the legal vacuum. It had to levy equitable taxes in a region in which real taxes were unknown. It had to write its own constitution and did so, in a text that was passed unanimously by all parliamentarians except the ex-Communists.

Similarly, administrators had to trim the oversized GDR bureaucracy they inherited by 40% and drop half the featherbedded professors' positions – in addition to identifying and removing the old *Stasi* networks. Interior Minister Heinz Eggert, an easterner from Mecklenburg to the north, says that at the beginning he went to bed every night not knowing, fortunately, what he would face the next day. He had to implement the complex western legal system overnight. He had to find the best candidate to run the state *Verfassungsschutz*, the equivalent of the FBI – and appointed a woman to the job, a first in the Federal Republic. He had to retrain the undermanned police away from political control to riot control – and to preventive action that might avert more Hoyerswerdas. Along the way, he relieved the police of functions they traditionally performed (and grumbled about performing) in the west – like enforcing pub closing hours. And all these things he did like the other Saxons, with zest.

Unfortunately, in the end Ossi Eggert proved no more immune to the temptations of power than various Wessis before him. He resigned in mid-1995 after multiple allegations of homosexual harassment of subordinates in the ministry. Biedenkopf was unable to find an Ossi to replace him.

All in all, Biedenkopf and his team – with easterners initially as ministers of justice, environment, and science and the arts as well as of the interior – figured they had only five years to experiment before structures in the east would get as ossified and hard to change as structures in the west. In education they cut down on the interminable years many students in the west take to get university degrees – and developed the Technical University in Leipzig as a center for applied research of use to industry. In the secondary schools they kept the eastern 12-year system rather than importing the western 13-year scheme, and argued that the west too needs to streamline education if it wants to stay competitive in the twenty first century.[50]

Most of all, Biedenkopf – who has long since earned the honorary title of 'Wossi', or a Wessi whom the Ossis have accepted as one of their own – champions Saxony shamelessly. Back in the nineteenth century, he stresses, Saxony was Germany's industrialized heartland when today's high-tech Baden-Württemberg was still a cow pasture – and Saxony expects to return to its original role. Easterners were more optimistic about the future than westerners in the 1995 new year's surveys, he points out, and that too should teach the westerners something. And if part of all this hype is a calculated thumb-in-your-eye to the chancellor who hounded Biedenkopf out of Christian Democratic politics in Western Germany a decade ago, that certainly doesn't bother the Saxons.

How long will it take east and west to 'grow together,' as Willy Brandt prophesied?

A generation, think Valentine Kosch and Dietrich Schröder.

But no more than a generation, thinks Kurt Biedenkopf.

Notes

1. Interviews in 1993 and 1994.
2. Daniela Dahn and Fritz-Jochen Kopka, 'Und diese verdammte Ohn-macht,' *Report der unabhängigen Untersuchungskommission zu den Ereignissen vom 7–8. Oktober 1989 in Berlin* (Berlin, 1991), pp. 240–41; Neues Forum Leipzig, *Jetzt oder nie-Demokratie: Leipziger Herbst '89* (Leipzig, 1989), pp. 88, 92; Armin Mitter and Stefan Wolle (eds), *Ich liebe euch doch alle . . . Befehle und Lageberichte des MfS, January- November 1989* (East Berlin, 1990), pp. 113–38. Information about Schabowski from interviews with him in 1990 and 1992.
3. Interview, 13 March 1995.
4. See Lt., 'Die Stasi plante Internierungs- und Isolierungslager', *Frankfurter Allgemeine Zeitung*, 12 April 1995, p. 1.
5. Interviews in 1993 and 1994.
6. Willy Brandt, ' . . .was zusammengehört', *Reden zu Deutschland* (Bonn, 1990).
7. This rise was registered immediately and concretely in the widespread acquisition of new cars and consumer white goods. According to a Family Ministry poll, 46% of east German households said their standard of living had risen by late 1991; 15% said it had fallen. By summer of 1992 three- quarters of households had freezers, half had video recorders, and almost a fifth had computers. ('Umfrage über Lebensstandard ost-deutscher Familien', *Frankfurter Allgemeine Zeitung* (hereafter *FAZ*), 29 August 1992. Telephones would take longer. In 1990 there were only 12 phones per 100 inhabitants; it would take until the beginning of 1995 for this figure to rise to 34 and to a projected 1997 to reach the west German level of 51. (Stü., 'Telekom beschleunigt den Netzausbau in Ostdeutsch-land', *FAZ*, 10 February 1995; 'Drei Millionen neue Telefon-Anschlüsse', *FAZ*, 1 March 1995, p. 2.
8. See Organization for Economic Cooperation and Development, *Germany* (Paris: OECD, July 1992); and Irwin L. Collier, Jr, 'German

Economic Integration: The Case for Optimism', University of Houston, May 1992.

9. See Manfred Wegner, 'German Unification and Europe: A Zero-Sum Game?', *AICGS Seminar Papers 9* (Washington: American Institute for Contemporary German Studies, September 1994).

10. One of the first was Hans-Joachim Maaz, *Der Gefühlsstau: Ein Psychogramm der DDR* (Berlin: Argon, 1990).

11. See Hans-Jürgen Ewers, 'Aufbau der Verkehrsinfrastruktur in den neuen Bundesländern', *Beilage zum Parlament: Aus Politik und Zeitgeschichte* B 5/93, pp. 23–33.

12. See Klaus H. Götz, 'Rebuilding Public Administration in the New German Länder: Transfer and Differentiation', *West European Politics*, 6,4 (October 1993), pp. 447–69.

13. Interview. For an argument that challenges this conventional wisdom and says restitution would create more problems than it would solve, see David Southern, 'Restitution or Compensation: The Open Property Question', *German Politics*, 2,3 (December 1993), pp. 436–49.

14. Helmut Wiesenthal, 'East Germany as a Unique Case of Societal Transformation: Main Characteristics and Emergent Misconceptions', Max-Planck-Gesellschaft, Arbeitsgruppe Transformationsprozesse in den neuen Bundesländern 94/8. For a report on one legal contest for ownership in Leipzig, see 'Falsche Erben', *Der Spiegel*, 9 January 1995.

15. For one discussion of the striking failure of the SPD to recreate a robust party in what had once been its stronghold in the east, see Stephen J. Silvia, 'Left Behind: The Social Democratic Party in Eastern Germany', *West European Politics*, 16, 2 (April 1993), pp. 24–48.

16. For an analysis of the PDS vote, see Jürgen W. Falter and Markus Klein, 'Die Wähler der PDS bei der Bundestagswahl 1994' *Beilage zum Parlament: Aus Politik und Zeitgeschichte*, B 51– 52/94 (December 23, 1994). For an analysis mid-way between the two general elections the east Germans voted in, see Matthias Jung and Dieter Roth, 'Politische Einstellungen in Ost- und Westdeutschland seit der Bundestagswahl 1990', *Beilage zum Parlament: Aus Politik und Zeitgeschichte*, B 19/92, 1 May 1992, pp. 3–16.

17. In a casual conversation in a train in western Germany in 1991 one retired east German couple explained matter-of-factly how difficult their financial situation had become with increased rents and prices and how they had to grow their own vegetables to eat within their budget. When asked if it had been better in the old days, the wife, incredulous that anyone could ask such a question, responded 'Oh no! Because of the freedom!' Their frugal eating habits, it transpired, not only let them travel extensively throughout Germany on senior-citizen train tickets; a few months earlier they had even visited a relative in the United States for the first time in their lives.

18. See Nicholas Eberstadt, 'Demographic Shocks in Eastern Germany, 1989–93', *Europe–Asia Studies*, 46,3 (1994), pp. 519– 33. Other sources give outmigration of only 600,000, but add to that some 350,000 net commuters. Hans-Joachim Veen, director of research at the Konrad Adenauer Foundation, sees the drop in marriages and births not as a

shock, but as east German young people 'writing their own biographies for the first time'. They no longer automatically married their boyfriend or girlfriend at a certain age (younger than their west German counterparts) and had children right away, but took more time to travel and explore first the new worlds that had opened up to them.

19. Treuhand spent DM44 billion on clean-up of mines, nuclear plants and other polluters (Treuhandanstalt, p. 13). For one estimate of a DM100 billion bill for the clean-up of military sites alone, see hal., 'In Deutschland 240,000 belastete Flächen?' *FAZ*, 25 January 1995 p. 1. See also, e.g., Judy Dempsey, 'Big coalfield reclamation agreed', *Financial Times*, 7 December 1994, p. 6; and hal., 'Bund und Länder weiten Hilfe für die Altlastensanierung im Osten aus', *FAZ*, 21 December 1994, p. 11.

20. For an assessment of the east German economy as of the day of unification, see Leslie Lipschitz and Donogh McDonald (eds.), *German Unification: Economic Issues* (Washington: International Monetary Fund, December 1990). For a later evaluation, see Ullrich Heilemann and Reimut Jochimsen, *Christmas in July? The Political Economy of German Unification Reconsidered* (Washington: Brookings Occasional Paper, 1993).

21. See, for example, two studies by Manfred Wegner, 'German Unification and Europe: A Zero-Sum Game?', *AICGS Seminar Papers 9* (Washington: American Institute for Contemporary German Studies, September 1994); and 'Produktionsstandort Ostdeutschland. Zum Stand der Modernisierung und Erneuerung der Wirtschaft in den neuen Bundesländern', *Beilage zum Parlament: Aus Politik und Zeitgeschichte*, B 17/94 (April 29, 1994, pp. 14–23). One vigorous dissent to the mainstream view can be found in Jörg Rösler, 'Privatisation in Eastern Germany – Experience with the Treuhand', *Europe-Asia Studies* 46,3 (1994), pp. 404–517.

For an evaluation of Treuhand at midpoint, see Christian Watrin, 'Germany's Economic Unification Two Years Later', *AICGS Seminar Papers 4* (Washington, American Institute for Contemporary German Studies, January 1993). For an assessment by Treuhand's President Birgit Breuel as the Trust Agency closed shop, see her interview, 'Wer hört die Signale?', *Die Zeit*, 6 January 1995 (US edition), p. 4. For other appraisals, see the entire edition of *Beilage zum Parlament: Aus Politik und Zeitgeschichte* B43–44/94 (October 28, 1994); enn., 'Noch über Jahre Finanztransfers in den Osten', *FAZ*, 17 December 1994, p. 13; 'Abschied eines Buhmanns', *Der Spiegel*, 19 December 1994; enn., 'Aus einer Treuhand werden vier Gesellschaften und eine Anstalt', *FAZ*, 29 December 1994, p. 10; Judy Dempsey, 'The end of the sales', *Financial Times*, 30 December 1994, p. 12; Jl., '500 Milliarden DM im Osten investiert', *FAZ*, 19 January 1995; and the Deutsches Institut für Wirtschaftsforschung (DIW) Wochenbericht of January 19, 1995, 'Gesamtwirtschaftliche und unternehmerische Anpassungsfortschritte im Ostdeutschland'.

For the 1995 dispute about fraud and waste – which easterners interpreted as yet another anti-eastern attack by westerners – see, e.g.,

'Milliardengrab Aufschwung Ost', *Der Spiegel*, 13 February 1995, cover story; enn., 'Die neuen Länder wehren sich: öffenliche Mittel sinnvoll und zukunftsorientiert eingesetzt', *FAZ*, 15 February 1995; Jens Reich, 'Nun mal halblang', *Die Zeit*, 17 February 1995, p 1; ' "Schwachsinn in Potenz" ', *Der Spiegel*, 20 February 1995, pp. 18–21; and Ulrich Schäfer, 'Sag mir, wo die Milliarden sind', *Die Zeit*, 24 February 1995, p. 17.

22. The Bonn government, averse to reestablishing the old Junker estates in the east and evicting east German families that had been living on these lands for two generations, was happy to record that Moscow insisted on excluding its expropriations in the 'East zone' between 1945 and 1949 as a precondition for German union. This position was challenged in court by west German estate heirs, but was judicially sustained. See Klaus Krause, 'Enteignungsopfer der Kommunisten geben noch nicht auf', *FAZ*, 8 December 1994, p. 3; and Uwe Wesel, 'Halbe-halbe', *Die Zeit*, 10 February 1995, p 21.

23. See Wolfgang Vehse, 'Privatization German Style: A Look Inside the Practices and Policies of the Treuhandanstalt', a paper presented at the NATO economics colloquium, Brussels, June 29–July 1, 1994. Text distributed by NATO. See also the overviews in Deutsches Institut für Wirtschaftsforschung (DIW) and Institut für Weltwirtschaft an der Universität Kiel, with the Institut für Wirtschaftsforschung Halle, 'Gesamtwirtschaftliche und unternehmerische Anpassungsfortschritte in Ostdeutschland', 19 January 1995; and Michael Heise, 'Wirtschaftspolitik zur Verbesserung der Standortbedingungen in den neuen Bundesländern', *Beilage zum Parlament: Aus Politik und Zeitgeschichte* B 17/94 (April 29, 1994), pp. 24–30.

24. Treuhandanstalt, *Informationen* (final edition), 21 December 1994; Vehse. For a study of one sector, see 'Investment and Ownership in a Volatile Economy: Big Banks and the Case of the East German Economic Transition', *Politics and Society* 22,3 (September 1994), pp. 389–420.

25. See Wegner, 'German Unification and Europe . . .'

26. DIW, 'Wochenbericht 6/95', 9 February 1995.

27. See 'Die Tariflöhne im Osten erreichen 84 Prozent des Westniveaus', *FAZ*, 8 February 1995, p. 13; and 'Zum überleben zuviel', *Die Zeit*, 31 March 1995, p. 27.

28. DIW, 'Wochenbericht 8/95', 23 February 1995; 'Töpfer: Mieten im Osten sind tragbar', *FAZ*, 17 December 1994.

29. Wegner, *op. cit.*; enn., 'Noch über Jahre Finanztransfers in den Osten', *FAZ*, December 17, 1995.

30. Wegner, 'German Unification and Europe . . .'

31. According to Friedrich Bohl, Kohl's chief of staff, as reported in 'Drei Millionen neue Telefon-Anschlüsse', *FAZ*, 1 March 1995, p 2. See also DIW, 'Wochenbericht 4/95', 26 January 1995.

32. See Ralf Neubauer, 'Die Vertreibung findet nicht statt', *Die Zeit*, 17 March 1995, p. 32.

33. See Adalbert Rückerl, *The Investigation of Nazi Crimes 1945–1978* (Heidelberg, C. F. Müller, 1979); and Gerhard Werle and Thomas Wandres, *Auschwitz vor Gericht* (Munich: C. H. Beck, 1995).

34. One of the most famous accusations of the older generation was Alexander and Margarete Mitscherlich, *Die Unfähigkeit zu trauern* (Munich: Piper, 1967, 1991).
35. Lothar Gall, Gerald D. Feldman, Harold James, Carl-Ludwig Holtfrerich and Hans E. Büschgen, *Die Deutsche Bank 1870–1995* (Munich: C. H. Beck, 1995).
36. For two explorations of some of the issues, see Eckhard Jesse, ' "Vergangenheitsbewältigung" nach totalitärer Herrschaft in Deutschland', and Stephan Hilsberg, 'Vergangenheitsaufarbeitung als Bewährungsprobe der Demokratie', *German Studies Review, Special Issue: Totalitäre Herrschaft – totalitäres Erbe*, pp. 157–71 and 213–18 respectively.
37. See Joachim Gauck, *Die Stasi-Akten. Das unheimliche Erbe der DDR* (Reinbek: Rororo, 1991); Wolf Biermann, *Der Sturz des Dädalus oder Eizes für die Eingeborenen der Fidschi-Inseln über den IM Judas Ischariot und den Kuddelmuddel in Deutschland seit dem Goflkrieg* (Cologne: Kiepenheuer & Witsch, 1992); Biermann, 'Das Kaninchen frisst die Schlange', *Der Spiegel*, 2 March 1992, pp. 40–51; Biermann, ' "A la lanterne! à la lanterne!" ', *Der Spiegel*, 21 September 1992, pp. 81–92; Gauck, 'Das Erbe der Stasi-Akten', *German Studies Review* (Fall 1994), pp. 187–98.
38. For the account of one of these spontaneous citizen occupations of *Stasi* headquarters, see Untersuchungsausschuss der Stadt Greifswald, *Abschlussbericht* (Greifswald, 1990). No other equally complete secret-police archive has ever become available to outsiders. The much more gradual yielding of power by the Communist regimes in Poland and Hungary in 1989, for example, gave security forces there ample opportunity to destroy or falsify documents.
39. See, for example, afk, 'Vaatz kritisiert westdeutsche Politiker/Ostdeutsche Appelle gegen ein Ende der Vergangenheitsaufarbeitung', *FAZ* 31 October 1994, p. 7; Günther Gillessen, 'Vom Leben in Diktaturen/Joachim Gaucks Erfahrungen', *FAZ*, 7 November 1994, p. 16; Judy Dempsey, 'Stasi amnesty call hits raw nerve in unified Germany', *Financial Times*, 7 November 1994, p. 1; and lt., 'Diepgen will Stasi-überprüfungen einschränken', *FAZ*, 6 January 1995, p. 4; Vera Gaserow, 'Henry K. zieht jetzt einen Schlußstrich', *Die Zeit*, 24 February 1995, p. 17; Rita Süssmuth, 'Die Stasi-Akten müssen geöffnet bleiben', *Die Zeit*, 24 February 1995, p. 12; Sp., 'Erste Bilanz der Gauck-Behörde', *FAZ*, 25 February 1995; Johannes Leithäuser, 'Akteneinsicht statt blutiger Revolution', *FAZ*, 4 March 1995, p. 4; Sigrid Kneist, 'Stasi-Akten nicht schließen', *Tagesspiegel*, 12 March 1995, p. 9; Ws., 'Wieder mehr Anträge auf einsicht in die Stasi-Akten', *FAZ*, 21 March 1995, p. 5; and Richard Schröder, 'Laßt sie auf ihren Ladenhütern sitzen!', *FAZ*, 21 March 1995, p. 38.
40. For an account of the first high-level convictions, see Rainer Frenkel, 'Die DDR vor Gericht', *Die Zeit*, 21 January 1994, p. 40.
41. For consideration of some of the legal issues in the trials of the border guards and of Politbüro members, see Ralf Altenhof, 'Die Toten an Mauer und Stacheldraht', *Deutschland Archiv* 4 (April), 1992, pp. 430–32; Dieter Blumenwitz, 'Zur strafrechtlichen Verfolgung Erich Honeckers:

Staats- und völkerrechtliche Fragen', *Deutschland Archiv* 6 (June), 1992, pp. 567–79; Peter Jochen Winters, 'Was Erich Honecker den Deutschen politisch angetan hat, kann kein Strafgericht sühnen', *FAZ*, 31 July 1992, p. 3; Rainer Frenkel, '. . . getötet zu haben, ohne Mörder zu sein?', *Die Zeit*, July 31, 1992, p. 3: Hans Schüler, 'Die Schuld der Gesellen', *Die Zeit*, 31 July 1992, p. 3; and Rudolf Augstein, 'Ein politischer Prozess', *Der Spiegel*, 3 August 1992, p. 22.

42. See Ws., 'Sieben ehemalige Mitglieder des Politbüros angeklagt', *FAZ*, 15 March 1995.

43. For criticism of this asymmetry, see Rolf Lamprecht, 'Ungleiches Recht', *Der Spiegel*, 3 April 1995, p. 33. The two convictions may not hold up on appeal, since the Berlin district court that gave the rulings explicitly contested the much more reserved opinion of the federal appeals court. The district court accepted evidence of political intervention in GDR courts by the Politburo as adequate proof of a judge's perversion of justice. The appeals court, on the contrary, interpreted the unification treaty's provision that existing GDR law shall be the measure for any acts committed in the GDR to mean that individual arbitrariness must be proven. See Peter Jochen Winters, 'Wo beginnt die Rechtsbeugung?', *FAZ*, 1 April 1995, p. 10.

44. See Jan Wielgohs and Helmut Wiesenthal, 'Konkurrenz – Ignoranz – Kooperation: Interaktionsmuster west- und ostdeutscher Akteure beim Aufbau von Interessenverbänden', Arbeitspapier 94/9; Michael Brie, 'Die Ostdeutschen auf dem Wege vom 'armen Bruder' zum organiseirten Minderheit?' Arbeitspapier 94/4; and other working papers issued by the Arbeitsgruppe Transformationsprozesse in den neuen Bundesländern in the Max-Planck-Gesellschaft.

45. See Ulrich Mählert, 'Nur falsche Wege im Labyrinth', in the *Süddeutsche Zeitung*, 1 April 1995, p. IV, a review of the book edited by Rainer Eckert, Ilko-Sascha Kowalczik and Isolde Stark, *Hure oder Muse? Klio in der DDR. Dokumente und Materialien des Unabhängigen Historiker-Verbandes* (Berlin: Gesellschaft für sozialwissenschaftliche Forschung, 1994).

46. See 'Suppe ohne Salz', *Der Spiegel*, 10 April 1995, pp. 76–8.

47. Helmut Wiesenthal, 'East Germany as a Unique Case of Societal Transformation: Main Characteristics and Emergent Misconceptions', Max-Planck-Gesellschaft, Arbeitsgruppe Transformationsprozesse in den neuen Bundesländern', Arbeitspapier 94/8, pp. 10f. See also the Arbeitsgruppe paper 92/1, Christiane Bialas and Wilfried Ettl, 'Wirtschaftliche Lage und soziale Differenzierung im Transformationsprozess', pp. 46f.; and the paper 94/4, Michael Brie, 'Die Ostdeutschen auf dem Wege vom 'armen Bruder' zur organisierten Minderheit?' pp. 23ff. See further Helmut Wiesenthal, 'Tarifautonomie in de-industrialisiertem Gelände', *Kölner Zeitschrift für Soziologie und Sozialpsychologie*, September 1994, pp. 425–53.

48. 'Eine Nation zu werden ist schwer', *FAZ*, 10 August 1994, p. 5.

49. Sozialismus an sich . . .', *Der Spiegel*, 15 August 1994, p. 111.

50. See, for example, Brigitte Mohr, 'Weit über den Lehrplan hinaus/Beispiele innovativer Schulen in den neuen Bundesländern', *FAZ*, 2 Novem-

ber 1994, p. 14. On administrative reform, see Günter Dill and Klaus Ehrhart, (eds), 'Gebiets- und Verwaltungsreform in der Freiwilligkeits-phase in Sachsen und Thüringen', Konrad-Adenauer-Stiftung Interne Studien und Berichte Nr. 52/1993.

5   European and Foreign Policy

The Cold War ended rather like Beethoven's *Missa Solemnis*. There was no grand recessional, no cumulative detonation of the nuclear forces that had held Europe in terror of war (and therefore in peace), in some inexorable coda. Instead, with a few swift chords, the post-World War II system simply stopped. The deft modulations into ultimate silence stunned everyone. But in retrospect, all agreed sagely that the end had been inevitable. Dona nobis pacem.

On the face of it, German adjustment to the abrupt disappearance of the bipolar world should have been far more difficult in the foreign than in the domestic arena. By definition, there was no common heritage to reclaim in inter-state relations, no shared Fontane meadows and Caspar David Friedrich cliffs, no solid Deutschmark to clasp as one's own. On the contrary, across Europe the shared history was one of mutual recrimination, of religious bloodletting, then in a more secular age a century and a half of cumulative French– German enmity, of amoral shifting alliances executed without reference to trust or friendship or NATO's latterday proclamation of common values.

To be sure, life would become more relaxed as Soviet divisions departed German soil for the first time in 45 years. By the time the Russians fulfilled their pledges in 1994 and removed all troops, Germany would have a year's – rather than a few hours' – notice of any improbable Soviet attack, But the world would also become vastly more complicated. The old division and rigidity – but also the old calculability – would vanish. In their place would be fluidity and surprises and a less inhibited exercise of individual national interests. The prospect should have unnerved the Germans, who more than most crave stability and predictability and incremental change.

As the clear and present Soviet danger no longer compelled the Western alliance to stick together, then, the biggest unknown was how the Western European allies would themselves react. Would they dismantle a NATO now seen as superfluous, race each other to claim

174

a 'peace dividend' in cutting defense spending – and leave neglected bits of an atomized Europe vulnerable to the nibblings of petty aggressors? Would the erstwhile Western European allies, absent any exterior Soviet discipline, fall out among themselves? What could hold the world's most long-lived alliance together any longer? What could prevent America's and Germany's and France's intense economic rivalry from tearing them apart?

Under the new circumstances, perhaps the comforting Kant-derived theory that liberal democracies don't fight each other was wrong after all.[1] Perhaps Europe's warring tribes had just deceived themselves in thinking that their alliance was anything more than a fleeting anomaly that would now revert to a more normal Hobbesian state.[2] Maybe the alliance had been only artificial, no more than a reflex during the forty years of existential Soviet threat and counterbalancing American presence in Europe. Maybe the post-World War II suspension of the periodic European calls to arms, the sublimation of the West Europeans' own feuds (Greece and Turkey excepted), was only an interregnum.[3]

No one expected the French and the Germans to hit the trenches against each other very soon, of course. No one would deliberately resort to war. After Wilfred Owen and Erich Maria Remarque and the carnage of World War I there was no longer the glorification of battle of a century earlier, no expectation that the terrible flames of combat would forge sons of the assorted fatherlands into heroes of self-sacrifice and bravery. Yet even in a nuclear age few were sure that the perceived utility of war or even a drift to war had really been banished in the West Europeans' dealings with each other. At best, neo-realists and structural realists argued, a return to balance-of-power jostling would make us all long for the simplicities of the Cold War.[4]

Uncertainty was heightened by doubts about Washington's continued commitment to Europe. What could now keep the US engaged in the old continent as a balancer among the West Europeans, a provider of the necessary leadership that the British would otherwise hardly cede to the French, nor the Dutch to the Germans? In US economic interests, trade with the Pacific Rim was supplanting the traditional primacy of Europe. And sentimentally, the increase of Hispanics and Asians in the demographic mix was weakening the traditional trans-Atlantic affinity. Americans, seeing themselves as Europe's altruistic rescuers of last resort in two world wars, had in any case never intended to keep troops in the old world on a permanent basis. They underwent recurring cycles of wishing to abandon the whole endeavor, to bring the boys (and girls) home and let the ungrateful Europeans pay for their own defense. Now the American taxpayers had their chance.

The final element of unpredictability, many thought, was Germany itself. Europeans, most emphatically including the Germans, were haunted by the disaster of the previous two ascents of this ill-starred land in a century. With its economic dominance of Europe and with a population instantly grown a third larger than France, Britain, or Italy, might Bonn now begin to assert itself in ways it had not been able to do for four decades? The end of German division removed the constraints on Bonn, commentators argued, tempting it to throw its weight around. At worst, Germany might become an aggressive 'Fourth Reich'.[5] At best, even if it stayed in the alliance, Bonn might 'hollow out' its commitment to NATO, evict allied troops from its territory, and give rise to new instabilities and miscalculations.[6] What could possibly prevent a 'renationalization' of security as Germany, no longer dependent on Washington's guarantees, shook off the irritations of unequal American patronage? Didn't the strains about nuclear weapons in the 1980s suggest that the Germans, unnaturally suppressed over 40 years, would break out of the encumbering American traces at the first opportunity? Wouldn't east Germans' generic abhorrence of any military alliances sap the united country's commitment to NATO? And even though their alibi for not joining allies in unpleasant operations in the Mideast or elsewhere 'out of [NATO's] area' was now gone, wouldn't the Germans still shirk their larger duties and thereby provoke Congress to call the GIs home?[7] Hadn't the Germans, the authors of Auschwitz, forfeited forever the right to unification?[8] Wouldn't Germany, fully sovereign at last, now require its own nuclear weapons as the ultimate status symbol?[9]

The subtext of this concern was the almost universal rejection by Europeans of Francis Fukuyama's thesis about the end of history.[10] In Europe, at least, just the opposite was true, they thought: history, frozen for two generations, would now resume with a vengeance.

But which history? The ghosts of the past were varied. Arguably, after 3 October 1990 the new Germany was more akin to the post-Bismarck Wilhelmenian order than to the Yalta order that had just passed. Germany no longer straddled the East–West faultline. It was once again in the middle geographically and politically, lacking natural barriers, a land of transit to other lands, too small to enforce its will on others, but far too strong to submit gladly to others' will. It was a country of 'eternal beginners' that was beginning yet again, a land in which no national government had ever before lasted long enough to legitimize itself.[11]

Under the new–old circumstances, might the Germans' restless romantic soul now seek to resolve the perennial identity crisis by supporting neo-Nazi thugs in the streets and forsaking the Western anchor so assiduously crafted by Konrad Adenauer?[12]

No, replied the German and American governments flatly – and, various others thought, either disingenuously or naively. The US, a congenital believer in second starts (and anyway bigger than Germany, and far away), trusted German democracy. Or at least the nucleus of Bush Administration insiders who were designing European policy did. This third rise of Germany would be different, they preached, as they framed in intimate consultation with Bonn the strategy and tactics of the '2 + 4' negotiations that would unify Germany in one telescoped year.[13] European Community President Jacques Delors agreed, and arranged for the swift incorporation of eastern Germany into the EC.

London and Paris were far more dubious about German redemption, and far more impressed by the Wilhelminian balance-of-power analogy. Apart from the inconvenient risk of nuclear annihilation, they had lived quite comfortably with the Cold War. Fission of Germany into two semi-sovereign states had solved *their* German problem, and they had banked on the permanence of the provisional. François Mauriac's turn of phrase about loving Germany so much that he was glad there were two of them had become conventional wisdom. So had Lord Ismay's quip about NATO's keeping the Soviets out, the Americans in, and the Germans down. The postwar surrender of empire had been hard for Paris and London, but they had both found compensation as members of the exclusive nuclear club, veto holders in the UN Security Council – and guarantor- occupiers, along with the US, of Germany. Unification would imperil this status, would devalue the bomb while revaluing the mark.[14]

However often NATO might have endorsed German unification over the decades, then, the British and French (and the Italians) understood that such pledges were merely lip service. Nobody other than the Germans really supported union, they knew, but the litany pacified the Germans. It therefore came as a shock, after the Berlin Wall fell, to discover that Washington really did believe in German self-determination – and even intended to accelerate the process to finish the merger before Soviet opposition to it hardened.

Trying to stave off the evil day, British Prime Minister Thatcher initially lectured the Germans that they should not act selfishly now, but should wait another generation before even thinking of union. Otherwise they could topple Gorbachev, imbalance Europe, and jeopardize the growth of new democracies in Central Europe. She lobbied further for a post-Yalta settlement that would be decided by the four World War II victors rather than the Germans themselves. Most famously, she gathered experts on Germany to analyze the land to the east and came up with the inventory of fearsome traits starting with 'angst, aggressiveness, assertiveness' – a list that more than one political cartoonist saw fit to apply to Thatcher herself.[15]

French President François Mitterrand was more tactful in public, but he shared the same hope of blocking or at least postponing German unification. In conspicuous allusion to the Franco-Russian alliance against Germany of a century earlier, he flew to Kiev within weeks of the fall of the Wall to solicit Gorbachev's help in hindering German unification. Shortly thereafter he scheduled a visit to East Germany behind the back of his close ally Kohl and, instead of joining George Bush in allaying Polish fears about possible German border claims, fanned the Poles' protests about Kohl's equivocation as the chancellor maneuvered to neutralize the German far Right. In addition, in what the Germans suspected was the start of the feared each-man-for-himself 'renationalization' of defense, he announced that French troops would now leave German soil for good. Initially, all of Bonn's importunings to leave at least token French forces in Germany availed nothing.[16]

Mitterrand was the first to yield to the inevitable. Once again, as in the 1980s, he calculated that the only way to circumscribe Germany's growing power was to embrace it. In the new situation Paris could no longer maintain the illusion of previous decades that Germany would provide the brawn, France the brain, of Europe. A larger, fully sovereign Germany two generations after Hitler was less and less inclined to pay France the moral and political deference of earlier years. And after the Cold War Paris's nuclear weapons and even the will to project forces abroad translated into far less international influence than did the banal Deutschmark. Averting unilateral German action by binding Bonn into closer European union was the best Paris could hope for.

This would unfortunately curtail France at the same time as it would curtail Germany – and it would risk magnifying German might by Europe's mass – but it would still hazard less than relinquishing Bonn to unilateral action. Formally, France would have to yield more of its sovereignty to such integration; factually, since the Bundesbank already dictated economic policy to all of Europe, France might even benefit from gaining at least one voice in fundamental European financial decisions.

Mitterrand therefore proposed a European central bank and European monetary union, and a few months later, at the chancellor's insistence, joined Kohl in proposing European political union.

The French President was pushing on an open door. Though in the shock of 1989/90 few of his European allies believed him, Kohl was as intent on integrating Europe as he was on unifying Germany. He doubted whether the next generation of Germans, which had not itself experienced the devastation of World War II, would be as pro-European as his own. He too wanted to bind his country irrevocably, to the EC as to NATO. He said time and again that the unification of Germany must be the catalyst for rather than the brake on the unification of Europe – and, citing Thomas Mann, that what resulted must be a European Germany and not a German Europe. He endorsed Mitterrand's ideas – provided only that the European central bank be independent of government, on the model of the Bundesbank, and make monetary stability its first commandment.[17]

With the French–German engine for Europe thus back on track, and with German unification assured for the end of 1990, Bonn could now define its new foreign policy. For all the tectonic change, it exhibited remarkable continuity.[18]

POST-NATIONAL, RISK-AVERSE

To the practitioners in Bonn's foreign ministry, all the concerns that Germany might turn into a loose nineteenth-century cannon-ball seemed ludicrous. They knew their Federal Republic to be resolutely post-national, with a conservative distaste for risk and, for all the reverence for establishment consensus, with robust democratic checks on excess. As confirmed pragmatists – this marks perhaps the greatest difference of all from the nineteenth-century pretensions of Bismarck's successors – German diplomats might smile at the formal academic school that sought to refute neo-realism by noting the taming influence of pluralist domestic politics on foreign policy.[19] Yet instinctively they sympathized with that persuasion.

Had the kind of conjecture about an overnight flip in German foreign policy been made about other, 'normal' countries, it might have been dismissed as an amusing fantasy. But since it addressed a nation that had inexplicably slid from civility to barbarity within living memory, it was taken very seriously indeed. Five decades after Hitler, the impossible negative burden of proof was still placed on the Germans, to demonstrate that they were *not* gearing up to betray the West, were *not* carving out for themselves an exclusive sphere of influence in Mitteleuropa, were *not* turning neo-Nazi. Especially in the year 1992 – as the unification mini-boom ended, the German economy tipped into an 18-month decline, Europe plunged into its worst recession in a half century, and 17 firebombings or other racist murders were committed in Germany – many neighbors feared a return of the old demons. They might suddenly be more concerned about German weakness than strength, but their apprehension about a German resort to the illegitimate right was the same.

Typically, for years afterward, for lack of any more contemporary footage, the one film clip a cameraman shot of a small right-wing German gang would keep reappearing on world TV, alarming viewers anew with tin drums and swastika derivatives. Racist violence in Germany, understandably, would attract far more extensive coverage in world media than racist violence in Britain; spurts of the nationalist Republikaner over the 5% minimum for seats in regional German legislatures would draw far more publicity than Jean-Marie Le Pen's steady double-digit support at national level in France. And subliminally these images would justify far more anxious scrutiny of Germans' than of others' foreign policy.[20]

To calm allies' worries, officials in Bonn pointed to German rejection of national particularism and to internalization of a pan-European ethos to a greater degree than in any other EC land. Pride in being a European matched pride in being German in the high 60s and 70s percentiles.[21] Readiness to renounce national independence in favor of a European political union was a high 43% in west Germany, 54% in east Germany.[22] More anecdotally, European decals on cars were and are popular. And although young Germans no longer demonstrate passionately for a united Europe as in the 1950s, they move across borders with an ease their elders never imagined, feeling as much at home on King's Road or the Champs Elysées as on the Kurfürstendamm.

Moreover, the Germans have by now internalized as well the open society conferred on them by the Americans, British and French – and the constraints that pluralism places on chauvinism in a medium-sized country. They are puzzled by the mesmerism Hitler exerted over their grandfathers. They sense stability, decency, and, ultimately, that long-sought German legitimacy, in Adenauer's unassuming Bonn republic. Until 1989 they had doubts about their untested aptitude for a political system they had neither won for themselves nor adhered to through a major depression or other catastrophe; in 1989 their doubts evaporated with the East German embrace of that system and their own discovery of how well they weathered the whirlwind of unification. So confident are they now that they are even willing, after venting their qualms, to entrust the survival of their democracy to a reinstated capital of Berlin and to what Adenauer, mistrusting his compatriots, regarded as the Asian steppe starting in Braunschweig.

It's easier for the Germans than for any of their allies to be post-national, of course. They have the unique advantage of having been defeated and having their nationalism utterly disgraced in 1945. Unlike the French, they feel embarrassed by any mention of ethnic glory. Unlike the British, they live in the present and have no occasion for nostalgia for World War II. Unlike the Americans, they are a small enough, Idaho-sized, nation to know how vulnerable they are in an interdependent world in which they export a third of their GDP, billions of dollars can shift hands instantaneously, and the Deutschmark is everyone's second reserve currency. Any initial resentment of defeat has long since given way to the realization that they live much better now in every sense than they would have done had they won the Second World War.[23]

Moreover, as the world's third largest economy, controlling, willy-nilly, the third of world production in the European economic area, Germany can afford to be generous politically. It benefits more than any other country from the single European market (even if it also pays the most for it). Its exports, the bulk of which go to Europe, generally lead the country's growth. The Deutschmark today is the equivalent of Bismarck's Prussian army of 1871; with its authority now established, it hardly needs to be brandished. Without trying, Germany is, economically, once again Europe's 'demi-hegemon'.[24] Yet with nine neighbors and the longest borders in Europe, it also understands the need to jawbone compromises.

Clearly, what impels foreign policy in Germany, as elsewhere, is not altruism, but self-interest (even if politicians are still reluctant to utter this dirty word aloud in the post-Hitler era). Yet the striking aspect of Germany's stance is the regularity with which the popular consensus chooses enlightened, long-term self-interest over short-term gain, especially in European Community (now European Union) matters.

Thus, citizens who still can't quite believe their good fortune in avoiding any runaway inflation since the 1940s balked initially at surrendering their 'beloved Deutschmark' to the European Monetary Union planned for 1999, opinion polls showed – but they nonetheless have given no significant votes to parties that flirt with anti-Europe populism. Taxpayers who grumble about plowing an annual 5% of GDP into investment in eastern Germany (but still reelect the chancellor who made them do it) rarely complain that they are also the paymasters for 28% of the EU budget. In Germany the litmus of protectionism is limited, specific, and negotiable, rather than (as in France) emotive and policy-driving. In Germany officials are happy to continue giving the small members a disproportionately strong voice in the EU. Most broadly – and most puzzlingly for Anglo-Saxons – the efficient Germans reason that it is worth subordinating swift unilateral action today to the cumbersome forging of EU coalitions for the sake of institution-building tomorrow. Conservatives, Social Democrats, Liberals, and even the Greens all concur that their country should be bound to Europe.

Kohl, Europe's senior statesman by now, manifestly speaks for his compatriots in arguing that Germany must above all avoid Bismarck's old nightmare for this land in the middle: being surrounded by a hostile coalition. In this limited sense a nineteenth-century analogy is apt.[25] Yet the underlying realism of the 1990s is utterly different from that of the 1890s; today's realism recognizes that this latest ascent of Germany will end in ruin unless it is based on the full, voluntary cooperation of other Europeans.

Should Otto von Bismarck-Schönhausen return today, he would no doubt have very mixed feelings. He would honor the necessary restraint in dealing with neighbors; after his own unification by 'blood and iron', he had himself declared Germany 'saturated'. On due reflection, he might even approve Bonn's acceptance of the permanent loss of more than a quarter of German territory since his time.

He would surely be dismayed, however, by Bonn's current reliance on the capricious instrument of voluntary European cooperation rather than solo German bravura in balancing power. And while he would admire Kohl's mastery of federal German politics as local 'Oggersheim' politics writ large, he would scarcely comprehend Kohl's extension to Europe of that same local politics writ even larger, with daily telephone deals with Madrid and Stockholm. Nor would he approve the unique socialization of Germans at large, over decades of obligatory weaving of their economy, security, and even polity into a

European web, to dealing with Europe as fundamentally an issue of domestic rather than foreign policy.

BISMARCK'S HEIRS

For Kohl, unlike for Bismarck, post-nationalism and warding off of the nightmare of a hostile coalition translated with Germany's last unification of 1990 into four concrete priorities in foreign policy: first, preservation of American engagement in Europe; second, 'deepening' of the European Community in the direction of political as well as economic union; third, a corollary 'widening' of the EC to the east to assimilate the emerging democracies into the Western club of security and prosperity; and fourth, assurance to a still-nuclear Russia that the end of its external and internal empires would not shut Moscow out of Europe, especially during the four-year period until completion of Soviet troop withdrawal from the heart of Europe.[26]

To these was added a fifth, subordinate desire: to play, eventually, an international political role commensurate with Bonn's economic might, both in European crisis management and in the United Nations, in the form of a permanent seat in the Security Council.[27]

The first precept was just the reverse of the estrangement from the US that was widely expected once Germany ended its existential dependence on Washington. The new, mature cordiality was based partly on deep gratitude to the US for what Foreign Minister Hans-Dietrich Genscher called the 'seamless' bilateral cooperation in winning unification.[28] But it was also eminently rational. On the one hand, Bonn wished to reassure its nervous European allies that they would not be left alone with the German elephant. On the other hand, Bonn itself disliked the prospect of being left alone with its sometimes parochial European friends.

In fact, the US security commitment continued to be as needed in multipolar as in bipolar Europe. America's Minutemen and Pershings were blessedly irrelevant now, except as abstract reinsurance – but with the end of the European peace wrought by nuclear terror, Washington's airlift, real-time intelligence, and the painstakingly constructed integrated military NATO command were more necessary than ever before in a new, operational sense. Security, it quickly became apparent, would be even more complicated in a world of local warlords undisciplined by the old superpower rigidity. Indeed, the savage war on the European fringes in ex-Yugoslavia would soon induce NATO to fire the first shot in anger in its entire lifespan.

More broadly, the German appeal to the Americans to stay engaged in Europe was an explicit call for continued US leadership – a call that Genscher's successor Klaus Kinkel was far less inhibited about proclaiming in public than were his British and French counterparts. Despite intensive efforts to 'deepen' the EC – and despite French lobbying for exclusively European structures to fill what the French assumed would be a void after inevitable American withdrawal – the Europeans still quarreled too much among themselves to accept any single European political authority. Leadership on tough issues still had to come from the outside power that Europeans might chafe under, but nonetheless trusted more than they did each other.[29]

From the German point of view, there was also a new need in the post-Cold-War world for an American presence farther east. Certainly in still-nuclear Ukraine, America's leadership was indispensable – and was forthcoming, after the election of reforming president Leonid Kuchma in mid-1994 – in a region that few Russians viewed as legitimately independent after three centuries of Russian–Ukrainian union. And throughout the whole arc of lands released from the Russian empire a vigorous American presence was especially welcome to the Germans, given the dearth of other Europeans there – to allay Central European paranoia about being left alone with the Germans.

In narrower bilateral terms, American–German contact remained unusually close, even if it could not conceivably maintain the intensity of 1989/90. This continuing collaboration resulted in part from the deliberate cultivation by Richard Holbrooke of a role for Bonn in Washington's day-to-day wrestling out of policy during his 11 months as US Ambassador to Germany in 1993/4, in part from American conviction that despite all the pious German avowals about a 'common foreign and security policy', real power still lay not in Brussels, but in Bonn.

Bonn's second foreign-policy precept carried with it the compulsion to continue the 'alliance within the alliance' with France. This was tricky psychologically, since the whole post-war assumption of Paris – in the cliché, France would be the guiding rider, Germany the obedient workhorse, of Europe – had now collapsed. However loathe the French were to admit it, unification 45 years after Hitler marked a new beginning for this now fully sovereign Germany. Bonn's part compulsory, part voluntary postwar apprenticeship to France was over. As a reward for its good citizenship over four decades in first soliciting Paris's prior moral imprimatur for any foreign-policy initiatives, Bonn now hoped to launch ideas of its own on occasion – without having its motives automatically impugned. Yet it still knew that only when it worked together with Paris would the Germans' desired European integration proceed. Kohl therefore (like Helmut Schmidt before him) was willing to humor France to a degree the British found exasperating, even on issues like free trade, where German interests paralleled London's far more than Paris's.[30] Kohl, however, now expected to be treated as an equal by France, and not as a supplicant.[31]

Unlike the first two precepts, Germany's third axiom – incorporating the new Central and East European democracies into the European club – was new. It followed logically from the second, however.

In the short-term view, West Germany might well have abstained on Central Europe, pleading preoccupation with the difficult digestion of the GDR's rubble and 16 million new citizens who expected to attain Western well-being instantly. But it had some pangs of conscience in realizing that its own postwar prosperity was built partly on Soviet victimization of East Europeans and erection of an iron curtain that let modernization proceed in Western Europe without being overstrained by claims from the east. Moreover, Bonn was plagued by premonitions of turmoil next door should the new democracies flounder – and of an influx of refugees to Germany should living conditions in Poland, Czechoslovakia, and Ukraine deteriorate badly.

Long-term prudence therefore prevailed. Western Europe could not long remain a haven, the Germans reasoned, if it built a new iron curtain of its own, walling off affluence in the west from poverty in the east. Germany, suddenly freed from being the tense frontline state politically, had no wish to remain 'the east of the West' economically and socially.

As soon as Germany was unified and his government had full jurisdiction over pan-German borders, then, Kohl confronted what remained of the once-powerful lobby of the twelve million Germans expelled from the east after World War II. The price of Germany's realization of its four decades' old dream of union, he bluntly told a convention of expellees that booed him for it, was final legal recognition of the permanence of the Oder–Neisse boundary and loss of that quarter of old German territory awarded to Warsaw and Moscow in 1945. The Federal Republic's constitution was modified to remove any expectation of acquiring further territory; Article 23, under which the last government of the GDR was able to join the Federal Republic instantaneously, was struck from the document. For the first time in centuries, Bonn was saying, the Poles (and Czechs) need not feel squeezed between predatory Germans and Russians.

Beyond settling this long-unfinished business from the past, Germany further set itself the task of becoming Central Europe's 'lawyer' or 'advocate' within the EC. It began prodding the EC to give a formal promise of eventual membership to the Central Europeans[32] (a prospect the British supported, since London hoped that 'widening' to an even more diverse membership would preclude in practice the dreaded 'deepening' of the EC). Bonn also recruited Paris to regular trilateral ministerial meetings with Poland, the largest of the Central European states. And beyond that, a host of governmental and non-governmental German programs joined other Western efforts in offering training for Central European business managers, military officers, parliamentary staffs, and the hosts of other professionals needed to make pluralism work.

Looking farther east, Germany's fourth, and vaguest, precept involved a search for ways to assure the Russians that they would not be shut out of Europe (unless, of course, they shut themselves out). Tangibly, Bonn pledged $46 billion to the Soviet Union, with more than a tenth of this going to build housing for army officers returning from assignment in Germany. More intangibly, Kohl made a point of consulting President Mikhail Gorbachev, then President Boris Yeltsin, on issues affecting Russia.[33]

A fifth postulate, which loomed especially large for Germany's allies, was a rethinking of the use and abuse of military force in the service of foreign policy. Before unification, the particular application of German post-nationalism by the '68 generation' of agenda-setting left intellectuals, publicists, Greens, and Social Democrats had often enough been nuclear pacifism and moral condemnation of American exercise of power in the world. That criticism, in turn, had often irritated American (and British and French) officials in the 1980s, especially in the running quarrels over new Pershing missile deployments and dispatch of NATO forces to regions outside the NATO treaty area.

With unification, the center–right government in Bonn wished to steer Germans to a rather different concept of morality. Precisely because the SS and Wehrmacht had committed such atrocities in the past, it reasoned, Germany could not remain neutral when decency and peace were threatened in the present. Germany was too big and had too large a claim on its conscience to abstain in the world. It needed to accept its share of responsibility for crisis management. It should seek a permanent seat on the UN Security Council when the post-Cold-War reorganization of this body occurred, the Foreign Ministry eventually decided (after first hoping that a common EU foreign and security policy would develop fast enough to justify a common European seat). And Bonn could only be given that seat by the other major powers if it was as willing as they were to pledge blood as well as treasure to agreed actions.[34]

All told, these principles represented evolution, not revolution, in Bonn's foreign policy.

DETOURS EN ROUTE TO MINSK

If what seemed so obvious and sensible to the Germans seemed so murky and fraught to other Europeans, there were several reasons for this. The first was that the flow of relative power to Germany wrought by unification was profoundly unsettling for its formal peers of Britain, France and Italy. In their efforts to temper or delay their own loss of influence, others sometimes read into German actions more ulterior motives than the Germans attributed to themselves. Germany's unusual openness in foreign policy – a lesson of democracy the young Federal Republic carried a good deal further than its mentors – offered little defense against such imputations. All the foreign ministries with more secretive traditions probed anyway, as in countless Yiddish jokes, for the real, hidden explanations.[35] Besides, the continuing post-Hitler taboo on mentioning 'national interest' and the German consensus itself tended to militate against as sharp a public articulation of ends and means as in countries where foreign policy was more controversial. Bonn's priorities were often implicit rather than explicit, and therefore subject to misinterpretation.

The second reason was that intentions do not ensure successful execution. The messy outside world required premature responses from Germany (as from others), while it was still overwhelmed by the complexities of unification and before its foreign principles had taken form in operational policy.

The first test was the war in the Persian Gulf. At the time, the Bush Administration saw this allied action as a 'defining moment' on the way to the 'new world order' that would succeed the Cold War. Later, Bush's dispatch of an American-led expeditionary force to push back Iraq's conquest of Kuwait would be seen instead as the last cry of the old American intervention. Thereafter the US would still protect Israel, but unrelated aggressions in the third world would not seem as urgent with the Cold-War intensity gone. American military spending would in any case drop sharply, and, especially after the debacle of the UN efforts to separate warlords in Somalia, the 'Gulf syndrome' would prevail in the US. As the sardonic summary had it, this would preclude sending US forces abroad except in those cases in which the enemy had no airpower or electronics and was in a desert with no place to hide.

In the next several years America's own growing antipathy to dispatching GIs overseas would relieve the pressure on Bonn to ante up money and/or German soldiers for allied operations out of area. But as the brief war raged in the Gulf in early 1991, various commentators in other NATO states thought the moment of truth had come in which unified Germany would have to prove its loyalty to the West by participating – or else reveal its ultimate disloyalty.

The confrontation was exacerbated by ten days of government 'radio silence' in which the nuclear pacifist demonstrators of the 1980s again took to German streets to denounce the Western war in Kuwait, German TV gave abundant coverage to the two or three American army deserters and the gallant Germans hiding them – and German officials made no public effort to rebut the imperious censure of the US. Street slogans of 'No blood for oil' elicited from American critics a repetition of the countercharge that German firms – similar business by American companies had not yet been revealed – were willfully exporting chemical weapons materials to Iraq's 'Auschwitz in the sand'.[36]

The confrontation was also aggravated by the conspicuous refusal of a number of Germans already in uniform to go to Turkey to service 18 German Alpha Jet fighters deployed there in symbolic support of the allied Gulf operation. To those servicemen (and Social Democrats) who argued that the action might provoke Iraq, their refusal was the logical extension of the prerogative of every individual to decide the rights and wrongs of foreign policy. To many of Germany's allies, such à-la-carte claims showed a self-indulgent readiness to welcome the alliance during the 40 years in which it protected the Federal Republic, only to reject it as Germany no longer needed alliance solidarity, but Turkey did.

Aptly enough, in the same way that the Gulf war would turn out to be the last large-scale American intervention, so these revived peace demonstrations would be the last large-scale German protest against US military action. Though few Americans noticed the phenomenon (and the Bonn government itself apparently couldn't quite believe it), German public opinion actually supported the Western operation in the Gulf from the beginning by a solid 56%.[37] And that support solidified once Iraqi Scud missiles – especially Scuds that might at any moment be armed with chemical warheads provided by rogue German businessmen – started to fall on Israel.

Here was a real 'defining moment', for the German elite. Iraq's threat to Israel combined with the special obligation of Germans to Jews after the Holocaust and changed overnight the moral paradigm in public discourse. In a world of manifest bullies, pacifism was no longer automatically moral, war automatically immoral when conducted by authorities for whom a citizen felt responsible. The German left split into factions that traded vehement accusations about the Gulf war and anti-Semitism.[38] In the most dramatic political consequence, the Greens forced the resignation of one of their own officials who repeated the previously politically correct line and in effect blamed the Israelis themselves for the Iraqi attacks on them.

For its part, the Federal Republic made a hefty contribution to logistical support from the German staging area for the Gulf expedition. It provided key ammunition stocks and tanks with chemical weapons sensors for US use. It supported participation by the Western European Union (WEU), the fledgling military arm of the EC, in the naval blockade of Iraq by NATO and other allies and sent German minesweepers and supply ships to the Mediterranean to free allied vessels for use in the Gulf. More publicly – and under more public pressure from Washington – it also paid the 16 billion Deutschmarks to the US for Desert Storm's defense of the common allied good, and to Iraqi neighbor states hardest hit by the embargo.[39]

Most significantly, perhaps – although its allies took little note of the move – Bonn further tightened bans on export of chemical and nuclear weapons components and their enforcement. Whereas it had previously argued that its open, export-dependent economy could not tolerate more intrusive government intervention and regulation, now it passed some of the toughest legislation in the world in this area, and strengthened enforcement. Among other sea changes, it overcame the strong post-Hitler resistance to extraterritoriality to make German executives liable in German courts for illegal export of weapons even when that export was conducted entirely outside Germany.[40]

Furthermore, the government determined to press ahead with 'normalization' and change the standard constitutional interpretation that until unification had consistently barred sending German soldiers on any operations outside the territory of NATO members. Without joining others in such actions, Bonn argued, Germany would be 'singularizing' itself and pursuing the '*Sonderweg*' or 'special way' aloof from the West that had led to such disaster under Hitler. Without demonstrating its responsibility by committing blood as well as treasure in time of need, the government contended, Germany would neither deserve nor win either the rotating seat coming open in the Security Council or a permanent seat later.

The second premature test of post-union foreign policy in ex-Yugoslavia did little to advance these German claims. As seen in retrospect, Bonn may have done no worse than anyone else in the West's woeful response to the Balkan savagery. At the time, however, other Europeans' sensitivity to any new assertiveness by Germany combined with general impotence and frustration, with memories of Nazi collaboration with thuggish Croatian puppets – and with romantic *Black-Lamb-and-Grey-Falcon* visions of the Serbs[41] – to heighten suspicion of Bonn in Paris and London.

The British Foreign Office in particular understood German pressure for EC recognition of Slovenia and Croatia at the end of 1991 as an attempt to reconstitute a special German sphere of geopolitical influence in the Balkans in collusion with Croatian heirs of the old Ustashi (and the half million Croats in Germany), with the Bavarian, Austrian, and German Roman Catholic hierarchies, and with suspect German nationalists at the *Frankfurter Allgemeine Zeitung*. In this view, recognition legitimated mistreatment by Croatia of its Serb minority[42] and made inevitable the spread of fighting to Bosnia – and Germany was deliberately condoning these iniquities in forcing its EC partners to recognize the new states. Bonn might now be acting out of weakness rather than strength – this was the period when British and French analysis shifted as the enormity of the cleanup task in eastern Germany became more apparent and the federal economy lurched into negative growth – but unwelcome German assertiveness could conceivably result from either cause.

Various German diplomats themselves, while uncomfortable with the fallout from recognition of Croatia and Slovenia, found geopolitical explanations absurd. They attributed the decision instead to Bonn's very real commitment to self-determination in the Balkans as well as in Germany, to a desire to internationalize the brutal Serb internal conquest in order to legitimize outside condemnation of it, and to Genscher's response to popular outrage at Germany's first living-room TV war.

As Yugoslavia disintegrated and the bloodletting got even worse, recriminations between the French and British on the one hand and the Germans on the other were joined by other allied polemics. The US, though it was initially glad to stay clear of the Balkan thicket, later reproached the British for keeping Washington at a distance and labelling the Yugoslav fighting an exclusively European affair. Even later the US, offended by the rape and seizure of territory in Bosnia but unwilling to risk its own men on the ground to reverse Serb advances, would find itself in conflict with the less sentimental British and French over successive peace proposals, the Serb humiliation of UN peace-keeping forces (including British and French troops), UN restrictions on supportive use of NATO airpower, and the regional arms embargo that disproportionately benefited the well-armed Serbs and penalized their Bosnian victims. Germany would generally sympathize with the US,[43] but like the US would not commit its troops to the ground. In this context the feud pitting the Germans against the British and French would be relativized.[44]

Faced with the threat that the quarrels over Yugoslavia might escalate beyond Serb defiance of NATO ultimatums and undermining of its credibility to a real fracture of NATO itself, all alliance members pulled together by winter of 1994/95, ordered damage control, and banned further recriminations.

MAASTRICHT

In the wake of Bonn's one initiative in the Yugoslav crisis came the Maastricht conference to set the terms for the European monetary and political union proposed by Mitterrand and Kohl. Yugoslavia and Maastricht were linked because of timing; desire to make a success of the forthcoming EC summit increased the pressure on other Europeans to fall into line with Bonn's wishes on diplomatic recognition in the Balkans.

Unlike the Gulf and Yugoslav wars, however, the reconstitution and redefinition of heartland Europe after the earthquake of 1989/90 was not a side issue that caught the Germans by surprise. It was no distraction from Bonn's central task of melding east and west Germany, but the logical extension of it to the immediate neighborhood. In the German view, the Maastricht conference would be far more of a barometer for twenty-first-century Europe than would Bosnia and Iraq.

In this context the forecast was at best stormy. It would be an exaggeration to call the summit a disaster, but in the EC tradition made familiar over decades, it was certainly an unhappy compromise. It came at a time when Europe was entering its worst recession since the end of World War II, and in periods of economic retraction the EC always tended to stagnate or even retrogress.

The Maastricht Treaty did set three brave goals for what would become the European Union after ratification: economic and monetary union, targeted for 1997 or for a fallback 1999; Bonn's pet 'common foreign and security policy' that was already being mocked by the disarray over Yugoslavia; and bundling together of transnational police, asylum, immigration, environment, and other regulations and functions of interior ministries. The EC states further left their door open to accept new members: Austria, Switzerland, and the northern Scandinavian countries in a first tranche, if they wished, and – though no firm promises were given initially – Central Europe in a second.

At German insistence, European Monetary Union (EMU) was made conditional on the meeting of tough financial criteria by a majority of states – and on preclusion of any 'gray zone' between circulation of old-fashioned national currencies and introduction of the new European currency unit. Later, Kohl would require as well siting of the European central bank and its forerunner in Frankfurt, where it might imbibe the non-inflationary spirit of the Bundesbank and demonstrate to voters holding German marks that it was so doing. In this one area the Germans would demand a strong German Europe rather than a flabbier European Germany.

Kohl had to abandon two further prerequisites he had originally set. The first was embedding EMU in a robust political union that could impose enough European-wide economic and social coherence to keep the common currency in internal balance. The second was filling the EC's gaping 'democratic deficit' by enlarging the powers of the European Parliament debating club.[45] France in particular was not yet willing to accord Bonn the 18 additional seats its increased population warranted. Nor, given the turf fight between France and Belgium, was the Parliament given a single locale to eliminate the constant shuttling back and forth of Euro MPs between Brussels and Strasbourg. Nor, as Britain and France both resisted Germany's push for more supranational rather than just intergovernmental mechanisms, did the European parliamentarians win enough increased competence to transform themselves from the European Commission's poodle into a real watchdog.[46]

Kohl lost too in his effort to bind the Germans irrevocably and automatically to monetary union, especially after the German constitutional court required Bundestag approval for such a step. And he failed to facilitate EC decision-making for a future unwieldy membership of two dozen by reducing veto privileges, curtailing the obstruction rights of member ministates, or changing rules for the rotating six-month presidency.

Kohl did finesse one of the trickiest issues, however, in managing to keep Britain engaged by letting it disengage. London had been a latecomer to the EC, partly because of its own aversion to submerging its identity in a continental amalgam, partly because of French President Charles De Gaulle's veto on British entry. Once it did join, it pressed for the real free trade zone that would arrive only in 1993 – and otherwise resisted any flow of political sovereignty from national capitals to Brussels. It abhorred Kohl's notion of 'deepening' political integration.

Kohl temporarily squared the circle by giving Margaret Thatcher's sudden successor, John Major, an opt-out that would let London stand aside without blocking those who did wish to proceed with the common European enterprise. The trade-off was Major's support for recognition of Croatia and Slovenia – and eventual ratification of Maastricht.

Afterward, the official reading in London was that Britain had triumphed in Maastricht in averting a dangerous 'federal' Europe. The media reading in the US, reflecting British cynicism, was that the EC had again shown its irrelevance to the real world. The official reading in Bonn was that whatever the problems, there was no alternative; the European Union was still doomed to succeed.

In the coming year, that German faith would be put to a severe test. Ordinary citizens found the hundreds of pages of Maastricht bureaucratize impenetrable. Danes actually voted against the treaty they feared would regulate their beloved tiny apples out of the market. Even the French, who feared the same indignity for their non-pasteurized Camembert, squeaked through with a positive referendum with only the slimmest of margins. In Germany itself the *Bild* tabloid screamed, 'They're taking away our lovely D-mark,' and was seconded by periodicals as diverse as the *Frankfurter Allgemeine* and *Der Spiegel*. Bavarian Premier Edmund Stoiber scoffed at 'esperanto money'; the august Bundesbank's President Karl-Otto Pöhl agreed. Dissenting politicians further followed the grand German postwar tradition in appealing an issue they had lost politically to the constitutional court.[47]

Conventional wisdom concluded that elite, out-of-touch officials across Europe had gotten too far ahead of their citizens. The concepts of transparency, accountability, and 'subsidiarity' (assigning competence in any issue to the lowest possible level of government) got a frantic new airing. European Commissioners actually began asking for outside opinions before sending legislative drafts to the European Parliament. Various French and English public figures sounded each other out on the common cause they might yet find (as against German enthusiasm for binding the separate nations ever closer) in championing an EC of Charles deGaulle's intact sovereign fatherlands and powerful national legislatures. German government and party spokesmen vowed to do a better job of educating their own voters the next time – and teaching the British that Germany's decentralized 'federalism' was not the dread British shibboleth of bureaucratic centralism but actually subsidiarity by a less highfalutin name.[48]

In the end, everyone did ratify the Maastricht Treaty, the Danes after some creative interpretation to justify a second referendum on an unchanged document, the Germans after their constitutional court ruled that surrendering bits of sovereignty to Brussels was legal so long as the Bundestag approved each step and – more problematically – that democratic accountability was preserved in the integration process. The Bundesbank kept interest rates high to squeeze inflation out of the heavy borrowing for union; the rest of Europe grumbled that its ensuing deeper and longer recession (and dearth of investment funds as rich Germany sucked up capital) constituted an involuntary tax that non-Germans too had to pay for unification. Structural unemployment on the continent climbed to 20 million. The European Monetary System exploded under speculation in late 1992, spewing out not only the British pound, but also the Italian lira. (The 'franc fort' escaped the same fate, thanks only to unprecedented joint intervention by the Bundesbank and the Banque de France.) The whole postwar Italian system collapsed as corruption charges eliminated one politician after another; the once activist Italy, preoccupied by internal crisis, now left the pan-European field to Germany, France and the Benelux countries. With some *schadenfreude* Eurosceptics in Britain noted that Germany itself was far from fulfilling EMU criteria – and that a club that could not hold a loose monetary system together would hardly be able to keep the much more difficult currency union intact.

Against this drama, it was anticlimax when the EC actually began its long-anticipated single European market on 1 January 1993, and even when the European Community became the European Union ten months later.

Yet the German government was determined to see forward movement in the accustomed trial-and-error pattern of two steps forward, one step back. It welcomed further EU agreement with the European Free Trade Association to form a combined 'European Economic Area' of 380 million, accounting for 43% of world trade. It was willing to twist arms and pay for Spanish fish and Arctic farms to enable three EFTA members – Austria, Finland, and Sweden – to draw the logical conclusion from that cooperative agreement and join the premier institution themselves by 1995. It continued to accentuate the positive in looking at the EU and to anticipate that 'Maastricht II' – the next Inter-Governmental Conference scheduled for 1996 – would in fact go further and write the real constitution for whatever form of confederation-plus would emerge.

THE US CONNECTION

The next major task in defining post-Cold-War Europe the German government saw as guaranteeing US engagement in Europe. Unlike the French, the Germans had bet that the Americans would stay, and they were doing everything in their power to encourage such continuity. They had already skirted various sensitivities in renegotiating a restricted status-of-forces agreement to replace the previous generous occupation rights of GIs in Germany. They had helped write, in November 1990, a grand new Trans-Atlantic Declaration (which was instantly forgotten by all). They had set aside strains over out-of-area operations as no longer relevant. Now, after the election of a new president who had ignored foreign policy and campaigned almost exclusively on domestic issues, they waited for the education of Bill Clinton.

Initially, they were not especially worried. They thought that after forty years the trans-Atlantic relationship had enough momentum to continue on its own for some time without any new political impulse. NATO should be able to ride out the momentary panicked casting about for a new rationale to replace the superpower enmity, they reasoned. The decrease of US forces in Germany to 100,000 should satisfy Congressional demands for cuts and more equitable 'burden-sharing' – but still leave both a coherent fighting force for emergencies and the necessary hostages to ensure Germany American nuclear protection. The general American public, habituated to NATO over decades in which its conscript sons spent pleasant years in Europe and often enough returned with German wives, continued to support the alliance.[49] In the Germany of the 1990s, moreover, NATO had ceased to be the bugaboo of the left it had been in the 1980s, as Washington's zeal for overseas intervention waned and the penchant for nasty violence in the Balkans and the ex-Soviet Union persuaded pacifist idealists that democracies might need armies after all to keep chaos from their doors and curb aggression in the neighborhood.

After the usual American foreign-policy vacuum in the year following a presidential election, though, the Germans did look for some confirmation from Clinton that Europe mattered to him. To be sure, it was a relief that Clinton was not repeating Bush's sharp 1991 warning to the Europeans that if 'your ultimate aim is to provide for your own defense, the time to tell us is today.'[50] But on the other hand, the welcome absence of American suspicion about European integration in a land now focusing on its Pacific rather than its Atlantic rim might reflect only indifference to Europe. One senior German diplomat expressed anxiety in December 1993 about what he saw as 'a critical period, comparable to the formative phase at the end of the 1940s, and just as important. We could get it right. We could get it terribly wrong,' he fretted, and end up with a corrosive resort to 'every man for himself'.[51]

When he finally did focus on Europe, Clinton did 'get it right', the Germans believed. He pushed through the Senate the reduction of trade barriers in the General Agreement on Tariffs and Trade that had been under negotiation for seven years and was the main deterrent to a trade war between the three industrialized blocs of the EU, North America and Japan. Then on his first official trip to Europe in January 1994 he warmed German hearts by endorsing integration on the continent, both in 'deepening' political cooperation among Western European members of the EU and in 'widening' the EU and NATO to welcome the new Central European democracies as future members. He also reversed Washington's initial misgivings about the joint 'Eurocorps' that Germany, France, Belgium, Spain, and Luxembourg were constructing and instead welcomed the WEU efforts as European assumption of some of the burden-sharing of security and costs that the US had been requesting for so long. In principle, he approved the concept of separate European or WEU military operations with NATO assets under 'Combined Joint Task Force' arrangements. On a subsequent trip to Berlin he joined in establishing US–EU study groups to address Central and East European issues, the fight against drug traffic and organized crime, and EU efforts to forge a common foreign and security policy.

Later in 1994, as schizophrenic new Republicans humiliated Clinton in the fall elections and brought in half-isolationist, half-unilateralist yearnings in foreign policy – and as differences over Bosnia policy threatened to split NATO and stall the whole idea of a Combined Joint Task Force – the Germans got more worried. They joined other Europeans in lecturing the Republican majority in Washington about the importance of Europe – but what they missed above all, as Clinton retreated even more into domestic preoccupation, was activist presidential leadership on behalf of the trans-Atlantic alliance. They welcomed it when Clinton at last decided that alliance solidarity must have priority in Bosnia – and promised to put US troops on the ground there to help evacuate UNPROFOR (UN Protection Force) peacekeepers should the latter withdraw and need to fight their way out of exposed positions. They welcomed even more the reassertion of real American leadership in the region once the Croat blitzkrieg cut Serb conquests to half of Bosnia's territory.

The Germans sympathized with the Bosnians as much as Congress did, but they were no more ready to commit hundreds of thousands of Bundeswehr soldiers to restore conquered Bosnian territory than Congress was to commit hundreds of thousands of GIs. In the end, for the same alliance reasons that moved Clinton to approve dispatch of an American division to the Balkans, Bonn approved dispatch of 4,000 Bundeswehr soldiers to the region.

'MITTELEUROPA'

The Germans' third basic policy aim – integrating the Central Europeans into Western Europe – had no single catalyst for decision to compare with Maastricht and the NATO conflict over Bosnia strategies. It was advanced instead by a myriad of small, discrete efforts to help shape the transformations to the east (especially after collapse of the Soviet Union in 1991), and to prepare the resulting new democracies for participation in the Western community.

The Germans started from the hypothesis that the real new dynamic of the *fin de siècle* was not recidivism to tribal feuds in the European periphery of the Balkans and Caucasus, but the swift spread of the improbable Western system of voluntary cooperation to Central Europe. If this intuition was correct (*pace* Fukuyama), then Central Europe's provisional escape at long last from the vicious cycle of history deserved robust Western support.

The eastern Slavs in Russia and Ukraine might be too big a mass and too removed from the Western mentality to be able to absorb much financial or institutional help from the West. But the West could hope to have some fundamental, benign impact on the smaller and more Western-oriented Baltic states, on Poland, Hungary, the Czech Republic, Slovenia, and (perhaps) Slovakia, with their more receptive infant civil societies.

What was needed, then, was a second creation worthy of Dean Acheson's and Robert Schuman's first. As brilliant improvisation brought security and prosperity to a ruined Western Europe after 1945 and made war there inconceivable, so should imaginative diplomacy now do the same for Central Europe.

No new Marshall Plan for the east would be realistic, the German government calculated. Bonn was in effect buying the retreat of the Soviet Army with its one-off transfer to the Soviet Union of $46 billion – and trying to channel as much of this wealth as possible away from mafia hands into housing for the thousands of homeless officers. But this sum was more in the nature of a ransom than an investment in the future. Even the east Germans, with habits and preconditions closest to the west Germans' and with the gift of $100 billion per year for the rest of the century, were struggling to make a success of the bewildering new system thrust upon them. Bonn had no substantial capital left for other projects – and no expectation, even if it did, that largesse farther east would do anything but disappear into the black hole of Swiss bank accounts.

Bonn could help the Central Europeans to help themselves, however, with technical and organizational and legal training. This it proceeded to do, with a plethora of governmental and private initiatives. The Central Europeans, striving to qualify as fast as possible in any case for EU membership, found some shortcuts to their political, economic, social and institutional transformation in adopting ready-made EU or German models. They welcomed all the additional Western assistance they could get in this process; more help came from Germans than from any other nation.[52] The think tanks connected with the mainstream German parties, repeating their service in helping establish democracy in Spain and Portugal in the 1970s, helped transmit political and social organizational skills. The Goethe Institute facilitated communication by spreading knowledge of the second lingua franca after English. Bilateral exchanges and workshops proliferated.

Whatever their old suspicions of overbearing Germans (and whatever the British and French suspicions about a German geopolitical sphere in the region),[53] the Poles, Hungarians, and Czechs in particular quickly came to see Bonn as their best friend in the EU.[54] They chafed under the slowness of the graduated opening of the West European market to their textiles and steel and berries, but in general they trusted that the Germans were doing as well as they could. Other EU members tended to ignore them, apart from the French, when the Germans dragged them along, and the British, whom the Central Europeans understood to be playing their own games to block 'deepening' by means of 'widening'. The Germans, by contrast, by December of 1991, won association agreements for the Visegrad states[55] of Poland, Hungary, and Czechoslovakia, with liberalized trade working toward a full free-trade zone. (The French, regarding the Visegrad states as German clients, subsequently got the same privilege for Bulgaria and Romania.) Industrial goods from these countries would enter the EU without tariffs by 1995, steel by 1996, textiles by 1997.

By 1993 the Germans further got the EU to give a firm promise of membership to these states whenever they might meet EU norms, and by 1994 to invite them to sit in on EU summits in the interim. By 1995 the EU would turn out a white paper detailing the specific harmonization needed in banking, transport, legal, environmental, social and other regulations for membership by about the year 2000 of these six, along with Slovenia, Cyprus and Malta. Entry of the three Baltic states was anticipated in the early twenty-first century. In a parallel process, Germany also spearheaded an associate partnership status in the Western European Union for the four Visegrad and three Baltic states, plus Romania and Bulgaria.

Germany was also the first, in a solo campaign by Defense Minister Volker Rühe, to press for early extension of NATO membership to the Central Europeans. When the Americans hesitated, the first step in this direction was a compromise 'Partnership for Peace' program worked out jointly by Washington and Bonn that would let individual Central European partners set their own pace in achieving compatibility with the integrated NATO military command. By 1994 the US took the lead in pressing for early clarification of conditions of eligibility to join NATO; Bonn, happy not to be out front, then deferred to Washington.

In Germany's bilateral relations with Central Europeans, tension between Czechs and Germans has lingered the longest. This is curious, since it was the Poles who suffered far more casualties in World War II than the Czechs – far more, in fact, than any other country except Luxembourg in proportion to population. Six million Poles, half of them Jews, died in World War II. The Czechs, by contrast, did not resist Nazi seizure of the Sudetenland in 1938 and therefore did not martyr their sons. They further had the closest historical and cultural links with Germany of any Central European state other than Austria. Back in the fourteenth century Prague had been the center of the Holy Roman Empire of the German Nation and the site of the first German university in Europe; up through the mid-twentieth century some of the purest German in Europe had been spoken in Prague.

What soured the relationship in the 1990s, however, was Bonn's refusal to give special compensation to Czech victims of the Nazis, and Prague's refusal to invalidate postwar expropriation of German property or even (with the important exception of President Vaclav Havel) to admit that injustice was done to Germans summarily expelled from Czechoslovakia in the revenge of 1945.[56] Resentment by Czechs of the more than 20 million annual German visitors to next-door Prague and of heavy German ownership of media in Bohemia added to strains.

Given the region's violent history, what is more surprising than Czech–German antagonism is the new mutual tolerance practiced by Germans and Poles. Shortly after unification there were some nasty drunken brawls at Frankfurt on Oder and other border towns, but these faded. There was also some ambivalence about German money as serious Western investment first began flowing in in 1995 following rescheduling of Polish debts. Basically, however, the Polish government and intellectuals welcome the German lobbying for their admission to EU and NATO membership – and welcome too the moderating effect the German Embassy in Warsaw has on demands by the German minority in Poland. By 1994 the Poles symbolized their growing trust by inviting the Bundeswehr Inspector General to participate for the first time in the commemoration at the Westerplatte of the outbreak of World War II. The Germans reciprocated, after a brief spat about Bonn's failure to invite the Polish president, by inviting Polish Foreign Minister Wladyslaw Bartoszewski to address an unusual joint session of the Bundestag and Bundesrat as part of Germany's own fiftieth anniversary commemoration of the end of the war.

On the same issues that are roiling Czech–German relations, Warsaw and Bonn have either moved further toward reconciliation or have simply agreed to disagree, and are going on to address more useful matters. As far back as 1965 the Polish bishops, in a controversial statement, asked forgiveness for the wrongs done by Poles to Germans expelled at war's end. Then Chancellor Willy Brandt began his *Ostpolitik* opening to the East, visited Poland, and at the Warsaw Ghetto kneeled in contrition in what has been known ever since simply as 'the kneefall'. And in the 1970s the German government paid the old Polish Communist government DM150 million toward war damages (though not toward still-outstanding compensation for Polish forced labor under the Nazis), and gave Warsaw additional credits of DM1 billion. The Polish government subsequently let 200,000 ethnic Germans emigrate to the Federal Republic.

At this point the German government has no wish to stir up the hornets' nest of old Junker property claims on lands which two generations of Poles have now inhabited – but it also has no wish to stir up a domestic hornets' nest among the German expellee organizations by saying so publicly. This silence the Warsaw government honors. And in the population at large, young Poles, far from visiting the anger of their grandparents upon the third generation of Germans, find it chic to wear Bundeswehr jackets, complete with German flag insignia, that they buy on King's Road.[57]

For their part, the Germans feel encouraged in their optimistic assessment of Central Europe by Poland's success in converting Solidarity's corporate politics of heroism of the 1980s to the messier democratic articulation of interests in the 1990s. Polish voters, despite their inexperience, have rejected both the easy demagogue and right-wing nationalists. The Sejm, despite a splintered parliament of almost three dozen parties, legislated harsh shock therapy – then rewrote voting rules in a way that got parliamentary parties down to a more responsible half dozen in the 1993 election. When the ex-Communists regained power in that 1993 election, they turned out to be not only real democrats, but also real defenders of the market and of disciplined budgets. And Poland became the first post-Communist country to come out of economic tailspin, with 4% growth in 1993, even in the midst of Western European recession, and 5% growth in 1994.[58] Moreover, the Poles have shed their traditional martyr complex to grope for compromise – and have deliberately joined the Ukrainians in burying the animosities of the past.

RUSSIA/UKRAINE/POLAND

Farther east, the trick for foreign policy is not managing the rise of new democracies, but managing the decline of the Russian ex-superpower. The West applauded the election of President Boris Yeltsin as a considerable improvement over the old succession by feud between shadowy patronage clans, and it was willing to cross its fingers and call the new process democracy by way of encouragement. But no officials in Bonn, Washington, or elsewhere in NATO capitals equated the lurch to some new 'time of troubles' in Moscow with the real planting of democracy and civil society in ready soil in Warsaw and Prague.

For the West in general and Germany in particular, managing the Russian decline was first perceived as avoiding two historically defined traps (or at least minimizing their impact): the kind of turmoil and violence that followed breakup of the Ottoman Empire, and the kind of humiliation and backlash that engulfed Weimar Germany. By the mid-1990s – although Bonn was even slower than Washington in drawing concrete policy conclusions from the shift – the task was increasingly redefined as getting the balance right between Russia, Ukraine and Poland.

The first period lasted until withdrawal of the last Russian troops from Germany, Central Europe and the Baltics in 1994.[59] In the 2 + 4 negotiations that effected German unification, the Americans and Germans, in remarkably close strategic and tactical teamwork, had promised Moscow that it would not be exploited, but would be treated with dignity, as it downsized. It would not be shut out, but would be granted its room in the 'common European house' that Gorbachev talked about so passionately.

This was the only prudent treatment of a country that was still a nuclear superpower, still had heavily armed divisions on the ground inside Germany – and still had plenty of resentful chauvinists around of the ilk of Vladimir Zhirinovsky, ready to lash out at the West and invent a 'stab in the back' legend similar to Hitler's in the Weimar Republic.

The West honored its promise. The Germans delivered their billions to the Soviet Union and its successor states and built officers' housing in Russia and Ukraine to full Western standards of quality. At home they not only averted any defacing of monuments to Soviet soldiers, but conscientiously tended and refurbished these memorials. They detered defections by making it clear that they would not grant asylum to Russian deserters. They further trained 12,000 Soviet Army men in accounting, management, and data processing, and met the payroll of the army's remaining stay in eastern Germany at fictional exchange rates and with a hard-currency largesse bewildering to conscripts used to wages of a few rubles a month. Until 1994 they also overlooked the massive smuggling in sealed trucks into Russian army barracks of cigarettes and just about everything else – and the concomitant build-up of Russian distribution and protection mafias in Berlin, Frankfurt and elsewhere.

The Germans drew the line, however, at giving the Russian troops that had threatened them for forty years the same warm farewell that they lavished on the American, British and French troops that had protected them for forty years. Despite Yeltsin's importunings, in summer of 1994 the Germans waved the Russians a separate goodbye from their country. The ceremony was polite, even when Yeltsin tipsily insisted on conducting the military band himself. It was not, however, a festival like the parallel farewell (from Berlin only, not from Germany) for the Western allies.

More substantively, Russia was invited to join an ad hoc 'Contact Group' along with the US, Germany, Britain, and France to coordinate Western and European intervention or passivity in ex-Yugoslavia. In part, this was a gesture to give Moscow high visibility in protecting its Serb clients; initially, there was even some thought that the Contact Group might eventually turn into another concert of powers like that after the Congress of Vienna to write agreed limits on Europe's quarrels. Obversely, the Contact Group represented an effort to keep Moscow engaged in sanctions against the Serbs at a time when Russian foreign policy was recoiling against earlier concessions to the West. Then too, the Contact Group provided a convenient figleaf in Soviet cantankerousness to cover the West's own disarray and inaction in Bosnia.

In a further invitation to join Western fora that was less welcome to the Russians, NATO also solicited Moscow's participation, first, in the new North Atlantic Consultative Council (NACC) and then in 1994 in the more ambitious 'Partnership for Peace' program that would prepare some (Central European) participants for eventual membership in the alliance. Here the Russians objected not only that they were accorded no special superpower status and rated no more than equal to all other ex-Communist states – but even that they had an inferior position and never would be considered for full membership themselves. German officials would confirm this reading in public; more cautious American officials would confirm it only in private.

Throughout this period the only remaining full superpower of the US took the lead in massaging and pressuring Moscow to implement its pledged troop retreat. Washington, backed by the EC/EU, also publicly urged the Baltic states to accord full civil rights to their Russian minorities so that maltreatment of them would give Moscow no pretext to delay withdrawals. At the same time the US made clear to the Russians that they could not prolong a *droit de regard* in their former empire in the Baltics and Central Europe either by strength of threat or by the weakness of pleading that worse Zhirinovskys would take over if the West didn't humor the nicer Yeltsins. Germany and the other NATO allies were essentially bystanders to this continued superpower duet.

The much more complex current phase of managing Russian decline requires finding the right equilibrium between Russia, Ukraine and Poland – and the right rhythm for EU and NATO expansion. Here the Germans play a larger role, indirectly, in reassuring both the Central Europeans and the Russians along the way. Yet from that summer day in 1994 when the Russians retreated and ended east Germany's de facto hostage status, the Germans' own interest in fitting Russia into the European framework has become less existential and more abstract.[60] The urgency is gone. Clearly, Bonn will not be donating further billions to Russia. Yet equally clearly, Germany as an anchor of stability and predictability in the EU and in Europe at large remains crucial for Russia. The familiar Kohl, Europe's senior statesman, Yeltsin sees as his best Western friend.[61]

Yeltsin's perceptions make EU expansion easier, NATO expansion more fraught. Given the previous Soviet hostility toward the EC, Russia is remarkably relaxed as the EU increasingly becomes the organizing field for Central Europe as well as the Baltic states. Moscow is unperturbed by the EU (and, by inference, WEU) plans to take in the Visegrad states by the end of this century and Estonia, Latvia and Lithuania early in the next century. Sometime in the past five years, it seems, Moscow accepted the American contention that the Baltic states, despite their incorporation into the Soviet Union in World War II, had been part of Moscow's external (East European), and not its much more sensitive, internal empire.

Western Europe's old and continuing security arm of NATO is a different matter. Partly because of Cold-War history, the Russians continue to oppose vehemently any expansion of this alliance to take in the former Warsaw-Pact countries that are clamoring for admission. In 1990 the West may have convinced Gorbachev and Soviet Foreign Minister Eduard Shevardnadze that everyone on the continent, including Russians, would sleep easier at night if the dynamic Germans were tied to NATO rather than left as a loose cannonball. With no comparable Russian awe of Poles, however, any similar argument carries little weight in Moscow in the present controversy. Nor have Western efforts to give Moscow a consolation prize by upgrading the Conference on Security and Cooperation in Europe (CSCE) to the Organization of Security and Cooperation in Europe (OSCE) had much success.[62] The OSCE is performing useful monitoring service, and at the EU's behest may even do so in Russia's mutinous region of Chechnya. But what Russia wants – and precisely what the West is unwilling to grant – is special deference, with a veto on slippage of Moscow's former clients into NATO. As of this writing it was not yet clear what sort of special consultations between NATO and Russia might constitute a sufficiently distinctive position to attract Moscow without at the same time worrying Warsaw.

At this point Germany is essentially deferring to the US on NATO expansion. German Defense Minister Volker Rühe launched the whole debate in 1993, asking that the West give security guarantees to the Central Europeans to underpin their new democracies.[63] When it looked briefly as if Yeltsin had no objections to NATO expansion, the US then took up the cause, only to retreat to the more ambiguous Partnership for Peace program when Yeltsin shifted to protest. Now both the State Department and the new Republicans in Congress are again pushing fast-track membership – while German Foreign Minister Klaus Kinkel has doubts, Chancellor Kohl has not committed himself one way or the other, and Bonn generally is helping delay the process.[64] The issue is thus typical of American–German dialogue after the Cold War: debate splits less on trans-Atlantic lines than on internal cracks, with some Americans and some Germans on both sides. In the end, Germany's official position will probably depend as much on Bonn's estimate of the constancy of Washington's current policy as on Germany's own substantive assessment.

Thus, both Rühe and American proponents of rapid expansion argue that Moscow's present weak period may not last – and now is the best time to press ahead and fill the security vacuum in Central

Europe before Russia recovers and refills it. Opponents contend that Poland is in fact the safest it has been in 300 years, and that a rush to haul it into the alliance might be counterproductive, diverting scarce resources away from needed economic to distorting military uses, and risking tipping Moscow into a new arms race or a hardline takeover in the Kremlin.

The most recent joker in this controversy is Ukraine. After three disastrous first years of independence and stagnation, the newly-elected President Leonid Kuchma in 1994 ended fears of secession, agreed to destroy Kiev's inherited nuclear missiles, got parliamentary ratification of the Non- Proliferation Treaty, and decreed real economic reform. Ukrainians suddenly have hope again,[65] and all three Western capitals that care about Ukraine – Bonn, Washington, and Ottawa – would like to reinforce that hope. Basically, the West wants to give Ukraine enough time, after three centuries as a Russian province, to invent a separate identity and acclimatize the still incredulous Russians to the alien notion that Ukraine is no longer theirs. Kiev, after initially opposing NATO membership for Poland as likely to draw a new west–east dividing line at the Polish–Ukranian border, has now concluded that its own interests are best served by approving NATO expansion and by pushing Ukranian cooperation with NATO as far as possible short of the explicit security guarantee for members.

After two years of joint handwringing about imminent debacle in Kiev, both Bonn and Washington are overjoyed by the turnaround. Neither imagines that Kiev itself could possibly join the EU or its sister NATO in the foreseeable future; with a population and territory equal to France's but a critically sick economy, Ukraine is simply too big, too underdeveloped, and too far east to be admitted to either the prosperity or security branches of the European club. But both Washington and Bonn want to help Ukraine through this transition; some in both capitals argue that such help requires maintaining a certain ambiguity at this point about NATO's interest in Ukraine and therefore in Poland too.

The difference here is that so far Bonn's broader support for Ukraine remains largely rhetorical. The US put together $900 million bilateral assistance over two years, got the Group of Seven industrialized nations to pledge $4 billion in support for reform in 1994, and persuaded the International Monetary Fund to link support for Russia with Russian debt relief for Ukraine in 1995. Germany, by contrast, gives little to Ukraine beyond the military housing it promised Gorbachev, and does not even have enough diplomats in Kiev to follow the political pulse there.

So far the indiscriminate Russian bombing of civilians in suppressing the Chechnya rebellion in 1995 does not significantly change the Russian equation for the Americans or the Germans. The Chechens, proud of their Caucasian warrior and smuggler tradition, and still angry at their brutal deportation by Stalin during World War II, are determined to continue guerrilla fighting until Moscow recoils from the mounting Russian death toll. The response of both American and German officials has been to hold their noses, condemn Russian inhumanity in Chechnya – but keep dealing with Yeltsin so long as he remains healthy enough to conduct business a few hours each morning. If *de facto* Western condoning of Russian cruelty in internal affairs can further be traded for Russian condoning of Ukrainian consolidation[66] and NATO expansion eastward, this implicit deal will be struck, Ottoman-Empire-style decay has in fact set in, not only in Chechnya, but also in Tadzhikistan, Nagorno Karabach, and elsewhere – but so long as it does not spill over the Russian fringes, the West will not want to get involved.

THE BUNDESWEHR ABROAD

In terms of specific German participation in any future OSCE or other peacekeeping operations, a quiet evolution has occurred that should take the sting out of old allied charges that Bonn is a freeloader and won't contribute its fair share to security. Germany began the expansion of the Bundeswehr's mission by sending mine-sweepers to the Persian Gulf in 1991, then providing two Transall C-160s for UN verifiers of Iraqi destruction of nuclear and chemical weapons, and flying humanitarian aid to Kurds in northern Iraq. As the public climate changed under the impact of Iraqi Scuds in Israel and daily TV evidence of the results of Western military inaction in Bosnia, the German government next gingerly sent 1500 Bundeswehr medics on a UN mission to Cambodia in mid-1992. The operation was successful, there was sympathetic television coverage of good deeds by Bundeswehr doctors – and the expected public storm did not erupt when the first bodybag came back with the German victim of a random street shooting. The government subsequently pressed the case that what had been treated in previous decades as a constitutional ban on sending armed German soldiers outside the NATO area was instead a policy decision – and with unification and the end of the Cold War, it was now time to change that policy.

By early 1993 – before NATO command teams loaned to UNPRO-FOR got exposed to fire on the ground in ex-Yugoslavia – German air force officers were flying in their usual multinational crews in NATO AWACS surveillance planes over Yugoslavia. They were grounded temporarily, pending constitutional clarification of their status, once NATO officers on the ground risked getting drawn into combat. In the meantime, Bonn scraped together 1700 armed soldiers from every conceivable unit to send on the ill-fated UN peacekeeping mission in Somalia. The German force stayed out of harm's way and gave good photo ops by building hospitals and wells. It pulled out without incident as the Americans retreated – though the exercise also convinced government and opposition alike that German operations abroad should henceforth essentially be restricted to Europe and its 'periphery'.[67] By early 1994 Germany further sent nine officers to join the first UN military observer mission in the former Soviet Union, in Georgia.

The slowest to join the emerging consensus have been the Social Democrats. In 1992 they had already brought suit challenging the constitutionality of participation by German ships in monitoring the arms embargo in the Adriatic. In 1993, in a bizarre twist, they were joined by the junior Liberal partners in the government coalition in what would be the defining appeal, over German participation in the AWACS flights over ex-Yugoslavia. At the time a number of Liberals regarded the suit as a matter of principle; in retrospect, others in the party tended to describe it more instrumentally, as an effort to clarify the legal situation before making any further Bundeswehr commitments.

In the end, the court agreed in mid-1994 with the government position that dispatch of German soldiers does not violate the constitution per se, and is a matter for political rather than juridical decision. It added, however, in what the Social Democrats immediately claimed as their victory, that the government must get parliamentary approval for every German military operation outside of NATO.[68] Since that judgment, debate has ceased to have the apocalyptic aura of the 1980s' missile dispute and has devolved to more routine evaluations of objectives, means, and practicalities. The gravest issue became the question of whether the Bundeswehr, already halved from its 700,000 strength at the time of merger of the West and East German armies, could maintain the numbers and the budget to constitute the rapid-reaction forces that the new era would require.[69]

Along the way, the Social Democrats modified their 1980s' pacifist sympathies somewhat. A fierce debate began in the party in 1988, before unification, and ended in a kind of truce in 1993. In the party resolution of that year the SPD approved selective use of the Bundeswehr in UN 'blue helmet' peace*keeping* but not peace*making* operations abroad – and not in NATO operations without a UN or CSCE aegis. Long-time foreign-policy spokesmen for the party like MP Karsten Voigt found the distinction an impossible one and tried subsequently to expand the party's interpretation of the resolution. The left wing, especially in the persons of party deputy chairman Heidi Wieczorek-Zeul and Saarland Premier Oskar Lafontaine, successfully resisted such accommodation.[70] The 1994 chancellor candidate and party chairman Rudolf Scharping basically evades substantive discussion of the issues altogether and criticizes particular operations rather than principles.

Yet as public opinion changed, so too did the focus of the SPD opposition on military affairs. By 1995 the Social Democrats were criticizing the government not only for closing too many military bases, but also for asserting that the Bundeswehr must never go where Hitler's Wehrmacht once had gone. Wouldn't it be better to send German troops to near-by Macedonia than to far-away Somalia, Scharping took to asking.[71]

The shift of the Greens away from their old across-the-board derision of NATO was even more striking. By the mid-1990s the pragmatic 'Realos' had defeated the 'Fundamentalists' within the party. Joschka Fischer had long since donated to a museum the famous sneakers he wore on taking his first oath of office as a state minister in Hesse, and he was now sartorially indistinguishable from other MPs as he strode to the Bundestag podium to berate the government for being too soft on Russian brutality in Chechnya. Outraged as well by the treatment of Bosnians in ex-Yugoslavia – and already being courted by some Christian Democrats for eventual future coalitions – the Greens were far less dogmatic about use of the Bundeswehr abroad than was the left wing of the SPD.[72] Nor were they the ones to recall Bismarck's dictum that the Balkans were 'not worth the bones of a single Pomeranian grenadier'.

By five years after unification, then, in a striking break with the past, Bonn did in fact send Pomeranian grenadiers to the Balkans, in the form of Tornado fighters equipped with unique anti-radar electronics, prepared to help evacuate UNPROFOR peacekeepers from ex-Yugoslavia. (Less controversially, it also dispatched a full military hospital to Split.) So far had the consensus moved that in the parliamentary vote the question was no longer – as it would have been even six months earlier – how many Liberals might defect from the thin government majority – but rather how many centrist Social Democrats and Greens would defect from their party's line to swell the majority of the governing coalition. Bonn could at last argue to those considering upgrading its rotating seat on the UN Security Council to a permanent one that it was now in a position to provide its share of military personnel for crisis management.

Politically, the rest of the world was already convinced of Germany's clout in any case. In one not untypical week in spring of 1995 the Italian and Thai prime ministers, the South Korean President, and the Russian Minister of Culture all visited Germany; Foreign Minister Kinkel helped broker an agreement in Bonn between Muslim and Croat officials for common administrative structures in Bosnia and the return of refugees; Chancellor Kohl announced a DM50-million program to eradicate child labor around the world; Kohl helped stabilize the franc during exchange-rate turbulence by praising the strength of the French economy; and Defense Minister Rühe was in the US with his American, British and French counterparts to coordinate strategy on Yugoslavia and NATO expansion in the second quad meeting since the Western troop withdrawal from Berlin. In addition, Kinkel, as one of the troika of EU foreign ministers – the unwieldy but functioning institution of past, present, and future holders of the EU's six-month rotating presidency – got Yeltsin to accept a permanent OSCE mediation mission to the secessionist republic of Chechnya, in return for unfreezing an EU-Russian trade pact; and media continued to dissect a middleman attempt by Germany to secure release of an Israeli pilot held for nine years in Iran.

Moreover, by now, in one of the least noticed but most significant diplomatic shifts, the Netherlands has decided that its future lies with this united, democratic Germany, and with the French-German teamwork that Bonn attaches such value to, whatever the current bilateral vicissitudes. For years the Netherlands was the largest or second-largest exporter to Germany; the guilder was tied to the mark; Queen Beatrix's consort was German. Yet hostility and mistrust from the days of Nazi occupation lingered on, more powerfully even than in Poland.[73] Over the years the Netherlands deliberately cultivated the British and trans-Atlantic link as an escape route from Germany's Europe. Dutch Prime Minister Ruud Lubbers opposed German unification in 1989/90 (and subsequently failed to get Kohl's crucial backing to succeed Jacques Delors as EU President). And the greatly overweight vote of small countries in the EU – which Bonn now wishes to reduce to less than a veto – was a talisman.

After several years of especially strained bilateral relations, Dutch–German reconciliation finally came in a five-hour confidential talk in The Hague in January 1995 between Kohl, Dutch Prime Minister Wim Kok, and two dozen other Dutch opinion leaders.[74] A continuing formal dialogue of elites of the sort the Germans like was also launched to assure future good relations.

NATIONAL INTEREST AND THE SPLITS

So where does all this leave foreign policy five years after German unification and recovery of full sovereignty?

Certainly it leaves Germany pursuing its own 'national interests', a phrase the center is finally reclaiming from the borderline right.[75] By now, however, these interests savor less of Kaiser Bill than of Adenauer – and they are being advanced not in a balance-of-power clash, but in tedious bureaucratic maneuvering in the confederation-plus of the EU and the confederation-minus of the trans-Atlantic community. The Germans will put muscle into their EU diplomacy by threatening to go it alone if their European partners will not integrate further. But their own preference is clear. They have resoundingly answered the question – Which history? – by rejecting the Congress of Vienna, Versailles and Yalta, and embracing instead the unpretentious Bonn Republic, and Europe.

Moreover, the German elite has rallied to this answer with a matter-of-factness and unanimity that belie the tectonic change in Europe, epicenter Germany, of the 1990s. Continuity, stability, and predictability mark the German evolution, despite all the turbulence in the environment. Of course the Germans want the US to stay in Europe. Of course they want to promote further integration in Western Europe. Of course they want increasingly to draw the new democracies to the east into the Western club. Of course they continue to shun exorbitant and politically useless nuclear weapons. Of course, in an interdependent world, nationalism is eccentric.

There were debates – one real, one aborted – on two narrower issues: use of the Bundeswehr abroad and surrender of the Deutschmark. But the course has by now been set on the first, leaving aside institutional differences between the Defense and Foreign Ministers about when and where to intervene,[76] and the second debate all officials are confident of winning, now that the European central bank will be situated in Frankfurt.

Apart from these specifics, the fundamental post-Cold-War choices followed so seamlessly from what preceded them that they never seemed like choices. Foreign policy was no issue in the 1994 general election, and the only general criticism that opposition leader Scharping can now muster in this area is the charge that the Kohl government is 'half-hearted' in pursuing European integration.

In many ways even the tactics remain the same as they were before unification: first, coordinate European initiatives with Paris (and ignore French flirtations with Russia over Serbia, Iran, and Ukraine). Next, solicit the views and modifications of the Benelux, and now Scandinavian, countries – and of Italy, insofar as Rome can be distracted from its domestic crisis long enough to focus on Europe. Last, proceed without waiting for the slowest (British) caboose, but give the United Kingdom an opt-out along the way, and let it jump on at the very last second when it decides it does not want to get left behind after all. When needed to break out of deadlock, dig deeper into the German pocket and pay a bit extra for polar-circle cows or 20,000 more tons of North Atlantic haddock.

Above all, in every case wait for the logic of events to move Europeans toward commonality – for the French, after excluding the Germans from the fiftieth anniversary of the Normandy invasion, to invite the Bundeswehr to join the 14 July 1994 Champs Elysées parade for the first time; for French industrialists to assert their own free-trade interests against French peasant protectionism; for the new Labor Party to win a general election and bring Britain fully into Europe; for the Dutch to stop demonizing the Germans (and the French). In the meantime, have as many youth exchanges as possible, and let fledgling British diplomats, fresh from Foreign Office secrecy, be stunned by the openness they find working in staff positions in the German Foreign Ministry.

In practice, the elite consensus on expanded international commitments tends to complicate rather than simplify post-unification diplomacy. The country's graduation from political dwarf to regional giant has brought Germany greater exposure, and far greater demands on its money, mediation, and massage. Inevitably, it will have to respond with more vigor to human-rights violations abroad, whether in Bosnia, Chechnya, or Kurdistan. Inevitably, more and more outside conundrums will spill over into German domestic politics. The half million refugees from ex-Yugoslavia who now live in Germany will grow. Some of the Kurds who have come to Germany for asylum will bomb Turkish businesses nightly – yet various Social Democratic *Länder* will defy the federal government and refuse to expel Kurdish aliens so long as they are not guaranteed safety from persecution in Turkey. And however much Bonn may want to foster regional stability by supporting the Ankara government against fundamentalist Islamic threats, it will be forced by popular outrage to suspend aid to Turkey with every presumed use by Ankara of German-supplied military equipment to mow down Kurds.

At the same time, the rich Germans will be expected to contribute heavily to the economies of new EU member states, to the Maghreb, to non-proliferation costs, to environmental clean-ups, to replacement of dangerous nuclear plants to the east, to investment in Central Europe and the Middle East, to the international fight againt drugs and crime. Their pleas that they are overstretched by the drain of $100 billion a year to eastern Germany will not excuse them in the eyes of the claimants.

As in the past, Bonn's attempts to accommodate its allies and clients will thus require a constant *Spagat*, or the splits. Yet such *sowohl als auch* ('both X and Y') equivocation will risk offending partners who want clear decisions from this bigger and now sovereign Germany. Washington will expect German activism in promoting NATO expansion eastward at a pace matching EU expansion. Paris will expect Bonn's help in strengthening the WEU, while London (and Washington) will insist on continued primacy for NATO. Balancing EU and trans-Atlantic commitments, NATO and the European 'pillar', France and the US, Western and Eastern Europe, Central Europe and Russia, widening and deepening of the EU – and joining NATO allies in out-of-area operations and doing the tough political spadework to make this step domestically acceptable – will be tricky.[77]

Even in the area where Bonn exerts the most vigorous leadership – the EU – it cannot expect to achieve many of its stated goals at the benchmark Inter-Governmental Conference of European heads of state and government in 1996. The IGC, or 'Maastricht II', will not write the EU constitution the Germans wish for. It will not offset the EU's 'democratic deficit' and distance from individual citizens. It will not resolve the tension between the real political union the Germans want and the Gaullist edifice of still powerful sovereign states that the French and British envision. It will not settle the contest between the incompatible French and German concepts of a two-speed Europe, with Bonn seeking temporary 'concentric circles' open to future accession by all qualified entrants, and Paris seeking a more permanent 'variable geometry'.[78] Indeed, Maastricht II will not get much beyond lowest-common-denominator decisions. And it certainly will not convince the skeptical Americans that in serious issues they should deal with the EU as a whole rather than with Bonn bilaterally.

The only thing the IGC will accomplish, German planners now anticipate, is incremental progress in 'common foreign and security policy'.[79] Yet however meager the headway, they figure that all participants will want to sell this as a success – and get on with preparations for the next major step of integration, European Monetary Union. Despite exchange-rate turmoil in early 1995, German government officials (if not German bankers) still expect to launch a single European currency by the turn of the century. They believe the required majority – seven excluding opt-outs, and possibly even eight states – will meet the EMU inflation, budget, and debt criteria by then.[80] They are confident that this time the Bundesbank under its new president will back EMU, even if Germany can't marshal parallel progress toward political union.[81] They think that by giving the issue a full public airing – though they keep postponing this moment of truth – they can persuade German voters that they will be gaining broader European stability rather than endangering Germany's own famed stability.

Furthermore, taking the long view, they point to vastly greater European integration by this turn of the century than the wildest optimist would have dared predict in 1945. The French and Germans are friends, against all the probabilities of history. The single European market is a reality, and outsiders are clamoring to join the EU and reproduce its institutions on their own soil. Western stability and even prosperity are spreading eastward. There is an unprecedented daily coordination of policies in Western Europe, at least in low politics – and so much transparency that no one can produce unpleasant surprises in high politics. The European Court, almost unnoticed, has established its supranational authority, somewhat on the pattern of the expansion of US federal powers a century ago under the Interstate Commerce Clause. The Schengen accord for free travel across the borders of seven EU states has been implemented, more or less, only ten years late. A limited 'Europol' police force is beginning to operate. France, Germany, and probably Britain are forming an unprecedented joint military procurement agency.[82]

Even in the more difficult medium term, the Germans also seem to be confident that they and the French can overcome bilateral tensions that grew after successful German pressure for accession to the EU of Bonn's partners of Austria, Finland, and Sweden – and after publication in fall, 1994 of an IGC proposal issued by the conservative caucus in the Bundestag.[83] Polemics about the proposal focused largely on the concept of a 'core Europe' of France, Germany, and the Benelux countries – Italy was conspicuously excluded – that would integrate faster than other EU members. What agitated the French the most, however, was the paper's challenge to Paris to put its money where its mouth was, stop playing its own balance-of-power games against Germany, and end its ambivalence about the political union that the French and Germans had broached in concert. French suspicions about an exclusive zone of influence by Germany to its east and north might well be realized, the paper warned, rattling Bismarck's sword, if France did not stop stalling on any 'concrete steps of integration'. Furthermore, the paper announced, some French movement on a European cartel office, extravagant agricultural subsidies, and cooperation between NATO and the WEU would be necessary.[84]

Paris could not answer the German challenge definitively before its presidential election in spring of 1995. The German threat to act unilaterally may have had some impact on the Gaullists, however, since all candidates subsequently declared their allegiance to Europe.[85] The Germans let up on their pressure for a time, produced some more money to balance widening of EU membership to the north and east with attention to French concerns in the Mediterranean[86] – and waited for the next opportunity to move two steps forward in the EU before sliding one step back.

The German elite consensus on ends, ways and means can only be envied by the less coherent post-Cold-War France, Britain and US. 'The Germans [finally] know who they are,' declares one American diplomat, surprised by his own conclusion after years of despairing about the Germans' long-running identity crisis. 'The French used to be puzzled about why the rest of the world wasn't like France,' comments a German with equal reverse surprise; 'now they're puzzled about what's so special about being French.'

For years to come, no doubt, various non-German think-tanks will continue to sponsor conferences with provocative titles like 'Germany's New Assertiveness' or 'Unified Germany: Stabilizer or Threat?' Various British and French officials, and even the occasional American, will continue to suspect the Germans of colluding with the Russians at the expense of Central Europe, or of colluding with Central Europeans at the expense of London and Paris.

Over the years, however, the assessments of such conferences will increasingly have to be that Germany is genuinely post-national, is thoroughly European, in a way that none of its allies yet is. Unification did not, after all, reclothe the Germans in jackboots or spiked helmets. They are the same rumpled, quizzical selves that they were before union, mixing competence and self-doubt, anxiety and efficiency, seeing through a glass darkly, but figuring, on balance, that if they kept staring it down, the glass will eventually have to lighten up. Oddly enough, the congenitally pessimistic Germans agree with Walter Hallstein, the first President of the Common Market Commission, in proclaiming, 'Anyone who doesn't believe in miracles isn't a realist.'

Notes

1. The classic exposition of this view was set forth by Michael W. Doyle in 'Kant, Liberal Legacies and Foreign Affairs', Parts I and II, *Philosophy and Public Affairs* 13, 3 (Summer 1983) and 13, 4 (Fall 1983), pp. 205–35 and 323–53 respectively.
    For ongoing debate on this issue and the revival of interest in Immanuel Kant see, *inter alia*, the edition of *International Security* 19,2 (Fall 1994); and Pierre Hassner, 'Beyond the Three Traditions: The Philosophy of War and Peace in Historical Perspective', *International Affairs* 70, 4 (October 1994).
2. For a presentation of this point of view prior to the fall of the Berlin Wall, see Josef Joffe, *The Limited Partnership: Europe, the United States and the Burdens of Alliance* (Cambridge, 1987).
3. John Lewis Gaddis has been exploring this hypothesis in papers presented at various academic conferences.
4. The most famous proponent of this view was John Mearsheimer in 'Back to the Future: Instability in Europe After the Cold War', *International Security* 15, 1 (Summer 1990), pp. 5–56; and 'Why We Will Soon Miss the Cold War', *Atlantic* (August 1990), pp. 35–50. Subsequent discussion of this thesis can be found in *International Security* 15/2 (Fall 1990) and 15, 3 (Winter 1990/91).
5. See Conor Cruise O'Brien, 'Beware, the Reich is Reviving', *The Times*, 31 October 1989.
6. See Ian Davidson, 'Atlantic Alliance Fails to Read the Writing on the Wall', *Financial Times*, 12 July 1990, p. 2.
7. Ronald D. Asmus, 'Germany in Transition: National Self- Confidence and International Reticence', RAND Note N-3522–AF. Santa Monica, California: RAND, 1992.

8. It was a German, novelist Gunter Grass, who made this accusation in the most categorical fashion, in *Two States One Nation* (San Diego, 1990).
9. See John Mearsheimer, 'Back to the Future'.
10. Francis Fukuyama, *The End of History and the Last Man* (New York: Free Press, 1992). For one of the earliest statements of the contrary thesis, see Misha Glenny, *The Rebirth of History: Eastern Europe in the Age of Democracy* (London, 1990).
11. See the summary of the historical debate by Arnulf Baring, 'Germany, What Now?', in Arnulf Baring (ed.), *Germany's New Position in Europe – Problems and Perspectives* (Oxford, 1994), pp. 1–20. For more accusatory formulations of the question, see, among others, A. M. Rosenthal, 'Let's Keep Hearing About the German Yesterday', *International Herald Tribune*, 5 February 1990, p. 8, and Martha Gellhorn, 'Ohne Mich: Why I Shall Never Return to Germany', *Granta* 42 (Winter 1992). For a wary, but not accusatory, evaluation, see Fred Kempe, 'Restless Germany Rummages for a Foreign Policy', *Wall Street Journal* (Europe), 2 February 1995, p. 6. For a relaxed acceptance of Bonn's 'normalization', see Manfred G. Schmidt, 'Political Consequences of German Unification', *West European Politics* 15, 4 (October 1992), pp. 1–15; and Philip H. Gordon, 'The Normalization of German Foreign Policy', *Orbis* 38, 2 (Spring 1994), pp. 225–43. For one historian's dismissal of comparisons with Prussian Germany, see Rudolf von Thadden, 'Kein Preußen und kein Gloria', *Die Zeit*, 7 April 1995, p. 1.
12. The most controversial challenge to the axiom of 'binding [Germany] to the West' was posed by a younger generation of the new post-Wall right in Rainer Zitelmann, Karlheinz Weißmann, and Michael Großheim (eds), *Westbindung. Chancen und Risiken für Deutschland* (Berlin, 1993). It should be noted that the questioning of Germany's Western links was directed rather more at the country's other European allies than at the US.
13. See George Bush's support for unification even prior to the opening of the Berlin Wall in his interview with R. W. Apple, Jr, 'Possibility of a Reunited Germany Is No Cause for Alarm, Bush Says', *New York Times*, 25 October 1989. For accounts of the intimate American-German relationship in the 2 + 4 negotiations in 1990, see Elizabeth Pond, *Beyond the Wall: Germany's Road to Unification* (Washington, 1993); Stephen Szabo, *The Diplomacy of German Unification* (New York, 1992); Horst Teltschik, *329 Tage* (Berlin, 1991); Richard Kiessler and Frank Elbe, *Ein runder Tisch mit scharfen Ecken* (Baden-Baden, 1993); and Philip Zelikow and Condoleeza Rice, *Germany Unified and Europe Transformed* (Cambridge, MA, 1995). The 'two' in 2 + 4 referred to West and East Germany, the 'four' to the US, the Soviet Union, Britain and France.
14. Oddly, adjustment to the new German reality was much easier for the man on the street than for the political class in France. Surveys first showed majority French approval for German unification in 1983/4. By October and December 1989 surveys sponsored by the US Information Agency gave 71% and 59% overall French approval respectively. See

Ingo Kolboom (ed.), *Vom geteilten zum Vereinten Deutschland: Deutschland-Bilder in Frankreich* (Bonn, 1991), p. 30; and USIA, Research Memorandum, 14 February 1990, pp. 1 and 3.
For discussion of Britain's efforts to adjust down and still 'punch above its weight', see 'Punched Out', *The Economist*, 25 March 1995, p. 48; and Joe Rogaly, 'The Lion Studies its Navel', *Financial Times*, 1 April 1995, p. I.

15. See 'Thatcher Sees East European Progress As More Urgent Than Germans' Unity', *Wall Street Journal*, 26 January 1990, p. A12; 'Alle gegen Deutschland – Nein!', *Der Spiegel*, 26 March 1990, pp. 182–7; Horst Teltschik, *329 Tage*, pp. 115–16, 134, 148, 171; Volker Gransow and Konrad H. Jarausch (eds), *Die deutsche Vereinigung: Dokumente zu Bürgerbewegung, Annäherung und Beitritt* (Cologne Wissenschaft und Politik, 1991), pp. 16–62; Timothy Garton Ash, 'The Chequers Affair', *New York Review of Books*, 27 September 1990, p. 65; Dominic Lawson, 'Saying the Unsayable', *Orbis* 34 (Fall 1990), pp. 505–7.

16. See Horst Teltschik, *329 Tage*, esp. pp. 60–61, 372; Karl Kaiser, 'Germany's Unification', *Foreign Affairs* 70 (1990–91), p. 191; and Jochen Thies, 'German Unification – Opportunity or Setback for Europe?', *The World Today* 47 (January 1991).

17. Interview, Horst Teltschik, 16 November 1989; see also Teltschik, *329 Tage*, pp. 60ff. and 72ff. Conventional wisdom, even in Germany, still interprets the goal of monetary union as a victory for French policy over German resistance. This misunderstanding arose in part because Kohl was glad to let the French claim a triumph (and convert this into French support for closer EC political union as well), in part because for tactical reasons, Kohl wanted to let some key *Land* elections finish before saying much publicly about EMU.

18. For overviews of Bonn's foreign-policy choices as perceived in Germany, see Klaus Kinkel, 'Deutschland in Europa', *Europa-Archiv* 49,12 (25 June 1994), pp. 335–42; Klaus Kinkel, 'Deutsche Außenpolitik in einer neuen Weltlage', speech to the Deutsche Gesellschaft für Auswärtige Politik, 24 August 1994 (Foreign Ministry Press Release 1090/94); Karl Kaiser and Hans Maull (eds), *Deutschlands neue Außenpolitik, Vol. 1* (Munich, 1994); Hans-Peter Schwarz, *Die Zentralmacht Europas. Deutschlands Rückkehr auf die Weltbühne* (Berlin, 1994); Jens Hacker, *Integration und Verantwortung. Deutschland als europäischer Sicherheitspartner* ((Bonn, 1995); Hanns W. Maull, 'Japan und Deutschland: Die neuen Großmächte?' *Europa-Archiv*, 10 November 1994, pp. 603–10; and contributions by Werner Weidenfeld, Karl Kaiser and Josef Joffe in *Internationale Politik* 50, 1 (January 1995).

19. The most specific and detailed application of this debate to Germany is Peter Katzenstein's chapter, 'Taming of Power: German Unification, 1989–1990', in Meredith Woo-Cumings and Michael Loriaux, *The Past as Prelude: History in the Making of a New World Order* (Boulder, 1993), pp. 59–81. See also Katzenstein's *Policy and Politics in West Germany: The Growth of a Semi-sovereign State* (Philadelphia, 1987). For a comprehensive presentation of the neo-realist view, see Kenneth N. Waltz, 'The Emerging Structure of International Politics', *International*

Security 18, 2 (Fall 1993), pp. 44–79. See also discussion of the German examples cited in that article, in Elizabeth Pond, 'International Politics, Viewed from the Ground' and Waltz's reply, *International Security* 19, 1 (Summer 1994), pp. 195–9.

20. Roger de Weck, Editor-in-Chief of *Der Tagesanzeiger* in Zurich, attributes the unreasonable 'stubborn search for reasons to fear Germany' not only to history, but also to envy and resentment. He notes the contradictory nature of anxiety that Germany will withdraw from the EU, but also that the 'EU is . . . nothing more than a masked instrument of German power.' Essay in 'Statesman and Pragmatist Humanist,' proceedings of the InterAction Council (New York: 1995), pp. 149ff.

21. See Allensbach surveys from 1982 through 1991 in Elisabeth Noelle-Neumann and Renate Köcher, *Allensbacher Jahrbuch der Demoskopie 1984–1992* (Munich, 1993), pp. 394 and 1011.

22. In 1991. As disillusionment with the Maastricht Treaty set in, this readiness dropped by 1993 to 32% in west, 25% in east Germany. Hans-Joachim Veen and Carsten Zelle, 'Zusammenwachsen oder Auseinanderdriften?', Konrad-Adenauer-Stiftung Interne Studien 78, p. 42.

23. The FORSA Institute found in May 1994 that 64% of Germans thought Nazi ideas were 'false and bad'; 56% thought Germany started World War II; and two-thirds thought it a good thing that Germany lost the war and would not have wanted to live in Germany had it won (Andreas Juhnke and Charlotte Wiedemann, 'Die Deutschen und die NS-Vergangenheit', *Die Woche*, 1 June 1994, pp. 1ff.).

24. Baring traces this coinage, which was applied to the post-Cold War world by Jochen Thies and Hans-Peter Schwarz, to Ludwig Dehio in 1961. Baring, *Germany's New Position in Europe*, p. 17.

25. See, e.g., Kohl's plea to the British not to revert to an anti-German coalition in his speech at St Antony's College in Oxford, 11 November 1992. Bundespresseamt, *Bulletin No. 125/1992*, 25 November 1992, p. 1142.

26. One of the most succinct formulations of these foreign-policy goals is to be found in the Defense Ministry's post-Cold-War White Book. Germany's five 'central interests' are identified as 'preservation of the freedom, security and welfare of Germany's citizens'; 'integration with the European democracies in the European Union'; the 'Trans-Atlantic alliance with the US'; 'a bringing in of our eastern neighbor states to Western structures and formation of a new, cooperative-security order encompassing all the states of Europe'; and 'worldwide observance of human rights'. Bundesverteidigungsministerium, *Weißbuch* 1994, p. 42.

27. The discussion of German perceptions of foreign policy in this chapter is based essentially on interviews in the five years since unification with, among others, Chancellor Helmut Kohl; Foreign Minister Hans-Dietrich Genscher; Saxony Minister-President Kurt Biedenkopf; Wolfgang Schäuble, CDU caucus leader in the Bundestag; then Christian Democratic Union General Secretary Volker Rühe; Karl-Heinz Hornhues, Chairman of the Bundestag Foreign Affairs Committee; Joachim Bitterlich, Peter Hartmann, and Horst Teltschik, successive chief foreign-

policy advisers to Chancellor Kohl; Michael Mertes and Eduard Ackermann, successive chief advisers to Kohl on domestic policy; Uwe Kästner and Claus J. Duisberg of the Chancellery foreign-policy staff; Konrad Porzner and Hans Georg Wieck, Presidents of the Federal Intelligence Service; Major General Klaus Naumann, at the time deputy chief of staff, Politico-Military Affairs and Operations, Armed Forces Staff; Hans-Heinrich Weise of the Defense Ministry Planning Staff; General Franz-Joseph Schulze (retired); in the German Foreign Ministry: successive political directors Wolfgang Ischinger and Jürgen Chrobog, State Secretaries Hans-Friedrich von Plötz and Dieter Kastrup, Coordinator of US-German Relations Werner Weidenfeld, policy-planning directors Frank Elbe, Konrad Seitz and Klaus J. Citron, policy planning staff members Joachim von Arnim and Rudolf Adam, German representative to the EU Committee of Permanent Representatives Dietrich von Kyaw, Minister-Director of the Directorate for Central and Eastern Europe Ernst Jörg von Studnitz, director of foreign press relations Henning Wegener, Ambassador to the United Nations Hans-Otto Bräutigam, Ambassador to Ukraine Alexander Arnot, Minister Thomas Matussek in the Washington Embassy; Alexander Vershbow and Jenonne Walker, US National Security Council staff; in the US State Department: Assistant Secretary of State for European and Canadian Affairs Richard Holbrooke, Holbrooke's chief deputy John Kornblum, coordinator of aid for the former Soviet Union Thomas Simons, Director of Office of Analysis for Western Europe and Canada, Intelligence and Research, Bowman Miller, Ambassadors to Germany Charles E. Redman, Robert Kimmitt, and Vernon Walters, Deputy Chief of Mission to Germany J.D. Bindenagel; Sir David Gillmore, permanent under secretary of state and head of diplomatic service in the British Foreign Office; British Ambassadors to Germany Nigel Broomfield and Christopher Mallaby; Pauline Neville-Jones, British minister to Germany; Jan G. van der Tas, Ambassador of the Netherlands to Germany; Dominique Chassard, French minister to Germany: Dominique Moisi, executive director of the French Institute for International Relations; Hans-Joachim Falenski, senior foreign policy adviser to CDU deputy parliamentary caucus leader; Karsten Voigt, foreign-policy spokesman for the Social Democratic Bundestag caucus; Karl Kaiser, Director of Studies of the German Society for Foreign Policy; Polish Ambassador to Germany Janusz Reiter; NATO spokesman Jamie Shea; Chairman of the Konrad Adenauer Foundation Gerd Langguth; Andreas Meyer-Landrut, chief of the office of President Richard von Weizsäcker; EU Ambassador to Poland Alexander Dijckmeester; in Poland: Deputy Defense Minister Jerzy Milewski; Under Secretary of State for European Integration and Foreign Assistance Jacek Saryusz-Wolski; Senate adviser Artur Hajnicz; Professor Jerzy Holzer; Sejm members Janusz Onyszkiewicz, Bronislaw Geremek, and Jerzy Szmajdzinski; then Senior Deputy Director of the Polish Institute for International Affairs Henryk Szlajfer and Institute Fellow Mieczyslav Tomala; Polish journalists Adam Krzeminski and Karol Szyndzielorz; and German Minister to Poland Wolfdietrich Vogel.

28. Interview, 28 August 1992.
29. For advocacy of US–German cooperation in foreign policy from the American side, see Daniel S. Hamilton, 'Beyond Bonn: America and the Berlin Republic', (Washington: Carnegie Endowment Study Group on Germany, 1994). For advocacy of trans-Atlantic cooperation in security policy in general, see Nanette Gantz and John Roper (eds), *Towards A New Partnership: US–European Relations in the Post-Cold War Era* (Paris, 1993).
30. For the French side of the duet at various points since unification, see Ingo Kolboom, *XIV. Deutsch–Französische Konferenz: Deutschland und Frankreich im neuen Europe* (Bonn, 1991), *Vom geteilten zum Vereinten Deutschland: Deutschland-Bilder in Frankreich* (Bonn, 1991), and 'Die Grande Nation zur Disposition', *FAZ*, 14 August 1993, in unpaginated weekend insert; Stanley Hoffmann, 'France: Keeping the Demons at Bay', *New York Review of Books*, 3 March 1994, pp. 10–16; and Joseph Fitchett, 'Candidates in France Shift Debate Away From Europe', *International Herald-Tribune*, 19 March 1995, pp. 1, 10.
31. The bluntest statement of this insistence came in the CDU/CSU Bundestag caucus paper 'Überlegungen zur europäischen Politik' of 1 September 1994. The reunification of Germany and especially the return of Central Europe as a theater of action for Germany, the paper said, meant that 'the room for movement for Germany is now the same as for all of its Western partners'. The context was that Germany itself wishes to be bound into the EU – but if France is not willing to treat Germany as an equal, Bonn too has alternatives.
    For a critical view of responses by France to its post-Cold-War dilemmas, see Anand Menon, 'From independence to cooperation: France, NATO and European security', *International Affairs* 71, 1 (January 1995), pp. 19–34.
32. One aspect of Germany's highly mediated democracy is a far greater willingness by political elites to disregard public opinion on issues they find important than is evident in the US. Despite polls showing that only 24% of Germans want to take Central European countries in as EU members, all the main German political parties, including the Greens, support this goal. These poll results were presented in 'Erweitern oder vertiefen?' *Der Spiegel*, 5 December 1994, p. 144.
33. For an analysis of the evolution in Russian foreign-policy thinking, including the turning away from accommodating the West after late 1992 and Russian disappointment with relations with Germany, see Hannes Adomeit, 'Russia as a "great power" in world affairs: images and reality', in *International Affairs* 71, 1 (January 1995), pp. 35–68.
34. The government approached this hot potato only gingerly. For the classic, blunter presentation of the government's view, see Hans-Peter Schwarz, *Die gezähmten Deutschen: Von der Machtbesessenheit zur Machtvergessenheit* (Stuttgart, 1985).
35. The classic version of the joke has two Jews meeting on the train and probing each other about why they are there. The first says he is going to Minsk to buy wheat, whereupon the second of course deduces that he is really going to Warsaw to buy flour. After various convolutions the

second concludes that the first actually is headed for Minsk and gets angry at the patent attempt to deceive him by telling the truth: 'You tell me that you're going to Minsk to buy wheat. I'm supposed to think that you're going to Warsaw to buy flour. But I know that you're really going to Minsk for wheat. So why are you telling me a lie?' Uriel Weinrich, *College Yiddish* (New York, 1974, p. 96).

36. William Safire first coined the phrase about Iran's Rabta facility.

37. In western Germany. In eastern Germany the plurality was lower, at 36%, as against 22% (42% undecided) who would have preferred to leave Kuwait in Iraqi hands in order to avoid war. The poll was taken in February 1991. Elisabeth Noelle-Neumann and Renate Köcher, *Allensbacher Jahrbuch der Demoskopie 1984–1992*, Vol. 9 (Munich, 1993).

38. See Elizabeth Pond, 'After Gulf War: A Drive Toward European Unity', *Boston Globe*, 31 March 1991; Andrei Markovits and Jürgen Hoffmann, 'Ein amerikanischer Jude und eine deutsche Friedensrede', *Frankfurter Rundschau*, 16 February 1991, p. 6; Andrei Markovits, ' "Die Linke gibt es nicht – und es gibt sie doch" ', *Frankfurter Rundschau*, 16 February 1991, p. 6 and 'Eine nüchternde Erfahrung', *Die Zeit*, 22 February 1991; Rainer Erd, 'Deutsche Linke an die Front?', *Frankfurter Rundschau*, 20 February 1991, p. 4); 'An der deutschen Heimatfront', *Der Spiegel*, 4 March 1991, pp. 238–45; and Henryk Broder, 'Unser Kampf', *Der Spiegel*, 29 April 1991, pp. 255–67.

39. See Karl Kaiser and Klaus Becher, *Deutschland und der Irak-Konflikt: Internationale Sicherheitsverantwortung Deutschlands und Europas nach der deutschen Vereinigung* (Bonn, 1992).

40. See Harald Müller, 'German Foreign Policy after Unification' in Paul B. Stares (ed.), *The New Germany and the New Europe* (Washington, 1992), esp. pp. 139–50.

41. Rebecca West's classic *Black Lamb and Grey Falcon* (New York: Viking, 1941) sympathetically portrayed Yugoslavia and depicted especially the pre-World War II tensions between spontaneous Serbs and overbearing Germans.

42. Germany specifed formally in early December 1991 that respect for minority rights was one of the criteria for recognition. In the view of the British and French, however, diplomatic recognition proceeded so fast that Croatia felt no pressure to demonstrate compliance.

43. One Bundestag staff member recalled the period when Germany was trying to get its European partners to support the US proposal to lift the arms embargo and 'Kinkel would come back from Brussels every Monday, throw up his hands, and say "we got outvoted 11 to one." '

44. Some echoes of the original condemnation of Germany can still be heard today. For a more even retrospective distribution of Western blame, however, see Misha Glenny, 'Yugoslavia: The Great Fall', *New York Review of Books*, 23 March 1995, pp. 56–65; and Sabrina Petra Ramet, 'The Yugoslav Crisis and the West: Avoiding "Vietnam" and Blundering into "Abyssinia" ', *East European Politics and Societies* 8, 1 (Winter 1994). For an argument against blaming the worsening of the war on Germany's 'premature' recognition of Croatia and Slovenia, see Mark

Almond, *Europe's Backyard War: The War in the Balkans* (London, 1994).

45. Members of the European Parliament, which was established to provide the same kind of popular representation for the EC as a whole that national parliaments do for member states, were first elected by direct vote in the 1970s. They cannot originate legislation and still have few other powers. As a consequence, few of them are young future leaders in their countries; more are senior politicians who have been rewarded with a sinecure after a lifetime of national service.

46. The Commission, the EU's executive arm, consists of the President (Jacques Delors from the mid-1980s to the mid-1990s, Jacques Santer since then) and his cabinet of commissioners with specific portfolios. The Commission in Brussels spends the EU's money, is the sole originator of EU legislation, directs the EU bureaucracy, and is otherwise immensely powerful. It has sometimes been viewed by Germans as the proto-government of a future European political union. It is definitely not viewed in that light by the British and French, who want the member national-states to continue as the top decision-makers in the form of the 'European Council', or thrice per half-year summits of heads of government or state. In practice, much of the EU's business is carried out by the Council of Ministers (periodic meetings of foreign or finance or other national ministers) and by the less well known Committee of Permanent Representatives (appointed by government chiefs) residing in Brussels.

47. Among the most famous appeals were the 1952 Social Democratic constitutional challenge to rearmament under the European Defense Community Treaty and the 1973 Bavarian challenge to the Intra-German Basic Treaty. See Donald P. Kommers, *Judicial Politics in West Germany: A Study of the Federal Constitutional Court* (Beverly Hills/ London, 1976).

48. In fact, activism in the 1990s by German *Länder* intent on clawing back powers that had seeped away from them to Bonn over the previous four decades could turn out to be one of the most potent defenses of subsidiarity in the EU. The *Länder* insisted on revising the German constitution to guarantee EU consultation with the *Länder* on areas originally reserved to them in the Federal Republic. The most significant early application was a 1995 German constitutional court ruling that the European Council could not set European content quotas for TV broadcasts. See fr., 'Der Bund muß bei europäischen Entscheidungen auf die Länder Rücksicht nehmen', *FAZ*, 23 March 1995, p. 1. For French pressure on the EU to restrict American and other foreign programming on European stations to 49%, see Tom Buerkle, 'EU Does About-Face on Television Quotas', *International Herald-Tribune*, 23 March 1995, p. 1.

49. The Chicago Council on Foreign Relation 1995 edition of 'American Public Opinion and US Foreign Policy' showed that two-thirds of all Americans and 98% of the elite continued to support active foreign engagement by the US. In positive rating of foreign countries Germany held its fourth place, tied with Mexico, after Canada, Great Britain, and Italy. See John E. Rielly, 'The Public Mood at Mid-Decade', *Foreign*

Policy 98 (Spring 1995), pp. 76–93; and C. K., 'Das Virus des Neoisolationismus hat Amerika nicht erfaßt', *FAZ*, 16 March 1995, p. 5.

50. See Alan Cowell, 'Bush Challenges Partners in NATO Over the Role of the US', *New York Times*, 8 November 1991, p. 1.

51. For a description of more general European nervousness about Clinton in this period of limbo, see Lionel Barber, 'EuroThrash: Our Allies Up in Arms', *Washington Post*, 24 October 1993, p. C1.

52. In monetary terms, the OECD calculated that in 1992 Germany donated $3.9 billion, or almost half of the total $8.1 billion development aid by OECD member states to Central and Eastern Europe. (The second largest donor, the US, gave $700 million.) If all official and private sources are included, Germany gave some 60% of the total $15.1 billion OECD aid. These figures include money for housing for military officers returning from Germany. Press release of the German Embassy in Kiev, 11 May 1994. See also 'EC Says 57% of Aid to Soviets Is German', *International Herald-Tribune*, 22 January 1992, p. 2, and Wolfgang H. Reinicke, 'Toward a New European Political Economy', in Paul Stares (ed.), *The New Germany and the New Europe* (Washington, 1992), p. 192.

In trade, Germany is the leading partner of virtually every Central and East European country. Total two-way trade with the region topped DM100 billion for the first time and surpassed German-American trade in 1994, with especially dynamic growth with the 10 states associated or soon to be associated with the EU: Poland, Hungary, the Czech and Slovak Republics, Estonia, Latvia, Lithuania, Bulgaria, Romania, and Slovenia. See Stü., 'Kräftiger Zuwachs im Osthandel', *FAZ*, 31 March 1995, p. 17; and hig., 'Osteuropa erreicht als deutscher Handelspartner das Niveau Amerikas', *FAZ*, 8 April 1995, p. 14.

As of this writing, it is still too early to judge what the eventual German share in investment in the region will be, before the expected surge in Western investment in Central and Eastern Europe in the late 1990s. The UN's Economic Commission for Europe calculated in spring 1995 that the US has provided more than half of long-term $118 billion investment committed to Central Europe and the former Soviet Union. $82 billion of this is earmarked for oil and gas projects in Kazakhstan and Russia. Turkey held second place with 13%, while Western Europe as a whole provided about 25% of the total. See Frances Williams, 'Investors Head for Kazakhstan', *Financial Times*, 28 March 1995, p. 7.

53. For the expectation of strong continuity in a risky search for a German sphere in central Europe, see James Kurth, 'Mitteleuropa and East Asia', in Meredith Woo-Cumings and Michael Loriaux, *Past as Prelude: History in the Making of a New World Order* (Boulder, 1993).

For a British analysis of the view that there is a necessary conflict between Kohl's 'Rhineland,' pro-European views and a more national 'Eastern orientation', see A. J. Nicholls, 'Germany and the European Union: Has Unification Altered Germany's European Policy?', *IHJ Bulletin* 14, 3 (Summer 1994), International House of Japan, Tokyo, pp. 1–7. Nicholls places the *Frankfurter Allgemeine Zeitung* and the Bundesbank in the national camp and in opposition to European

Monetary Union. He thinks the pro-European inclination will prevail, however.

54. This attitude is perhaps to be expected among elites. What is more remarkable is the shared popular regard for Germany. The EU's 1995 opinion survey question 'Where does our country's future lie?' with a choice of only two answers (USA or EU) nonetheless elicited the spontaneous addition of 'Germany' (and of no other single country) from a significant number of respondents in every Central and East European country. In Hungary 9% added Germany, in Poland 7%, in the Czech and Slovak Republics 2% and 1%. These answers were in addition to overwhelming pluralities for the EU of 22%, 37%, 40%, and 32% respectively. European Commission, *Central and Eastern European Eurobarometer* (Brussels, March 1995).

55. The name derives from the summit of these states' leaders in the Hungarian city of Visegrad in February 1991. The intent was to seek strength in numbers both in moving away from the still existing Soviet Union and in petitioning to join the EC at a time when France was vetoing the Central Europeans' bid for associate membership. Their cooperation disintegrated as each of the capitals – especially Prague after Czechoslovakia split into two nations – sought to outbid the others for the West's favor. See Rudolf L. Tokes, 'From Visegrad to Krakow: Cooperation, Competition, and Coexistence in Central Europe', *Problems of Communism*, November-December 1991, pp. 100–114; Milada Anna Vachudova, 'The Visegrad Four: No Alternative to Cooperation?' *RFE/RL Research Report* 2, 34 (August 1993), pp. 38–47; and Christoph Royen, 'Die 'Visegrad' – Staatengruppe: Zu früh für einen Nachruf', *Europa-Archiv* 49, 22 (25 November 1994), pp. 635–42.

56. On the Czech-German spat, see Hansjakob Stehle, 'Alte Hypotheken', *Die Zeit*, 17 March 1995, p. 10. On the expulsion of Germans from the Sudetenland, Poland and Königsberg/Kalingrad, see John Sack, *An Eye for an Eye* (New York: Bowker, 1993) and Alfred M. de Zayas, *The German Expellees: Victims in War and Peace* (New York, 1994).

57. See Michael Ludwig, *Polen und die deutsche Frage, Mit einer Dokumentation zum deutsch-polnischen Vertrag vom 17. Juni 1991* (Bonn: Europa, 1990); Hans-Adolf Jacobsen and Mieczyslaw Tomala (eds), *Bonn Warschau: Die deutsch-polnischen Beziehungen 1945–1990: Analyse und Dokumentation* (Cologne: Wissenschaft und Politik, 1991); Wojtek Lamentowicz, 'Erwartungen an Deutschland', *Internationale Politik* 50, 1 (January 1995), p. 37ff.; Michael Ludwig, 'Die eigenen Sünden werden bewußt', *FAZ,* 23 February 1995, p. 8; Andrzej Szczypiorski, 'Das Ende aller Zivilisation', *Die Zeit*, 24 March 1995, p. 64; and Michael Ludwig, 'Gute Absicht, zweifelhafte Wirkung', *FAZ,* 16 March 1995, p. 6.

58. The Polish Central Statistical Office officially calculates 1993 growth at 3.8% and estimates 1994 growth at 4.5%. Privately, some economists estimate 6% growth for 1994. Interviews with Polish officials. See also *Financial Times* special section on Poland, 28 March 1995, pp. II and VII.

59. See Claus J. Duisberg, 'Der Abzug der russischen Truppen aus Deutschland', *Europa-Archiv* 49, 16 (25 August 1994), pp. 461–9.

60. One of the unexpected consequences of this shift, with immense ramifications for Germany's economic and foreign policy, Bundesbank President Hans Tietmeyer notes, is that the Deutschmark is now a safe haven whenever there is currency instability in the world. Until 1994, so long as eastern Germany could become hostage to Russia at any moment, this was not the case. The 1995 market revaluation of the world's second reserve currency by 20 pfennig against the dollar dramatized this change. Tietmeyer to the Bertelsmann workshop of American journalists, Gütersloh, 20 March 1995.

61. See Bruce Clark and Chrystia Freeland, 'Still master of the Kremlin', *Financial Times*, 17 March 1995, p. 15.

62. The 1975 Helsinki Conference on Security and Cooperation in Europe, with participation by the US, Canada, and all European states except Albania, was not a binding treaty. It nonetheless defined a common commitment not to change European borders by force – and, for the first time, formally blessed the concept that violation of human rights in any one country is not only a domestic issue, but is a matter of legitimate international concern. In 1990 there was much speculation that the CSCE might become the framework for security east of Germany. As the Central Europeans rejected being shunted off to the CSCE and clamored instead to get into NATO, however – and as the Soviet Union split up in 1991 and its dozen-plus successor states all joined CSCE, the institution lost its glamor. It was upgraded to the *Organization* of Security and Cooperation in Europe in 1995, but its secretariat remained minuscule.

63. Volker Rühe, 'Shaping Euro-Atlantic Policies: A Grand Strategy for a New Era', Alastair Buchan Memorial Lecture, International Institute for Strategic Studies, 26 March 1993. Text distributed by the German Defense Ministry.

64. For recent American articulation of the arguments, see Richard Holbrooke, 'America: A European Power', *Foreign Affairs*, March/April 1995, USIS Information and Texts No. 18, Z 12481 B; Ronald D. Asmus, Richard L. Kugler, and F. Stephen Larrabee, 'NATO Expansion: The Next Steps', and Michael E. Brown, 'The Flawed Logic of NATO Expansion', *Survival* 37, 1 (Spring 1995), pp. 7–33 and 34–52 respectively. For Rühe's championing of swift expansion, see his speeches at Stanford University on 27 February, Council on Foreign Relations, New York City on March 1, and Georgetown University on 2 March 1995 (texts distributed by the German Defense Ministry). For a negative German analysis, see Klaus Kinkel, 'NATO Requires a Bold But Balanced Response to the East', *International Herald Tribune*, 21 October 1993; and Karl-Heinz Kamp, 'The Folly of Rapid NATO Expansion', *Foreign Policy* 98 (Spring 1995), pp. 116–29.

65. Discounting 20% undecided, 72.8% thought Kuchma is making 'progress in keeping the promises he made during the campaign, and [should be given] more time to make the other changes he promised.' 27.2% disagreed. By contrast, on the same scale, only close to 16% approved, while 84% dispproved, of the job parliament is now doing. The poll was conducted in December 1994 by the Kiev International Institute of Sociology for the Washington-based International Foundation for Elec-

toral Systems and distributed by the foundation in an 'Analysis of Preliminary Results' on 18 January 1995.

66. See Matthew Kaminski and Chrystia Freeland, 'Kiev tightens Crimean grip as Moscow's back is turned, *Financial Times*, 23 March 1995, p. 3: and Kaminski and Freeland, 'Ukraine signs accord on Russian debt', *Financial Times*, 21 March 1995, p. 2.

67. See, for example, 'weniger forsch', *Der Spiegel*, 3 April 1995, pp. 72–4. German diplomats profess some puzzlement as to what the European 'periphery', as coined by Defense Minister Rühe, actually means. In line with the consensus that the Bundeswehr should stick closer to home in the future, however, the Bonn government did decline to send any Bundeswehr units to Angola.

68. For press coverage of and commentary on the decision see, e.g., Claus Gennrich, 'Kinkel: Jetzt sind wir frei – wenn der Sicherheitsrat zustimmt', *FAZ*, 14 July 1994, p. 1; and Ulrich Fastenrath, 'Was ist der Bundeswehr nach dem Karlsruher Spruch erlaubt?' *FAZ*, 22 July 1994.

69. Between 1990 and 1994 German defense spending dropped from 3.3% of GDP to 2.8%. The Defense Ministry has now been promised a constant DM47.5 billion, or about a third of annual transfers to eastern Germany. See fy., 'Bilanz und Programm der deutschen Sicherheitspolitik,' *Frankfurter Allgemeine Zeitung*, 16 March 1994, p. 1; and Deutsche Presse-Agentur (dpa)/Reuter, '49 Milliarden Mark neue Schulden', *Süddeutsche Zeitung*, 1 April 1995, p. 5.

   For a preview of Defense Ministry thinking about the uses of the Bundeswehr once Russian troops left Germany, see Dieter Mahncke, 'Wandel im Wandel: Bundeswehr und europäische Sicherheit', *Beilage zum Parlament: Aus Politik und Zeitgeschichte*, B 15–16, 9 April 1993, pp. 40–46.

70. See Lafontaine interview, 'Keine Tornados nach Bosnien', *Die Zeit*, 24 March 1995, p.4; ban., 'Lafontaine widerspricht Scharping', *Frankfurter Allgemeine Zeitung*, 3 February 1995; and Günter Bannas, 'Bei der Seeheimern erntet Verheugen nörgelnde Unruhe', *Frankfurter Allgemeine Zeitung*, 18 March 1995, p. 3.

71. Scharping at the Bertelsmann workshop for American journalists, Gütersloh, 19 March 1995. See also Günter Verheugen interview, 'Kohls gefährlicher Sonderweg', *Focus*, 25 February 1995, pp. 24–6.

72. See Gunter Hofmann, 'Was wollen sie, wofür stehen sie?', *Die Zeit*, 17 March 1995, p. 5f.; and sto., 'SPD und Grüne kritisieren Rühe', *Frankfurter Allgemeine Zeitung*, 16 March 1995, p. 4. For the first major renunciation of pacifism by Greens under the impact of the war in ex-Yugoslavia, see the interview with Helmut Lippelt, a member of the party's executive committee, ' "Die Lager müssen befreit werden" ', *Der Spiegel*, 24 August 1992.

73. The most recent opinion survey on the subject sponsored by the Clingendael Institute in The Hague, for example, showed that 56% of Dutch youth from 15 to 19 years old had a negative view of Germans. Some 71% thought Germans want to dominate others; 60% found them arrogant; 46% even found them warlike. (Lutsen B. Jansen, 'Bekannt und unbeliebt', March 1993). One exasperated Dutch ambassador to

Germany finally chided his compatriots in print for endorsing anti-German attitudes in good society in a way no other xenophobic expression would be tolerated in this scrupulously liberal society.

74. For a discussion of Dutch–German relations prior to this meeting, see Marten van Traa, 'Wohlbekannt, aber unbeliebt?', *Europa-Archiv* 49, 17 (10 September 1994), pp. 491–8.

75. See the deliberate use of the phrase in President Roman Herzog's keynote speech at the fortieth anniversary of the German Society for Foreign Policy, 'Die Globalisierung der deutschen Außenpolitik ist unvermeidlich', *Bulletin*, Presse- und Informationsamt der Bundesregierung, 15 March 1995, pp. 161–5; and Wolfgang Ischinger and Rudolf Adam, 'Alte Bekenntnisse verlangen nach neuer Begründung,' *FAZ*, 17 March 1995, pp. 8f. Herzog confronted the taboo head on, asserting, 'Just now one again reads a lot about the contradiction between a foreign policy based on interests and one based on responsibility. Realists, according to the stereotype, conduct a policy of interests, idealists a policy of responsibility. [But in reality] German interests and German responsibility for the world community are the same thing.' Herzog further called for an end to the German 'freeloading' in security.

The Social Democrats, who in the 1980s castigated NATO missile deployment as a reprehensible 'policy of interests' and urged greater accommodation of the Soviet Union as a more moral 'policy of responsibility', still choke on the word. When asked point-blank if he is comfortable with the phrase 'national interest', SPD leader Scharping squirms and finally speaks only of 'European interests'.

For the sometimes more Wilhelminian use of 'national interest', see Rainer Zitelmann, *Wohin treibt unsere Republik?* (Frankfurt/Berlin, 1994).

76. See Werner Perger, 'Auf der Lauer', *Die Zeit*, 3 March 1995, p. 5.

77. For a discussion of these contrary claims before unification see, for example, David P. Calleo, *Beyond American Hegemony: The Future of the Western Alliance* (New York, 1987). For a discussion after unification, see Timothy Garton Ash, 'Germany's Choice,' *Foreign Affairs* 73, 4 (July/August 1994), pp. 65–81; and 'The European Disunion,' *Time*, 19 September 1994 (international edition), p. 67. For a German criticism that Foreign Minister Kinkel, all too conscious of the contradictory demands on German foreign policy, seems incapable of articulating priorities, see Günther Nonnenmacher, 'Woran Kinkel leidet', *FAZ*, 7 April 1995, p. 1.

78. See the interview with Wolfgang Schäuble, ' "Die D-Mark ist nicht alles" ', *Der Spiegel*, 27 March 1995, pp. 22–5.

79. Interviews. See also the interview with Schäuble published in the *Financial Times*, 'Kohl's loyal lieutenant', 21 March 1995, p. 14. For the common reading before the Schäuble interviews in the *Financial Times* and *Der Spiegel* (see previous note) that Germany would insist on parallel progress toward political union before agreeing to monetary union, see Ian Davidson, 'Answer to the puzzle', *Financial Times*, 15 March 1995, p. 12, and the *Financial Times* editorial 'Britain and Euro-defence', 23 March 1995, p. 13.

80. The seven would be Germany, France, the Benelux countries, Austria, and possibly Ireland. Denmark might bring the number to eight.

81. For an argument by the Bundesbank President that political union is necessary, see Hans Tietmeyer, 'Europäische Währungsunion und Politische Union – das Modell mehrerer Geschwindigkeiten', *Europa-Archiv* 49, 16 (25 August 1994), pp. 457–60.

82. See Bernard Gray, 'France, Germany offer UK role in arms group', *Financial Times*, 28 March 1995, p. 16; and 'Attack the frontiers', *Economist*, 8 April 1995, pp. 18f.

83. 'Überlegungen zur europäischen Politik', 1 September 1994, distributed by the CDU/CSU caucus. It is commonly referred to as the 'Lamers–Schäuble paper' after caucus chief Wolfgang Schäuble and foreign-policy spokesman Karl Lamers. For press coverage, see C. G., 'CDU und CSU wollen Kerngruppe in der EU stärken', *Frankfurter Allgemeine Zeitung*, 2 September 1994, p. 1; and Quentin Peel and Michael Lindemann, 'CDU proposes an EU top five', *Financial Times*, 2 September 1994. For a counterproposal by the EU affairs committee of the French National Assembly that seeks to strengthen the inter-governmental Council of Ministers over the EU Commission, see David Buchan, 'Pressure in France to curb power at EU centre', *Financial Times*, 17 February 1995, p. 2. For a plea for French-German cooperation in building Europe, west and east, see Dominique Moisi and Michael Mertes, 'Europe's Map, Compass, and Horizon', *Foreign Affairs* 74, 1 (January/February 1995), pp. 122–34. For other discussions of French-German vicissitudes, see Ingo Kolboom, 'Dialog mit Bauchgrimmen? Die Zukunft der deutsch–französischen Beziehungen', *Europa-Archiv* 49,9 (10 May 1994), pp. 257–64; Renata Fritsch-Bournazel, 'Paris und Bonn: eine fruchtbare Spannung', *Europa-Archiv* 49, 12 (25 June 1994), pp. 343–8; Dominique Moisi, 'Insecurities, Old and New, Plague the Paris-Bonn Axis', *Wall Street Journal Europe*, 7 February 1995, p. 8; Daniel Vernet, 'Die französischen Erwartungen', *Internationale Politik* 50, 1 (January 1995), pp. 41f.: and David Buchan, 'France seeks to deepen ties with Germany', *Financial Times*, 20 February 1995, p. 2.

84. For another comprehensive reform concept for the EU written by a primarily German committee for the Bertelsmann research project on 'Strategies and Options for Europe,' see 'Wider die Erosion von innen', *Frankfurter Allgemeine Zeitung*, 14 July 1994, p. 8.

85. See David Buchan, 'Chirac sets out foreign agenda', *Financial Times*, 17 March 1995, p. 2; and David Buchan, 'French candidates fight on common EU ground', *Financial Times*, 20 March 1995, p. 3. For an overview of French-German relations and an appeal to Britain to join the other two, see Michael Stürmer, 'An open relationship', *Financial Times*, 27 January 1995.

86. In spring of 1995 the EU was projecting aid of just under 7 billion Ecu for the Central and East European states, just over 5 billion Ecu for the Mediterranean countries. Lionel Barber, 'EU points the way for six would-be members', *Financial Times*, 11 April 1995, p. 2.

6 Whither Germany?

Bliss it was not, in that dawn of the new millennium, to be alive in Germany. But then where was it? Germany was at least finally normal – 'stink normal', in the Berlin argot – and that was good enough for those previously resigned to division, a peculiarly intense nuclear threat, Honecker's boring custodial state, and Hitler's all too exciting Third Reich. Today's Germans like just fine to be predictable, consistent, reliable – and immobile to the point of one court's ruling that a person receiving unemployment benefits is entitled to turn down a job in the neighboring district because of the cultural stress the alien environment might subject him to.

Even the whirlwind of 1989/90 failed to disturb the tranquility – some said false tranquility – at the German eye of the storm. The Federal Republic grew overnight from 61 million to 78 million. It regained sovereignty – but it also lost the ability to hide behind others. Even more than before, Germany became the regional giant that all petitioners came to, whether for money or for clout. Even more than before, Helmut Kohl – the industrialized democracies' only surviving statesman after political attrition in England and France – became the fixer of first and last resort.

Yet as German commentators noted *ad nauseam*, unification was accompanied by no summons to blood, sweat, and tears – and by no spontaneous voluntarism of starry-eyed idealists moving to the new frontier. The government simply set up the Treuhandanstalt in Göring's old Nazi Aviation Ministry and left it to the bureaucrats to sort out the privatization bids, unmoved by any special lofty vision. For their part, the western *Länder* also drafted large numbers of civil servants to go east on two-year loan, but the spirit of most was less one of adventure than of obligatory inconvenience. Young law graduates from the glut who could not snare the few good jobs in the west jumped an entry grade or two when they went east – but still surprisingly few of them chose to do so. And western taxpayers, when dunned a 'solidarity surcharge' on their income tax, paid up, but without enthusiasm. There were few heroics – and there was lots of grumbling.

There was also something a good deal nastier as that xenophobic violence spread from Hoyerswerda in Saxony, to Rostock in Mecklenburg, to Mölln in the west, killing 17 victims and terrorizing hundreds or thousands more in the unhappy year of 1992. What was even more disturbing than the drunken youths who threw gasoline bombs into Vietnamese or Romany or Turkish hostels were the hundreds of onlookers in Rostock who cheered the skinheads on, night after night, as the police were excruciatingly slow in stopping the assault.

The recession and long-term structural unemployment too added to the foreboding. Not only did west Germany have to renovate a desolate east German economy. It discovered that its own illustrious model was looking shabby. It lacked the venture capital and high tech of Silicon Valley, Japan, and the new Asian tigers. Its wages, and its state levies of 44.5% of GDP, were too high. To an increasing number of Social Democratic mayors as well as to the conservatives in general, it seemed that Germany's famous small- and medium- sized businesses were being strangled by red tape, minute regulations, overlong university education – and compulsory 6.30 p.m. store-closing hours that kept consumers harassed, policemen overworked, and hard-working Turkish entrepreneurs poorer than they would otherwise wish.

There was also something profoundly unsettling in the east–west dissonances. Germans were dealing with Germans, after all, with the same grim and glorious national memories, the same temperament, the same thundering Reformation, the same *Innerlichkeit*, the same Faustian temptations. To be sure, the last forty years had pulled the Germans in different directions. West Germans, in ways that still surprised them when they thought about it, had finally carried the Protestant ethic to the logical political conclusion of Western liberal democracy – yet some corporate aspects of this particular version of the genre would not be all that unfamiliar to east Germans. East Germans had internalized yet again the lesson of passivity and obedience to the hierarchy – yet the habit of conformity this lesson taught wasn't all that strange, in a rather different context, to West Germans. They should be growing together, as Willy Brandt said. And maybe Berlin and Brandenburg were 'fusing' in a rational way that the sclerotic irrational *Länder* in the west seemed incapable of doing. But somehow the Berlin theaters, cafés, and even orchestras in east and west kept nurturing their separateness. Kreuzberg and Prenzlauerberg remained two different worlds. Cologne remained remote from Leipzig.

Even more distressing in a political sense was a disaffection from the centrist parties, measured not only in regional votes of up to 11% for the Republikaner (in Baden-Württemberg in spring of 1992) and other far-right parties, but also in the drop in loyal support for the mainstream parties and the rise in swing votes. Back in 1980 the three main parties took 98% of the ballots, and 60% of these came from faithful supporters who provided stability by always voting for the same party; only 24% were floating votes. By 1990 only 88% went to the three main parties of the CDU/CSU, the Social Democrats, and the Liberals, with only 44% loyal voters and 41% floaters. Moreover, election turnout fell in the same decade from 89% to 78%; contentment with democracy dropped from 90% to 79%; the number doubting the truthfulness of political leaders rose from 33% in 1977 to 40% in 1992; and those with confidence in government and parliament fell from 70% in 1980 to 42% in 1991.[1]

Both the level of violence and the degree of political 'sulkiness', as it was called, were minor by comparison with the US, but they seemed to presage breakdown to Germans. Talk about an economic, political and even moral crisis swept the editorial pages. Had the self-correction of democracy ceased to function? Had the Germans' creeping consensus slowed to such a crawl as to constitute stagnation? Had the Germans' suspicion that they were about to lose their Deutschmark aborted their European consciousness? Was democracy, bestowed on the Germans by Western conquerors and unwrested by themselves (until now, in eastern Germany), finally going to face the lethal test of economic depression that everyone had been waiting for for 40 years?

Farther afield, did the backlash to the Maastricht Treaty signal the demise of European cooperation all around? Did the ejection of the British pound and the Italian lira from the more rudimentary European exchange-rate mechanism preclude any more ambitious European Monetary Union? And if the European bicycle stopped, wouldn't it fall back into a perilous every-man-for-himself? Was ex-Yugoslavia after all the wave of the future, obliterating even NATO in its wake?

There were no dramatic answers to these questions and doubts, no flashes of lightning that dispelled the malaise. But imperceptibly the apprehension lifted, and the old consensus reasserted itself, in steady, unspectacular adaptation to the new cosmos. The Bundestag quietly amended the constitution to declare unification complete and foreclose any future attempts to reclaim Polish territory – and to restore to the *Länder* competences they had forfeited to the center over four decades. After ten years of vacillation, parliament also finally expanded nursing care for the elderly, but otherwise trimmed social benefits; and after a similar gestation period it launched a major 20-year program to expand railway links and connect them with neighbors. After objecting for years that its open trading system didn't allow such intrusive intervention, the Bundestag also passed exemplary laws against export of components for weapons of mass destruction. And after years of resistance, all major German nuclear suppliers acepted full International Atomic Energy Agency safeguards.

Under what looked like no more than glacial movement, other institutions also adapted. The central government and the *Länder* wrestled out the equity and the details of their shares in the $100 – billion annual costs for the rehabilitation of eastern Germany. The constitutional court, by a vote of five to three, reversed the court's 4:4 decision of a decade earlier upholding criminal punishment for pacific sit-ins outside missile sites. With this, the 10,000 men and women convicted for 'intimidation' back in the prehistoric era of Pershing deployment in the 1980s could appeal their judgments.

Wage negotiations also resumed their famed harmony. The obvious economic strains gave employers a lever with which to regain competitiveness as trade unions accepted wage hikes lower than productivity gains. And the even more desperate situation in the east let employers there deviate from the industry-wide contracts that prevailed in the west as workers in various plants decided they would rather have work at lower wages than see their plants go bankrupt.

To the chagrin of the 'post-industrialist' left, the consensus system further worked to reassert old-fashioned 'materialist' concerns about jobs and careers above urges to clean up the environment and redistribute more wealth. In part, this represented the usual retreat in a period of recession from the luxury of generosity. In part, it was the misfortune of the more programmatic left to have chosen, once again, the route that would alienate voters, as when it opposed German rearmament, firm ties to the West and the EC, and, finally, sotto voce, German unification. Most conspicuously, the last choice spawned a new intellectual generation; the "89ers', whose conditioning event was the fall of the Berlin Wall, rebelled against the "68ers,' the intellectual agenda-setters, if not the political power-holders, for 20 years.[2]

The fierce internecine and left–right disputes over east German novelist Christa Wolf, post-modernism, the liberation of literature from political correctness, the merger of the east and west Berlin PEN club and writers' unions, the Gulf war, and dispatch of the Bundeswehr outside the NATO area faded. The environmentalist Greens in particular, returning to the Bundestag in 1994 after a clear victory of 'Realos' over 'Fundis' in the party, shed their earlier belligerence and prepared for the eventual day of coalition even with the conservatives. The conservatives reciprocated, and reserved one vice-president's slot in the Bundestag, for the first time, for a Green. The party brought with it the first ethnic Turk to be elected to parliament. For the first time, too, it took the portfolio of a classic ministry, justice, in Hesse. In the end, Germany's consensus system was not sabotaged by the Greens, as the conservatives had feared when the maverick party sprang up in the 1980s. Instead, the system absorbed the Greens, and was reinvigorated by them.

In the most crucial issue of halting violence against foreigners, consensus took a new form as hundreds of thousands of Germans marched with candles to show solidarity with murdered Turks – and to demonstrate to the Rostock onlookers that even passive condoning of xenophobia is wrong. Police work gradually improved, and the first prison sentences for perpetrators of anti-foreign violence made clear to would-be imitators that this was no game.

After ten years of inconclusive debate, too, the Bundestag passed a further constitutional amendment restricting the conditions under which foreigners could apply for asylum. Opponents of the change feared it would end the most open asylum policy (as distinct from immigration) in European practice. The government argued instead that it would cut the dangerous support for right-wing Republikaner among unemployed Germans who resented all the welfare payments to Tamils and Ghanaians.

In the first year of practice the new provisions certainly did reduce the number of newcomers. The 1992 peak of 438,000 asylum seekers (out of a total of 700,000 refugees, asylum seekers, and ethnic German immigrants that year) dropped to 323,000 in 1993. Specifically, the number of applicants in the six months after the change went into force in July, 1993 – 99,000 – was less than half the first six-month figure of 224,000. Germany still takes in more asylum seekers than the rest of the EU combined, and 87% of Germans support the right to political asylum.[3] But 70% of Germans prior to the constitutional amendment also thought Germany should take in fewer asylum seekers.

The amendment did pacify these voters. After its passage, opinion surveys showed a steady drop in sympathy for the Republikaner from 5% or 6% in the first half of 1993 – enough to win seats in any Bundestag election – down to 4% by December 1993, 3% the following June, 2% in August and September, and a negligible figure by the time of the actual election in October 1994. Voters' ranking of 'asylum seekers and foreigners' in Germany as the problem that most worried them ebbed correspondingly; it topped the list until the amendment was passed, then fell behind unemployment and the long recession.[4]

In this new area of primary concern, an economic upturn in fact began toward the end of 1993 in the west and even more in the east. Hope returned. People started to reconstruct stable lives and expectations out of the comprehensive cataclysm they had been through.

The timing could not have been better for Kohl. As he launched his general election campaign in early 1994, he trailed his Social Democratic rival, Rudolf Scharping, by 18 points;[5] at the kickoff CDU convention he had to exert every effort to persuade the party faithful not to give up and concede defeat then and there. As the economy continued to improve, however, so did his ratings. By October all the dissatisfied easterners and disgruntled westerners nonetheless gave Kohl's coalition a narrow but functioning majority.

By the new year of 1995 the Allensbach Institute recorded the highest jump in optimism in 35 years. By later that year the standard of living in the east was surging past Greece's (sunshine not factored in). The first twinges of a new envy of eastern investment and lean-production industry emerged among west Berliners and west Germans. German growth was up to 3% (8.5% in the east), and despite a debt burden absorbing 24% of revenues, Germany looked as if it would meet the EMU guidelines by the turn of the century. Structural employment persisted, but at least the jobless figures settled down to an overall 9% (14% in the east). German machine tool exports continued to stream abroad, despite a *de facto* 7% Deutschmark revaluation that logically should have priced them out of the market.

Somewhere along the way, too, all the old 1980s' talk about a German identity crisis evaporated. The EU, though it backed away from writing a new European constitution, headed toward economic and monetary union – and agreed on the concrete guidelines for admitting Central European members. Mitterrand retracted his earlier threat to pull French troops out of Germany, and the Gaullists, *faute de mieux*, accepted the utility of European integration. NATO held together.

All told, the united Germans could look back at their first five years and say, with the famous jibe about Wagner, that the music hadn't been as bad as it sounded.

Yes, the record of Germany is unsatisfactory. It should admit it is an immigration land – one of the most desirable ones in the world, in fact – and pass the appropriate legislation. It should make it easier for

Turks who speak perfect Swabian to become citizens – and other parties besides the Greens should elect some of those Turks who are citizens to parliament. It should pull up its competitive socks in industry and E-mail, and regain a work ethic. It should cut stultifying subsidies. Dynamism should replace entropy. Germany should further get the Ossis and Wessis talking to each other more than they do. It should articulate lucid priorities in foreign policy and not try so hard to be liked by everyone from the Chinese to the Fiji Islanders. It should do better at reconciling the French and Americans, NATO and WEU, widening and deepening. It should wring more money out of the EU to help stabilize Ukraine. It should persuade Turks to like Kurds, and Greeks to like Turks, and Russians to like Chechens, and Armenians to like Azeris, and Serbs to like Bosnians.

But then so should everybody else. Germany's new normality presumably grants it the same tolerance for mistakes that others enjoy.

Given the alternatives of history, maybe that is very Heaven after all.

Notes

1. Konrad-Adenauer-Stiftung surveys.
2. See Patrick Süskind, 'Deutschland, eine Midlife-crisis', Der *Spiegel*, 17 September 1990, pp. 116–25; Hermann L. Gremliza, *Krautland einig Vaterland* (Hamburg: Konkret, 1990); Ulrich Greiner, 'Flucht in die Trauer', *Die Zeit*, September 18, 1992, p. 69; Heinz Bude, *Das Altern einer Generation. Die Jahrgänge 1938 bis 1949* (Frankfurt: Suhrkamp, 1995); and Claus Leggewie, *Die 89er: Porträt einer Generation* (Hamburg: Hoffmann & Campe, 1995). For a skeptical view of the whole notion of political generations, see Warnfried Dettling, 'Die Achtundsechziger und die Neunundachtziger', *Die Zeit*, 7 April 1995, p. 29. For a contrarian new-right view that Germany has drifted to the left since unification as recycled east German Communists have reinforced the western '68ers, see Rainer Zitelmann, *Wohin treibt unsere Republik?* (Frankfurt and Berlin: Ullstein, 1994).
3. Ronald J. Bee, 'New Challenges to Germany: Foreigners and the German Response' (Washington: AICGS Seminar Paper 7, March 1994), p. 7.
4. The percentage of respondents listing foreigners and asylum seekers as their first concern was 67% in December of 1992, about 50% in the first seven months of 1993, going down to 32% in September and October, 29% in November, and 26% in December and January 1994 (Politbarometer Forschungsgruppe Wahlen, Mannheim).
5. Politbarometer January 1994. Forschungsgruppe Wahlen, Mannheim.

Bibliography

Acton, John Emrich Edward Dalberg, *Essays in the History of Liberty*, Indianapolis 1985

Albert, Michel, *Capitalisme contre Capitalisme*, Paris 1991, English translation, London 1993

Allemann, Fritz Rene, *Bonn ist nicht Weimar*, Cologne 1956

Backer, John H., *Winds of History*, New York 1983

Bade, Klaus J., *Vom Auswanderungsland zum Einwanderungsland?* Berlin 1983

Bagster-Collins, Elijah W., *The Teaching of German in Secondary Schools*, London 1904

Baring, Arnulf, *Deutschland, was nun?* Berlin 1991

Baring, Arnulf, ed., *Germany's New Position in Europe - Problems and Perspectives*, Oxford 1994

Barrico, Alessandro, *L'Anima di Hegel e le Mucche del Wisconsin*, Milan 1992

Berghahn, Volker, *The Americanisation of West German Industry*, New York and Leamington Spa 1986

Biermann, Wolf, *Der Sturz des Dädalus oder Eizes für die Eingeborenen der Fidschi-Inseln über den IM Judas Ischariot und den Kuddelmuddel in Deutschland seit dem Golfkrieg*, Cologne 1992

Binder, David, *The Other German*, Washington 1975

Blackbourn, David, *Class, Religion and Local Politics*, New Haven 1980

————, *The German Bourgeoisie*, London and New York 1991

Bleek, Wilhelm and Hanns Maull, *Ein ganz normaler Staat?*, Munich 1989

Bohley, Bärbel, *40 Jahre DDR*, Frankfurt 1989

Böll, Heinrich, *Billard um Halb Zehn*, Cologne 1959, English translation New York 1962

Bolaffi, Angelo, *Il Sogno Tedesco*, Rome 1993

Brandt, Willy, '. . .was zusammengehört,' *Reden zu Deutschland*, Bonn 1990

Breuilly, John (ed.), *The State of Germany*, London and New York 1992

Brubaker, Rogers, *Citizenship and Nationhood in France and Germany*, Cambridge, MA, and London 1992

Buchholz, Jochen, *Parteien in der Kritik*, Bonn 1993

Bude, Heinz, *Das Altern einer Generation. Die Jahrgänge 1938 bis 1949*, Frankfurt/Main 1995

Calleo, David P., *Beyond American Hegemony: The Future of the Western Alliance*, New York 1987

Calleo, David, *The German Problem Reconsidered*, Cambridge and New York 1978

Calvocoressi, Peter and Guy Wint, *Total War*, Harmondsworth 1972

Cipolla, Carlo M., *Wirtschaftsgeschichte und Weltbevölkerung*, Munich 1972

Clinton, Bill and Albert Gore, *Putting People First*, New York 1992

Dahrendorf, Ralf, *Gesellschaft und Demokratie in Deutschland*, Munich 1965

Deak, Istvan, *Germany's Leftwing Intellectuals*, Berkeley 1968

Dettling, Warnfried, *Das Erbe Kohls*, Frankfurt 1994
————, *Perspektiven für Deutschland*, Munich 1994
Deutscher Sonderweg, Mythos oder Realität?, Munich and Vienna 1982
Dickstein, Dagmar (ed.), *Wovon wir künftig leben wollen*, Munich 1994
Diner, Dan, *Ist der Nationalsozialismus Geschichte?*, Frankfurt 1987
Dönhoff, Marion Gräfin *et al.*, *Weil das Land sich ändern muss*, Reinbek 1992
Dyson, Kenneth (ed.), *The Politics of German Regulation*, Aldershot 1992
Edinger, Lewis J., *Kurt Schumacher*, Stanford, CA 1965
Education at a Glance, OECD Indicators, Paris 1993
Edwards, Jeremy and Klaus Fischer, Banks, *Finance and Investment in Germany*, Cambridge 1994
Eley, Geoff, *From Unification to Nazism*, Boston 1986
Eschenburg, Theodor, *Die Herrschaft der Verbände*, Stuttgart 1955
European Commission, *Central and Eastern European Eurobarometer*, Brussels, March 1995
Fukuyama, Francis, *The End of History and the Last Man*, New York 1992
Gall, Lothar, Gerald D. Feldman, Harold James, Carl-Ludwig Holtfrerich, and Hans E. Büschgen, *Die Deutsche Bank 1970–1995*, Munich 1995
Gantz, Nanette and John Roper, eds., *Towards A New Partnership: US–European Relations in the Post-Cold War Era*, Paris 1993
Garton Ash, Timothy, *In Europe's Name*, New York 1993
————, *The Magic Lantern*, New York 1990
Gauck, Joachim, *Die Stasi-Akten. Das unheimliche Erbe der DDR*, Reinbek 1991
German Studies in the United States, Madison 1976
Giersch, Herbert *et al.*, *The Fading Miracle*, Cambridge 1992
Gimbel, John, *Science, Technology and Reparations*, Stanford, CA 1990
Gitmez, Ali and Czarina Wilpert, 'A Micro-Society or an Ethnic Community?' in John Rex *et al.* (eds.), *Immigrant Associations in Europe*, Aldershot 1987
Glenny, Misha, *The Fall of Yugoslavia*, London 1992
Glenny, Misha, *The Rebirth of History: Eastern Europe in the Age of Democracy*, London 1990
Glotz, Peter *et al.*, *Die planlosen Eliten*, Munich 1992
Goethe, Johann Wolfgang von, *Goethe's Faust*, bilingual, trans. by Walter Kaufmann, Garden City, NY 1963
Gransow, Volker, and Konrad H. Jarausch, eds., *Die deutsche Vereinigung: Dokumente zu Bürgerbewegung*, Annäherung und Beitritt, Cologne 1991
Grass, Günter, 'Rede vom Verlust' in *Reden über Deutschland*, Munich 1992
————, *Hundejahre*, Neuwied am Rhein, 1963, English translation New York 1965
————, *Two States One Nation*, San Diego 1990
Gremliza, Hermann L., *Krautland einig Vaterland*, Hamburg 1990
Growth, Competitiveness, Unemployment: The Challenges and Ways Forward into the 21st Century, Brussels and Luxembourg 1994
Guehenno, Jean-Marie, *La Fin de la Democratie*, Paris 1993
Hacker, Jens, *Integration und Verantwortung. Deutschland als europäischer Sicherheitspartner*, Bonn 1995
Hamilton, Daniel S., *Beyond Bonn: America and the Berlin Republic*, Washington 1994

Hamilton, Stephen F., *Apprenticeshop for Adulthood*, New York and London 1990

Hardach, Karl, *The Political Economy of Germany*, Berkeley, Los Angeles and London 1980

——, *Historikerstreit*, Munich 1987

Hofmannsthal, Hugo von, *Der Rosenkavalier*, Frankfurt 1962

Hohoff, *Johann Wolfgang von Goethe*, Munich 1989

Howe, Frederic C., *Socialized Germany*, New York 1916

Huckemann, Stefan and Ulrich van Suntum, *Beschäftigungspolitik im internationalen Vergleich*, Gütersloh 1994

Jäckel, Eberhard, *Frankreich in Hitlers Europa*, Stuttgart 1966

Jacobsen, Hans-Adolf and Mieczyslaw Tomala, eds., *Bonn Warschau: Die deutsch-polnischen Beziehungen 1945-1990: Analyse und Dokumentation*, Cologne 1991

James, Harold, *A German Identity*, London 1990

Joffe, Josef, *The Limited Partnership: Europe, the United States, and the Burdens of Alliance*, Cambridge 1987

Joppke, Christian, *Mobilizing Against Nuclear Energy*, Berkeley, Los Angeles and Oxford 1993

Kaiser, Karl and Klaus Becher, *Deutschland und der Irak- Konflikt: Internationale Sicherheitsverantwortung Deutschlands und Europas nach der deutschen Vereinigung*, Bonn 1992

Kaiser, Karl and Hans Maull, eds., *Deutschlands neue Außenpolitik*, Band 1, Munich 1994

Katzenstein, Peter, *Policy and Politics in West Germany: The Growth of a Semi-sovereign State*, Philadelphia 1987

Kennan, George F., *The Decline of Bismarck's European Order*, Princeton 1979

Keynes, J. M., *The Economic Consequences of the Peace*, New York 1920

Kiessler, Richard, and Frank Elbe, *Ein runder Tisch mit scharfen Ecken*, Baden-Baden 1993

Knight, Uta and Wolfgang Kowalsky, *Deutschland nur den Deutschen?*, Erlangen, Bonn and Vienna 1991

Kolboom, Ingo, ed., *Vom geteilten zum Vereinten Deutschland: Deutschland-Bilder in Frankreich*, Bonn 1991

Kolboom, Ingo, ed., *XIV. Deutsch-Französische Konferenz: Deutschland und Frankreich im neuen Europa*, Bonn 1991

Kramer, Alan, *The West German Economy*, New York and Oxford 1991

Lampedusa, Giuseppe Tomaso di, *Il Gattopardo*, Milan 1960, English translation New York 1960

Le Gloannec, Anne-Marie, *L'Etat de l'Allemagne*, Paris 1995

——, *La Nation orpheline*, Paris 1989

Leggewie, Claus, *Die 89er: Porträt einer Generation* Hamburg: 1995

Lehmann, Albrecht, *Im Fremden ungewollt zuhaus*, Munich 1991

Lippmann, Walter, *US Foreign Policy*, Boston 1943

Lipschitz, Leslie and Donogh McDonald, eds., *German Unification: Economic Issues*, Washington December 1990

Luce, Henry, *The American Century*, New York 1941

Ludwig, Michael, *Polen und die deutsche Frage, Mit einer Dokumentation zum deutsch-polnischen Vertrag vom 17. Juni 1991* Bonn, 1990

Maaz, Hans-Joachim, *Der Gefühlsstau: Ein Psychogramm der DDR*, Berlin, 1990

McAdams, A. James, *Germany Divided*, Princeton 1993

McClelland, C.E., *State, Society and University in Germany*, Cambridge 1980

McGhee, George C., *At the Creation of a New Germany*, New Haven 1989

McKinsey Global Institute, *Manufacturing Productivity*, Washington, DC, 1993

Maier, Charles S., *The Unmasterable Past*, Cambridge 1988

Manifest der 60, Das, Munich 1994

Margolies, Silvia R., *The Pilgrimage to Russia*, Madison 1968

Marschalk, Peter, *Bevölkerungsgeschichte Deutschlands*, Frankfurt 1984

Marsh, David, *The Germans*, London 1989

Marx, Henry, *Deutsche in der neuen Welt*, Braunschweig 1983

Marx, Karl and Friedrich Engels, *Ausgewählte Schriften*, Berlin 1953

Matthias, Erich, *Sozialdemokratie und Nation*, Stuttgart 1952

Michels, Robert, *Zur Soziologie des Parteiwesens*, Leipzig 1911

Miegel, Meinhard and Stefanie Wahl, *Das Ende des Individualismus*, Bonn 1993

Milward, Alan S., *The European Rescue of the Nation-State*, Berkeley 1992

Mitchell, B.R., *European Historical Statistics*, London 1980

Mitscherlich, Alexander and Margarete, *Die Unfähigkeit zu trauern*, Munich 1967, 1991

Mollo, John, *Military Fashion*, New York 1972

Mommsen, Wolfgang, *Max Weber and German Politics*, Chicago and London 1984

Murphy, Richard C., *Gastarbeiter im deutschen Reich*, Wuppertal 1982, English translation Boulder, CO, 1983

Namier, Sir Lewis B., *The Revolution of the Intellectuals*, Oxford and New York 1992

Nicholls, A.J., *Freedom with Responsibility*, Oxford 1994

Noelle-Neumann, Elisabeth, and Renate Köcher, *Allensbacher Jahrbuch der Demoskopie 1984–1992*, Munich 1993

Noelle-Neumann, Elisabeth, *Demoskopische Geschichtsstunde*, Zurich 1991

O'Brien, Conor Cruise, *The Great Melody*, London 1992

Oeberg, Sture and Helene Boubnova, 'Ethnicity, Nationality and Migration', in Russell King, *Mass Migration in Europe*, London 1993

Olson, Mancur, *The Rise and Decline of Nations*, New Haven and London 1982

Pappi, Franz Urban, 'Die deutsche Gesellschaft in vergleichender Perspektive', in Karl-Heinz Reuband *et al.* (eds.), *Die Gesellschaft der Bundesrepublik in vergleichender Perspektive*, Opladen 1995

Paret, Peter, *Yorck and the Era of Prussian Reform*, Princeton 1966

Pflueger, Friedbert, *Die Zukunft des Ostens liegt im Westen*, Duesseldorf 1994

Philipsen, Dirk, *We were the People*, Durham, NC, 1993

Platzer, Hans-Wolfgang and Walter Ruhland, *Welches Deutschland in welchem Europa?*, Bonn 1994

Poidevin, Raymond, *Les Relations economiques et financielles entre la France et l'Allemagne*, Paris 1969

Pond, Elizabeth, *Beyond the Wall: Germany's Road to Unification*, Washington 1993

Putnam, Robert D., *Making Democracy Work*, Princeton 1993

Ranke, Winfried (ed.) *August Sander, Die Zerstörung Kölns*, Munich 1985

Rückerl, Adalbert, *The Investigation of Nazi Crimes 1945–1978*, Heidelberg 1979

Russell, Bertrand, *Freedom versus Organization*, New York 1962

Scharpf, Fritz W., 'Die Handlungsfähigkeit des Staates' in Beate Kohler-Koch (ed.), *Staat und Demokratie in Europa*, Opladen 1992

Schäuble, Wolfgang, *Der Vertrag*, Stuttgart 1991

———, *Der Zukunft zugewandt*, Berlin 1994

Scheuch, Erwin, *Wie deutsch sind die Deutschen?*, Bergisch-Gladbach 1991

———, and Ute Scheuch, *Cliquen, Klüngel und Karrieren*, Reinbek 1992

———, ' "Fremdenhass" als akute Form des Rechtsextremismus' in Konrad Loew (ed.), *Terror und Extremismus in Deutschland*, Berlin 1994

Schimank, Uwe *et al.* (eds.), *Coping with Trouble*, Frankfurt and New York 1994

Schneider, Peter, *Paarungen*, Berlin 1992

Schoenbaum, David, 'The World War II Allied Agreement on Occupation and Administration of Post-War Germany', in Alexander L. George *et al.*, *US–Soviet Security Cooperation*, New York and Oxford 1988

———, *Zabern 1913*, Boston and London 1982

Schwarz, Angela, *Die Reise ins Dritte Reich*, Göttingen 1993

Schwarz, Hans-Peter, *Die gezähmten Deutschen: Von der Machtbesessenheit zur Machtvergessenheit*, Stuttgart 1985

Schwarz, Hans-Peter, *Die Zentralmacht Europas. Deutschlands Rückkehr auf die Weltbühne*, Berlin 1994

Seitz, Konrad, *Die japanisch-amerikanische Herausforderung*, Munich 1991

Silverberg, Robert (Paul Hollander), *Political Pilgrims*, New York 1981

Smith, Jean Edward, *Lucius D. Clay*, New York 1990

Smyser, W. R., *The Economy of United Germany*, New York 1992

Sombart, Werner, *Warum gibt es in den Vereinigten Staaten keinen Sozialismus?*, Tübingen 1906, English translation White Plains, NY 1976

Spotts, Frederic and Theodor Wieser, *Italy: A Difficult Democracy*, Cambridge 1986

Stares, Paul B., ed., *The New Germany and the New Europe*, Washington 1992

Szabo, Stephen, *The Diplomacy of German Unification*, New York 1992

Stern, Carola, *Willy Brandt*, Reinbek 1988

Stokes, Gale, *The Walls Came Tumbling Down*, New York and Oxford 1993

Taylor, A. J. P., *The Course of German History*, New York 1946

———, *The Struggle for Mastery in Europe*, Oxford 1954

Teaching German in America, Madison 1988

Teltschik, Horst, *329 Tage*, Berlin 1991

Thatcher, Margaret, *The Downing Street Years*, New York 1993

Thurow, Lester, *Head to Head*, New York 1992

Tocqueville, Alexis de, *Democracy in America*, New York 1956

Trumpener, Ulrich, *Germany and the Ottoman Empire*, Princeton 1968

Van der Wee, Herman, *Prosperity and Upheaval*, Berkeley and Los Angeles 1987

Waigel, Theo and Manfred Schell, *Tage, die Deutschland und die Welt veränderten*, Munich 1994

Wallach, Jehuda L. *Anatomie einer Militärhilfe*, Düsseldorf 1976
Weber, Max, 'Der Nationalstaat und die Volkswirtschaft' in *Landarbeiterfrage, Nationalstaat und Volkswirtschaftspolitik*, Tübingen 1993
———, 'Politik als Beruf', Tübingen 1993, English translation in Hans Gerth and C. Wright Mills, *From Max Weber*, New York and Oxford 1958
Werle, Gerhard and Thomas Wandres, *Auschwitz vor Gericht*, Munich 1995
White, Theodore E., *Fire in the Ashes*, New York 1953
Williamson, Samuel R., *The Politics of Grand Strategy*, London and Atlantic Highlands, NJ, 1990
Wilpert, Czarina, 'Demographische Entwicklung und Migration' in Ingrid Gogolin (ed.), *Kultur- und Sprachenvielfalt in Europa*, Munster 1991
Woo-Cumings, Meredith, and Michael Loriaux, *The Past as Prelude: History in the Making of a New World Order*, Boulder 1993
Wordsworth, William, *The Prelude*, Oxford 1959
Zitelmann, Rainer, Karlheinz Weißmann, and Michael Großheim, eds., *Westbindung. Chancen und Risiken für Deutschland*, Berlin 1993
Zitelmann, Rainer, *Wohin treibt unsere Republik?*, Frankfurt/Berlin 1994
Zundel, Rolf, *Das verarmte Parlament*, Munich 1980

Index

Aachen, 9
Acheson, Dean, 198
Adenauer, Konrad, 45, 51, 56, 67, 159, 177, 181, 211
Alcatel, 114
Allemann, Fritz René, 13
America Online, 91
American Telephone & Telegraph, 90
Angst, 14
Armenia, 10, 236
Arndt, Ernst Moritz, 20, 23, 31, 54
Asians, 175
Asylbewerber, 20
Audi, 117
Aussiedler, 20, 58, 59, 70, 72
Ausländische Mitbürger, 57
Austria, 3, 9, 192, 195, 215
Austrian Empire, nationalities in, 21–2
Azeris, 236

Baden-Württemberg, 154, 166
Baltic States, 204
Banque de France, 194
Baring, Arnulf, 44
Bartoszewski, Wladyslaw, 200
BASF, 114
Bavaria, 21, 65
Bavarian Christian Social Union (CSU), 69
Bavarian Dental Association, 97
Bavarian Motor Works, 114, 117, 123
Bayer, 114
Belgium, 1, 5, 17, 117, 123, 196, 215
BellSouth, 91
Berlin, 8, 9, 15, 161, 181, 210
Berlin Wall, 1,3, 8, 15, 19, 43, 51, 112, 147–8, 153, 177
Bernart, Helmut, 99–100
Bertelsmann, 91, 114
Bertelsmann Foundation, 107
Bethe, Hans, 14

Betriebsverfassungsgesetz , 98
Biedenkopf, Kurt, 49, 55, 110, 165, 166, 167
Biermann, Wolf, 160
Bild, 193
Bioengineering, 88
Bismarck, Otto von, 3, 6, 16, 19, 23, 92, 96, 179, 181, 182, 183, 209, 215,
Blitzkrieg, 14
Blunck, Lilo, 126
Bonaparte, Napoleon, 16, 112
Bonn, 16, 17, 19
Born, Max, 14
Bosch, 114
Bosnia, 190, 197, 203, 207, 209, 210, 212, 236
Bracher, Karl-Dietrich, 54
Brandenburg, 154, 162
Brandt, Willy, 15, 49, 71, 113, 152, 167, 201, 231
Breuel, Birgit, 157
Briand, Aristide, 11
British Telecom, 90–1
Bulgaria, 5, 149, 199
Bundesbank, 14, 17, 50, 51, 108, 126, 159, 178–9, 194
Bundesrat, 108–9
Bundestag, 87, 90, 100, 109, 193, 209, 215, 232–3, 234
Bundeswehr, 154, 197, 207–11, 233
Bush, George, 3, 178, 196

Cable & Wireless, 91
Catholics, 21–2, 23, 152, 190
Central Europe, 185–6, 192; democracy in, 178
Charlemagne, 17
Chechnya, 205, 207, 209, 212
Chile, 10; Honecker dies in, 161
Christian Democratic Union (CDU), 19, 62, 65–6, 70, 87, 94, 106, 108, 117, 164, 167, 232

Churchill, Winston, 103
Cinema, 15
Citizenship, 26–7; law, 23, 57–8,
    70–1
Clinton, William Jefferson, 195, 196,
    197
Cohn-Bendit, Daniel, 17, 68
Cold War, 2, 159, 174–5, 205, 207;
    German attachment to, 177
Cologne, 11, 12
Compuserv, 90
Computers, industry, 88–9; public
    attitudes about, 89; modem
    prices, 90
Conference on Security and
    Cooperation in Europe (CSCE),
    205, 209
Congress of Vienna, 6, 203, 211
Constitution, 61–2, 89, 92–3, 99;
    Basic Law, 28
Corporations, governance, 98, 100–2
Craig, Gordon, 44
Cranach, Lucas, 12
Croatia, 190, 210
Currency exchange, 14, 156, 194, 210,
    232
Cyprus, 199
Czech Republic, 5, 198, 199–201
Czechoslovakia, 146, 149, 185–6

Daimler-Benz, 112, 114, 125
De Gaulle, Charles, 194
Delors, Jacques, 177, 210
Delors White Paper, 64, 119
Demography, 18, 20, 63–4, 109, 124
    (*see also* emigration,
    immigration, population)
Deportation, 28
Denmark, 1, 193
Deutsche Bank, 112, 114
Deutsche Telekom, 90–1, 114, 125
Deutschmark, 3, 59, 66, 112, 126,
    174, 178, 181, 182, 193, 211, 232
Diehl, Roland, 123
Dohnányi, Christoph von, 56
Dohnányi, Klaus von, 56
Dortmund Chamber of Commerce,
    125

Dow Chemical, 122
Dresden, 111, 154; violence in 146–7
Dresdner Bank, 125
Dürer, Albrecht, 12
Düsseldorf, 111

EKO Steelworks, 122
East Berlin, 17, 55, 146–7, 149, 161
Eastern Europe, 1, 113
Eberstadt, Nicholas, 155
Economy: GNP, 14, 114; inflation,
    14; wages and benefits, 14, 105;
    public spending, 15; relation to
    Europe, 52; projections, 67–8;
    dilemma of capital, 110;
    economic planning, 92; currency
    reform, 92; GNP growth, 93;
    social market economy, 93–4;
    international comparisons, 96;
    entrepreneurship, 94; savings,
    95, 112, 120; public debt, 95;
    capital reconstruction of East
    Germany 111; per capita
    production, 114; exports, 114–
    15; environmental investment,
    116; entrepreneurial presence in,
    123; contributions to EU budget,
    182
Edelausländer, 63
Education, 15, 116–17, 124
Eggert, Heinz, 166
Emigration, 22
Employment, 53, 59–60, 87; of
    women, 68
Engholm, Björn, 61
Erhard Ludwig, 107
Eucken, Rudolf, 11
Eurocorps, 51, 196
European Commission, 119
European Community, 1, 179, 181,
    183, 186, 190 191–5; attitudes
    about unemployment, 118
European Free Trade Association,
    195
European Monetary Union, 182, 194,
    214, 232, 235
European Union, 90, 91, 151, 157,
    192, 196, 198, 199, 210, 211, 213,

235; attitudes toward union, 66–7, 180; unemployment 120; need for outside leadership, 184; 1996 intergovernmental conference, 195, 213; Europol and European Courts, 213

Extracommunitari, 63

Fallersleben, August Heinrich Hoffman von, 23, 54

Fechter, Peter, 8

Federal Republic of Germany (West Germany), 1, 2, 6, 12, 15, 16, 17, 19, 113, 147, 149, 152, military presence in, 13; conscientious objection in, 13; unification vote, 46; opinion about unification, 48–9

Fest, Joachim, 17

Financial Times, 16, 97, 114

Finland, 195, 215

Fischer, Joschka, 48, 209

Flick Friedrich, 25

Fontane, Theodor, 152, 174

Foreign policy: devotion to European unity, 180–3; American involvement in Europe, 183–4; Franco–German relations, 184–5, 212; modification of constitution, 185; central Europe, 185–6; Russia, 186; use of military, 186–90

France, 1, 6, 21, 57, 92, 113, 114, 115, 117, 123, 152, 175, 176–7, 178–9, 184–5, 187, 193, 195, 196, 203, 215, 236

Frankfurt on Main, 152

Frankfurt on Oder, 9, 111, 147–50, 200

Frankfurter Allgemeine Zeitung, 17, 190, 193

Frankfurter Rundschau, 17

Fraunhofer, 117, 123

Frederick the Great, 113

Free Democratic Party (FDP), 108

Fremdarbeiter, 57

French Revolution, 16

Friedrich, Caspar David, 174

Fukuyama, Francis, 176, 198

Furmaniak, Karl, 96

Garton Ash, Timothy, 44

Gastarbeiter, 14, 20, 24, 28–9, 57, 61, 72

Gates, Bill, 98

Gauck, Joachim, 160

Gauweiler, Peter, 66

Gazprom, 122

Geissler, Heiner, 68

General Agreement on Tariffs and Trade (GATT), 196

Geneva convention, 28

Genscher, Hans-Dietrich, 183, 184, 190

Georgia, 208

German Aerospace (DASA), 91, 118

German–American Academic Council, 108

German Chamber of Industry and Trade, 107

German Democratic Republic (East Germany), 14, 16, 18, 19, 26, 113 birthrates in, 2; Soviet military presence in, 13, 174, 198; unification vote, 46; German identity of, 47–8; public spending, 112; privatization of industry 121; fall of, 146–52; production in, 152–3, 154, 156; Soviet occupation of, 157; ex-Nazis in, 158–9; politburo in, 146, 149–52; national defense council, 161–2; Socialist Unity Party, 146, 155; outmigration from, 155–7

German Empire, 5, 7, 9, 16

German Federation of Industry, 118

German Institute for Economic Research, 119, 120

German Question, 19, 30

German unification, 2,

Gerster, Johannes, 70

Gewandhaus Orchestra, 148

Giscard d'Estaing, Valéry, 65

Glasnost , 32

Globke, Hans-Maria, 159

Greece, 157–8, 175, 236
Green Party, 14, 17, 48, 69, 182, 186, 189, 209, 210, 233–4
Greifswald, 88
Grossdeutsch, 18
Group of Seven (G–7), 206
Goethe, Johann Wolfgang von, 2, 56, 152; *Faust*, 91
Goethe Institute, 198
Goodhart, David, 97
Gorbachev, Mikhail, 15, 46, 147, 178, 186, 205
Gulf War, 50, 51, 67, 160, 187–9, 207, 233

Habermas, Juergen, 31
Hackenberg, Helmut, 148, 149
Haffner, Sebastian, 26
Haider, Jörg, 64–5
Hallstein, Walter, 216
Hamburg, 60, 152
Hanover, 21
Harvard Business School, 107
Hauptmann, Gerhard, 11
Havel, Vaclav, 200
Health care, 3, 96; dental prophylaxis, 96
Heine, Heinrich, 152
Heinemann, Gustav, 7
Helsinki Final Act, 27
Herzog, Roman, 65
Hesse, 21, 150, 209, 234
Hesse, Hermann, 11
Heyse, Paul, 11
Hispanics, 175
Historikerstreit, 8, 117
Hitler, Adolf, 6, 17, 19, 54, 65, 92, 99, 159, 180, 184, 190, 202, 209, 230
Hobbes, Thomas, 175
Höchst, 114
Hoffmann, Stanley, 50, 54
Holbrooke, Richard, 184
Holocaust, 8, 155, 189
Holy Roman Empire, 16, 200; national composition of, 20
Holzer, Werner, 17
Hondrich, Karl Otto, 117
Honecker, Erich, 19, 32, 146–7, 149, 161, 230

Hoover, Herbert, 92
Horsley, William, 70
Hoyerswerda, 50, 64, 166, 230
Hungary, 3, 5; borders opened, 146

IG-Farben, 25
IG-Metall, 57, 114
Immigration,1,17, 24–6, 27–8, 53, 54–7, 62–3, 68–73, 109–10, 149, 235–6; ethnic Germans, 55, 154; voting trends relating to, 64–5; violence against immigrants, 65, 230
Independent Women's Association, 163
Independent Union of Historians, 163
International Atomic Energy Agency, 233
International Monetary Fund (IMF), 206
Internet, 89–90; *datenautobahn*, 115
Iraq, 187–9, 207
Ireland, 5
Iron Curtain, 51
Israel, 188–9
Italy, 5, 115, 176, 177, 187, 215

Japan, 14, 115, 117, 124, 196
Jena, battle of, 111
Jews, 1, 21–2, 58, 155, 189, 200
Johnson, Lyndon, 50
Joll, James, 8

Kaliningrad (Königsberg), 9, 154
Kant, Immanuel, 175
Kanther, Manfred, 62
Kastenbauer, Joseph, Dr, 97
Keynes, John Maynard, 52
Kinkel, Klaus, 184, 205
Kirghizstan, 10
Kleindeutsch, 18
Kleist, Heinrich von, 8
Klinger, Fred, 121
Kohl, Helmut, 3, 15, 45, 49, 58, 61, 64, 65, 69, 70, 89, 104, 105, 106, 107, 108–9, 123, 178, 179, 182, 183, 185, 186, 191, 192, 193, 205, 210, 211, 212, 230, 235

Kok, Wim, 211
Kosch, Valentine, 146, 148, 149, 153
    162, 167
Koestler, Arthur, 150, 162
Krenz, Egon, 147, 148, 149
Kronawitter, Georg, 70
Krupp (Fried. Krupp A. G.), 25
Kuchma, Leonid, 184
Kultur, 11
Kurdistan, 212
Kurds, 63, 207, 236
Kuwait, 187

Labor, 57, 98–9, 114; work week, 14;
    immigrant labor, 29; industrial
    unions, 93; wages, 101;
    vocational training, 101; eastern
    trade unions, 163
Lafontaine, Oskar, 56, 209
Lampedusa, Giuseppe Tomasi di, 113
Le Carré, John, 161
Le Pen, Jean-Marie, 64, 180
Leipzig, 15, 45, 111; demonstrations
    in, 146–9; Technical University
    of, 165
Lessing, Friedrich, 152
Leutheusser-Schnarrenberger,
    Sabine, 71
Lubbers, Ruud, 210
Luther, Martin, 152
Luxembourg, 1, 114, 199, 215
Luxemburg, Rosa, 8

Maastricht Treaty, 50, 66, 191–5,
    197, 232
Macedonia, 209
Mahler, Gustav, 9
Mafia, 203
Mainz, 3
Maizière, Lothar de, 48, 56,
Maizière, Ulrich de, 56
Major, John, 193
Malta, 199
Mann, Thomas, 10, 179
Märkische Oderzeitung, 147, 150
Marsh, David, 16
Marshall Plan, 93, 198
Marx, Karl, 5
Masur, Kurt, 147, 148

Mauriac, François, 177
Max Planck Institutes, 15, 112, 163
McKinsey Global Associates, 101–2
    Melville, Herman, 87
Mengele, Josef, 87
Mendiburu, Helios, 56
Merkel, Angela, 162
Metallgesellschaft, 118
Mezzogiorno, 55, 121, 158
Miegel, Meinhard, 67, 109
Mielke, Erich, 147, 148, 161
Migration, 18
Millowitsch, Willy, 57
Milward, Alan, 53
Mitscherlich, Alexander, 47
Mitteleuropa, 180
Mitteleuropaeisch, 19
Mitterrand, François, 178, 179, 191,
    235
Modell Deutschland, 90
Mölln, 50, 60, 231
Mommsen, Theodor, 11,17
Morgenthau Plan, 92
Munich, 11, 60
Museum of German History, 8
Museum of the Federal Republic, 8

Nagorno Karabach, 207
National identity, 18, 19, 23, 46–7;
    post-national identity, 52–4, 181,
    183, 216
Nazi era, 7, 16, 99, 155–8, 160, 230
Neo-Nazis, 60–1, 177, 180; racist
    violence, 180
Netherlands, 1, 97, 114, 175, 210–12,
    215
Nietzsche, Friedrich, 1
Nippon Telephone & Telegraph, 90
Nixdorf, 88, 114
Nobel Prize, 11, 14–15
Noelle-Neumann, Elisabeth, 164
Nolte, Ernst, 8
North Atlantic Consultative Council
    (NACC), 203
North Atlantic Treaty Organization
    (NATO), 13, 30, 51 174–6, 183,
    186, 191, 195–7, 204–5, 207–8
    213, 215, 232, 233, 235–6;
    attitudes about, 51–2, 165;

North Atlantic Treaty Organization (NATO) (*cont.*) Germany as potential hegemon 175–7, 179; partnership for peace, 199–200, 203
North Rhine–Westphalia, 154
Northern Telecom, 91
Nuclear power, 2, 87–8; attitudes about, 14;
Nuclear waste, 14, 88
Nuclear weapons, 14, 232
Nuclear Non-Proliferation Treaty, 14, 206

Oberndörfer, Dieter, 69
O'Brien, Conor Cruise, 43
Oder–Neisse line, 19, 185
Oggersheim, 182
Olson, Mancur, 94
Organization for Economic Cooperation and Development (OECD), 95, 98, 123
Organization for Security and Cooperation in Europe (OSCE), 205, 207, 210
Ossis, 18, 72, 151, 153
Ossietzky, Carl von, 11
Ostpolitik, 14, 20, 69, 104
Ottoman Empire, 4, 202, 207
Owen, Wilfred, 175

Party of Democratic Socialism (PDS), 66, 69, 155, 164
Pauli, Wolfgang, 14
Perestroika, 32
Pflüger, Friedbert, 44
Pirincci, Akif, 57
Pöhl, Karl Otto, 17, 194
Poland, 5, 6, 19, 21, 147, 151, 178, 185–6, 198, 199, 202–7, 232
Political asylum, 28, 62–3, 234–5
Politicians and parties, 105–7
Population, 20–1, 57, 64; birthrates compared with other EU members, 64
Portugal, 157, 199
Post-nationalism, 181, 183
Potsdam Accords, 92
Prague, 146, 200

Prantl, Heribert, 62
Prodi, Romano, 120
Protestants, 21–2, 47, 152
Prussia, 5, 16, 21–2, 24, 45; military reform 111–12
Puzo, Mario, 150

Queisser, Hans Joachim, 123, 124
Quidde, Ludwig, 11

Reagan, Ronald, 49, 60, 105, 106
Reformation, 47
Refugees, 71–2, 213
Remarque, Erich Maria, 175
Renan, Ernest, 6
Republikaner, 69, 180, 231–2
Reunification, 16, 43, 152–4, 185; 1989–90 public opinion about, 46–7, 164; costs of, 49, 111, 120; Kohl's pragmatic approach to, 49–50; institution-building in east, 162–4; demography of, 155; economic problems, 154–8; trials for GDR crimes, 159–62; eastern growth compared with EU average, 157; 2 + 4 negotiations, 177, 202; obstructions to 177–8
Reuter, Edzard, 17, 125
Reuter, Ernst, 17
Revolution of 1848, 7
Rohwedder, Detlev, 157
Romania, 5, 149, 199
Rommel, Manfred, 17
Rosenkavalier, Der, 4
Rostock, 160, 230
Rühe, Völker, 65, 205
Rühmann, Heinz, 57
Russia, 183, 186, 196, 198, 202–7, 236
Russian Empire, 10, 21
RWE, 114

Sachs, Hans, 96
Sachs, Nelly, 15
Saint Nicholas Church (Leipzig), 146–8
Sander, August, 12
Saxony, 21, 154, 165
Schabowski, Günter, 146, 147, 149, 150, 151, 162

Scharpf, Fritz, 112
Scharping, Rudolf, 89, 209, 211, 235
Schäuble, Wolfgang, 49, 54, 71, 154
Scheel, Walter, 67–8
Schengen accord, 214
Schlüter, Harm, 117
Schmalz-Jacobsen, Cornelia, 70
Schmidt, Helmut, 17, 49, 56, 107, 108, 185
Schneider, Peter, 88
Schönhuber, Franz, 31, 65
Schröder, Dietrich, 147, 148, 151, 153, 162, 167
Schröder, Gerhard, 68
Schuman, Robert, 92, 198
Seiters, Rudolf, 61
Sejm, 207
Serbia, 5, 236
Shevardnadze, Eduard, 205
Shop hours, 99–100, 126, 231
Siedler, Wolf-Jobst, 44
Siemens, 112, 114, 124
Silesia, 21
Simitis, Spiros, 56
Singapore, 117, 126
Slovakia, 198
Slovenia, 190, 198
Social Democratic Party (SPD), 23, 61, 62, 65, 69–70, 87, 89, 99, 106, 109, 126, 162, 182, 186, 188, 208, 232
Solingen, 51, 58
Somalia, 188, 208, 209
Sombart,Werner, 89
Sonderweg, 8, 51, 96
Soros, George, 107
Spain, 114, 196
Speer, Albert, 17
Spiegel, Der, 48, 55, 117, 193
Sprint, 91
Stalin, Josef, 207
Standortdebatte, 119, 126
Standort Deutschland, 90
Stasi, 147–9, 160
Stern, Fritz, 44
Stoiber, Edmund, 193
Stolpe, Manfred, 162
Strauss, Franz, 107

Strauss, Richard, 4
Stresemann, Gustav, 11
Stunde Null, 5
Stuttgart, 17
Süddeutsche Zeitung, 62
Sweden, 114, 195, 215
Switzerland, 97, 114, 192

Tadzhikistan, 207
Taylor, A.J.P., 7
Telecommunications, 89–91, 114, 115; marketing of, 90; EU leasing fees, 90; fiber-optic network, 90; phone volume, 91
Teltschik, Horst, 123
Thatcher, Margaret, 43, 105, 106, 177–8, 193
Thierse, Wolfgang, 162
Thyssen, 91, 114
Thyssen Foundation, 107
Tiananmen Square massacre, 46, 146–7
Trans-Atlantic Declaration, 195
Treaty of Versailles, 6, 16, 211
Treuhand Trust Agency, 88, 121, 122, 155, 156, 157, 158, 162, 230
Turkey, 175, 188, 213
Turks, 12, 29–30, 31, 53, 58, 59, 65, 69, 234, 236
Turner, Ted, 98
Tychner, Janusz, 62

Übersiedler, 70
Ukraine, 185, 202–7, 236
Umsiedler, 58
Unemployment, 194; compared with other industrialized nations, 95; created by unification, 111
Union of Soviet Socialist Republics, 6, 8, 19, 202–7; Moscow coup, 149; market collapse in, 156
United Kingdom, 1, 10, 22, 57, 114, 115, 117, 123, 152, 176, 187, 195, 203; Conservative Party, 106; attempt to delay reunification, 177–8; Maastricht, 191
United Nations, 5; security council, 177, 183, 187; UN Protection Force (UNPROFOR), 197, 208;

United Nations (*cont.*) German
  medics in Cambodia, 207
United States, 3, 10, 22, 52, 97,
  114, 115, 187–8, 195, 203;
  Republican Party 106, 197, 205;
  Reagan Adminstration, 111;
  commitment to Europe, 175–6;
  trust in German democracy, 177;
  missiles in Germany, 183

Veba, 114
Veen, Hans-Joachim, 164, 165
Verfassungpatriotismus, 31
Verfassungsschutz, 166
Vergangenheitsbewältigung, 158,
  160–1
Viab, 91
Viag, 91
Vocational education, 15
Vogel, Hans Jochen, 61
Voigt, Karsten, 209
Volkswagen, 112, 114
Volkswagen Foundation, 107

Warsaw, 146, 200
Watzal, Ludwig, 45
Weber, Max, 91, 122
Wegner, Manfred, 156, 158
Wehrmacht, 159, 186, 209
Weimar Republic, 7, 8, 16, 65, 95, 98,
  202
Weizsäcker, Richard von, 49, 65, 68
Weltanschauung, 14
Wende, 48, 104

Wessis, 18, 151, 153
West Berlin, 17, 55
West Point, 10
West Prussia, 91
Western European Union (WEU),
  189, 196, 204, 213, 215, 236
Westerplatte, 200
Wharton School, 107
Wieczorek-Zeul, Heidi, 209
Wiesenthal, Helmut, 163, 164
Wirtschaftswunder, 72
Wischnewski, Hans-Jürgen, 56
Wolf, Christa, 233
Wolf, Markus, 161
Wordsworth, William, 43
World Economic Forum, 114
World War I, 5,7, 10, 16, 19, 26, 175
World War II, 2, 4, 5, 13, 16, 23, 101,
  103, 178, 179, 181, 185, 192, 200,
  204, 207
Wossi, 166
Wötzel, Roland, 147, 148, 149

Yalta Conference, 176, 211
Yeltsin, Boris, 186, 202, 203, 205,
  207,
Yugoslavia (and ex-Yugoslavia),
  183–4, 190–1, 196, 203, 208;
  Slovenian and Croatian
  independence, 50, 51

Zeiss, 122
Zelle, Carsten, 164
Zhirinovsky, Vladimir, 202, 204